BRITAIN, EGYPT AND THE MIDDLE EAST

Britain, Egypt and the Middle East
Imperial policy in the aftermath of war 1918–1922

John Darwin

St. Martin's Press New York

St. Martin's Press, Inc., 175 Fifth Avenue, New York, NY 10010
Printed in Hong Kong
First published in the United States of America in 1981

ISBN 0–312–09736–0

Library of Congress Cataloging in Publication Data

Darwin, John.
Britain, Egypt, and the Middle East

Bibliography: p.
Includes index.
1. Near East—Foreign relations—Great Britain.
2. Great Britain—Foreign relations—Near East.
I. Title.
DS63.2.G7D37 1980 327.41056 80–14718
ISBN 0–312–09736–0

For G. M. Darwin

Contents

Preface

This book has been written as a contribution to the study of Britain's imperial decline in the twentieth century. Its aim has been to trace the reaction of the directors of British imperial policy to the problems and opportunities which the Great War and its aftermath created for them in Egypt and the Middle East, regions which had been considered of fundamental strategic importance to Britain since the early nineteenth century. The years of the aftermath have a special significance for the historian of the later phase of British imperialism. The First World War has often been seen as the great watershed in Britain's imperial career, the prelude to an era in which the rise of colonial nationalism and the decline of her economic and military strength enforced a gradual retreat from the grandiose legacy of the Victorians. Moreover, in the four years after 1918 these newfound weaknesses appeared to show themselves as Britain struggled against powerful nationalist movements in Ireland, India and Egypt and became embroiled in costly local conflicts in the Middle East. In their response to the challenge of Egyptian nationalism and in their estimate of Britain's strategic necessities in the Middle East, it is possible to see at work some of the most influential assumptions that guided British policy-makers in imperial questions up until the cataclysm of the Second World War.

Neither this book nor the research that it required would have been possible without the help and encouragement I have received. I owe a great deal to those who taught me as an undergraduate at St John's College Oxford and to the friendly and bracing atmosphere of Nuffield College. Above all I owed a great debt of gratitude to the late Jack Gallagher.

I should like to acknowledge the assistance of the Research Board of the University of Reading and of the staffs of the institutions whose records and archives I have consulted. I should also like to thank the editor of the *Cambridge Commonwealth Series* for his help and advice.

Quotations from the Austen Chamberlain Papers are made with the kind permission of the University of Birmingham; those from certain letters in the Montagu Papers by kind permission of the Master and Fellows of Trinity College Cambridge. Transcripts of Crown-copyright records in the India Office Records appear by permission of the Controller of Her Majesty's Stationery Office.

Abbreviations in Notes

A.C.	Austen Chamberlain Papers
Addit. Milner Papers	Additional Milner Papers, Bodleian Library, Manuscript Collection
Balfour Papers	British Library Additional Manuscripts, A. J. Balfour Papers
B.L.P.	Bonar Law Papers
CAB.	Cabinet Records, Public Record Office
Chelmsford Collection	Chelmsford Collection, India Office Library, Mss. Eur. E. 264
C.I.G.S.	Chief of the Imperial General Staff
Curzon Collection	Papers of 1st Marquess Curzon in Foreign Office Records (F.O. 800) Public Record Office
Curzon Papers	Papers of 1st Marquess Curzon in India Office Library, Mss. Eur. F 112
D.B.F.P. Is.	*Documents on British Foreign Policy*, First Series
D.C.S.M.	Documents Collected for the Special Mission to Egypt
Fisher Papers	Papers of H. A. L. Fisher
F.O.	Foreign Office Records, Public Record Office
I.D.C.E.	Inter-departmental Committee on Middle East Affairs
L.G.P.	Lloyd George Papers
Lothian Collection	Papers of 11th Marquess of Lothian, Scottish Record Office
Milner Collection	Papers of 1st Viscount Milner in Public Record Office
Milner Papers	Papers of 1st Viscount Milner in Bodleian Library, Oxford
P.R.O.	Public Record Office
S.S.C.	Secretary of State for the Colonies

S.S.I.	Secretary of State for India
A. T. Wilson Papers	Papers of Sir Arnold Wilson, British Library, Additional Manuscripts
Worthington-Evans Papers	Papers of Sir L. Worthington-Evans, Bodleian Library

Introduction

The history of the British Empire in the twentieth century is the history of an imperial system exposed twice in thirty years to all the strains and hazards of wars that extended over three continents and left in their wake violent discontinuities not only in the international system but also in the internal structure of almost every state and empire which had participated in, or been drawn into, the conflict. Inevitably, this fact alone impresses upon British imperial history since 1914 a character signally different from that of the previous century.

Perhaps because of this, and because by 1960 the last vestiges of Britain's existence as an independent world power had all but disappeared, historians have sometimes tended to regard the outbreak of the First World War as the decisive turning-point in Britain's imperial experience, separating the era of strength and success from the era of decline and dissolution. Nor is this division entirely lacking in plausibility. After 1914, or, more accurately, after 1918, the ability of the British to control their vast empire appeared less certain than before. The rejection by the white dominions of any subordination to the mother-country, and their progress towards full national sovereignty, seemed more definite and unequivocal. At the same time the British were confronted in Ireland, Egypt and India by nationalist movements which struck deeper roots and which devised more effective tactics against the exercise of imperial authority than their predecessors in colonial politics. Britain's own economic power, the driving force behind her imperial expansion and her world-wide influence in the nineteenth century, looked less awesome after the strains of the Great War and with the marked growth in the industrial and naval power of the United States and Japan. Lastly, after 1918, with the full emergence of a mass democracy in Britain, coupled with the development of deep-seated social and economic problems, the ability of British governments to divert resources into the protection and defence of Britain's imperial system seemed increasingly doubtful, and the preoccupation of politicians with issues of domestic rather than international significance correspondingly greater.

If on grounds of this kind the First World War is seen as the decisive watershed in the history of the British imperial system, and if thereafter its eventual disintegration within two or three generations was highly probable, then the troubled aftermath of the war should provide some insight into the beginnings of decline: the failure of those who directed and controlled the imperial system to manipulate its various components so as to benefit the system as a whole; their inability to protect British and imperial interests from the onslaught of colonial nationalists in the dependencies; their loss of confidence in the old techniques of imperial rule; and their gradual retreat from the mentality and ethos of imperialism. At first sight, the reaction of the policy-makers to the growth of unrest and non-cooperation in Ireland, India and Egypt between 1918 and 1922, and their willingness to concede formal independence on the one hand or more rapid progress towards self-rule on the other, seems to confirm such a diagnosis. But the historian who concludes from the twists and turns of imperial policy in these years that the symptoms of decay were already far advanced, and that the imperial system had already entered its final crisis, has also to take account of developments less easily portrayed as evidence of impending collapse. The British imperial system had, after all, survived the war with its political structure largely intact, and survived a war which was the graveyard of four rival empires. It had weathered internal and external strains which proved too much for its principal competitors of the pre-war years. Moreover, at the end of the war, it displayed a striking capacity for further expansion in Africa and the Middle East – expansion which brought the empire to its maximum territorial extent in 1921.[1]

How are these apparently divergent tendencies in the workings of the imperial system to be reconciled? How did the directors of imperial policy justify the impulse to expand Britain's imperial commitments at the very moment when a substantial devolution of power in her existing dependencies was taking place? Did the foundation of a new *imperium* in Africa and the Middle East by the same government which licensed constitutional reform in India betoken a new orientation in the imperial system away from the old reliance upon British supremacy in South Asia? Or was it merely the last spasm of a dying imperialism? Was this latest enlargement of the imperial embrace marked by a new approach to the relations between Britain and her overseas subjects and clients? And what did the effort to widen the scope of British influence reveal about the nature of imperial power in the age of trusts, mandates and self-determination? What hopes and expectations, what anxieties, lay behind Britain's management of nationalist unrest after 1918? How far were the policy-makers moved by the belief that the system of whose viability the late Victorians had been generally confident[2] was now so vulnerable to internal dissidence that its fall could not be postponed for long? Did policy-makers sense new international constraints upon their freedom of action? Lastly, to what extent were their dispositions a consequence of novel political circumstances at home?

It is beyond the scope of this study to direct these questions at the whole range of Britain's international and imperial policies in the crowded period of the aftermath. But it may be profitable to search for some of the answers in the policies of the Lloyd George coalition government towards two areas, both of which had long been seen as vital to the strength and security of the imperial system, and both of which provoked an intense and almost continuous debate among ministers during the life of the coalition Cabinet after 1918. The first of these is Egypt, where the British encountered a nationalist movement which tested not only the power and influence of the imperial presence, but also the extent to which ministers and their advisers were prepared to accommodate the demands of colonial nationalism; and the lengths to which they were ready to go to suppress or defuse a campaign of non-cooperation. The salience of Egypt in the structure of imperial defence lends a broader significance to the ideas of ministers as to how Britain's political control along the Nile should be remodelled. The second focus of inquiry is the Middle East, by which is meant broadly the Asian lands which had formed part of the Ottoman and Persian empires before 1914. It was this wide region which saw after 1918 the most spectacular expansion of British power in the twentieth century and which raises therefore a series of questions about the methods and motives of imperial policy in the early post-war years. For Britain's activity there has all the appearance of confusion and uncertainty, of erratic responses to varying circumstances: thus the unbending hostility to Turkish nationalism; the promotion of an Arab nationalism in Iraq; the conversion to the language of trusts and mandates; the quest for paramountcy in Persia; the reference to the strategic needs of India; the indifference to the entreaties of the Indian government for the conciliation of Turkish and Persian nationalism. What consistencies of purpose, it may be asked, lay behind these varying expressions of ministerial will? What understanding of Britain's future as a world and imperial power sustained those who defended devolution in Egypt and expansion in the Middle East?

Taken together, Egypt and the Middle East may allow some

conclusions to be drawn about the post-war character of Britain's Eastern empire which, with the white dominions, formed the core of her world-system. For the analysis of British policy in them both leads inevitably to a consideration of India's place in the calculations of the official mind, and to an assessment of the impact of constitutional change in this second pivot of the Victorian empire upon the wider strategies of the policy-makers. But throughout, the main focus of enquiry has been upon the ideas, the thoughts and motives of those in London who were charged with the administration of foreign and imperial affairs: primarily, that is to say with the leading ministers of the coalition. The view of Egypt and the Middle East that is taken here is the view from Downing Street, Whitehall and occasionally Westminster. For this reason, the internal politics of Egypt, the Arab lands, Turkey and Persia have only been very briefly touched upon, and then only where they are essential to an understanding of the formulation of policy in London. The development of the indigenous politics of Egypt and the Middle East states, which has been traced in the work of Kedourie[3] and others, lies outside the bounds of this study except in so far as the actions of ministers were guided by their comprehension of it. Rather the object has been to show the way in which decisions on imperial questions were reached in London, to see the particular policies applied in Egypt and the Middle East in the wider setting of the Anglo-Indian relationship, and to grasp the connection – too often neglected – between British activity in the *Arab* Middle East, above all in Iraq, and the strategies which the policy-makers tried to follow in Turkey and Persia. For it is argued here that only by linking their dispositions in Baghdad to their diplomacy at Constantinople and Teheran can the true meaning of the policy-makers' plans for the different parts of the Middle East be properly comprehended.

It remains to make a final disclaimer regarding those areas whose place in British imperial policy is to be investigated. In Part III, which deals with the problems of expansion in the Middle East, it is with Britain's efforts to exert her influence in Turkey, Persia and Iraq that we shall be primarily concerned. Palestine, Trans-Jordan and Syria get short shrift, especially after December 1919; the Arabian peninsula is neglected altogether. This is largely a faithful reflection of the main preoccupations of ministers. Syria passed out of their immediate concerns once the decision had been taken that it should be yielded to the French in exchange for an enlarged Palestine and Mosul; only the sensitivity of its French administrators to political events elsewhere in the Middle East gave it any subsequent prominence in the calculations of British policy since ministers were anxious not to re-open the rancorous quarrel which Syria had occasioned with the French in 1919. The administration of Palestine and Trans-Jordan excited little controversy and not much interest among ministers once their frontiers with a French-dominated Syria had been settled. The burden of their military costs caused irritation; and the danger that planting a member of the Hashemite family as the king of Trans-Jordan might provoke a French protest produced a brief flutter in March 1921. But, in general, the shape of the imperial presence and the character of imperial policy in these two mandated territories were not seriously at issue between 1918 and 1922, and did not react significantly upon the larger structure of the imperial system in a way that was characteristic of the affairs of Turkey, Persia and Iraq. Palestine at this period was a problem of secondary importance. Only when the accelerated flow of Jewish immigrants in the 1930s produced a fierce Arab reaction, encouraged by Britain's enemies in Europe, did the policies which the British pursued there begin to affect their whole strategic and political position in the Middle East. Finally, the Arabian peninsula merited no ministerial consideration at all. Its future within the British sphere of influence was unquestioned; nor was any change contemplated in the methods by which that influence was to be exercised. For as in the case of Palestine and Trans-Jordan, the nature of Britain's policy there was subordinate ultimately to the success or failure of an imperial design which was hinged upon Turkey, Persia, Iraq and Egypt.

Part I

Imperial Policy and British Politics

1 The Traditions of Imperial Policy and the Leaders of the Coalition

Imperial policy after 1880

Before 1914, there seemed little that Britain could gain from changes in the structure of international politics or the distribution of world power. The most predictable shifts in the balance of world power seemed more likely to weaken than to strengthen the security of her far-flung imperial system. The advance of Russia towards the frontiers of the Indian Empire and into the Chinese Empire had been held in check; the encroachment of German influence in the Middle East and in south central Africa partially arrested. But despite this, there could be no reason to suppose that the tighter international constraints with which the British world-system had had to reckon since the end of the 1870s would be loosened. Nor that the rise of new industrial powers with imperial ambitions could be reversed by a new surge of expansion that would roll back the forward movement of Britain's rivals.

In recognition of these facts, Britain's foreign policy in the two generations before 1914 was fundamentally defensive in character, geared not to the enlargement but to the conservation of her mid-Victorian pre-eminence in the trade and diplomacy of the world outside Europe. The makers of policy were not indifferent to Britain's purely commercial interests and were sympathetic to the task of resisting competition from the new industrial economies of Europe and America. But their prime concern was the defence of the structure of military and diplomatic power which had underwritten Britain's economic expansion in the past and which was the ultimate guarantee against a future war of attrition by her imperial rivals. Only if this structure were maintained could there be any firm assurance that Britain's vast sea-borne trade, and the markets which they served, would not suffer the same fate as had once overtaken the sea-borne empires of Portugal and Holland.[1]

The defensive strategy of the policy-makers varied, inevitably, from region to region, and from place to place. In the Western hemisphere, in Latin America, where Britain's principal rival was the United States, the directors of policy recognised the dangers of a confrontation so near the seat of American power, and the advantages of collaboration in a region of unstable politics for the better protection of all foreign interests. And despite their resentment at the emergence of a more forceful American diplomacy, policy-makers in London took heart from the narrow geographical ambit of America's pretensions, seeing her as a regional not a world power: with no aggressive designs on the core of the British imperial system.[2] But in the Eastern hemisphere, this relaxed and pragmatic approach to international rivalries did not prevail, since here the basis of British power, and the character of its enemies, seemed very different.

East of Suez, the advancement of British trade and the safety of the sea routes which it used, appeared to depend upon the control of India, itself a market, a supplier and a centre of investment of the utmost importance to Britain's international trading system.[3] The creation of a formal empire in India had allowed the British to penetrate with greater ease the economies of China and the Malay archipelago; but it had also committed them to the defence of a sub-continental land mass with frontiers that could not be guarded by sea-power alone. Thus Britain's development in the nineteenth century into the foremost commercial power in Asia had emphasised not only the immense value of India both for itself and as the key to the trade of East Asia, but also the acute vulnerability of this fruitful Anglo-Indian partnership to the growth of rival political influences along India's strategic frontiers.

By the 1880s, these strategic frontiers had become almost unimaginably far-flung, embracing Burma, central Asia, Persia, the Ottoman Empire, and the varied polities of northern, eastern and southern Africa. In all these places, the British struggled to preserve regimes that would deny strategic advantages to their imperial rivals: Russia, France, and subsequently Germany. At the same time, this task was growing more difficult as the effects of modernisation and westernisation generated political movements often hostile to British influence and its local agencies.[4] The directors of policy in London, while anxious to protect the multiple benefits of their Anglo-Indian security system, were forced in these circumstances to make caution and flexibility the watchwords of their diplomacy: to weigh carefully the costs and risks of political intervention. In general, however, their efforts to defend the imperial system which they had inherited, with its overlapping spheres of formal and informal influence, led them to adopt two contrasting solutions. In the Ottoman Empire, in Persia, and on Britain's economic frontier in China, the aim of policy was to uphold the integrity of the existing political systems and to oppose any project for their partition or annexation. In Egypt, the Transvaal and elsewhere, more direct methods were applied to restore, by coercion if necessary, the primacy of British interests.

Behind these divergent approaches there lay, nevertheless, a common adherence to the old rule of economy of effort. For in Turkey, Persia and the Far East, the alternative to the conservation of three crumbling empires was a military confrontation with rival powers whose superiority on land could not be counter-balanced by the use of British sea-power. Thus in the Near East, British diplomacy (after a brief flirtation with Salisbury's plan for planting military consuls in the strategic zones of Turkey-in-Asia) clung grimly to the hope that constitutional evolution in Turkey would reverse the apparently inevitable collapse into disintegration. (One result of this was that Grey greeted the Young Turk revolution with an enthusiasm that was later to seem somewhat misplaced.)[5] In Persia, only the evident futility of trying to exclude the influence of the Russians from the capital of the Qajar Empire led the policy-makers to accept her partition into spheres of influence.[6] In China, the similar proximity of Russian power to the imperial capital at Peking, the presence of French and German interests, and the impracticability of any attempt to establish formal control over the vast commercial hinterland of the Treaty Ports, had long since converted British policy-makers to the prime necessity of bolstering, rather than subverting, the instruments of traditional indigenous authority, while striving to prevent a monopoly of political and financial influence passing to their rivals.[7]

Different calculations in respect of Egypt and southern Africa produced a different technique, though even here it is likely that the policy-makers underestimated the duration and difficulty of the operations to which they committed themselves. In both places it appeared that the political framework on which Britain's strategic interests depended could not survive without immediate intervention; that their geographical location would allow Britain's military power to be used to its greatest effect; and that failure to act promptly would result in the creation of new frontiers of insecurity for the Anglo-Indian system. With so much at stake, the policy-makers surrendered to the temptation to seek clear-cut political solutions which would obviate the debilitating round of compromises and concessions which afflicted their diplomacy elsewhere, and yield lasting advantages to their long-term defensive strategy. The outcome was the 'temporary occupation' of 1882, and the South African War of 1899–1902.

The reflexes of ministers and their advisers to the opportunities and dangers which faced the imperial system in the late nineteenth century were conditioned not only by their view of the strategic foundations of British world power, but also by their keen sensitivity, appropriate in practitioners of parliamentary politics, to the dangers of allowing the burden of empire to press too heavily on the resources of the metropolis. Denied the institutional peculiarities which shielded the proponents of French territorial aggrandisement from the parsimony of the legislature, the directors of British policy had no inclination to make expansion a principle of their diplomacy. Committed already (after 1889) to a costly programme of naval construction, they dared not contemplate large permanent additions to Britain's military capabilities on land. Nor were they eager to present Parliament with the financial consequences of administering new territories deficient in taxable commodities. The defence of the Empire's strategic frontiers on land had, therefore, to be met so far as possible from the military and economic resources of Britain's dependencies: by using the sub-imperialism of the colonies to further the objectives of a master-plan laid down in London.[8] Only when the inadequacy of these local resources threatened to unbalance the larger structure of imperial defence could ministers in London normally be prevailed upon for reinforcements.[9]

It was, of course, by no means impossible to gain parliamentary sanction for intervention and annexation in pursuit of imperial security, as Rosebery demonstrated in Uganda, and Chamberlain, more dramatically, in South Africa. But such expedients were unwelcome to ministers who were exposed either to radical distaste for military adventure[10] or to conservative alarm at the social consequences of high taxation.[11] They were in general profoundly sceptical of the electorate's enthusiasm for empire and its defence, whatever febrile passions the efforts of the jingoes might arouse. The apparent failure of Chamberlain's great programme for tariff reform and imperial unity to educate public opinion in the dangers facing the imperial system confirmed the pessimism of those whose understanding of the electorate was based upon the chastening experience of the Midlothian election of 1880. To a vigorous proconsular spirit such as Milner's, the apathy or ignorance on which imperial unity foundered was especially demoralising. 'One must unfortunately explain to these d—d fools', he wrote to Amery, 'why we want . . . an Empire, and it pinches one in dealing with the methods of maintaining it.'[12] The hardy few who demanded national military service as a cure for the weaknesses revealed by the Boer War encountered a public indifference no less crushing.

The sense of an imminent crisis in the struggle to defend the imperial system against its rivals which galvanised the directors of policy in the years during and immediately after the Boer War,[13] thus found no real echo in the political nation at large, and was certainly too confined in its effects to generate a wider political support for the schemes of Joseph Chamberlain and Milner. The rejection of their far-reaching and drastic remedies[14] was, however, made much easier by the development of an alternative response to the danger that Britain's overseas interests might collapse under the combined onslaught of her colonial rivals. The diplomatic method identified with Balfour and Lansdowne among the Conservatives, and with Grey, especially, among the Liberals, did not, of course, exclude the possibility of imperial integration as a means of reviving British power. But, by allaying colonial tensions with France, by removing the threat of a combined assault on Britain's international position, and by capitalising on Russian willingness to seek a temporary truce in the long cold war between the two great European empires in Asia, it demonstrated the feasibility of preserving the essentials of world power without a sweeping and painful reconstruction of Britain's politics and economics.

The conservatism of British attitudes about the extent to which imperial commitments should be allowed to impinge upon the immediate preoccupations of domestic politics or disturb strategies worked out for the advancement of party interests at home, was no less marked in the management of colonial politics in their internal aspect. There was little sign before 1914 that the pressure of domestic opinion would enforce changes in the mode of British control in those regions where the imperial presence intervened directly in the ordering of local affairs. So long as colonial administrations kept order and remained solvent, they had little to fear from public opinion at home. Only when their ability to govern effectively and without recourse to imperial reinforcements of money and men was called into question did London proffer, or impose, its own views on constitutional reform.

Where imperial policy in the decade before 1914 displayed reforming or liberalising tendencies, it had usually been in response to the threat that, without the timely redeployment of the imperial factor, British authority, and the wider interests of the imperial system, would be jeopardised or become more difficult and costly to sustain. Thus it was the certainty that the 'Lyttelton constitution', with its very limited concession to self-government, would be unworkable and would wreck the fragile basis of Anglo-Boer cooperation, not an excess of democratic enthusiasm, that lay behind the decision of Campbell-Bannerman's ministry to grant responsible government to the Transvaal in 1906.[15] The same kind of calculation was at work in Gorst's short-lived experiment in the partial retraction of British influence from the internal politics of Egypt.[16] In India, constitutional change before 1914, far from being imposed over the heads of the guardians by a mother-country impatient of authoritarian bureaucracy, was tailored to the enlarged financial and political requirements of the *Raj* itself;[17] while the Indian government received what Balfour termed a 'blank cheque'[18] to operate the 1909 reforms to its own satisfaction. Where debate and disagreement occurred over these and other colonial issues, the differences revolved not around the ends of imperial policy but around the means whereby Britain could continue to enjoy the advantages of paramountcy without plunging the imperial system into crisis, or imposing a greater burden of military or administrative expenditure upon herself.

In the last years before 1914, Britain's relations with those regions of formal control and informal domination that were part of her world-system seemed, therefore, to be characterised by adherence to a number of cardinal principles which regulated the actions and reactions of the policy-makers. Firstly, there was general agreement that the era of territorial expansion was at an end; that further extensions to the formal empire of rule were more likely to weaken than to strengthen the foundations of British world power. The task of the statesman was to defend and consolidate, not to enlarge. Secondly, the course of politics both at home and in the dominions had appeared to demonstrate the impracticability of any large scheme for the closer integration of the mother-country and the settler colonies so as to share the burdens of world power more equally between the societies of Greater Britain.[19] The colonies remained determined to preserve their financial and legislative autonomy; while in Britain, popular sentiment and powerful vested interests combined in defence of a liberal trade policy the destruction of which had seemed the price of imperial unity. Continued enjoyment of the benefits of free trade and of a largely untrammelled control over the foreign policy of the Empire thus went hand in hand with the privilege of defending imperial interests out of the resources of Britain herself, or those of India, whose military value remained of great importance. Thirdly, international experience since the Boer War confirmed the policy-makers in the belief that an intelligent diplomacy could conserve for Britain the most valuable fruits of past expansion and exploit the weaknesses and divisions of her imperial rivals in the interests of imperial security. By this means, and by such regional pacts as the Anglo-Japanese alliance, or the informal accommodation with the United States in the Western hemisphere, the increased burden of defence expenditure, primarily on naval construction, could be kept within limits acceptable even to the party of Morley and Lloyd George.[20] Friendship with France and better relations with Russia encouraged all but the most resolute pessimists to hope that the divergent interests of the European colonial empires would not lead ineluctably to Armageddon, and that collaboration and cooperation between them were possible.[21]

Diplomatic success strengthened the fourth principle upon which foreign and imperial policy was founded. For despite the mutual jealousies which lay beneath the surface of Anglo-Russian relations even after 1907, and the growth of a forceful German *Weltpolitik*, especially in the Middle East, it still seemed safe to rely upon the arts of influence and persuasion, with the aid of certain financial inducements, to maintain Britain's strategic and commercial interests where military intervention would have been dangerous or counter-productive. Even after Turkey's loss of her European provinces, the integrity of her Asian empire continued to serve as the main defence for Britain's predominance in the Persian Gulf and the Indian Ocean; and the protection of British commercial and political influence in southern Mesopotamia remained a viable proposition.[22] In Persia, although the encroachment of Russian control worried and irritated the Foreign Office, British policy continued to turn upon the maintenance of an integral state – albeit divided into spheres of influence – and upon a form of cooperation with the Russians.[23] And in China, Grey's diplomatic defence of British interests in the last years of peace was generally successful.[24]

Lastly, in their approach to the government of their dependencies, the policy-makers respected the long-established convention of imperial policy that whatever degree of internal autonomy might be conceded, Britain's colonies and protectorates would not be allowed to pursue foreign policies at variance with the interests of the imperial system as a whole, as these were conceived in London. In questions of peace and war, the authority of the King-Emperor, advised by British ministers, was to be enough to determine the fate of every component of the formal empire – dominions, protectorates and crown colonies alike. In those dependencies which had made some progress towards autonomy, the necessity of ensuring a local regime that would conform to this iron rule was a prime consideration in the internal policies pursued by the British. Where the concession of local self-government was only a remote possibility, the preservation of a social and political structure compatible with British paramountcy was, similarly, the overriding preoccupation of the policy-makers, and led them in places to eschew economic development where it appeared to conflict with the conservation of pliable and cooperative social groups.[25]

On the eve of the First World War, the British imperial system seemed to have attained – however temporarily – a notable freedom from the pressures and burdens which had afflicted it during the 1880s and the period of the South African war. No large-scale nationalist movement hampered the operations of colonial governments or threatened the unity of the imperial system. Nor was their emergence readily foreseeable. The most virulent colonial nationalism outside the home islands, that of the Afrikaners, had been appeased by the concession of responsible government and then smoothly harnessed to imperial purposes (or so it appeared) by the creation of a united South African dominion. Fractiousness in Egypt and in some Indian provinces was inconvenient, but while Egyptian and Indian nationalists were unable or unwilling to rally mass support they remained a local rather than an imperial problem, requiring local solutions. Certainly there was little sign that the growth of nationalist politics in either of these vital components of the imperial system would limit their strategic and military usefulness to Britain or disrupt the network of imperial defence. London for its part showed no inclination and perceived no necessity to contemplate changes that would give Indians and Egyptians a real measure of control over the defence and foreign policies pursued in their name. Indeed, across the whole span of imperial commitments, the absence of any serious colonial revolt seemed to offer tacit proof that the intelligent direction of colonial rule could satisfy imperial requirements without awakening a general hostility and resentment among the subject peoples of the Empire. In these circumstances, there was little reason for the policy-makers in London to envisage any drastic alteration in the methods by which imperial control was exerted; and some reason to regard the likely tempo of political change, especially in Britain's African and Asian dependencies, as slow and predictable.

The same general stability prevailed also in the external defences of the imperial system. Since the Boer War, successful diplomacy and favourable circumstances had greatly eased the difficulties which had oppressed ministers in 1900–1901. The defence of imperial interests around the world did not seem incompatible with the existing level of military expenditure. Nor were ministers confronted by the painful necessity, recurrent since the 1880s, of licensing a forward policy in order to protect the existing frontiers of the imperial system. There seemed little reason to expect a serious deterioration in the strategic conditions which governed the safety of Britain's global interests. And while that remained true, ministers could hope to hold in check the most damaging sources of instability in imperial affairs: for nothing was likely to call the existing structure of imperial interests or the established pattern of colonial rule more rapidly into question than the imposition of a heavier military and administrative burden on the British and colonial taxpayer.

On both the internal and external front, therefore, there was in the period immediately prior to the outbreak of the war a striking absence of the kind of pressures which combined after 1918 to enforce a reappraisal of the scope of Britain's imperial interests and some adjustments in the exercise of imperial control. The great inflation of imperial commitments and the intimidating concatenation of nationalist upheavals in Ireland, Egypt and India which broke over the heads of the coalition ministry were problems whose scale and severity had no precedent in imperial policy in the decade before 1914. But the confidence which this may have bred was based ultimately on the readiness of the policy-makers to subscribe to political and strategic propositions which, while they did not discount the dangers of international aggression, tended to assume that the emergencies which might arise would be brief in duration and limited in geographical scope. They were reluctant to conceive of British involvement in a world-wide conflict upon the outcome of which would depend not merely the continuation of Britain's influence in a particular region but her survival as an imperial power in a recognisable form.

However the outbreak of war and its rapid extension to the Middle East and Africa created circumstances in which the validity of this and of the other guiding principles of imperial policy was soon to be questioned or rejected. By 1916 it was no longer certain that forward policy and territorial expansion had become obsolete in imperial diplomacy, especially in the Middle East where, as we shall see, the dissolution of the pre-war assumptions of British policy was particularly dramatic. By the middle of the war, too, the belief that Britain should have secure access to vital strategic materials such as oil was beginning to influence the outlook of ministers and their advisers.[26] And as the struggle to defend her maritime and imperial interests while waging war in France began to tell on Britain's economic resources and manpower, the closer integration of the formal empire appeared more and more necessary. Moreover, in Egypt, India and elsewhere, the policy-makers were driven to reverse their old priorities in the effort to mobilise economic resources for the war, with the result that the burden of imperial rule bore increasingly heavily on Britain's colonial populations.

But if the war saw the overthrow of some long-standing dogmas of imperial policy, it also served to reinforce others. For the future of British policy in Egypt and the Middle East, one of the most important effects of the war was its emphatic vindication of India's importance in the imperial system as a reservoir of military power. In the first months of the war, India sent troops to join the British Expeditionary Force in France and Belgium, to strengthen the imperial garrison in Egypt, and to join the assault on Germany's colonial outpost in East Africa. But her true value was seen when Turkey joined the Central Powers in October 1914, for the task of defending Britain's vital strategic interests in the Middle East devolved in large measure on the Indian army. India provided more than one third of the military manpower of the Egyptian Expeditionary Force which was eventually under Allenby to evict the Turks from Palestine and Syria. In Mesopotamia Indian manpower, by the time of the armistice, was providing much more than half the fighting strength of the imperial force as well as 100 000 non-combatants to service its requirements.[27] Indeed, as the war went on, India's reserve of manpower was tapped with increasing thoroughness.[28] All in all, India, which prior to 1914 had never despatched abroad a military formation exceeding 18 000 men,[29] had sent overseas more than 600 000 soldiers and nearly half a million non-combatants and followers.[30] Taken together these totals matched the contribution of all the white dominions combined.[31]

In addition, India had begun to assume after 1916, and at London's prompting,[32] the role of supply base for imperial forces east of Suez.[33] The development of her industrial capacity became an object of imperial policy. 'The war', declared the Montagu–Chelmsford Report in 1918, 'has thrown a strong light on the military importance of economic development . . . the possibility of our sea communications being temporarily interrupted forces us to rely on India as an ordnance base for protective operations in Eastern theatres of war.'[34] And as late as June 1918, Milner, as a member of the supreme directorate of strategy, was warning that France and Italy might be driven out of the war; that the 'German–Austrian–Turko–Bulgar bloc will be master of all Europe and Northern and Central Asia'; and that in the 'New War' that would follow when 'the fight will be for Southern Asia and above all for

Africa . . . success may largely depend on what supplies we can get from India and Australia'.[35] Had Milner's nightmarish vision come true, the defence of what Amery called 'the Southern British world which runs from Cape Town through Cairo, Baghdad and Calcutta to Sydney and Wellington'[36] – the core of Britain's presence in the Eastern world – would have rested even more heavily on the Indian Empire. Even as it was, the vital importance of political stability in India during the later years of the war supplied what was perhaps the decisive argument in the winning of ministerial approval for constitutional reform in 1918.[37]

Thus when ministers and their advisers came to take stock at the end of the war, they surveyed an imperial system which had been subjected to strains and stresses undreamt of in 1914, but whose management all over the Eastern world still seemed to depend on the relationship between Britain and India. But before examining in more detail the evolution of post-war imperial policy in Egypt and the Middle East, it is necessary first to glance briefly at those ministers who were to play the largest part in the shaping of that policy.

The Leaders of the Coalition 1918–1922

The task of resolving the issues of imperial policy after 1918 fell upon the coalition government which Lloyd George had first created in 1916 and which, with certain modifications of personnel and method, remained in office after the general election of December 1918. The direction of imperial policy remained, therefore, substantially in the hands of those who had presided over its wartime development from 1916, although the political and institutional changes brought by peace enlarged the influence of some ministers and diminished that of others.

At the head of this powerful assembly of political and administrative talent was Lloyd George, his energies unexhausted by thirteen years of office and four years of war. Although before 1914 Lloyd George had taken only a 'spasmodic interest' in foreign and imperial affairs,[38] and had founded his career upon social questions, by the end of the war his interests had undergone an almost complete transformation. For he had emerged not only as the prime author of the mobilisation of the war economy in Britain, but also as an international statesman, sharing with Woodrow Wilson and Clemenceau the highest responsibility for constructing the peace settlements of Europe and the Middle East. In this role, the scope of Lloyd George's authority, and his ability to conduct a personal diplomacy, often independently of the Foreign

Office, has frequently been noticed. But the wide discretion which he was able to exercise long after 1918 was less a consequence of machiavellian disregard for the niceties of constitutional practice than a product of the special circumstances of the war. Before 1918, and for many months after, the inter-relation of strategy and diplomacy at the highest level, and the structure of inter-allied cooperation created in the last two years of the war, made the day-to-day involvement of the Prime Minister an almost indispensable necessity for progress in peacemaking.

Even after the signature of the German peace treaty in June 1919, Lloyd George's main preoccupation in foreign affairs continued to be the settlement of Europe. At home, the multifarious problems of economic readjustment, and the management of labour unrest – regarded as Lloyd George's special field of competence – constantly claimed his attention. After the end of 1919, Ireland took up more and more of his time and energy. For these reasons, and because he lacked knowledge and experience of imperial politics in their internal aspects, Lloyd George was content to leave the problems of government in Egypt to his colleagues, and had little to say about the intricacies of its administration until constitutional reform there became a focus of ministerial disagreements, and of die-hard resentment against the coalition. At this stage, when imperial policy threatened to help overturn his government, Lloyd George became directly involved in devising solutions not for the political conflicts of Egypt, but for those between the different arms of the imperial government and its parliamentary critics.

This detachment from imperial questions, except where they impinged upon domestic politics, extended also very largely to the conduct of British policy in Persia and Mesopotamia. In 1920, certainly, Lloyd George was reluctant to quarrel with Curzon and Milner over Persia, although he had no enthusiasm for Curzon's Persian project and tweaked his ear about it on occasions. Only when the costs of occupation became a political issue at home did he begin to take an interest in the mode of imperial control to be employed in Mesopotamia. But notoriously this detachment did not apply in the case of Turkey.

By contrast with the pragmatism of his approach to German and Russian questions,[39] Lloyd George's burning commitment to the destruction of Turkey as a European power, or as an expansive force in Asia, has often appeared curiously irrational. Yet, for all that Lloyd George's imaginative conception of Turkey may have been influenced by a Gladstonian loathing for its methods of government, by a nonconformist passion for the liberation of oppressed Christians in Asia

Minor, or by an intense admiration for the arch-exponent of Greater Greece, Venizelos, it is unlikely that he viewed his ideas on Turkey as the mere indulgence of emotion and prejudice. Lloyd George was not a man whose politics were ruled only by intense commitments, emotional or personal. He had, after all, been a member of a government which had felt itself first betrayed and then humiliated by the war policy of the Turks. His enthusiasm for an Anglo-Greek partnership to rebuild imperial security in the eastern Mediterranean after the collapse of the old reliance on Turkey was widely shared in the government, and was sustained not only by a fear of Turkish revival, but also, until the summer of 1922, by the evidence of Greek military prowess and determination. Despite disagreements over method and timing, therefore, the basic elements of his Near Eastern policy were accepted by his senior colleagues and upheld by the Cabinet.[40]

In his conception of Britain's world power and imperial interests, Lloyd George was not a prey to any dogma, nor the devotee of any school of imperial thought. He was 'glued to no economic system'.[41] But neither was he inclined to conceive of Britain's place in the world in novel terms. In so far as any systematic ideas may be deduced from his policy, they reflected an acceptance of the broad principles of imperial policy by which pre-war Liberal governments had abided; a readiness to buttress the pre-war imperial system against a recurrence of the crises which had overtaken it between 1914 and 1918; and a certainty that the benefits of imperial power should not inflict greater costs on the mother-country after the war. None of these was surprising in a man who had served at the Treasury before the war, and who, as Prime Minister, had fully accepted the necessity of defending the strategic frontiers of India, and of the imperial system as a whole, in the arduous campaigns of the Middle East conflict.

If these were the notions which informed Lloyd George's thinking in questions of imperial policy, he was rarely disposed to state them candidly, or to adopt uncompromising postures on imperial, or other questions. For this lack of candour, which seemed to characterise his governing method, for the readiness to deploy, without any personal commitment, a bewildering variety of solutions to the problems which confronted the government, the explanation lay partly in Lloyd George's instinctive reluctance to confide fully in his colleagues – a reluctance commonplace in prime ministers and compounded in Lloyd George's case by the uncertainties of coalition politics. But it was also the result of his need to remain in touch with his colleagues' thinking in many fields where his own knowledge and expertise could only be scanty. Thinking aloud, often rather mischievously, and testing, by audacious statements, the opinions of fellow ministers became a favourite method for extracting decisions from the Cabinet,[42] and for avoiding the premature disclosure of his own preference where to do so might endanger his ultimate authority as head of the government.

For more than half of his post-war premiership, Lloyd George's leadership of the government was sustained not only by his genius in political relationships, and by the suppleness of his ideas, but also by the advice and support which he received from Bonar Law as leader of the Conservative party. Bonar Law had, indeed, played a crucial part in bringing Lloyd George to the premiership in 1916, and could view his qualities with a dispassion rare in the Conservative party. For he lacked any feeling for the historic and aristocratic traditions of the Conservative party and was conscious of the disparity between his own social provenance and that of the Cecilian dynasty he had replaced.[43] But if he was denied the advantages of social prestige, and if a refined member of his political audience could feel 'rather as if I were addressed by my highly educated carpenter',[44] Bonar Law's talents as a parliamentarian, his skill in detecting and controlling movements of party opinion, and his professionalism and sensitivity in the management of the party in the country[45] made his commitment to the coalition, and to the continuation of Lloyd George's premiership after 1918, a factor of signal importance in the stability of the government.

In the aftermath of his defeat and rejection as party leader, Austen Chamberlain once stigmatised Bonar Law as a weak man 'who has always leaned on some man stronger than himself – be it Lloyd George or be it Carson'.[46] But despite their close relationship, and despite Law's willingness to see Lloyd George enjoy the full panoply of prestige as head of the government, his role was never that of the Prime Minister's tool. For although he appeared indifferent to the creative functions of policy-making and was outshone in this regard by his more brilliant colleagues, his influence on the government's decisions was powerful and consistent. By taking as his constant theme the need to respect the feelings of the coalition's phalanx of Conservative supporters, and the limits imposed by wider political and financial realities, he served as a check on the extravagances of Lloyd George and his fellow ministers, and as a reinforcement to Lloyd George's own insistence on the primacy of domestic considerations where these appeared to conflict with imperial policy. On occasions his language to the Prime Minister could be very firm.[47] In return, Lloyd George showed a deference to Law's judgment which he reserved for that of no other minister, and was plainly discomfited by his retirement for reasons of health in March 1921. 'I miss your counsel more than I can tell you . . .', he wrote feelingly to Law, as one perplexity after another crowded in upon him. 'Come back as soon as you can. . . .'[48]

Bonar Law's successor as leader of the Conservative party, and as second minister in the government, was Austen Chamberlain.[49] Chamberlain was an experienced departmental minister and had associated himself closely with the campaign for tariff reform before 1914 and with the reform of Indian government in the later years of the war. After 1918, however, his principal preoccupation had been with finance, and, like Law, he had intervened scarcely at all on imperial questions except to warn against the consequences of incurring further military expenditure.[50] He was an ardent coalitionist who wished to move towards a fusion of the anti-socialist parties.[51] After his elevation as party leader, he also became devoted to Lloyd George, and to his retention as the head of the coalition. But Chamberlain fell heir to a difficult political legacy. His accession to the leadership coincided with the rapid growth of anti-coalition feeling in the Conservative party, the containment of which was beyond his political gifts. Lacking Law's personal standing, and his skill in managing the party machine,[52] he never enjoyed the latter's personal influence over the Prime Minister. For his part, Lloyd George, while appreciating Chamberlain's loyalty to him, never accorded overmuch respect to his capacities as party leader, and tended, after Bonar Law's withdrawal, to rely less upon a close collaboration with the established Conservative leadership than upon the support of a fluid coterie of favourites and confidants whose relations with the Conservative party were not always characterised by mutual trust and esteem.

The commanding heights of the coalition were occupied by ministers whose attitudes in imperial questions were, to a considerable extent, governed by the necessity to take a broad view of the ministry's varied responsibilities in the domestic and international sphere alike. Lloyd George's contribution to the formulation of Turkish policy was of decisive importance, but the framing of imperial policy in the rest of the Middle East and in Egypt was, in the first instance, the province of departmental ministers, principally Balfour, Curzon, Milner, Churchill and Edwin Montagu.

Of these, the most senior, although far from the most influential, was Balfour, whose ministerial experience stretched back to 1885, and who occupied the Foreign Office from 1916 until the end of the War Cabinet in October 1919.[53] But by 1918, when Balfour was seventy, his interventions in the making of policy were circumscribed by fatigue, illness and old age,[54] all of which made him reluctant to engage in sustained controversy, or the routine of departmental business. At the beginning of 1919, when he accompanied Lloyd George to the Paris Peace Conference, Balfour handed over the day-to-day management of the Foreign Office to Curzon and remained Foreign Secretary in name only until October. He continued, however, to play a part in the direction of foreign and imperial policy through his support for the main elements of the Lloyd George–Curzon strategy for Turkey, and by acting as the principal British representative at the Washington naval conference in 1921–2.

Balfour had firm and well developed views on imperial questions which owed something to his own long experience of foreign and colonial affairs, and much, perhaps, to the influence of his uncle, the third Marquess of Salisbury. He was a vehement critic of the principle of extending representative institutions to peoples without European political traditions and denounced on these grounds both the Morley–Minto reforms in 1909, and Montagu's proposals eight years later.[55] The distinction he commonly drew between European and Oriental communities may have made him particularly sympathetic to the eviction of the Turks from Europe. But the impact of Balfour's ideas on the internal government of Britain's dependencies was not great; even over Ireland, where the spirit of 'Bloody Balfour' still moved within him, his attachment to the coalition led him ultimately to repress his discontent with the Treaty.[56] Where he wielded a larger influence was on the more general question of Britain's international position after the war.

Balfour was deeply committed to the preservation and consolidation of Britain's imperial power. He favoured in 1918 the extension of British paramountcy over the Arab provinces of the Ottoman Empire as a cure for the security problems that Turkish rule had made so formidable.[57] But he did not believe that the expansion of imperial power could go very far without exposing the imperial system, whose vulnerability had been his special concern as Prime Minister, to all the hazards of the crisis years of 1900–1904. He had no taste for the drastic programme of reform once championed by Joseph Chamberlain and Milner. And his view of British power, formed in its essentials in the later nineteenth century, was keenly sensitive to the existence of post-war rivalries, and to the necessity of conciliating both France and the United States, whose naval ambitions became his special concern.

Balfour's place at the Foreign Office was taken by Curzon who stayed there until the end of the coalition in October 1922. But even before his move to the Foreign Office, first as a *locum tenens* and then with the full authority of Secretary of State, Curzon, as a member of the War Cabinet since 1916, had exercised a continuous influence over the government's strategy and policy, above all in the Eastern theatre of war. His knowledge of the region between Syria and India and extending north into Russian Central Asia, founded upon travel, study and viceregal experience, was unrivalled by that of any other minister. Curzon was a natural choice for the chairmanship of the Eastern Committee of the War Cabinet set up in March 1918 to coordinate strategy and politics in the Eastern war, and, on his entry into the Foreign Office, he carried with him much of the programme which he had formulated during the lifetime of that committee. As Foreign Secretary, the conduct of policy towards Turkey and Persia were his special responsibilities; while in Mesopotamia he enjoyed an authority moderated by the need for close inter-departmental cooperation and eventually transferred altogether to the Colonial Office. The affairs of Egypt were also his direct concern since their supervision had been reserved to the Foreign Office even after the 'veiled protectorate' was unveiled in 1914.

In 1918, Curzon appeared the most striking exemplar of proconsular attitudes in British politics, 'the most able, [and] the most eloquent, exponent of that sane imperialism to which this country is wedded as a necessity of its existence'.[58] He was identified, above all else, with the strenuous maintenance of British supremacy in India, and with the belief in India's prime importance as the second pivot of British world power. His 'indocentric' view of the imperial system, derived, perhaps, from the exercise of supreme power in India, had made him indifferent, even hostile, to the enthusiasm of Joseph Chamberlain and Milner for the closer integration of Britain and the settler colonies before 1914.[59] After 1918, Curzon dedicated himself to securing India's frontiers, and the strategic routes to India, against any future onslaught, and regarded this as the first priority of imperial diplomacy. His conviction that this purpose could only be served by the destruction of Turkey as an expansionist power, and as the seat of pan-Islamic sentiment, became, as will be argued, the key to his policy in the Middle East.

In popular conception, Curzon survives as a minister of a peculiarly inflexible cast of mind, with a personality by turns humourless, pompous and petulant. Curzon had, indeed, an acute sense of the dignity of his office and a sensitivity to personal criticism, accentuated, perhaps, by poor health, which made him a ready victim for Lloyd George's mischief. But his private pomposity has been exaggerated[60] no less than the rigidity of his political ideas. Curzon was deeply committed to the defence of Britain's Eastern Empire, but his attachment to India did not lead him to conclude that it could only be defended by the application of the classic Indian methods of direct rule and close administration in ever widening spheres. In Persia, Iraq and Egypt, as will be seen, he moved in the opposite direction. 'With all his merits', Lloyd George remarked at the height of the Egyptian negotiations in 1921, 'our George is not quite the man to negotiate with the inferior races.'[61] But Curzon did negotiate because, like most of his colleagues, he believed that the imperial system relied on techniques of political control which must vary from place to place; even if they all subserved the ultimate purpose of upholding imperial security and excluding foreign influence from its nerve-centres.

Curzon was not the only former proconsul to serve in the coalition government, since the war had also rescued Milner from the political oblivion to which the failure of tariff reform and his defects as a parliamentary politician[62] had condemned him. As a member of the War Cabinet between 1916 and 1918, Milner applied his administrative abilities to the problems of mobilising the war economy to the full and impressed Lloyd George by his readiness to adopt the most radical expedients.[63] As Secretary of State for War in 1918, and a member of the supreme directorate of strategy, Milner's relations with Lloyd George were necessarily close and generally harmonious. But by the end of the war, his own exhaustion, and Lloyd George's impatience with his declining effectiveness as an administrator (as Lloyd George saw it), precipitated his departure from the War Office and ended any real intimacy between him and the Prime Minister. From 1919 until early in 1921, Milner remained in the government as Colonial Secretary but grew increasingly disillusioned with its lack of direction and with the cold reception which was accorded to his proposals for constitutional reform in Egypt.

Before 1914, Milner had been chiefly distinguished for his uncompromising defence of British supremacy in southern Africa and for his ardent support for the political union of Britain and her colonies of settlement. In the pursuit of Britain's imperial interests, he had, wrote a hostile critic, 'the spirit of a Torquemada, ruthless, unbending, fanatical'.[64] As a minister during the war, Milner had widened his political experience and had made, perhaps, an important transition from a proconsular to a ministerial mentality. But there is no sign that in doing so he had shrugged off the preoccupations of his earlier career. He continued to be passionately devoted to the principle of imperial unity and was eager to make the wartime structure of cooperation between Britain and the dominions – through the Imperial War Cabinet and the Imperial War Conference – a permanent part of the imperial system.[65] He fiercely resisted any concessions to dominion autonomy that would cast doubt on their automatic obligation to join Britain in any future war as being 'incompatible with the existence of the British Empire as a political unit'.[66] Nor did he question the necessity to exclude any rival power from 'that great sphere of British influence extending from the centre of East Africa, through the Sudan, Egypt, Arabia and the Persian Gulf to India, which is the real British "Empire" apart from the Dominions'.[67] It remained to be seen how these trenchant views on the structure of the imperial system would be expressed in his attitude to the post-war extension of British influence in the Middle East, and to the issues of imperial control in Egypt.

Of the two Liberal ministers whose departmental responsibilities were colonial and imperial, Churchill was by far the more forceful and effective. But although as Secretary of State for War from 1919 to 1921, and as Colonial Secretary thereafter, he took a prominent part in the making of policy in the Middle East, the free play of his ideas was narrowly circumscribed by the intense pressure first for rapid demobilisation and then for stringent economy. As the head of two departments whose expenditure was abnormal by pre-war standards, Churchill was naturally sensitive to charges of profligacy. The reconstruction of his political career from the ashes of 1915 and the Dardanelles Commission Report appeared to depend upon great delicacy in his handling of parliamentary and especially Conservative opinion. Perhaps for this reason, Churchill became in 1920 the fiercest critic within the government of the over-extension of its military commitments in Persia and Mesopotamia, and the scourge of Curzon's great project for Anglo-Persian partnership.

But this did not betoken any frailty in his devotion to the imperial foundations of British world power. Churchill believed strongly in preserving the imperial system and Britain's supremacy within it. He opposed releasing Egypt from formal allegiance to the King-Emperor. And although he became the instrument of the coalition's efforts to place imperial control in Iraq on a more economical footing, he showed, for all his earlier criticisms of policy there, no sign of wishing to abandon an effective British control over the international aspects of Iraq politics. Nor was he less than firm in his support for the exclusion of the Turks from the Dardanelles after 1918, and for the reduction of Turkey to the status of a small Asian power without imperial pretensions.

Churchill's imperial ideas were, in all essentials, rooted in the imperial system which he had known, and helped to manage, before 1914. He had no interest in radical plans for its territorial enlargement or political integration. He remained a free trader. Like Balfour, Lansdowne, and Grey before the war, he regarded with satisfaction the structure of British power which had been established by the end of the nineteenth century, and was reluctant to contemplate either a renovation of that structure or the adaptation of British society for imperial reasons.

Montagu's perceptions of imperial policy throughout his period of office as Secretary of State for India from 1917 until his enforced resignation in March 1922, were dictated by his readiness to view all imperial problems through the prism of Indian politics. Before 1914 and after 1917, his whole experience of empire lay in the toils of Indian administration,[68] and India absorbed almost all his energies and the resources of his imagination. To this special and narrow approach, Montagu added a further crucial ingredient. Almost from the beginning of his involvement in Indian affairs, he became convinced of the need to substitute 'cooperation and devolution'[69] for the authoritarian traditions of the *Raj*, to widen the participation of Indians in government and attach them morally and politically to the imperial system. In 1917, when Lloyd George appointed him to the India Office in the wake of Austen Chamberlain's resignation (following the Mesopotamian Commission report), Montagu was able to superimpose elements of this programme upon the devolution proposals for India which were already being considered. In 1918 he put forward with the Viceroy, Lord Chelmsford, a comprehensive scheme for introducing limited responsible government into the Indian provinces and enlarging the representative institutions of the central government in New Delhi.

After this, all Montagu's actions were geared to the rallying of Indian opinion to the reforms which bore his name, and to resisting any tendency in wider imperial policy which might strengthen those in India whose interest lay in rejecting or destroying his constitutional innovations. Montagu's opinions on Egyptian policy, and, above all, on the tangled web of Britain's policy towards Turkey, reflected his intense preoccupation with the conciliation especially of Indian Muslims whose hostility appeared the greatest barrier to success in India. But despite the intelligence of his arguments, his influence on the ultimate direction of policy in the Middle East was minimal. His hypersensitive temperament,[70] attested by his correspondence, was ill-suited to his political role, and embarrassed and irritated his colleagues. Indeed, his only real hold on office after 1918 lay in the fear of senior ministers that his removal would prejudice the chances of political stability in India;[71] and perhaps also in Lloyd George's reluctance to displace a Liberal minister with Asquithian connections that had once been close. Montagu's influence, therefore, was generally confined to Indian affairs, and was only effective in a wider sphere when he combined with the Viceroy in refusing to use Indian resources for imperial purposes on a large scale after 1919. But despite the heavy engagement of Indian money and men in the conquest and occupation of Mesopotamia and Persia, his use of even this sanction, as will be seen, could only be sparing and occasional.

Despite their diverse political backgrounds, and the differences of emphasis and approach in their ideas, the leading ministers of the coalition shared in 1918 a common conviction that Britain's place in the world was founded upon her possession of a great overseas empire. All of them had served before 1914 in or under ministries which had regarded the defence of the imperial system as a fundamental obligation of any British government. All of them had taken part in a wartime government which had been dedicated not merely to the resistance of German hegemony in Europe, but also to the protection of Britain's world empire against the results of a German–Austrian–Turkish victory – a victory whose impact on the stability of Britain's position east of Malta would have been profound. Where their opinions diverged was not over the desirability, or even the necessity, of maintaining the world-system which the late Victorians had bequeathed; but rather over the best means by which it might be reinforced against pressures from without and dissidence from within.

Between them, the ministers described above were those most continuously involved in the formulation and discussion of imperial policy in Egypt and the Middle East. Others such as Herbert Fisher and Worthington-Evans played a marginal role in Cabinet debates. There were, of course, other influences at work. Imperial policy could not be solely the work of ministers. But in all important decisions which are traced in later chapters, it was the judgment of ministers, and their willingness to use or misuse the advice they received from their offices, that really counted. The leading ministers of the coalition were, in any event, a forceful group who were little inclined to adopt uncritically the suggestions of their advisers. But they had to deal not only with subordinate officials, but also with proconsuls whose advice was harder to ignore: Sir Percy Cox in Persia and Mesopotamia and Lord Allenby – the 'Bull' – in Egypt. The contribution of these men to policy will be better related in subsequent chapters. But before turning to the development of ministerial policy in Egypt and the Middle East, some account must first be taken of the domestic considerations which informed the Cabinet's approach to imperial issues.

2 The Domestic Origins of Imperial Policy

Introduction

Between 1918 and 1922, the policy pursued by the Lloyd George coalition in Egypt and the Middle East was shaped not only by the political realities which confronted the agents of British power in Turkey, Persia, Mesopotamia and on the Nile, but also by the limits which were imposed on ministers by the terms of their parliamentary authority in Britain. The makers of policy could not ignore, even if they hoped to influence, the views of those upon whose support their exercise of power depended; nor seek the backing of their followers for imperial policies which affronted the economic and political orthodoxies that were accepted by the broad spectrum of political opinion.

On two aspects of imperial policy it was particularly important for ministers to take into account the movement of domestic opinion; for the integration of new regions into the imperial system, and the reform of imperial administration in Egypt, could not be undertaken without reference to Parliament. The first raised the question of how far the assumption of new financial and military commitments would be acceptable to the representatives of an electorate groaning under the accumulated burdens of the war. The second, how far these same representatives would be willing to loosen the bonds of political control, or, indeed, preserve them in any form, in a zone where British paramountcy had long been regarded as fundamental to the defence of the Empire.

Ministers were naturally unwilling to embark upon policies which the pressure of public opinion might force them to repudiate, to the general detriment of the government's political authority. But in the years immediately after 1918, the exercise of political judgment was rendered particularly difficult by a variety of novel circumstances and considerations. It was not easy to predict what effect the enormous cost and suffering of the war would have upon public attitudes towards the defence of empire, especially where it might involve further heavy expenditure or military conflict. Nor could the response of the huge new electorate to the problems of adjusting the imperial system to post-war conditions be easily foretold. The entry of new forces into the political arena, in the form of an enlarged and independent Labour party and a vastly stronger trade union movement, added to these uncertainties. And if the prolongation of the coalition, and the scale of its electoral triumph in 1918, provided some assurance that mass politics would not impose radical changes in imperial policy, ministers could not be sure, particularly after the end of 1919, how long the alliance of parties would continue; or what alignment of political forces would take its place. They had, moreover, to reckon with the tensions of party cooperation at a time when it proved difficult to isolate imperial issues from other questions which, as in the case of Ireland, aroused violent passions in the majority party and threatened the dissolution not merely of the coalition but of its constituent elements as well. What follows here is a survey of those aspects of domestic politics which appeared to ministers to constrict significantly their freedom to defend, enlarge or modify Britain's imperial system.

Demobilisation, Security and Finance

Almost as soon as the war ended in Europe and the Middle East, the question of how long Britain would maintain the vast armies which had taken shape in the second year of the war became a political issue of the most urgent kind. For the military power which had secured victory in Europe and underwritten the expansion of British influence in the wide region between Greece and Afghanistan was founded upon a system of conscription the extension of which into peacetime seemed likely to rekindle the controversy which had attended its inception in 1916; and to force ministers into early decisions about the scale and nature of Britain's post-war military resources.

The first signs of this occurred immediately after the German armistice in November 1918, when, to the horror of Sir Henry Wilson, Chief of the Imperial General Staff, recruitment to the army under the Military Service Acts was halted.[1] Milner as War Minister wrote promptly to Lloyd George warning that 'unless some provision is made for recruiting and keeping men, you run the risk of finding yourself without an army at all in 6 months'; and arguing the need for a substantial military arm in 'the disturbed state of Europe, and [with] the revolutionary tendency, greater or less in all countries . . . '.[2] But, as Milner himself recognised, the proposal to continue compulsory military service at the war's end was unlikely to be popular or politically attractive.[3] Lloyd George, preoccupied with the coming election and with the problems of economic dislocation, showed at this stage, as later, a marked indifference to the anxieties of the War Office, and, far from intervening to preserve the manpower for the overseas garrisons, publicly berated Milner 'in the presence of a large number of people, many of them not ministers',[4] for the slow progress of demobilisation, and provoked him to seek a discharge from his duties at the War Office.

At the end of 1918, ministers faced in fact two inter-connected problems in the field of military manpower. The first was how large an army should be maintained after hostilities had terminated and on what basis it should be recruited; the second was the mode of demobilisation which would be applied to all those not required for further military service. This latter question had indeed been resolved – or so it had seemed – by an elaborate system which would release men from the army as the economy was reorganised to assimilate them. But this orderly reduction of the conscript army was abandoned within two months of the armistices as troops at Dover and Folkestone rebelled against the prospect of embarkation for France to relieve units scheduled for an earlier return to civilian life, and as the reaction against a demobilisation scheme which made no allowance for the length of war service spread within the army. Over the protests of Sir Eric Geddes,[5] whom Lloyd George had appointed to coordinate demobilisation, Churchill, who had replaced Milner at the War Office, quickly scrapped the industrial basis on which men were to be released and applied a simple rule of 'first in, first out'.

What the Dover and Folkestone mutinies appeared to reveal was a depth of feeling against compulsory military service abroad which surprised, and perhaps unnerved, ministers who were already apprehensive of the effects of economic dislocation on mass opinion.[6] Churchill and his military advisers on the other hand, faced with the imminent dissolution of the army or its decline 'into a rabble',[7] were anxious as a matter of urgency to combine demobilisation with a scheme that would enable them to recruit and retain sufficient men for the armies of occupation, at least until the peace treaties were signed and ratified. But their efforts in this direction encountered criticism and opposition from Bonar Law and Austen Chamberlain in London, and from the Prime Minister, now ensconced in Paris. Thus Bonar Law, with whom Churchill discussed the War Office's proposal to maintain a conscript army in excess of a million men, while recognising that 'something must be done, and done quickly', was fearful that continued conscription would come under attack, and anxious to avoid 'making a proposal for an army of this size on the meeting of Parliament'.[8] On 17 January Churchill aired at a meeting of the War Cabinet his suggestion for keeping the 1·7 million men who had joined the army in 1917 and 1918 in uniform for a further period, gradually reducing the number to a million.[9] Lloyd George, however, was alarmed by the scale of the War Office's plans, and displeased that so sensitive an issue should have been discussed by ministers before he had been consulted.[10]

Although Churchill, with the forceful advocacy of his military advisers behind him, eventually extracted a grudging acquiescence to his plans from Lloyd George and the War Cabinet, the prospect of prolonged peacetime conscription was viewed with evident distaste by the Prime Minister, by Bonar Law as leader of the Conservative party, and by Austen Chamberlain, who had become Chancellor of the Exchequer early in January. Lloyd George had been reminded by Christopher Addison, as the coalition Liberal minister with the main responsibility for social policy and for keeping in touch with working-class opinion, that continued recruitment under the Military Service Acts would be unpopular and would provoke industrial unrest[11] – a judgment which repeated attacks by the leaders of the Triple Alliance of miners, railwaymen and transport workers seemed to vindicate.[12] Bonar Law, who had also to take account of commercial and industrial opinion, predicted 'formidable opposition' to continued conscription;[13] while Chamberlain, facing a herculean task at the Treasury, regarded the army as a prime target for major economies.[14] At their prompting, Churchill agreed in August 1919 to bring conscription to an end in the following March, and to impose such cuts in army manpower as would reduce it by the close of the financial year to some 10 per cent of what it had been at the time of the armistices.[15]

It was plain, therefore, within a few months of the cessation of hostilities, and long before the political settlement of Europe and the Middle East had assumed any permanent form, that domestic political and financial considerations, as these were conceived by the most powerful members of the coalition government, would rule out any attempt to place Britain's emergence as a great land power after 1915 on a lasting basis. Indeed, by August 1919, Lloyd George was insisting that the army, far from expanding its peacetime strength, should be reduced below the troop levels of 1914 – an argument which the notorious Ten Year Rule was intended to buttress and justify. The priorities of domestic politics thus precluded from the earliest moment any radical shift in the military foundations of imperial power in peacetime.

The abandonment of the principle of compulsory service as the basis of Britain's military power restored in effect the familiar pattern whereby the defence of imperial interests devolved upon a regular army of long-service volunteers. But although the swift end to the wartime experiment in conscription may have forestalled a wider controversy over the imperial purposes to which much of the army was dedicated, especially in the Middle East, it did not resolve the question of how large a military establishment would be required to secure the gains of victory in 1918. Nor did it signify a firm decision by ministers to tailor their political objectives in the imperial sphere to those levels of military spending which they believed acceptable to domestic opinion.

Churchill, on whom fell the task of constructing a new regular army, at first intended that it should be larger than the army of 1914, with a strength of some 209 000 men.[16] But this assumption that the army's commitments would merit an increase in its resources was immediately attacked by Lloyd George and found such disfavour in all parts of the political spectrum that at the end of the coalition government the Conservative campaign guide for the election of 1922 could announce with pride and pleasure that the estimates for 1922–3 had assumed a smaller army in terms of manpower than had been maintained in the last year before the war.[17] This approach to military requirements was partly a consequence of the compound pressures for demobilisation and public economy; but it also drew strength from the fallacious belief, nurtured paradoxically by the war, that the defeat of the Central Powers in Europe had liquidated the major military problem which confronted the British imperial system. But, as the War Office was at pains to point out, the pre-war army, 'though organised to meet an emergency on the continent, had been designed, so far as its strength was concerned, solely with a view to the defence of the Empire'[18] and thus could not logically be reduced for *European* reasons. Furthermore, as both Churchill and the Chief of the Imperial General Staff emphasised, the coming of the armistices had not brought an end to Britain's military obligations in the two great theatres of war in Europe and the Middle East.

As it turned out, the course of British diplomacy in 1919 did allow a rapid contraction of the great expeditionary force which had been assembled in Europe but continued to require the maintenance of large garrisons in the Middle East to secure the objects of what was in essence an *imperial* policy. Sir Henry Wilson made this point repeatedly in the spring and summer of 1919 when the army's future was under constant review.[19] The prolongation of the military occupation of the Middle East was not, however, the only call on the army's services in the first months of 1919. A series of political crises within the imperial system itself made necessary the diversion of British troops as local disorder threatened the authority of civil government. 'Insurrection in Egypt and revolt in India', noted the Chief of the Imperial General Staff in April 1919, had resulted in 'urgent demands for reinforcements which are too well found and too insistent to ignore'.[20] The Third Afghan War, although brief in duration, added a further strain in the spring of 1919. 'In the Middle East, including Egypt, and in India,' Churchill told the Cabinet in July, ' . . . we must maintain our forces at full strength.'[21] Nor were these imperial crises confined to distant provinces of the Empire. By the summer of 1919, the progress of nationalist insurgency in Ireland was demanding, on Churchill's reckoning, an enlarged imperial garrison of some 60 000 men – a force very nearly as large as that maintained in normal times in India. Thus, even admitting that home defence would not impose a real burden on the army 'for years to come', there seemed, to the generals at least, little scope for reducing the army below its previous peacetime establishment since, in Wilson's gloomy prophecy, 'we are much more likely to need troops of an expeditionary nature for our overseas possessions today than we were in 1914'.[22]

These reflections prompted Wilson, as the professional head of the army, to insist as early as April 1919 that the urgent priority of military policy was to concentrate the army's shrinking manpower in what he called the 'coming storm centres' of the Empire in Ireland, Egypt and India, and to eschew military adventures in far-off places without immediate significance for imperial defence.[23] Wilson added to this list a further centre of disturbance and disaffection, not on the periphery of the imperial system but in its metropolitan heart in industrial Britain. For in 1919, the demolition of the war economy, and the accommodation of industry to the new economic climate of peace, was manufacturing unrest on a scale which appeared too great for the resources of the civil arm alone. Strikes in the coal fields, strikes among the cotton operatives, strikes on the Underground, above all the threat of a triple strike of miners, railwaymen and transport workers, alarmed a government which, after the trauma of October 1917, tended, perhaps, to view all symptoms of industrial unrest with an exaggerated fear and suspicion, and to detect proletarian revolution in every manifestation of working-class discontent.[24]

As Wilson predicted, the Cabinet's determination to suppress political dissidence, particularly within the United Kingdom, constantly distracted the army from the task of supporting Britain's diplomacy in Europe and the Middle East. As the reductions in army manpower bit deeper in 1920, the War Office's attempts to juggle with its diminishing reserve of infantry battalions became more frenetic and Wilson's comments on the Cabinet's military policy more acerbic. In the summer and autumn of 1920, the government's military dispositions seemed indeed a chronicle of desperate improvisation. In May, General Macready, the new Commander-in-Chief in Ireland, asked ministers to send a further eight battalions to help in the struggle against the republican army.[25] The Cabinet, while anxious to meet this request, recognised the force of Wilson's warning that the transfer of such a large proportion of the troop reserve remaining in Britain would leave 'very little for our own internal troubles'.[26] Macready was asked to hold over his request for as long as possible, while Wilson returned to the War Office to brood on the army's weakness in every theatre.[27] In June, the danger of an advance by Kemalist troops to Constantinople, overthrowing in the process the peace settlement which the Allies had planned for Turkey, provoked another emergency debate among ministers at which Churchill and Wilson reiterated the army's inability to provide reinforcements in one theatre except 'by withdrawing troops from another'.[28] In July, as Macready again asked for more men, as the necessity arose for sending fresh drafts to India, and as the Irish situation seemed to grow worse, Wilson pressed again for a rationalisation of Britain's military commitments and in particular for the withdrawal of the battalions in northern Persia.[29] In August, with a miners' strike hanging over them, ministers prepared to reverse their earlier dispositions and withdraw ten battalions or more from Ireland for service in England,[30] a proposal which, Macready declared, would lead to the collapse of the Royal Irish Constabulary, and of his whole security policy in Ireland.[31] 'The Cabinet policy', observed a harassed Wilson with understandable bitterness, 'has completely outrun their military power.'[32]

The same pattern recurred in the spring of 1921 when ministers struggled to find enough troops for Ireland, for police duties in Silesia, and for internal security at home in the event of the miners' strike widening into a triple strike of railwaymen and transport workers as well. But what is revealing about the reaction of ministers to these recurrent crises of military power is their reluctance to find any incompatibility between the range of the army's tasks and commitments and the fundamental principle of military policy laid down by Lloyd George in August 1919 and accepted without formal debate by his colleagues that the post-war army should be held at or below the troop strength which had prevailed before 1914. The unwillingness of ministers to revise this estimate of the defensive needs of the imperial system, to which the War Office was forced to adhere once demobilisation was complete, reflected the conviction, which was subscribed to across the whole political spectrum, that the electorate would not tolerate proportionately higher levels of military spending than could be justified by reference to pre-war precedents. Instead, the search for relief from the continual round of military emergencies led ministers to consider such expedients as the 'Special Gendarmerie' that Churchill proposed for Ireland; the formation of similar forces to keep order in Egypt and Iraq; the introduction of 'air control' in Iraq, Ireland and even Britain; the raising of Dominion volunteers to serve as reinforcements in Iraq in September 1920; and the imposition of a heavier military burden on India than she had borne before 1914. It may also have encouraged the War Office's efforts to modify the terms of Britain's mandates so that troops raised in the new African territories wrested from Germany might legitimately be deployed elsewhere in the imperial system.[33] Yet for all the unremitting pressure on the army, and for all that the Cabinet was so frequently confronted with the harsh realities of Britain's military weakness, the army's difficulties were for the most part only indirectly acknowledged in the formation of Britain's policies in Egypt and the Middle East. Wilson's objections to keeping troops in north Persia were ignored or overridden in 1920; his anxieties about retaining a small and vulnerable garrison in Iraq after the bulk of the occupying force had departed were discounted in 1922. In these circumstances, and especially after the abrupt change in the Cabinet's Irish policy in July 1921, Wilson's relations with ministers deteriorated and he came increasingly to feel that his professional advice counted for little with them,[34] an assessment which the readiness of ministers to license a further reduction in army manpower through the instrument of the Geddes Committee seemed amply to confirm.

In general, ministers showed no inclination to take seriously the War Office's estimates of the numbers of troops which would be needed to sustain their objectives in different parts of the world, and were unmoved by Wilson's awful warnings of imminent catastrophe in the various sectors of military involvement. Perhaps the absence of a major military disaster between 1918 and 1922 fortified the complacency of ministers and undermined Wilson's credibility. But in one important respect the perennial optimism of the ministers about the army's ability to square any circle was modified by caution. For while ministers were reluctant to withdraw from regions under military occupation at the end of the war without some guarantee that an acceptable successor regime would be set up, they were equally reluctant to assume fresh military obligations for which no precedent, however recent, could be found. It was this latter reservation which, as will be seen, was to discredit the attempt of Curzon, Balfour and Lloyd George to gain Cabinet sanction for the eviction of the Turks from Constantinople in January 1920,[35] and which made the containment of Turkish nationalism the object not, for the most part, of military endeavour but of a machiavellian diplomacy. Ministers baulked at vigorous political intervention beyond the tidemark of wartime occupation. But with this exception, there is little sign that the Cabinet's political strategy in Egypt and the Middle East was shaped *primarily* by a sense of deficiency in military power, or that ministers cherished political objectives which military weakness alone denied them.

Behind this dogged determination to stretch the reserves of military power to the limit and to ignore the strains which this imposed on an army in the throes of post-war contraction and reorganisation, there lay an awareness that the real constraint on the expansion of imperial power, formal or informal, was not so much military as financial. From the first month of peace, the coalition was committed to the pursuit of economy in order to achieve a rapid reduction in the size of the debt accumulated in the war years.[36] In 1919, however, the necessity to meet financial commitments arising out of the war, inevitable delays in demobilising the army, and substantial increases in many items of expenditure such as the pay of the services, postponed retrenchment and enforced further borrowing. The real turning-point in the Cabinet's financial policy, and the real beginning of post-war financial stringency, came with the acceptance by ministers of the report of the Cunliffe Committee on Currency and Foreign Exchanges in the early part of 1920.

The Cunliffe Committee, which was chiefly concerned with Britain's position in international trade and finance, laid great stress on the damage which was being inflicted on these sensitive sectors of economic activity by the inflationary pressures of continued government borrowing.[37] The force of their arguments gained strength from the political complexion of the coalition's parliamentary supporters and from the anxiety of ministers not to be seen to defy the canons of financial orthodoxy. Certainly, Chamberlain's decision to act immediately on the Committee's advice and to check inflation by putting an end to all further borrowing produced a dramatic change in the political context of financial policy. For the Chancellor of the Exchequer intended not only to finance all expenditure out of revenue but to add to that expenditure the cost of redeeming a proportion of the war debt so as to reduce the long-term burden of debt-servicing. The consequence of this sharp change of policy was the imposition of heavier taxation (especially through higher rates of Excess Profits Duty) which aroused keen resentment among the Coalition's Conservative followers in the Commons during the budget debates of 1920.[38] Thereafter, ministers were under constant pressure to make convincing economies in government spending and to apply far more stringent controls on expenditure than in the first year of peace, since distaste for the unpalatable medicine which Chamberlain had administered found vent in widespread denunciations of government extravagance – especially among Conservatives. In June 1920, both Lloyd George and Chamberlain were warning that defence spending in particular must be reduced;[39] while by July the tide of public criticism had so unnerved some ministers that – in anticipation of the Geddes Committee of a year later – the appointment of a committee of 'impartial and unprejudiced persons' – not ministers – to review the whole field of public expenditure, and to educate public opinion in the government's difficulties, was seriously canvassed.[40]

In this climate of opinion, no minister of either coalition party was eager to be publicly identified with proposals for expenditure beyond what was deemed both acceptable and unavoidable. Neither of these criteria could be convincingly applied to the level of defence spending, nor, emphatically, to the cost of the military occupation of Mesopotamia and Persia two years after the Turkish armistice. Thus the atmosphere of the Commons debates on the coalition's policies in these places became noticeably chillier between June and December 1920, when the government encountered open criticism not just from the opposition parties but also from Conservative members, a small number of whom voted with the opposition at the division. In these circumstances, it is likely that the embarrassment of having to seek a supplementary estimate to cover expenditure in Mesopotamia – the occasion of the December debate – at a time when even the ordinary estimates were causing unease strengthened the hand of those ministers who regarded an imperial policy so dependent on military power as a dangerous hostage to political fortune.

Already by the end of 1920, therefore, the need to save money had become an important factor in the political viability of the coalition's imperial diplomacy. Ministers were unable to contemplate, particularly, any commitment which would delay the swift reduction of the army to its pre-war size and cost. To some extent this may have reflected an unthinking conservatism in their approach to economics and imperial defence; but it was also a consequence of the novel burdens which the war had laid upon public finance. New items of social expenditure which it was inexpedient to abandon in the disturbed political conditions of the aftermath, and, above all, the inescapable requirements of debt-servicing, which absorbed a third of gross expenditure in 1922,[41] inevitably focused attention upon the armed services, and upon overseas military spending, as sectors where major savings could be made without serious repercussions for the government's domestic popularity.

In 1921, the onset of economic depression, for which Chamberlain's plans had made no allowance, intensified all these pressures, since it appeared to substantiate the claim that the weight of taxation was bearing too heavily upon incomes and profits. As trade fell off and unemployment grew, the 'genuine alarm throughout the constituencies',[42] which Lloyd George observed, threatened to erode the loyalty of coalition Conservatives, worried by the rapid progress of Rothermere's Anti-Waste League and the by-election defeats of coalition Conservative candidates at the hands of 'ruthless economy' independents.[43] 'The middle classes mean to insist upon a drastic cut-down,' Lloyd George told Chamberlain in June 1921. 'Nothing will satisfy them next year except an actual reduction in taxes.'[44] The defeat of the official Conservative at the St George's election, he went on, represented 'the real sentiment which may overwhelm us if we do not deal with it in time'.[45] The shared determination of Lloyd George and Chamberlain to preserve the coalition's authority among Conservatives, and to appease the discontent of their supporters in the country, lent, in the summer of 1921, a fresh urgency to the search for economies; and led eventually to the adoption of a device which ministers had rejected the previous year: the appointment of a committee of non-ministerial experts to review expenditure. The main result of this review was the imposition of further reductions in the army, navy and air estimates for 1922–3.[46]

The financial anxieties which beset ministers after 1918 were indicative of more than just the temporary difficulties which attended the normalisation of financial policy after a period of heavy extraordinary expenditure. For they were a reflection also of the new uncertainties in Britain's economic circumstances, and of the structural weaknesses which the war had served to reveal and to create. The dislocations of the economy in 1919, the short-lived boom of 1920, and the depression which set in in 1921 were a prelude not to the full revival of Britain to her nineteenth-century pre-eminence as a commercial and financial power, but rather to her relative decline as an industrial producer in the world market and, even more, to her decay as the heart and centre of international finance. As the economic costs of the war made themselves felt, the old confidence in the strength of Britain's industrial and commercial resources drained away to be replaced by a growing sense of the fragility of her position. The rapid growth of rival industrial economies, and the intractability of the problem of war debts served notice that the economic foundations upon which imperial expansion and imperial security had been built in the past could not sustain any further enlargement of the burden imposed on them by the structure of British world power.

For much of the immediate post-war period, therefore, the imperial policies of the Lloyd George coalition were pursued amid domestic circumstances which made severe retrenchment a condition of political survival. It was upon this assumption that the plans of the policy-makers for a permanent British presence in Mesopotamia, Persia and elsewhere had to be made once the euphoria of victory gave way to more sober feelings. The effect was not to overthrow the whole strategy for the defence and expansion of British influence in Egypt and the Middle East since financial constraint at home was only one – even if an important one – of the several elements of the problem. Nevertheless, to a greater extent, perhaps, than any other single factor, the sense of financial vulnerability underlined the hazards of novel or expensive modes of imperial administration at the moment when the orientation of imperial policy, particularly in the Middle East, seemed erratic and undecided; and provided a forceful reminder that 1919 was not to be the dawn of a new and more grandiose imperial age; and that the old financial disciplines of imperial policy, familiar to Gladstone and Salisbury, prevailed, and in a form which was, if anything, more stringent than ever before.

The Politics of the Coalition

In their approach to the issues of imperial policy that were raised in Egypt and the Middle East after 1918, ministers were necessarily swayed by more than just the practical considerations of military power and financial resource. The impact of domestic politics upon their calculations could not be contained merely by a recognition that there was a limit to the sacrifices in money and men which the mother-country would make to retain or extend British control in regions of strategic importance. For political and parliamentary opinion in Britain, while it was highly sensitive to such logistical arguments and traditionally suspicious of ministers who appeared to treat them lightly, was responsive also to convictions and beliefs which were more than simple rationalisations of economic self-interest or military weakness. The long experience of colonial empire had entrenched powerful sentiments about the correct modes of imperial rule and, even more, about the proper management of colonial politics: sentiments and prejudices whose most ardent exponents were to be found in the dominant party of the Lloyd George coalition.

In the coalition government of 1918 to 1922, however, it was not at first entirely clear in what way and to what extent opinion in Britain on questions of imperial policy had been modified by the war and by the political and economic circumstances of the aftermath; nor how far domestic opinion of any kind would trench on ministerial authority. In the first months of 1919 there seemed amid the turmoil of demobilisation and economic readjustment at home, and the search for a German settlement in Europe, a general indifference to the government's efforts to uphold British power in India, Egypt and even in Ireland.[47] Ministers were largely free to devise and apply policies without regard to the House of Commons, or to the views of their back-bench supporters,[48] perhaps because the large intake of new Conservative members needed time to take stock of the ministry and the tendency of its decisions.

By the end of the year, however, with the signs of a growing popular discontent with the coalition, reflected in a steady stream of by-elections,[49] the attitude of the policy-makers towards parliamentary opinion had become less olympian, while their actions came to be scrutinised more critically by their followers. In part, this change may have been due to the government's inevitable failure to restore economic and financial stability as rapidly as had been expected. But it also owed much to the difficulties that grew out of the peculiar political foundations on which the authority of the ministers depended.

The coalition over which Lloyd George presided after the election of 1918 had been acquiesced in by the leaders of the Conservative party to ensure a smooth transition to peace and reconstruction in a period when electoral uncertainties consequent upon the war had been compounded by the great extension of the franchise under the Representation of the People Act of 1918. To Bonar Law, writing in the last weeks of the war, it appeared that the Conservative party in its pre-war incarnation 'will never have any future again in this country';[50] that without an accommodation with Lloyd George and a section of the Liberal party, social legislation would become a battleground of political forces increasingly driven to the extremes of radicalism and reaction.[51] To secure agreement over a programme of reforms 'as little revolutionary as possible'[52] was, therefore, a cardinal justification for retaining Lloyd George's services as Prime Minister and for prolonging the structure of political authority established in 1916. But although Bonar Law recognised the theoretical attractions of absorbing Lloyd George and his following into the body of a reorganised Conservative party[53] – as the Liberal Unionists had ultimately been absorbed – no real attempt was made in this direction when the wartime alliance of parties was renewed. Hesitation among coalition Liberals at the prospect of permanently separating themselves from the mainstream of the Liberal party in the country, and a surviving attachment to the old articles of the Liberal creed,[54] helped to preserve the temporary and provisional character of the partnership and encouraged expectations of an eventual revival of party warfare along familar pre-war lines.

Coalition Liberal contrariness was symptomatic of the fluid political conditions which obtained in the aftermath of the war when the programmes and strategies of all parties hinged upon varying predictions of the effects of mass suffrage and the rise of the Labour movement. In both wings of the Lloyd George coalition there were those who believed that prolonged association would damage their standing in the eyes of their supporters in the electorate or precipitate dangerous alignments and confrontations in British politics. Sensitivity to such opinions reinforced, perhaps, the refusal of most coalition Liberal ministers to contemplate fusion in 1920,[55] despite Lloyd George's discovery that going on with coalition in its existing form would be 'suicidal'.[56] But although a respect for the shibboleths of Liberalism, and a desire not to drive the coalition Liberals into resignation and reunion undoubtedly had some influence on the political stance and policies of the Lloyd George Cabinet, the real issue in the internal politics of the coalition after the honeymoon year of 1919 was the assuagement of anti-coalition feeling among Conservatives in Parliament and in the constituencies.

At the heart of Conservative dissidence[57] lay the conviction, fortified by the electoral failures of coalition Liberalism, that partnership with Lloyd George and his followers as a means of staving off radical reform and the dominance of the Left was an asset of steadily diminishing value since Lloyd George's ability to manipulate working-class opinion seemed increasingly doubtful, especially after January 1920. At the same time, continued loyalty to Lloyd George by the Conservative leadership and his retention as the head of the government caused a sense of grievance, especially among Conservative supporters in those constituencies where coalition imposed a self-denying ordinance. For in seats held by coalition Liberals, the terms of the electoral alliance forbade the adoption of an official Conservative candidate, drying up the flow of subscriptions and removing the social and political incentives which helped to sustain party activity in the localities.[58] The effect of this discontent in the constituencies was to persuade some of the coalition's parliamentary supporters that a tighter rein was necessary on the actions of Lloyd George and that a closer watch should be set on the susceptibility of Conservative ministers to the influence of the Prime Minister. To others, it seemed proof of the need to break up the coalition at the earliest possible moment.

Although there is no sign that in 1920 any of the Conservative ministers in the government wished to subvert the coalition, or were particularly disillusioned with its performance, they were anxious, nevertheless, to remain in touch with political feeling among their followers, and, in defending the coalition, not to give substance to the criticisms levelled at it from within the Conservative party. Chamberlain's budget, Montagu's 'provocative and violent'[59] speech denouncing General Dyer's action at Amritsar, and Lloyd George's negotiations with the representatives of Bolshevik Russia,[60] all caused difficulties with Conservative back-benchers. Lloyd George, in deference to Bonar Law's judgment, bent with the breeze and ruled against the proposed levy on war profits as a fresh source of revenue. 'The fact is', said Fisher, 'that he can't hold his Tories if he combines negotiations with Krassin and the War Levy.'[61] Later in the year, the appeasement of Conservative prejudice forced Lloyd George reluctantly to expel the principal Bolshevik negotiator, Kamenev, on the grounds that he was helping to foment the widespread industrial unrest of the autumn.[62]

Despite these early warnings, it was not until Bonar Law's retirement in March 1921, with 'dangerously high blood pressure',[63] that the problem of Conservative discontent became of real importance in the construction of policy. Two issues in particular threatened the coalition Cabinet's parliamentary authority and influenced its approach to imperial as well as domestic politics. The first of these was the growing opposition to the level of taxation and public expenditure which has already been noticed and which, in the form of Lord Rothermere's Anti-Waste League, made striking advances in the middle-class suburban constituencies that were the heartland of Conservatism.[64] The 'drastic cut down' upon the necessity of which Lloyd George and Chamberlain, the new Conservative leader, were agreed, led to the sacrifice of Addison and to the creation of the Geddes Committee. It also made much more urgent the installation of a reliable Arab regime in Iraq where the dependence of imperial policy upon a costly garrison made it vulnerable to charges of waste, and where the reconciliation of economy and security seemed peculiarly difficult.

But the impact of Anti-Waste, largely anaesthetised as a political issue by the appointment of Geddes and his colleagues, was far outweighed by that of a second question which came in 1921 to dominate the internal politics of the Conservative party and the coalition alike. For with the abandonment of coercion in Ireland in July, and the beginnings of negotiation with Sinn Féin – skilfully presented by Lloyd George in Cabinet as being 'fair to the King'[65] – the most virulent prejudices in the Conservative party were roused from slumber. Bargaining with the leaders of the 'murder gang', and betraying the forces of loyalty and order in Ireland, were difficult, the coercion of Ulster impossible, to justify to the party of Salisbury, Balfour and Bonar Law. But the danger that Lloyd George and Chamberlain faced was not the repudiation by the Conservative party as a whole of any attempt to come to terms with Sinn Féin. 'There is an intense desire for peace,' Sir George Younger, the chairman of the Conservative party organisation, told Chamberlain in a confidential report on the state of feeling in the party. 'It would not be easy to kindle the flame which burnt so fiercely before 1914.'[66] The real threat to the coalition was the irreconcilable opposition of the fifty or so die-hards in the Commons to any form of Irish Home Rule, and the likelihood that by rejecting any compromise they would succeed in making the overthrow of Lloyd George the price of party unity.

In the Irish negotiations, the struggle to outmanoeuvre, discredit and disarm die-hard opposition led Lloyd George to insist upon the exclusion of Ulster from a compulsory membership of the projected Irish Free State, and upon a formal declaration of southern Ireland's allegiance to the Crown, as the price of independence. But in the autumn of 1921, it was not only in Ireland that British ministers confronted recalcitrant nationalists. Both in India and in Egypt the government had to decide how far it was willing to appease nationalist movements whose cooperation was deemed vital by its proconsular subordinates.[67] However different the circumstances, it was plain that a further round of concessions to Gandhi and the Egyptian pashas on the eve of the Conservative party conference at Liverpool in November 1921, at a moment when the Irish negotiations hung in the balance[68] (and with them the leadership of the Conservative party and the survival of the coalition), could only strengthen the die-hard claim that Lloyd George was engaged in the wholesale demolition of the British Empire. As the Cabinet grudgingly conceded the principle of diplomatic representation for an independent Egypt, and fretted at Reading's delay in gaoling Gandhi, Chamberlain warned Curzon of the existence of a 'compact nucleus of some fifty members who will vote against us on any motion relating to Ireland or India or on such questions as arose yesterday'. 'Our concessions to Egypt', he added, 'will alarm and irritate these same people.'[69] To Fisher, writing on the same day, it seemed that the Prime Minister was 'so anxious about Ireland that he dare not make concessions about Egypt'.[70]

The tensions and uncertainties surrounding the conclusion of an Irish treaty at the end of 1921 go some way towards explaining the reluctance of ministers to sympathise with the political difficulties which faced Allenby in Egypt and the Viceroy in India. They may also explain, if Fisher was right, why Lloyd George adopted an uncharacteristically rigid attitude towards political compromise in both cases, forcing Curzon to become the champion of appeasement in Egypt, and uttering resounding declarations of Britain's determination to uphold the *Raj* in India. For although the policy of treating with Sinn Féin was approved at the Conservative party conference, and the eventual agreement was supported by the great majority of coalition Conservatives in the House of Commons, Lloyd George and Chamberlain were unable in the ensuing months to exorcise the passions which had been aroused within the Conservative party. In retrospect, it seemed to Chamberlain that it had been the failure to reconcile the die-hards which led ultimately to the fall of the coalition. The Irish settlement, he told George Lloyd, had been

> accepted with reluctant relief and a good deal of anxious misgiving by the great majority of the Party, but bitterly resented as a betrayal by a small section of it. Gradually around this section all the discontents crystallised and under pressure of the machine . . . the feeling against the continuation of the Lloyd George premiership grew into a formidable force.[71]

Chamberlain's commitment to the coalition, which was fervent, enjoined, therefore, even after December 1921, great circumspection in the handling of issues which bore comparison with the Irish question and which might be used to mount a further attack on the coalition and the Prime Minister. It remained important to preserve the appearance of firm imperial control in Egypt and India, and to deny that the government was ready to bargain with extremism. 'Firmness and clearness of policy in India and Egypt are held to be vital,'[72] declared Walter Long, with all the authority of an elder statesman, in a survey of Conservative discontent early in 1922.

By the spring, however, Chamberlain was confident that die-hard influence in the party was on the wane,[73] helped by the successful reception of the Allenby Declaration[74] and the removal of the die-hards' *bête noire*, Montagu, from the India Office.[75] Despite continuing unease over Ireland and over the political consequences if Britain were to accord diplomatic recognition to Bolshevik Russia, he remained optimistic that the party would stay loyal to the coalition and that 'in course of time the moderate and imperial-minded Liberals . . . may be drawn into the Unionist party'.[76] But even if anti-coalition sentiment was not widespread in the party, there was nevertheless no certainty that Chamberlain's Conservative followers would agree to fight a further election as a coalition if Lloyd George continued at the head of the government. Towards the end of the summer of 1922, this special hostility towards Lloyd George, rather than the coalition, appeared to grow more marked.[77] Thus in September, Chamberlain was being warned by Derby, by Younger and by Leslie Wilson, Chief Conservative Whip, that such a course would be unacceptable to the bulk of the party and might result in his overthrow as leader.[78]

The final phase of the coalition's imperial policy in the Middle East was played out against this background of renewed uncertainty about the future of Lloyd George and, indeed, of Chamberlain himself. But if those who wished to eject Lloyd George from the premiership hoped to use the confrontation with Kemal at Chanak to isolate him from the senior Conservative ministers, they were frustrated by the shared conviction of Chamberlain, Balfour and Curzon that the Kemalists could not be allowed to take control of the Dardanelles.[79] Nor was there much sign that ministers feared a rebellion by Conservative members against the policy of resisting Kemal by force if necessary. What transformed the coalition's bold diplomacy into a domestic issue of lasting notoriety was not a Conservative revolt against its supposed recklessness, but rather the decision by Lloyd George and Chamberlain to use the striking success that they had achieved to reassert their political authority and carry the coalition forward to a general election with its leadership unchanged.[80] It followed that success at Chanak, not failure, made it necessary for Lloyd George's opponents in the

Conservative party to portray him as the practitioner of brinkmanship, and the policy which he and Chamberlain had pursued as *folie de grandeur*.[81] With so much at stake, the Prime Minister's enemies dared not let him pose as the heir of Palmerston and Salisbury; nor did they want to suffer the charge of unpatriotic opposition.

The failure of Chamberlain's attempt to beat down Conservative dissidence by making his own continuation as party leader dependent upon the preservation of Lloyd George in office[82] suggests, however, that a resolute policy in the Middle East was not enough to counter the powerful domestic influences which had eroded the authority of the Lloyd George coalition. Chamberlain's subsequent bitter resentment at the hostile attitude of the press, of the opposition, of Rothermere, Asquith and Grey towards the government's 'firmness'[83] may have reflected his later conviction that a Turkish war to defend Chanak would not have commanded the support of wider public opinion, as some ministers warned at the time.[84] For neither Lloyd George nor Curzon, as the real architects of British policy in the Middle East since 1919, had made serious efforts to enlist a broadly based political support for their purposes – partly, perhaps, because of their mutual jealousies. This neglect made it all too easy for the resistance to Kemalism to be lampooned as 'LG's insane love of the Greeks'.[85] Public indifference to an imperial strategy the meaning of which had been veiled in obscurity so long as it had been sustained by the convenient application of Greek manpower, could not be transformed overnight into jingo enthusiasm.

The composition of the House of Commons and of the coalition ensured that for the most part the parliamentary and political criticisms which made the greatest impact upon the policies of the ministers would be those which derived from their own disparate following. But although it would be unwise to attribute to the Labour party, as the main party of opposition, much influence if any over the formulation of imperial policy in Egypt and the Middle East, its unsympathetic attitude towards the government's strategies was a further domestic constraint upon ministerial freedom of action in the affairs of these regions. The leaders of the coalition were watchful in all spheres of government activity for issues which the Labour party might exploit to weaken the 'constitutional' parties. They did not wish to concede any hostage to a party of whose general intentions they were extremely mistrustful, and whose electoral progress it was the prime function of the coalition to obstruct. Thus though they might disregard Labour's criticisms in June 1921 of the retention of a garrison in Egypt and of British control over her foreign policy[86] – if only because of the strong countervailing pressure from their own followers – they showed more respect for the opposition's attack on the enlargement of imperial commitments in the Middle East. For on questions which involved continued military expenditure abroad the Labour party's attitude did not reflect merely the internationalist enthusiasms of the Cobdenites whom it had recruited from the old Liberal party. Labour's insistence on the need to cut military spending in the Middle East as well as in Ireland was more than a genuflection to its anti-militarist tradition. The reduction of 'unproductive' expenditure was instead one of a series of proposals for countering unemployment[87] which were meant to appeal directly to the trade unions and to working-class voters, and which purported to show how the policies of the coalition threatened the interests and the livelihood of the industrial population. Coupled with middle-class resentment against high taxation, the danger of appearing indifferent to the financial causes of mass unemployment in Britain hammered home ministers' realisation in 1921 that if imperial purposes were to be served at all in the Middle East it could only be by the most economical of methods, and by the use of great discretion in the open deployment of imperial power.

Conclusion

The imperial policy of the coalition government in Egypt and the Middle East was constrained in two different respects by the movement of domestic opinion in Britain, accentuated, even distorted, by the internal structure of the party alliance. Ministers were, in the first place, unable to license, even had they wished to do so, an expansion of British influence except where they could find political alternatives to the costly apparatus of direct rule and military occupation. Only Churchill's success in thus converting the basis of British authority in Iraq removed the coalition's policy there from the sphere of political controversy; while Curzon's inability to construct a pliant but effective regime in Persia greatly weakened the claim of his Anglo-Persian Agreement upon ministerial sympathies. Had the confrontation at Chanak turned into a major military commitment of indefinite duration, the same difficulty would probably have arisen. For whatever the dreams of ministers and their advisers when the prospect of military victory in the Middle East was unfolded at the end of 1918, it was clear within a few months of the armistices that there had been no such shift in political attitudes in

Britain as might liberate the policy-makers from the old requirements of strict economy in the use of men and money. The dogma that Britain's land forces in peacetime should be no greater than those which had been maintained before the war was never seriously challenged. And the special vulnerability of the coalition, for reasons which have been described, to middle-class resentment against high taxation for whatever purpose, coupled with the mushroom growth of new financial commitments in debt servicing and social services, ensured that the reduction of military and imperial expenditure to its pre-war standard would be rapid and ruthless.

For these reasons, reflecting as they did the preoccupation of domestic politics with the recovery of economic, financial and social stability in Britain, there was no fund of public enthusiasm for the expansion of imperial power on which ministers could draw. In Turkey, Persia and Iraq, it seemed safer to veil the real objects of policy and reduce to a minimum the direct application of British power and resources. But the indifference or hostility of domestic opinion to the forward movement of the Empire's strategic frontiers did not signal a new disillusionment with the value of Britain's imperial system as a whole. In so far as political opinion at home was registered in the conduct of policy towards Britain's established dependencies, it acted to restrain rather than promote the search for more flexible techniques of imperial control. The significance of this should not, however, be exaggerated. Constitutional change in India and Egypt did not become a political issue until Lloyd George's hold over the Conservative party was placed in jeopardy by his search for an accommodation with Sinn Féin, and it became convenient for his critics to view the coalition's policy in Ireland, India and Egypt alike as the short road to imperial collapse. Nor is it clear that die-hard pressure modified in a fundamental way the approach of ministers to the problems of imperial control even if it encouraged caution in their public dealings with nationalist leaders. Lacking radical purposes in their recasting of the imperial presence, the main care of ministers was to preserve the apparently seamless web of continuity in their relations with colonial nationalisms; their main anxiety lest what they viewed as necessary easements in the machinery of imperial rule might be damned by their critics as strengthening the forces of revolutionary extremisms dedicated to the overthrow of the Empire. For what domestic opinion appeared to require was not the rigid maintenance of direct rule but the appearance at least of order and discipline in the relations between the British and the societies where their influence was paramount. The experience of 1918 to 1922 seemed to show that while ministers could meet this condition, and avoid any drastic increase in the military and administrative costs of empire, they had little reason to fear that the coming of mass politics would impose a new orientation on their imperial diplomacy.

Part II

Problems of Political Control: Egypt

3 British Policy and the Origins of the Post-War Crisis

The Background to the British Occupation

The arrival of British troops in Egypt in August 1882 marked the first stage in the creation of a paramount authority in the country which Britain was to enjoy in various forms and under various guises until after the Second World War. During this period, no other foreign power was to exercise anything like the degree of influence over Egyptian affairs which Britain could deploy as a result of the political and military arrangements which were instituted after the destruction of Arabi's army at the battle of Tel el-Kebir in September 1882.

Fundamental to an understanding of the circumstances in which British intervention took place, and which allowed the elaboration of British control, is an appreciation of the extent to which Egypt's political stability had been eroded by the stresses of rapid and far-reaching social and economic change over the previous fifty years. For Egypt in the later nineteenth century was very far from being a backward oriental state sunk in the pathetic contentment of subsistence agriculture and traditional social forms. Rather had it become by the 1870s perhaps the most striking example of the penetration of European commercial and social influences in a non-European and non-Christian society, with a significant population of Europeans[1] and an increasingly heavy dependence upon the workings of the international economy.[2] As a result, Egyptian society suffered in an advanced form from the same kind of internal tensions as could be found in the less dynamic societies of Persia and China.

Nominally, Egypt, even before the occupation of 1882, was not a sovereign state but a tributary of the Ottoman Empire. In reality, since the collapse of Bonaparte's effort to construct an oriental empire on the Nile, it had enjoyed many of the attributes of an independent state as a consequence of the vigorous struggle which had been waged by Mehemet Ali, the founder of the dynasty which ruled in Egypt until 1952, against the suzerain power in Constantinople. It was this struggle which had set in motion the great changes in Egypt's social and economic organisation which were subsequently to determine the course of its politics. For Mehemet Ali's success depended upon his ability to eradicate the bonds of religious loyalty and cultural sympathy which bound Egypt to the capital of Islam, and to foster instead a secular patriotism focused upon the upstart dynasty he represented. Secondly, it depended upon the creation of a naval and military machine powerful enough to sustain him against the Ottomans and to make his authority supreme in Egypt – a war machine more sophisticated and expensive than anything hitherto supported by the resources of the country. With these two objectives, the Pasha set out to reconstruct the entire basis of landholding in Egypt to obtain a larger share of agrarian revenues for the state, and to assert his power in the countryside. At the same time, to finance his extensive purchases of military equipment abroad, he took up with enthusiasm the conversion of Egyptian agriculture to the production of a staple which would supply the foreign exchange he needed. That staple was cotton.[3]

This great programme for the creation of an Egyptian state, and for the centralisation of authority and wealth within it, played a crucial role in jerking Egypt into the modern world. For the two great changes inaugurated by Mehemet Ali worked to reinforce each other's effects. Thus the Pasha, in asserting the control of the dynasty over the distribution of landholding, was anxious that those who held land should be able to meet the increasingly heavy burden of taxation which he imposed. Those who defaulted suffered confiscation; and the land so obtained was granted under conditional tenures to those who appeared capable of paying the land tax and of enhancing the value of the soil.[4] Control of the land passed, as a result, into the hands of those who regarded it as a commercial as well as a social asset, and who were favourably inclined towards the production of commodity crops for the European market to meet their financial obligations to the state. The pressures of taxation and of commercial opportunity, therefore, steadily transformed, throughout the nineteenth century, the old social relations between the landholder and the peasant cultivators who tilled the soil; a trend which was accentuated by such institutional changes as the legitimisation of mortgage rights which came in 1875, and the increasing security of inheritance of land theoretically held from the ruler on the conditional tenures of *kharaj* and *ushur*.

In the first half of the century, Mehemet Ali and his successors had been able to strengthen their control over the countryside and to expand their revenues by installing a new landholding élite closely bound to their court and administration, and by an informal alliance with the agents of European commerce. But after 1850 the ruling dynasty increasingly lost control over the social processes it had instigated and over the new propertied class it had helped to create. For this the main reason lay in the inability of Mehemet Ali's successors to match their expenditure to their resources; and in their readiness to meet their financial difficulties by compounding their rights over the control and distribution of land for the payment in advance of taxation for which that land was liable. During the 1870s, the extension of this practice, notably through the *Muqabala* law, allowed almost all land holders to free themselves from the interference of the royal house and to invest their estates with almost all the characteristics of private property.[5] The effect of this change was to reduce substantially the power of the dynasty to enforce political and social discipline among the notables who now dominated the localities, and to make it more and more dependent upon their cooperation.[6]

This gradual shift in the politics of Egypt was sharply accelerated in the crisis years of 1876 to 1882. In 1876, the Khedive Ismail, the ruler, was no longer able to service the foreign loans on which his administration had come to depend, and became bankrupt. His attempt to restore his credit and salvage Egypt's public finances by appointing a commission of foreign experts who enjoyed the support of his overseas creditors and the confidence of the French and British governments might have resolved his financial difficulties but only at the expense of alienating those in Egyptian society whose assistance and loyalty were essential to the exercise of his political authority. For to give a commission, and especially a commission of foreign Christians, full powers to reform the revenue system and to revoke those concessions and immunities which had become the mainstay of the Khedive's financial policy in the interests of sound finance would signal an attempt to reverse the great changes in property relations upon which the wealth and status of the rural notables depended. It would risk, therefore, the opposition of all those who had served and exploited the old system. Yet were the Khedive to suppress the commission, he would cut off entirely the flow of foreign finance and place himself in the hands of the notables and landlords. Moreover, with Egypt's agrarian economy now so closely integrated into the operations of the international economy, to sunder the links between his regime and the machinery of international commerce would mean the destruction not only of the financial system upon which the dynasty's strength was built, but also of every major achievement of the ruling house since the beginning of the century.

In these critical circumstances, the first and foremost objective of Ismail was to preserve the authority of the Khediviate, and to avoid becoming the prisoner either of the notable class or of the foreign bondholders. To this end, he was prepared, if necessary, to look outside the political class and appeal to the traditional religious élite, the ulama, who had never been properly reconciled to the social and intellectual changes which had occurred,[7] but who retained a formidable influence over the mass of population;[8] and to the army. Thus, having reluctantly constituted a reforming ministry in partnership with the landlord class, Ismail first intrigued against it and then secured its downfall through a military demonstration.[9] But this bold attempt to free himself from the toils failed in the face of the irritation of the foreign powers; and when his formal suzerain in Constantinople ordered him to vacate the throne in June 1879, Ismail could rally no important sector of Egyptian society to his side. Even his abdication gained no respite for the dynasty whose functioning was increasingly a matter of indifference to those social forces – the landholders, the ulama and the army – whose interests were threatened by financial retrenchment or the augmentation of foreign influences. The mutiny of the army, the first and last resort of Khedivial power, and the acquiescence of the traditional and modern élites alike in the overthrow of Ismail's successor, revealed the political as well as financial bankruptcy of the new order which Mehemet Ali had founded.

Three generations of rapid change thus produced by 1882 a breakdown in the established forms of political authority in Egypt and opened the way for the emergence of a new and unpredictable regime to replace the old alliance of the dynasty, the propertied class and the agencies of commerce. The collapse of this alliance served moreover to emphasise the social conflicts which remained unresolved in Egyptian society: the disadvantages which accrued to the fellahin as a result of agrarian improvements;[10] the flight from the country to the towns;[11] the decline of the traditional urban economies as a result of the influx of Western manufactures and the obsolescence of the old caravan routes;[12] the failure of urban and educated Egyptians to make headway in the professions still dominated by foreigners[13] (with the consequence that public service became the vital channel of advancement); the failure to develop an industrial sector to siphon off the surplus of agricultural labour;[14] the continuing dissonance between that part of Egyptian society which was modernised and Europeanised, and the large part which remained under the influence of traditional religious and social ideas, and deeply hostile to the permeation of Western influences. All these features of Egyptian society survived British intervention in 1882 and aggravated the difficulty of anticipating and managing the movements of its politics.

The effect of British occupation was not therefore to halt the social and economic evolution of Egypt but rather to interrupt its political side-effects; to shore up the shaken authority of the dynasty as a means of preventing xenophobic or unreliable groups from controlling the country. Henceforth, the struggle between the competing elements of political society in Egypt had to take account of the British attitude; and the Egyptian protagonists strove to use the imperial factor for their own purposes. In the period with which we are primarily concerned, the internal evolution of Egyptian politics, and the outcome of the dynasty's struggle to preserve its old prerogatives, was still uncertain; for the court, despite its collapse in 1882, still retained under the British occupation a substantial influence in the localities through its holdings of land,[15] and wide patronage in the central administration. After 1882, much was to depend not so much upon a confrontation between the British on the one hand and the Egyptians on the other; as on the ways in which all the varied and inchoate political formations in Egypt could adapt the imperial presence to suit their own needs in local politics.

British Policy before 1914

The British had intended their appearance in Egypt to be brief but salutary: to provide an interval during which the forces of stability and progress would reassèrt themselves and continue Egypt's tradition of close association with Britain and France. To satisfy both international opinion and their own followers, British ministers tended to emphasise the temporary and provisional character of the occupation of 1882, and to stress their eagerness to withdraw from Egypt at the earliest possible opportunity. And even after this moment of withdrawal came to appear a mere fancy of the official mind, a convenient illusion, the British stuck resolutely to the appearances of a diplomatic rather than a colonial presence. Egypt was not annexed to the Crown. The British representative went undignified by the title of High Commissioner or Resident and remained a mere Consul-General. Egyptian affairs continued to be the province of the Foreign rather than the Colonial Secretary.

These devices could not, however, conceal the reality of the power which the British exercised in Egypt after 1882: a power founded ultimately upon the presence of their garrison and Britain's naval strength in the eastern Mediterranean. But what the British had to decide was how they proposed to use that power and what political arrangements in Egypt would best suit their requirement that British influence should be exercised informally through the Egyptian political system. Their first concern was, in fact, to persuade the Khedive, whom they had hoisted back on to the throne, to reorganise his shattered finances in accordance with British notions of financial administration, both as a means of strengthening Britain's claim to be acting as the trustee of all European interests in Egypt and as an essential precondition to the restoration of order in Egyptian politics. For so long as the guardians of the public purse in Cairo were reduced to the mortgaging of uncollected revenues, to defaulting on the pay of the bureaucracy and the army, and to making desperate and one-sided bargains with the propertied classes, there could be little hope of constructing a durable political settlement. In British eyes, insolvency and anarchy seemed but two sides of the same coin.

Sound financial administration was to be the pivot of Egypt's recovery from the breakdown of 1876–82. But the British also wished to introduce measures of constitutional and administrative reform to fortify the patient against a recurrence of the old symptoms. Thus the Dufferin Report of 1883 proposed to establish representative institutions in the form of an assembly and a legislative council, and to remodel not only the administration of the revenue but that of the army, of the police and of the intricate and politically sensitive irrigation system.[16] But if Dufferin himself was doubtful whether such improvements could be effected without firm and consistent British support,[17] Cromer, who arrived as Consul-General in the summer of 1883, was convinced that with the authority of the Khedive still in question the elements of a new equilibrium acceptable to Britain were lacking:[18] a conclusion which the political crisis occasioned by the loss of Egypt's empire in the Sudan, and the attempt to reform the police, appeared to confirm. The hallmark of Cromer's policy became, therefore, the search for a system in Egypt which would promote internal stability by the careful adjustment of the machinery of government; and which would, at the same time, preserve a paramount British influence, since it became increasingly clear as time passed that not even the most thorough-going or beneficial reform of Egyptian political life would render superfluous Britain's need to intervene periodically on behalf of her strategic and financial interests.[19]

Under Cromer's guidance, British control in Egypt rested upon four main principles of policy. First of all, Cromer obtained from his masters in London the assurances of the permanency of a British presence which were necessary if his words were to carry any weight in Cairo. Secondly, he established a close personal and political relationship with the Khedive Tewfik whose temperament and political judgment made him an ideal collaborator,[20] and who 'often used his influence'[21] to smooth the path of the occupying power – a willingness not unconnected, it may be thought, to the circumstances of his restoration. Thirdly, Cromer used his own financial abilities to help square the circle of Egyptian politics. The irritation provoked by administrative reform was soothed by the reduction of taxation and by the improvement of bureaucratic salaries.[22] By this, Cromer sought to restore a wider freedom of political manoeuvre to the Egyptian government and make it less vulnerable to popular discontent. Lastly, the fragile edifice of cooperation was buttressed by the continued presence of a British garrison and by the control which the British had established early on over the diminished ranks of the Egyptian army. A British *Sirdar* and an officer corps seconded from the British and Indian armies now stood between any future Arabi and a successful military revolt.

Events were to show that if Britain's indirect control of the government of Egypt were to function smoothly it was necessary to maintain all these four constituents in good order. Thus the great crisis of Cromer's regime which occurred in 1893–4 closely followed the death of Tewfik in 1891 and his replacement by Abbas II, who shared neither his pliable temperament nor his sense of dependence on the occupying power. The influence of the court ceased, as a result, to act as a check upon the resentments of the notables and was used instead to stimulate the articulation of anti-British feeling as a way of re-establishing the old alliance of court and country and freeing the Khediviate from its close identification with the alien occupation. Abbas demonstrated the new spirit of independence by replacing, without Cromer's sanction, the Egyptian premier by an 'anglophobe', Fakhry.[23] Cromer responded by obtaining reinforcements for the British garrison and leave from Rosebery to occupy government buildings if necessary.[24] But this action, effective in the short term, encouraged Abbas to rally a larger coalition against him. 'Nine tenths of the official class from the Khedive downwards', Cromer told Rosebery in December 1893, 'are as hostile as they can be.'[25] In the same month, the Legislative Council, hitherto a docile body, not least because of its domination by Khedivial appointments, refused to discuss the budget, denounced expenditure upon the British garrison and called for Britain's withdrawal.[26] In January 1894, the Khedive turned to the central pillar of Cromer's authority and incited a demonstration against the *Sirdar*, Kitchener. Cromer seized this opportunity to threaten Abbas with a direct confrontation that would have ended in his deposition. Abbas yielded and publicly retracted his criticisms of Kitchener.

The alarm caused by Abbas' intrigues prompted Cromer to modify the techniques of political control on whose efficacy the recent events had cast a shadow. After 1894 the imperial factor was re-deployed to monitor more effectively the links of patronage and persuasion which bound the localities to Cairo. One aspect of this was the influx of British officials in larger numbers and their more general penetration of the Egyptian administration.[27] A second was the appointment of a British adviser at the Ministry of the Interior to supervise internal security and keep watch on the activities of the provincial and district governors.[28] Then, under the Judicial Adviser, Scott, sweeping changes were made in the Native Judiciary which Milner summarised as 'the careful elimination of the less truthworthy elements of the old Bench, and the substitution of a number of new and better qualified men'.[29] The 'veiled protectorate' was on the march in search of fresh collaborators. At the same time, the effect of these measures was reinforced by the vigorous external policy of the occupying power after 1896. The reconquest of the Sudan under Kitchener confirmed the primacy of British military power in the Nile valley; while the outcome of the Fashoda crisis extinguished any hope that French intervention would weaken Britain's grip on Egypt.[30] In these circumstances, there was little incentive in Egypt to withdraw cooperation from the occupying power, and little evidence of any successful movement against the terms of British control. Meanwhile, Abbas, with his overt political activity closely supervised by Cromer and the phalanx of advisers, was reduced to patronising the coterie of salon politicians and journalists who, under the inspiration of Mustafa Kamil, preached an amalgam of local patriotism and pan-Islamic fervour.[31]

The marked tendency of Cromer's later policy towards the subordination of the Khedive, rather than an alliance with him, and towards a tighter control over the lower levels of Egyptian politics, was reversed by his successor as Consul-General, Sir Eldon Gorst. Gorst had been a protégé of Cromer's and had served in Cromer's time as Financial Adviser in Egypt, a post second in importance only to that of the

Consul-General himself. But Gorst believed that the regime over which Cromer presided in his later years had become too narrowly based and, by increasing the power and scope of British officials in the administration, ran the risk of alienating Egyptian opinion altogether.[32] In urging the creation of a more sympathetic political relationship between British and Egyptians, Gorst was probably assisted by the desire of Grey as Foreign Secretary to lend a less authoritarian cast to the Temporary Occupation and by the concern which Cromer's management of the notorious Denshawai incident had caused at home.[33] On his appointment, therefore, he set out to restore what he regarded as the older and purer tradition of Anglo-Egyptian cooperation. The Khedive was to be treated with a consideration and respect which Cromer had denied him, and his constitutional status given public recognition. The provincial and district governors were to be given greater freedom from their British watchdogs, the inspectors and advisers.[34] But more important still was the task of breathing life into the institutions which Dufferin had created. The Legislative Council and the General Assembly were given 'an opportunity of making their voice heard in matters of importance'.[35] The provincial councils were granted wider powers especially in the field of education.

The result of Gorst's experiment was not to produce a new harmony between the occupying power and its reluctant clients. His political initiative was greeted by renewed nationalist agitation and a general attitude of criticism and opposition which depressed him.[36] The reason for this discouraging response may not be hard to seek. For the significance of Gorst's actions in the context of Egyptian politics had been to re-open the internal conflicts which Cromer's policy had banked down. The new cordiality between Consul-General and Khedive was calculated to alarm all those who had welcomed, however privately, Cromer's suppression of the influence of the court.[37] At the same time, the relaxation of British control over the provincial councils and the Assembly encouraged the notables to defend themselves against both the Khedive and the Consul-General by appealing to anti-British feeling. 'The Council . . . and also the General Assembly', reported Gorst ruefully, 'displayed in 1909 and the first half of 1910, a steadily increasing tendency to become the mere instruments of the Nationalist agitation against the Occupation. . . .'[38] In 1910, this intransigence came to a head over Gorst's attempt to obtain from the Assembly an extension of the ninety-nine year concession held by the Suez Canal Company. Gorst's efforts to recruit support in the Assembly were a fiasco and the Egyptian ministers who had been entrusted with the winning of the new concession lost control of the legislature. The assassination of Butros Ghali, the premier, was the last straw. Gorst told Grey: 'The conclusion to be drawn is that the policy of ruling this country in cooperation with native ministers is, at the present time, incompatible with that of encouraging the development of so-called representative institutions . . . There can be no doubt as to which of these two courses should be preferred.'[39]

Frustrated and disillusioned, Gorst in the last months of his consulship returned to the Cromerian tradition of closer British control and sought and gained Grey's support for a policy of masterfulness.[40] But the real work of restoring a more vigorous imperial presence fell to his successor, the former *Sirdar* Lord Kitchener. The first care of the 'Butcher of Khartoum' was to convey to the Khedive that the days of 'al-Lurd' had returned. The new atmosphere of deference towards the ruler which Gorst had encouraged was abruptly exchanged for a perfunctory courtesy which recalled Cromer's schoolmasterish attitude to Abbas II.[41] Kitchener resumed Cromer's self-appointed role as the protector of the fellahin. His semi-regal tours through the provinces were designed to re-establish the authority and prestige of the occupying power in the localities and serve notice that the self-effacing policy of Gorst was no more.[42] The revival of the imperial factor was carried further in the agrarian legislation which Kitchener pushed through. The Five Feddan law, modelled upon the Punjab Land Alienation Act, gave statutory protection to the cultivators of five feddans[43] or less against expropriation for debt. It was made necessary, Kitchener told Grey, by the operations of 'small foreign usurers . . . scattered throughout the country and in the villages'.[44] But its political and social significance as a measure against peasant unrest and the aggrandisement of the larger landowners with their urban connections was unmistakable.

Kitchener followed this by the foundation of a Ministry of Agriculture to bring government more closely into touch with the agrarian economy, and, also in 1913, by the formation of a Ministry of *wakfs* (pious foundations) to regulate the methods by which the Khedive and the greater landowners relieved their estates from the full burden of taxation. Next he set about a reconstruction of the legislature aimed, as he had told Grey, at securing a 'fuller representation of the view of the smaller-landowning class'.[45] The old upper and lower houses were merged under the Organic Law of 1913, and more than two thirds of the membership of the new Legislative Assembly elected by simpler and more direct methods.[46] But this reform of the Egyptian political system yielded the British little immediate benefit. In the first session of the new assembly, wrote Graham,[47] 'the attitude of a large section of the Chamber towards the Government and the authorities generally was marked by such bitter and unreasoning hostility . . . that the conduct of State affairs was for the time being seriously affected'.[48] He had no doubt where the responsibility for this lay. 'Throughout the elections the whole influence of the Khedive in the country had been openly thrown against the Government and in favour of the Nationalists or other anti-governmental candidates'.[49] During the session, palace officials had appeared in the lobbies to encourage the opposition; members of the assembly summoned to the Khedive and either 'cajoled or intimidated'.[50] Saad Zaghlul, the Vice-President of the Assembly, was 'in constant communication with the Palace as to the best means of upsetting the ministry'.[51] The immediate cause of this new alliance against the British was Kitchener's proposal for a Ministry of *wakfs* which was seen by the Khedive and notables as an attempt to check their influence in the localities. But the deeper issue upon which the combination of court and country was founded was the whole policy of the occupying power since Gorst's retirement. For Kitchener's energetic campaign to capture influence in the provinces was a direct challenge to the social and political status of the Khedive and the greater landowners alike. The outcome of this latest phase in the triangular politics of Egypt remained, however, unresolved, as in the meantime Egypt herself became involved in a larger struggle of more momentous consequences.

It is difficult to see in the policies which the British pursued between 1882 and 1914 any marked progression either towards or away from a more rigid imperial control over the politics of Egypt which was consistently maintained. Still less is it possible to see any decline in the determination of the British to protect what they regarded as their essential strategic interest in the country. The varying political methods used to uphold this interest and to secure a sufficient measure of political cooperation to avert the necessity of direct rule or the enlargement of the garrison, both of which would have had embarrassing internal and international repercussions, do not suggest that there was any consistent approach to the question of how far Britain should intervene in the internal affairs of Egypt. Rather were Cromer, Gorst and Kitchener guided by what seemed the political necessities of the moment: striving always to ease the difficulties which the Residency faced in its efforts to recruit pliable ministers and ward off the attempts of the Khedive or the notables to use the imperial factor as a whipping boy in their struggles with each other. Sometimes it appeared best to conciliate the Khedive; sometimes to appease the notables; sometimes to try to outflank them both by a direct appeal to those outside the magic circle of pasha politics. In 1914, however, these gyrations were rudely interrupted as the requirements of the imperial factor were suddenly and sharply transformed.

The Impact of War upon British Policy

Egypt's experience of Kitchener's new order was brief. The European crisis of the summer of 1914 swiftly spread to engulf British interests in the eastern Mediterranean and to threaten the strategic corridor to India and the Pacific dominions. The incompatibilities of British policy in Europe, where alliance with Russia was essential to the defence of France and the Channel, and of British diplomacy in the Middle East, where British alignment with Russia propelled the Turks, with German prompting, into an attitude of hostility towards their traditional Mediterranean ally, became unmanageable. When Britain and Turkey went to war the implications for the whole position of the British in the Middle East, and in particular for their control of Egypt, were profound.

In their assessment of how political quiescence could be maintained in Egypt while the occupying power waged war on its constitutional suzerain, the acting Consul-General, Cheetham, and the senior advisers as well as the Foreign Office in London, were clearly influenced by the fiasco of the Assembly's first session. Anticipating the outbreak of the Anglo-Turkish war, Cheetham reported early in September 1914 that without the declaration of a British protectorate and the formal abrogation of Turkish sovereignty, the Interior and Financial Advisers 'could not guarantee either internal order or financial stability'.[52] Ministers would be afraid to remain in office, and Egyptian officials cooperating with the British would be exposed to allegations of treason. Yet without their support, it would be necessary to impose martial law and direct administration, a course which would create the maximum of political excitement. The logic of these arguments was a prompt declaration of Britain's desire to assume constitutional responsibility for Egypt, both to rally support to the ministers and to clear the way for the removal of the Khedive whose antagonism to British control had been clear enough before the emergency and whose wings both Kitchener and Graham had been eager to clip after the legislative experiment of 1914.

There was, however, no rapid decision on the exact form which the extension of British powers would take until the issue was precipitated by the declaration of martial law in Egypt on 2 November 1914, and the formal commencement of hostilities with Turkey, news of which was published in Egypt on 7 November. Meanwhile London vacillated between annexation proper and a protectorate. Having accepted Cheetham's request for a promise to 'accelerate progress towards self-government',[53] as the price of constitutional change, Grey proposed a little over a fortnight later to annex Egypt to the British Empire by order-in-council. This Cheetham and the advisers strongly opposed as unnecessary and unwise. Egyptian opinion, they argued, had accepted the new situation, but the chances of obtaining the collaboration of Hussein, Abbas' putative successor, and Rushdy as prime minister, would be jeopardised by full annexation, with the result that direct rule would become unavoidable. If this happened, warned Cheetham, with unmistakable emphasis, 'drastic precautionary measures would have to be taken'.[54] Indeed annexation would destroy the whole existing basis of Anglo-Egyptian collaboration, for

> Annexation must involve a more direct responsibility for Great Britain for higher standard of Government and for stricter protection of foreign interests. This would ultimately be attained but only by free displacement of native officials. Although increased efficiency might be appreciated, an influential class of malcontents would be created.[55]

This argument Cheetham supplemented with the potent threat of a backlash from the forces of organised religion:

> . . . most serious difficulty of governing without ministers will be severance of connections with religious elements whose future action is an uncertain and dangerous factor and cannot easily be controlled.[56]

As a final attack on the annexation project some three weeks later, Cheetham pressed the claims of the intended successor to the Khediviate, Hussein:

> Prince himself remarked to me in conversation that . . . if a Moslem Head of State was to give us effective help he must have prestige and be regarded as something more than a superior official.[57]

Cheetham's despatches torpedoed the case for annexation in London.

Grey gave way and the institution of a protectorate which did no more than transfer ultimate sovereignty over Egypt to the British Crown was announced in Egypt on 18 December 1914. A day later the news of Abbas's deposition and of his replacement as Khedive by Hussein was published in Cairo. Nor until 1917 was there to be a further challenge to the policy of continuity that Cheetham had championed.

The annexation debate was of major significance in the evolution of the Anglo-Egyptian connection and exercised a crucial influence on the framing of policy after the war. This was not only because Cheetham had prevented the drift towards direct rule at what seemed a propitious moment, but also because of his successful defence of the cooperative traditions of the Temporary Occupation. Cheetham brought into play two factors which Allenby was later to use with decisive effect. He insisted that the only alternative to working through the ministers and the 'native officials' was a massive extension of British responsibilities – a dangerous and expensive enterprise. Secondly he predicted that the abandonment of an Egyptian ministry would inflame the ulama, a prophecy calculated to unnerve a generation of policy-makers on whom the mahdist rising in the Sudan and the death of Gordon had been as influential, perhaps, as had been the circumstances of the Mutiny for the guardians of the *Raj*. And, significantly, the validity of Cheetham's policy was upheld by its apparent success – by the acquiescence, however grudging, of the various political groupings in Egypt including the ulama, in the transfer of sovereignty.

The orthodoxies of policy laid down by Cheetham were, nevertheless, to be tested by the circumstances of Britain's conduct of the war in Europe and the Middle East. By 1917, under pressure of economic and military necessity, the British were driven to exert more and more control over the Egyptian war economy and to remove its direction out of Egyptian hands altogether. Influenced, perhaps, by the inevitable growth under war conditions of British control of the Egyptian administration, Wingate, newly appointed as High Commissioner, wrote privately to Balfour in February 1917 urging on him the view that the 'changed political status of this country must inevitably lead to the Residency taking a greater part in administrative – as distinct from diplomatic – concerns'.[58] Therefore, the theoretical separation of powers, with a Residency responsible to London and British advisers responsible to Egyptian ministers, which had been the distinguishing feature of both the 'veiled' and the unveiled protectorates, should be abolished. Lord Robert Cecil, Balfour's deputy at the Foreign Office, echoing Wingate's logic, added the suggestion that Egypt should be handed over to the Colonial Office – a proposal which may have done something to rally support for Egyptian autonomy within the Foreign Office. Graham, the most senior official with direct experience of Egypt, wrote a lengthy memorandum which, while stressing the great importance of a firm foothold in Egypt to Britain's security in the Middle East, insisted that the 'maintenance of the present regime of a protectorate . . . is more in consonance with our true imperial interests'.[59] This observation was followed up by Hardinge who rejected Lord Robert Cecil's proposal on the grounds that annexation would have a bad effect in India and because the management of the large foreign interest in Egypt, especially that of the other Mediterranean powers, created special problems in Egypt which required the expertise of the Foreign Office.[60] These arguments Hardinge repeated to Wingate in a private letter early in May.[61]

But Wingate, who was increasingly anxious about the preservation of political stability after the death of the ailing Sultan Hussein, was reluctant to let the matter drop. Towards the end of July he sent Hardinge a memorandum by Clayton, Director of Military Intelligence in Cairo, the whole tone of which was strongly disposed towards annexation. Clayton's case rested upon assertions about the cardinal importance of Egypt to British control of the Middle East in the event of a failure to knock down the Ottoman Empire completely. Could British predominance in Egypt be assured, he asked, 'under the regime of a protectorate with a ruling dynasty which is of Turkish origin and cannot but be of Turkish sympathy'? He continued:

> From what may be termed the Imperial strategical point of view, therefore, it does not seem possible under the existing system to secure that complete and absolute control which is so necessary in Egypt where lies the keystone of our whole Near Eastern fabric.[62]

Wingate supported Clayton's reasoning and again appealed for a consideration of the 'form of Government . . . which will safeguard permanently and effectually the British position in Egypt'[63] once Hussein's influence was terminated by death. If annexation were decided upon, he claimed, it

> would be accepted passively, if without enthusiasm, by the bulk of the population and inasmuch as it implied a closer and more irrevocable link with the British power, would tend to facilitate and strengthen our control and influence in the administration of the

> country and ultimately to improve and solidify our relations with its natives.[64]

Implicit in these urgent representations from Clayton and Wingate were pessimistic predictions about the course of the war in the Middle East. Neither of them expected a clearcut victory over the Turks. Both anticipated a prolonged cold war with an Ottoman Empire which would have become the satellite of Germany. And both feared the effects of Ottoman survival upon Egyptian politics once the Sultan succumbed to ill-health. 'In the near future', wrote Wingate,

> we must expect political opposition to British control . . . and the facility with which that control is exercised will vary in inverse ratio to the military strength and political importance of the Turkish Empire.[65]

When the time came to consider the appointment of a new Sultan, he went on,

> were the influence of Turkey still strong and liable to be exploited by a strong anti-British combination . . . it would then be incumbent upon us to consider whether by perpetuating the existence of a native Sultan we should not be dissipating an authority which, if it is to gain the respect of an oriental people, must be powerful and concentrated.[66]

But strenuously argued as they were, the views of Clayton and Wingate made little impression on a Foreign Secretary who looked to Hardinge and Graham for advice on Egyptian affairs. And their disinclination to encourage radical change in Egyptian administration was reinforced by wider international considerations. 'Nothing could be more inopportune', wrote Hardinge,

> than any such administrative change at the present moment when the political situation in Syria and Arabia is in the melting pot and the chief concern of our policy in the Middle East . . . is to resist foreign encroachment and the pretensions of France and Italy in Arabia and the Red Sea.[67]

Before Hardinge's view prevailed, however, the issue was referred to a committee of the War Cabinet (comprised of Balfour, Curzon and

Milner) in deference, perhaps, to the fact that the demand for annexation was being advanced not only by Wingate within the Residency but also by the principal British representative in the Egyptian government, the Financial Adviser Lord Edward Cecil, who happened also to be unusually well-connected in British politics.[68] It was Cecil who argued before the committee in September 1917 that 'the whole constitution and internal government of Egypt was and must be in process of reconstruction . . . a complete change in the constitution and practice of the State was inevitable'.[69] The particular object of Cecil's reforming zeal was the system of Capitulations which had been left untouched in 1914 and which, through the extensive privileges of extra-territoriality which it conferred, in many cases on dubious grounds, was a source of administrative inconvenience particularly acute in war conditions. But Cecil's arguments carried in the end no more weight than Wingate's. Neither Curzon nor Milner would support him. Milner opposed annexation as unnecessary, although he favoured Egypt's transfer out of the hands of the Foreign Office. And prophetically he foresaw that while the diplomatic and international problems surrounding the British presence in Egypt had been simplified 'the internal questions – constitutional and administrative – are going to take their place and are likely to prove even more troublesome'.[70]

Even before the committee finally pronounced against annexation in February 1918, the issue had lost its urgency. Despairing, perhaps, of help from London, Wingate concentrated his attention upon securing the accession of Fu'ad once Hussein died. The successful installation of this apparently pliable monarch, and the general improvement of British military fortunes with the capture of Jerusalem in December 1917, eased the pressures which had provoked the Residency's call for constitutional change, although by the middle of 1918 Wingate was already coming to suspect the new ruler of the tendencies Cromer and Kitchener had found so reprehensible in Abbas II.

Thus the course of British policy in Egypt after the declaration of the protectorate in 1914 showed how far the assumptions behind Cheetham's polemic against annexation had become entrenched in the Foreign Office. Balfour and his advisers, for reasons both particular to Egypt and general to their Eastern policy, had refused to accept the case for altering the internal government of Egypt which had been left intact by the transfer of sovereignty in 1914. But their insistence to Wingate that the protectorate was working satisfactorily took little account of those changes which the war had wrought not so much in the formal constitutional structure of Egypt as in the fabric of its political life. As a result, they were little prepared for the agitation which arose as soon as the war ended; and still less for the violent outbreak of March 1919.

The Agitation and the Rising

The satisfaction expressed in London at the functioning of the protectorate seemed at first sight to be justified by the smoothness of Egyptian politics after 1914, a smoothness which appeared all the more remarkable after the turbulence of the Gorst and Kitchener period and at a time when Britain's war against Turkey might have been expected to rouse a fierce political and religious opposition to the protecting power. The political and constitutional changes carried through in 1914 appeared, whatever the Residency said, to have strengthened British influence and control and to have reinforced those buttresses of the imperial presence which Cromer had been concerned to erect. The declaration of the protectorate had removed any doubts about the determination of the British to preserve Egypt as a component of their imperial strategic system and to make full use of it in the Mediterranean and Middle Eastern conflict. Moreover, the dethronement of Abbas II, which was accomplished without difficulty in 1914, removed what the Residency had come to regard as the prime focus of opposition to British authority. 'Unless the difficulties of the Occupation . . . are to be seriously increased', Graham had remarked after the first session of Kitchener's new assembly,

> and we are to be faced with ministerial crises at the pleasure of the Palace, one of two alternatives must be contemplated: either the existing power of the Assembly must be curtailed or undue influence on its proceedings on the part of the Palace must be brought to an end once and for all. The former proposal is to be deprecated as retrograde and unpopular; the latter would not be attended with the same disadvantages.[71]

In the event, the war afforded the British the opportunity to adopt both alternatives simultaneously. The Legislative Assembly was prorogued indefinitely in the autumn of 1914; and the replacement of Abbas II by Hussein Kamel, another member of the dynasty, provided the British with a ruler of whose loyalty and cooperation they had no subsequent cause for complaint, and whose influence, like that of Tewfik, was mobilised on their behalf. The result of these two changes, and of the Draconian laws of assembly which were applied during the war, was, in effect, to place a moratorium on overt political activity and upon the open struggle for patronage and influence which had characterised the proconsulships of Gorst and Kitchener. The vast increase in the British military presence consequent upon Egypt's use as a base and transit camp for troops moving between the theatres of war, and upon the defence of the Canal against the Turks, was a further reinforcement to the persuasive powers of the Residency.

But, as Milner had sensed, it was far from clear how long this gratifying phase in Egyptian politics would last; nor whether the emergency measures of the war had solved the old problems of Anglo-Egyptian relations. Indeed, the first signs of a new period of unrest began to show themselves before the war was over. For although the succession of Fu'ad to the throne after the death of Hussein had helped to quieten the Residency's call for annexation in 1917, it was not long before the new Sultan[72] began to show something of the old spirit of Abbas. In December 1917 Wingate detected a mood of unwonted truculence among the Egyptian ministers although it was not clear how far they were acting under instructions from the palace.[73] By the end of the month, however, Fu'ad's attempt to revive the prerogative of appointing ministers of his own choosing, and his threat to go over the head of the High Commissioner,[74] showed that the resurgence of the court as an independent and unpredictable factor in Egyptian politics was beginning to make an impact on the functioning of the protectorate. The following summer saw a further deterioration, as Wingate viewed it, in the ruler's behaviour. Fu'ad had taken a marked dislike to Rushdy and Sarwat, both of whom the Residency regarded as useful servants of the protectorate. He began to intrigue against them and to consort with undesirables one of whom, Ismail pasha Sidky, was of 'marked Nationalist feeling'.[75] The Sultan himself was mouthing nationalist slogans. Wingate concluded somewhat bleakly: 'I hope that contact with affairs will gradually form the Sultan's mind.'[76]

The Sultan's attempt to rebuild the power and prestige of the dynasty by asserting its independence of the Residency formed a prelude to the agitation which culminated spectacularly in March 1919. Its effect was to stimulate political activity not only in Cairo but at the lower levels of Egyptian society where the patronage and favour of the ruler was also exercised. With the end of the war, the uncertainties generated by the more vigorous policy of the court were furthered by the anticipation of substantial changes in the constitutional machinery of the protectorate: an anticipation closely allied with apprehension among those whose political fortunes were unlikely to benefit from the assertion of the court's prerogatives. Thus, when Balfour decided to publish the terms of the Anglo-French declaration of November 1918 which promised a wide autonomy to the Arab provinces liberated from the Ottomans, Wingate was anxious about the effect of this pronouncement upon Egyptian opinion, and asked Balfour for guidance on future British policy in Egypt in the event of a campaign in the press.[77] But long before the Foreign Secretary or his advisers turned their attention to the question of how the protectorate was to be managed after the war, and with which elements in Egyptian society it was to collaborate most closely, the whole structure of indirect control as it had developed since 1914 was in serious disarray.

On 17 November 1918, Wingate reported to the Foreign Secretary that he had been visited by a number of prominent Egyptian politicians who had demanded a 'programme of complete autonomy' for Egypt, leaving under British supervision only the Debt administration and the facilities of the Canal. Significantly, when Wingate lectured them on the iniquities of agitation, they claimed that they had forsaken the old methods of Mustafa Kamil, and now enjoyed the full support of the Sultan Fu'ad.[78] In the same telegram Wingate added that the leaders of the ministry, the pashas Rushdy and Adly, had asked for permission to come to London to discuss the constitutional framework of the protectorate. Wingate believed that both they and the Sultan had been frightened by the new wave of agitation: 'There is little doubt', he told Balfour, 'that neither Sultan nor ministers feel strong enough to oppose nationalist demands however unacceptable they may be'.[79]

How far this was an accurate reading of affairs is open to question. Far more likely is it that the old antagonists of Egyptian politics had scented the coming of a new order and were shuffling into position in readiness for a further round in the struggle between the court and those who challenged its pretensions. But as this familiar tendency began to assert itself, the pattern of political alignment was suddenly and drastically modified by Egyptian reaction to the consequences which seemed likely to flow from the abolition of the Capitulations and of foreign extra-territorial privileges. For, perhaps as a gesture towards the Residency's complaints in 1917, Balfour had allowed the establishment of a commission under the Egyptian government (although its real masters were not in doubt) to inquire into the ways in which the inconveniences of foreign privilege might be removed. Sir William Brunyate, the Judicial Adviser, and also, after Lord Edward Cecil's death, the acting Financial Adviser, drafted a series of proposals for achieving a reform for which the Residency had hankered since Cromer's time. Brunyate's conclusions were radical. In a note forwarded to Wingate the day after the High Commissioner's confrontation with the dissident notables, he proposed the abolition not merely of the Capitulations but of the Kitchener constitution as well. They were to be replaced by a new bicameral legislature for which an upper house or Senate would be created to contain only a minority of Egyptians; the majority of its members being drawn from British officials or the representatives of the foreign communities whose old immunities were to be swept away. Moreover, this new upper chamber was to be the 'more serious legislative body'.[80]

The diplomatic and international considerations which prompted this constitutional device for protecting the interests of the foreign colonies while eradicating the last vestiges of foreign interference in internal Egyptian administration are clear enough. But the implications for the whole range of Egyptian politicians were unmistakable. Court and country alike were faced not with the inauguration of a fresh and unsatisfactory system of checks and balances but with a general tightening of British control and with a proposal which, if carried through, would diminish the political authority and standing of the native ruling class as a whole in favour of immigrant communities who, for all their wealth and privileges, had never been accorded any permanent voice in the government of the country. Little wonder that, as Allenby found, Brunyate became decidedly unpopular among Egyptians. Little wonder that the Egyptian premier, Rushdy, discovered unexpected advantages in the retention of the Capitulations.[81] Little wonder that these confidential proposals whose author was regarded, by virtue of his twin offices, as the second most influential representative of the protecting power in Egypt, quickly reached a wider political audience and eventually the Egyptian press.[82]

The effect of Brunyate's scheme, disseminated as rumour and speculation, was, however, to irritate and alarm a much larger constituency than the notable class and the court faction. It had caused a storm, wrote Walrond, a former private secretary of Milner, to his old master in January 1919.[83] The abolition of the Capitulations, it was widely rumoured, would mean the anglicisation of the language and practice of the law courts, a change that would threaten the status, the ambitions and the livelihood of Egyptian legal practitioners who were almost exclusively trained in the French tradition.[84] 'The proposed abolition of the Capitulations, legal reforms and advocacy of use of the English language in the Mixed Courts has . . . antagonised the lawyer class,'[85] observed a leading British businessman in a confidential report subsequently passed to the Milner Mission. Agitation by 'out-of-work lawyers' against the protectorate was also blamed for the later unrest in the provinces.[86] The alarm of the lawyers gave credibility to the fears of Egyptian officials that the expansion in the number of expatriate civil servants which had been a marked feature of the war, would be carried further and would lead to a contraction in the avenues of advancement as a flood of alien carpetbaggers washed over the ministries. Thus both these important groups in Egyptian society, whose loyalty to the protectorate was essential, became increasingly nervous and suspicious of British intentions. And amid the uncertainties opened up by the defeat of Turkey and the humiliation of the Caliph, their hostility to the direction in which the protectorate appeared to be moving began to be shared by the traditional religious élite of Egyptian Islam, the ulama, centred upon the great fortress of Muslim culture and religion in Cairo, the Al-Azhar. The formidable influence of the sheikhs, preachers and students of Al-Azhar, an influence of which the British had always been wary, carried the discontents of the notables deeper into the fabric of Egyptian society.[87]

Between November 1918 and March 1919, there was, therefore, a new and dangerous ferment in Egyptian politics the implications of which seemed to have escaped British officials stationed in the country. Wingate left from Port Said on 21 January 1919 to press his case for a constitutional conference and to be available for consultation in London. Meanwhile, a fierce rivalry ensued between different elements in the notable class for control over the new political forces which the agitation had thrown up. Cheetham, Wingate's deputy, reported reassuringly the growing friction between Zaghlul, who had placed himself at the head of those whose demands Wingate had heard in November, and the 'Old Nationalists'; and the decline of public interest in the 'doings of the extremists'.[88] Three weeks later he detected a general lowering of the political temperature. Rushdy and Adly pashas, who had resigned in protest against London's refusal to invite them to London for talks, had lost the temporary popularity which this had brought them. Zaghlul was being lacerated by the 'Old Nationalists' and was falling out of the public eye. 'The agitation which they have organised is dying out or is at any rate quiescent in the country at large . . .'.[89] Cheetham concluded that the 'present movement . . . cannot be compared with that of Mustapha Kamel', and asserted confidently that there was, in consequence, no reason for London's plans to be deflected by any false dawn of Egyptian nationalism.

The transformation of Egyptian politics which took place between this complacent appraisal and the violent disturbances which broke out all over Egypt less than three weeks later can only be tentatively surmised. Certainly the telegrams which raced from Cairo to London in early March suggest that the Residency had little grasp of the currents of opinion and excitement which erupted so spectacularly. What Cheetham saw was an attempt by Zaghlul and his confederates to frighten the Sultan into making common cause with them against the British, although the source for this interpretation he did not reveal.[90] The Sultan had 'earnestly appealed to me for protection against further insults' and this protection Cheetham pressed his masters to provide. 'Saad [Zaghlul] . . .', he wrote, 'is more dangerous than those interned at Malta since beginning of war. I recommend his immediate arrest and deportation and, for the sake of the Sultan's prestige, which is a political interest to us, I would beg for an early decision.'[91] Cheetham's analysis was sufficiently persuasive for Zaghlul's banishment to be sanctioned by London, but the truth was almost certainly more complex. For the agitation had, for all the preoccupations of the Residency, more than just an anti-imperialist face. It had cloaked a struggle for power between the Sultan and his aristocratic enemies which the intensity and scale of the unrest had made the more bitter. Whatever their original harmony at the time of the first approach to Wingate, the court faction and the dissident notables whom Zaghlul had formed into a party had drifted into mutual hostility. Whatever the substance of Zaghlul's interview with the Sultan – the immediate cause of his removal – it was clear that the Sultan had decided that the time had come to cut him down. The British served as a convenient instrument for this reassertion of dynastic power.

But certainly the British, and probably the Sultan, seriously miscalculated the situation in which they now found themselves by early March. British officials in Cairo and London made no allowance for, or failed to comprehend, the effect of the uncertainties they had created. They assumed that the agitation, and Zaghlul's attempt to direct it, could be quelled by the well-tried method of exiling its leadership, for pre-war experience had seemed to show the complete failure of pasha nationalism to strike any real roots in popular sentiment. In drawing this conclusion the British were, however, playing by rules which their own actions had outmoded. On 9 March 1919, Zaghlul and three of his associates were arrested and deported. On the tenth, Cheetham reported rioting in Cairo. By the fifteenth, the British were struggling to control disorders all over the Delta. On 17 March, Cheetham telegraphed the astonishing fact that 'we have no means of regaining control in Upper Egypt, from whence there is practically no news . . .'.[92] To their own surprise and horror, the British, by seeking to re-establish political discipline at the top, found themselves grappling with a rebellion which reached down to the base of Egyptian society.

It was this new dimension of colonial politics which threw the British so badly off balance. Fractiousness and indiscipline among the political élite was a familiar feature of the Occupation, and the British had come to expect violent rhetoric from the press and the threat of riots in the towns. But upheaval in the countryside and a revolt of the fellahin, apparently in sympathy with the deported pashas, was an unexpected and wholly unwelcome novelty. The rural cultivators had long been thought of as the bedrock of Britain's control of Egypt; their loyalty was thought to countervail the frothy nationalism of salon politicians in Cairo. Therefore the *jacquerie* of 1919 was to haunt those British officials in Egypt who cast round for an explanation of the March rising, and who were anxious to rebuild what they understood to be the old foundations of British influence. Far more than the stratagems of the pashas or the resentments of the towns, it was the inarticulate fury of the rural localities which preoccupied the official mind in 1919.

In reality, the rural disturbances were symptomatic of the same conflicts and tensions which animated Egyptian politics at a higher level. The social and economic changes which had helped to precipitate the crisis that brought about the Occupation of 1882 had not been checked by the arrival of the British. On the contrary, they had gone on apace. The erosion of customary tenures, the replacement of the old landholding stratum by 'a new class, the urban rich',[93] the appearance of large land companies, often owned by Europeans, in newly reclaimed parts of the Delta,[94] all acted as solvents upon the rural social hierarchy. Change of this sort may have influenced the land policy of the government which, at British prompting, disposed of public domain where possible in very small parcels: a policy designed to liberate the smaller cultivators from the hegemony of the large landowners.[95] This programme was carried out extensively in Middle Egypt between 1900 and 1906 and in the Fayyum between 1916 and 1922,[96] but as a palliative its effect is uncertain. However, some index of the strains imposed on rural society by these various aspects of 'modernisation' before 1914 may be found, perhaps, in the accelerating crime rate,[97] and in the growth of narcotic and alcoholic addiction.[98]

The unsettling effects of economic transformation before the war were greatly reinforced by the pressures of mobilisation after its outbreak, and by the construction of a war economy. After the March rising, it became commonplace among British observers to blame the rural insurrection upon the unfairness of the system of conscription to the Egyptian Labour Corps – which serviced the British armies in Sinai and Palestine – and of the compulsory purchase of camels and other livestock for the use of the army in Egypt. These impositions, often, so it was said, corruptly administered by subordinate Egyptian officials in the localities, were supposed to have aroused violent resentment among the cultivators. But although the need for draft animals and labour, which became particularly acute in 1917,[99] drove the British to interfere more and more in the countryside, the search for these two commodities, and the infliction of novel burdens on the fellahin were by no means the full extent of their wartime demands on Egypt. Because they turned Egypt into a vast base for their military operations in the eastern Mediterranean, the British were compelled, as the war went on, to exercise closer and closer control over the economy, the society and administration of Egypt and in doing so to trample upon old-established privileges, immunities and customs. Thus the proclamation of martial law in 1914 led inexorably to an ever-widening network of controls over the sale of alcohol, the availability of narcotics, the use of the railways and of other transport, and over the distribution of foodstuffs.[100] In May 1917, at the insistence of the military, a rigorous arms law was promulgated which debarred all but the royal family, the ministers and senior officials from keeping or bearing arms, a regulation which caused wide resentment,[101] and symbolised the growth of British political control.

These drastic additions to the scope of imperial control were disliked and resented among the notables and in the towns. In the countryside, where the weight of conscription, compulsory purchase and price inflation fell with great unevenness,[102] and where the war, while impoverishing some Egyptians, or driving them into reluctant service, had enriched others through the great rise in commodity prices, British interference could be directly associated with the appearance of new sources of friction and jealousy, and a further erosion of the old social structure. As a result when the agitation for autonomy broke out in late 1918, the countryside was very far from conforming to the idealised conceptions of the British official mind. Instead it resembled an economic and social battleground where competing groups struggled to gain most and lose least from the changes of the preceding decade and where the struggle had grown more intense in four years of war. The mutability of economic fortune had roused the provinces from their quiescence, while the leaders of rural society contemplated a renewal of the triangular conflict between the British, the court and its 'constitutionalist' opponents. When the restlessness generated by the rival campaigns of Zaghlul and the Sultan for increased power was compounded by a surge of religious feeling, all the confusions and bitterness of rural life were ignited in an explosion of resentment against the agencies of foreign influence. It was from these daunting manifestations of unrest and revolt that Cheetham concluded that the upheaval had a 'Bolshevik tendency',[103] and that the 'present movement in Egypt is national in the full sense of the word. It has now apparently the sympathy of all classes and creeds . . .'.[104]

Zaghlul and Egyptian Nationalism

Cheetham's alarming characterisation of the Egyptian disturbances was intended to awaken his masters in London to the gravity of the crisis which had suddenly enveloped British rule in Egypt and which seemed likely for a moment to lead to a revolt on a scale unparalleled in the Eastern Empire since the Indian Mutiny. The acting High Commissioner had after all to dispel the complacency which his own reports had encouraged and to prepare the ground for the kind of concessions which London had so far refused to consider. As it turned out the disorders in Egypt, widespread and violent though they were, failed to ignite an explosion capable of driving the British into the Mediterranean or the Canal: the concentration of British and Indian manpower, much of it in transit, was enough to make any such outcome improbable. Nevertheless, the great eruption of discontent had a deep significance for British policy in the country. For as the British came gradually and gloomily to appreciate, the remarkable feature of the disturbances was not that they arose as a spontaneous reaction against the impositions and unfairnesses of their war administration, as a sort of programmeless anarchy: on the contrary, the connection between the outbreak of violence and the Residency's attempt to cut off the head of Egyptian nationalism was unmistakable. Indeed, subsequent British inquiries seemed to confirm that the disturbances had been instigated by Zaghlul's supporters. The conclusion to be drawn from this was radical. No longer were Egyptian politics confined to the narrow and predictable activities of the pashas and the dynasty. No longer could the placidity and indifference of the urban and rural masses be relied upon to countervail the rhetoric of drawing-room nationalists. Instead, the ability of pasha politicians to mobilise popular support had to be reckoned with. Certainly after April 1919 the countryside subsided into passivity: self-interest alone dictated a more cautious attitude towards rural protest among the notables. But in the towns the days of pathetic contentment seemed to have gone for ever. After 1919 and throughout the inter-war years, the political volatility of the students and public servants, as well as of a wider spectrum of town-dwellers, became a permanent feature of the Egyptian political scene and fear of urban protest against a particular regime or government a vital element in both British and Egyptian calculations.

These new conditions in Egyptian politics were strikingly demonstrated by the emergence of the *Wafd* or 'Delegation' party (so-called from its claim to represent the Egyptian people and their demand for independence). The *Wafd* began as the group of notables who gathered round Zaghlul in November 1918 to press for greater Egyptian autonomy, a group which seems to have been rooted in Zaghlul's old following in the Legislative Assembly before its prorogation in 1914. The formation and dissolution of groups of disaffected notables was familiar enough to the Residency which probably expected that the rejection of Zaghlul's demands would quickly break up the party which had formed around him. Instead, however, Zaghlul's followers began to recruit adherents in the provinces and initiated an energetic propaganda campaign which presented Zaghlul as the chosen representative of the suspended assembly.[105] Moreover, Zaghlul and his committee, so Wingate told Balfour, were developing an organisation 'of which our knowledge is imperfect',[106] a confession whose truth swiftly became embarrassingly manifest.

The Residency's failure to monitor the growth of the *Wafd* is one indication of the novelty of its method and the relative obscurity of its adherents. For although Zaghlul's immediate followers included 'many rich and influential notables', it was far from being a party of landowners. Lawyers were especially prominent in its leadership alongside a number of civil servants. Both these latter classes had, as we have seen, strong objections to the direction in which the protectorate seemed to be moving, and much to lose from any drastic reorganisation of the law and administration that the British might carry through. They were also, perhaps, particularly receptive to Wilsonian ideas of self-determination whose dissemination British officials in the East constantly bemoaned. But the support which the *Wafd* drew from these groups had an additional value since the lawyers and public servants helped either to transmit its propaganda to a larger constituency of discontented or simply acquiesced in its generation. This was particularly important in preparing the ground for the strikes of public officials which greeted the arrest of Zaghlul and harassed the British for much of 1919. The 'effendi' class of officials was also crucial, as the British came later to believe, in spreading Wafdist propaganda in the countryside. The worst outbreaks of violence among the fellahin, Milner observed, 'took place in the immediate vicinity of the markhazes, or official centres'[107] and showed signs of official encouragement. Similarly, there were indications that the unrest in the provincial towns was promoted by the lawyers through the newer forms of association that had grown before and during the war.[108] Amine Youssef Bey, who was married to Zaghlul's niece, was a lawyer in Damietta and one of those sent out to recruit support in the provinces. Youssef was, by his own account, especially active among government officials in Tanta, Mansoura and Zagazig,[109] all of which became centres of disturbance in the March rising. But Youssef's contacts were not confined to government officials. Before the war he had been active in forming labour clubs in Damietta and in social work among the poor. During and after the war the disruption of Damietta's trade enlarged the scope of this charitable activity and Youssef himself helped to organise the supply of subsidised food to artisans and weavers afflicted by high prices. Elsewhere labour social clubs 'led movements for education and social benefits for workers'.[110] Activity of this kind by the social groups most sympathetic to Zaghlul thus opened the way for the recruitment of new allies in the towns, and for the rudimentary coordination of provincial protest. It helps to explain why the *Wafd* seemed capable of directing and controlling volatile elements in the towns, in itself a formidable addition to the armoury of pasha nationalism. But by the same token, it is a reminder that the *Wafd*'s effectiveness as a party of protest depended upon a climate favourable to its propaganda and the influence of its more prominent supporters.[111]

The *Wafd*, as its name proclaimed, was founded as the collective representative of the Egyptian nation. In fact, it was dominated throughout the period 1918–22 by the personality of Zaghlul. Indeed, during these four years and up until his death in 1927, Zaghlul overshadowed Egyptian politics altogether. Like Gandhi's or De Valera's, Zaghlul's political outlook and behaviour perplexed and irritated the British. He was and remained an enigma. Even his provenance was in doubt. 'A fellah of the fellahin,' said George Lloyd,[112] but it seems more likely that he was the son of a prosperous lesser landowner in the Delta who may also have been an *omdeh* or village headman.[113] On some of those British who met him Zaghlul left an impression of charm and geniality. 'A benevolent old gentleman with a twinkling eye', was how one official remembered Zaghlul's visit to London in 1920.[114] More often official judgments of him were both harshly critical and curiously inconsistent. He had, reported Graham in 1914, 'all the makings of a successful demagogue . . . his weak points are intense egotism, an ungovernable temper and a domineering manner'.[115] When Zaghlul sought office in 1917 the Residency was less impressed: 'He is now getting old and probably desires an income.'[116] A year later as Zaghlul's agitation got under way, Brunyate, the acting Financial Adviser whose opinion of Egyptian politicians was seldom high, attributed to him 'a curiously uncompromising character'.[117] But the Residency remained convinced that Zaghlul was now no more than a venal politician in search of a place. 'Saad Zaghlul is a demagogue', Wingate told Hardinge, 'and, even his own supporters admit, is to be bought by the highest bidder.'[118] He and Sidky, he assured Balfour, 'were disappointed politicians who would probably accept office on our terms but are barred by their personal antecedents'.[119] Not until much later did Zaghlul's claim to represent Egyptian national feeling begin to erode his unflattering reputation as a cynical opportunist whose first loyalty was not to *Misr* but to the poker table. On one issue, however, there was general agreement. As a parliamentarian, as an agitator or in the private colloquies where politics were conducted in the absence of representative institutions, Zaghlul displayed a character that was relentless, even intimidating. Subsequently he came to appear almost recklessly confident in his ability to command support. To the Cabinet in London he eventually became, as we shall see, a monster of unreason whose power to obstruct them transformed him into an ogre.

The political career that had led Zaghlul to the pinnacle of his reputation as the scourge of the imperial government is interesting and instructive. After an education at a village school and at Al-Azhar, he studied law and obtained a post in the judicial branch of government. In 1892, at the age of thirty-three or thirty-four, he was appointed a judge in the appeal court and associated himself with the reform of legal administration and the Sharia or religious courts. Sometime thereafter he was taken up by Princess Nazli and, apparently at her instigation, equipped himself for higher preferment by learning French and attending the French Law School in Cairo. He became the Princess's legal adviser and adorned the salons where much of Egypt's political life was spent. Then in 1906 he confirmed his membership of the political élite by marrying the daughter of Mustafa Fahmi Pasha, the Prime

Minister and Cromer's favourite, and crowned his triumph by being appointed Minister of Education with the Agency's approval. 'He possesses', declared the proconsul, 'all the qualities necessary to serve his country . . . he should go far.'[120]

Thus Zaghlul's career up until the age of fifty offered few clues to his later emergence as the foremost champion of Egypt's independence. If he shared the nationalism of Mustafa Kamil, or aspired to lead Egypt to freedom, he shrouded such thoughts with discretion. Once established as a minister, however, he began to display a personal independence and ambition which eventually brought him into conflict with the Khedive. In 1913, his unpopularity with the court and the belief that he was too influential with the Prime Minister brought his downfall. 'He's more trouble than he's worth,' said Kitchener, and Zaghlul left the ministry. But he did not retire gracefully into private life. Instead, with characteristic determination, he set out to rally support against the Residency in the Legislative Assembly of which he became Vice-President. This new career was cut off prematurely by the war and the indefinite prorogation of the Assembly. But in 1917 Zaghlul was once again a candidate for office in a reconstruction of the ministry. Once more his advancement was frustrated by the intervention of the Residency which was determined to preserve strict political discipline as the pressures of the war on Egyptian society multiplied.

Thus even before his appearance in front of Wingate at the end of 1918, Zaghlul was *persona non grata* with the Residency, and an object of suspicion to the dynasty. He had little reason to trust the benevolence of either and well knew that the sympathy of the Sultan which he claimed was unlikely to endure. Having moved into opposition to the Residency, he had little option but to seek a wider support to protect himself against a probable counter-stroke by the British and the palace. Circumstances, as we have seen, greatly facilitated his efforts; but for all that, it is unlikely that Zaghlul anticipated the fierceness of the Residency in March 1919 or the violence of the popular reaction which his arrest aroused. Still less could he have predicted the chain of events which was to take him to London in the summer of 1920. His political career, indeed, warns against the facile assumption that the change from collaboration to resistance, from involvement in the machinery of imperial control (as a minister) to the organisation of a nationalist resistance to it was necessarily the result of an intellectual or emotional conversion – in Zaghlul's case it would have been at the ripe age of sixty. Like other colonial politicians elsewhere, Zaghlul was prepared to switch from constitutional to agitational politics[121] as circumstance, opportunity or self-preservation dictated. Agitation required a different and fiercer rhetoric, and it led inevitably to confrontation with the imperial power. But it was also a clumsy and unpredictable instrument by which to promote constitutional change, carrying with it the risk of social upheaval unwelcome to his principal political allies. The supreme difficulty which confronted Zaghlul was that once the *Wafd* had been launched as the party of agitation its survival appeared uncertain unless the tempo of discontent could be maintained by the rejection of all compromise. Between 1919 and 1922 Egyptian politics and British policy were distracted alike by this conundrum.

In the spring and summer of 1919, British troops gradually restored order and suppressed an insurrection which claimed the lives of almost a thousand Egyptians and caused the death or injury of some seventy-five British.[122] Strikes and disorders continued in the towns, but there was no further outbreak of rural violence on anything approaching the scale of March. Contrary to Cheetham's apocalyptic expectations, the disturbances did not signal the beginning of a new era of mass nationalism in which court and country, pashas and fellahin, lawyers, officials and clergy united to drive the British into the sea. Nevertheless, it seems clear that the scale of the revolt dented for a time the confidence of the British in their ability to repress dissidence. And when British control in Egypt came under ministerial review in 1920–22, the uprising served as the implicit justification for constitutional change and the scrapping of the protectorate. Above all, perhaps, it set the seal upon the determination of policy-makers in London not to be drawn into annexation or the creation in Egypt of a direct administration on the Indian model. But the immediate effect of the agitation and the upheaval to which it led was to create a sharp conflict of opinion between the senior ministers of the coalition government; and it was from the effort to resolve that conflict that there derived the attempt to redefine the objectives and methods of imperial control in Egypt which forms the subject of the chapters which follow.

4 The Emergence of a Policy

Before the Milner Mission

At the outset of the political difficulties in Egypt at the end of 1918, the Foreign Secretary and his advisers in London, preoccupied as they were with the forthcoming Peace Conference, were not disposed to view with sympathy, or even patience, the demands of Egyptian politicians for constitutional change. Thus when Wingate reported on his interviews with the nationalist leaders and the two leading Egyptian ministers on 17 November 1918, Balfour was slow to reply, and when he did so made his irritation and disapproval clear. The Egyptian demands had, he said, created 'an unfortunate impression . . . I trust that they received no encouragement whatsoever from the Sultan and his ministers'.[1] There was no question, he went on, of Britain giving up her responsibility 'for order and good government in Egypt'.[2] Wingate's suggestion that the ministers might be allowed to visit London as a palliative he dismissed as 'inopportune'; the only concession to discontent that might be considered was an earlier suggestion of Wingate's for a commission of inquiry to visit the country.

Wingate was not inclined to accept this unyielding response and regarded matters in Egypt as being too urgent to wait for a commission. At the end of November he despatched to London a long survey of Egyptian politics in which he argued that although thus far 'political ferment . . . has . . . been confined to the aristocratic class and the intelligentsia', and had scarcely penetrated outside Cairo and the bigger towns, there were signs that a larger movement would be mobilised 'to show the Egyptians as . . . unanimous against an unsympathetic alien control'.[3] To counter such a movement, Wingate urged that the British 'put forward a liberal programme and . . . show our sympathy with reasonable Egyptian aspirations . . .'.[4] In December, he kept up the pressure on Balfour, and pressed again for permission for the ministers to come to London. This further appeal he backed by warning that the current agitation in Egypt represented 'something more than a fresh outcrop of Egyptian nationalist sentiment'[5] and by stressing the unease of the Sultan and the ministers and the need for a display of British confidence in them.

The urgency of the High Commissioner's tone extracted at the very end of the year a grudging concession. On 1 January 1919, Balfour telegraphed his willingness to receive the ministers, but not before March. Meanwhile Wingate might give assurances that the Brunyate proposals, which had sparked off the trouble, would not be implemented without consultation.[6] But Wingate was left in no doubt that his proceedings were ill-regarded in London. A private letter from Graham, Balfour's principal adviser on Egyptian affairs,[7] chastised the Residency for 'faulty staff work' in failing to detect collusion between the Sultan, Rushdy (the minister) and Zaghlul, who had assumed the mantle of nationalist leadership; and Wingate himself was criticised for appearing to countenance their demands.[8] Undeterred, Wingate now pressed for a further concession. The ministers, he said, were anxious that Zaghlul too should come to Europe, if only to discredit him, a request which he endorsed by implying that unless it were granted no Egyptian ministry would stand. 'Real cooperation with leading Egyptians', he observed, 'has in fact become an essential part of our machinery.'[9] Over the next three years the Residency was to repeat time and again this fundamental article of its faith.

Wingate's new appeal was held over while he travelled to London for consultation with the Foreign Office in advance of the scheduled visit of the ministers. Passing through Paris, Wingate saw Balfour, Hardinge, Lord Robert Cecil and Eyre Crowe, all of whom he found sympathetic.[10] But the supervision of Egyptian affairs, as Balfour explained to Wingate, was now the responsibility of Curzon as acting Foreign Secretary in London. When Wingate arrived there he found, however, a less congenial atmosphere than in Paris. Not until 17 February, a fortnight after his arrival, did Curzon consent to see him. The interview was not a success. Nationalist leaders, said the minister, should not be allowed to 'hold a pistol to our head'.[11] Curzon agreed, however, to refer Wingate's request, and his own opposition to it, to Balfour. But in his message he made clear the extent of his dislike of the High Commissioner's policy. The 'departmental view', he wrote magisterially, was against allowing the leaders of a 'disloyal' movement to come to London. Secondly, and somewhat disingenuously, he argued that to bring the nationalists over and then to snub them 'scarcely seems to savour of fair play and would be likely to increase the bitterness of their feeling against us'. Finally, Curzon questioned the urgency of Wingate's appeals for concessions to Egyptian opinion. Egypt, he said, could be governed for the moment; moreover 'indications have been received from Egypt that Sir Reginald Wingate's view of the matter is not shared in every quarter'.[12] For Cheetham, deputising for Wingate, was now reporting a decline in the tempo of agitation and the appearance of schism in the nationalist campaign. Curzon's estimate passed unchallenged in Paris. A few days later, after a further reassuring telegram from Cheetham, he instructed Cairo to make no more concession to the heads of the 'disloyal' movement since they 'would be likely to make illegitimate use' of it. The ministers would be allowed to come but not to dictate terms.[13]

At the end of February, therefore, at Curzon's command, the face of British policy was set firmly against the flexibility of approach for which Wingate had pleaded. An adjustment in the machinery of imperial control had not been ruled out, but the timing and substance of change were to be decided in London by the policy-makers, not in Cairo by the politicians. But in March the conditions which seemed to justify this unhurried attitude were abruptly transformed. Cheetham was now much less confident that political discipline could be maintained: Zaghlul's agitation was winning over the government officials and the advocates in the courts to non-cooperation; he was frustrating the formation of a ministry and intimidating the Sultan. He asked that Zaghlul and his principal associates be deported to India or Ceylon.[14] Curzon accepted this suggestion which was consistent with his own policy towards the nationalists and consigned Zaghlul and his friends to Malta. But his trust in Cheetham's judgment was misplaced. On 9 March the deportation orders were enforced. On the tenth Cheetham reported rioting in Cairo. The disorders worsened and spread to the provinces.[15] By 15 March the Residency's resolution had dissolved, and Cheetham was asking if he could let it be known that, as soon as the disturbances were over, London would receive a delegation of the 'advanced party' as well as the ministerial representatives. Curzon refused to consider this. But this time his policy did not go unquestioned in Paris. Impressed, perhaps, by what seemed in retrospect the accuracy of Wingate's warnings, and influenced, possibly, by Lloyd George and the Chief of the Imperial General Staff, whom Wingate had also met while in Paris, Balfour telegraphed to Curzon on 18 March dissenting from his reply to Cheetham.[16] This was an early warning of what was to follow.

Meanwhile the Cairo Residency continued to press for a gesture from London, and Cheetham for this purpose painted the upheaval in the most lurid colours as 'anti-British, anti-Sultanian, and anti-foreign. It has Bolshevik tendency, aims at destruction of property as well as communications.'[17] It was essential, he said, to rally an Egyptian element to ease the task of repression. All that Curzon would allow, however, was that he should take note of any proposals 'from responsible quarters' for reference to London.[18] But while Curzon was reiterating this policy of firmness, its downfall was being prepared. For at the end of March there arrived in Cairo in place of Wingate a High Commissioner whose political authority and personal determination were to ensure that the Residency's view prevailed over that of its formal superiors in the Foreign Office.

The High Commissioner was Field Marshal Lord Allenby, nick-named, not unjustly, 'the Bull'. In the spring of 1919, Allenby enjoyed an enviable reputation as the architect of victory in Palestine and what was perhaps a unique status in the eyes of Lloyd George, whose opinion of his generals was rarely flattering. In March he had been summoned to Paris in his capacity as the head of the military government in occupied Syria and Palestine[19] and as the most prestigious British official, civil or military, in the Middle East. The proposal to send him to Cairo to restore order originated, ironically, with Curzon; but it was rapidly seized on by Balfour who appointed him Special High Commissioner on 20 March 1919, theoretically for the period while Wingate was in England.[20] Allenby in his new role went immediately to Cairo to direct the repression. But if Curzon had hoped that this military proconsul would draw inspiration from the example of Kitchener, he was soon to be disabused. For Allenby accepted almost at once the need for the kind of concessions which Cheetham had urged on Curzon without success. On the last day of March, and after no more than a few days at the Residency, he told Curzon that the former ministers, now resigned, had recommended an end to the restrictions on travel which the Foreign Office had refused to lift for nationalist leaders wanting to go to Europe, and added his own estimate that this concession would 'automatically restore tranquillity and guarantee formation of a ministry'. With Curzon's concurrence, he went on, he intended to allow a passport to any Egyptian 'without reference to colour of their requirements', and ended his message unceremoniously: 'Please express approval.'[21]

Curzon had heard these arguments before from Wingate and Cheetham and liked them no better from Allenby. But when he denounced them to Balfour, the Foreign Secretary took Allenby's part. The special terms of Allenby's appointment, he said, meant that his advice 'cannot be disregarded . . . . It is important to avoid any appearance of mistrusting his policy.'[22] Curzon was not persuaded.

Accompanied by Graham and Wingate, whose expertise had hitherto been despised but whose opposition to the timing of Allenby's concessions made him a useful tool, Curzon tried to win over Bonar Law, and, through him, the Prime Minister in Paris. But Law was impressed neither by Curzon's arguments nor by Wingate's judgment.[23] On 4 April, Allenby again demanded Curzon's assent to his measures. This time there was no resistance for Curzon received a message from Lloyd George, for onward transmission to Cairo, which fully endorsed the High Commissioner's policy and which promised him 'every support' in carrying it out. All that Curzon extracted from this humiliating defeat was Lloyd George's cautious suggestion that Allenby might like to consider the possibility of a commission under Lord Milner to inquire into the future of the protectorate.[24] Armed with this authority, Allenby announced the end of restrictions on travel and obtained within a few days the release of Zaghlul and his confederates from detention on Malta.

Since mid-November, when Balfour had declined to let the Egyptian ministers come to London, British policy had changed markedly in its attitude to political unrest in Egypt. From chastising the Residency for so much as listening to the complaints of the ministers and those who demanded more radical change, the Foreign Office had been forced, by its authorisation of Allenby's concessions, to recognise implicitly the representative character of the nationalist movement which Curzon had stigmatised as 'disloyal'. Two connected factors may account for this striking reversal. The first was the embarrassing scale of the insurrection in Egypt which occurred at the moment when the government was preparing to obtain a general international recognition for the protectorate which had been declared in 1914; and at a time when the prospect of sending large reinforcements to Egypt in the aftermath of the January mutinies against foreign military service was particularly unwelcome.[25] The second was the enormous access of influence which Allenby's appointment gave to the voice of the Residency, and the confidence which Lloyd George, Balfour and Bonar Law reposed in his ability to quell the turbulence in Egyptian politics. Allenby's determination to make full use of his special status, and his lack of respect for what Curzon had called the 'departmental view', allowed the Residency to pursue for some months its search for alternative sets of Egyptian ministers without let or hindrance from London.

The idea of sending a commission to Egypt to examine the workings of the new system hastily inaugurated in 1914 was at least as old as

September 1917 when Hardinge had remarked on the need to modify the protectorate, 'to reduce friction with the Egyptians'.[26] It had been put forward by Balfour, and rejected by Wingate, as a sop to Egyptian discontent in December 1918.[27] Early in March 1919, however, Wingate himself revived the notion and pressed the Foreign Office to send a commission that would follow the 'Montague [*sic*] precedent' and help 'rally our well-wishers'.[28] Wingate's motive was plainly to find some way of moderating the policy of firmness which Curzon had refused to alter on his advice. Accordingly, his proposal received short shrift. Such a commission, said Graham, 'would resemble a rather feeble attempt to placate and postpone';[29] while Curzon could see 'no grounds for such a Commission which . . . may be interpreted as a mark of weakness'.[30] But a fortnight later, following the violent outbreak of mid-month, and Cheetham's warnings of the uncooperative mood of the moderates and extremists alike, Curzon had second thoughts. It would be difficult, he told Balfour, to get the native ministers to come to London without making unacceptable concessions; but a mission sent to Egypt could hear all sides without detracting from the prestige and authority of British policy. Milner, he added, shared his view and 'would greatly like' to lead the mission.[31]

Two days later Allenby's bombshell arrived in London. Thereafter, the despatch of a commission under Milner, at least in Curzon's mind, assumed a quite different importance as a device for checking the imprudence of the headstrong proconsul. On 1 April, when he appealed to Balfour to veto Allenby's concessions, Curzon urged the sending of a mission as an 'alternative policy'.[32] Two days later he repeated this appeal,[33] and used it in the effort to get Bonar Law's support for his protest.[34] Balfour and Lloyd George, as we have seen, refused to overrule Allenby; but in deference to Curzon, and to the indications that Milner agreed with him, they asked the High Commissioner to consider the proposal. Allenby, however, was understandably reluctant to have his policy monitored by an instrument of Curzon's choosing, and brusquely dismissed a commission as 'useless now'.[35] But his failure to suppress disorder completely, and the symptoms of unrest which persisted, gave Curzon his chance. In mid-April he asked Lloyd George to discuss the 'very serious position' in Egypt with Milner and himself, and pressed for a definite decision to send a mission under the Colonial Secretary.[36] Three days later he telegraphed in triumph to Allenby: 'His Majesty's Government desire to send' a commission of five under Milner, 'which will determine future form of British protectorate'.[37]

Curzon thus gained his immediate object of imposing some degree of control over the Residency. But what followed was a struggle between himself and Allenby over the use to be made of the mission. For Allenby, having agreed to the principle of an inquiry, wanted to deploy it as part of the Residency's longstanding objective of maintaining an Egyptian ministry in office at all costs. Thus on 23 April, following the collapse of the ministry of whose formation he had been boasting less than a fortnight before, and in the midst of a strike of government officials, he demanded the immediate announcement of a royal commission to come to the country. Whatever Curzon's view of this, Milner was adamant that the terms of the mission's inquiry should not be hurriedly announced in such circumstances.[38] To do so, he declared, 'would be a repetition . . . of the great blunder made by Allenby when, to save himself from being left without an Egyptian ministry, he made the concession about passports and the release of Zaghlul and Co'.[39] It was vital, he thought, to show the 'intriguing Pasha class' that 'we could and would do without them', as the only way of re-establishing the control exercised over Egyptian politics during the previous thirty years. The mission had, therefore, at all costs to 'be kept clear of the present crisis', and to avoid being caught up in the immediacies of local politics.[40]

So great was Curzon's desire to preserve Milner as leader of the mission,[41] that he acquiesced reluctantly in delay despite his continuing anxiety about Allenby's conciliatory attitude to the 'extremist' party in Egypt.[42] By midsummer, however, both he and Milner became suspicious that Allenby, having eventually found a new set of ministers, was trying to bury the mission altogether. For, echoing the view of the Sultan and the leader of the Egyptian ministry, the High Commissioner now wanted to postpone the mission until the end of the year or even until January 1920.[43] Curzon refused to consider this and laid down mid-October as the date of its departure. But while Allenby was vacationing in England in September, Cheetham, his deputy, began to report the mobilisation of protest against Milner's visit and the threats of the ministers to resign rather than negotiate with him.[44] Curzon temporised: the departure date would be held back until Allenby returned to Cairo and could consult the ministers there. This time Allenby was in a more compliant mood, aware, perhaps, after his discussions in London, that the mission which Curzon had announced as long ago as May could not be postponed indefinitely. On 11 November, almost a year after Wingate's notorious interviews, he asked that the mission start for Egypt 'as soon as it can'.[45] This time there were to be no second thoughts.

The origins of the Milner Mission lay, therefore, in the determination of both Curzon and Milner to subject Allenby's management of Egyptian politics to a closer and more rigorous scrutiny than Balfour or Lloyd George seemed inclined to give it; and in their shared unease at what appeared to be Allenby's clumsy and naive approach to the 'intriguing Pasha class' whose activities Milner characterised as a 'try-on'.[46] These two old proconsuls had little respect for Wingate's successor at the Residency. The Mission was a device to bring more experienced hands to the wheel, but also to circumvent the dangers of an open confrontation with a High Commissioner of whose ruthlessness in imposing his will there could be no doubt. For Curzon, Milner's presidency of the enquiry was sufficient guarantee that its findings would be consistent with his own view of the necessity to preserve political discipline in Egypt and the substance of imperial control. Neither he nor Milner could have foreseen, on the eve of the Mission's departure, the role which their creation was eventually to play.

The Mission in Egypt

The terms of reference with which the Milner Mission began its labours in December 1919 had been set out by Curzon some seven months before. The Mission, Curzon had told the House of Lords on 15 May, was 'to inquire into the causes of the late disorders in Egypt, and to report on the existing situation in the country and the form of the Constitution which, under the Protectorate, will be best calculated to promote its peace and prosperity, the progressive development of self-governing institutions and the protection of foreign interests'. Here, it might be thought, was a brief whose scope was clearly defined, and the implications of which were plain to all those who carried a responsibility for Egyptian affairs. But Curzon, who had drafted the original statement of the Mission's task, was himself to offer conflicting interpretations of his own pronouncement. Writing to Lloyd George in July, Curzon proposed as a member of the Mission Cecil Hurst, legal adviser at the Foreign Office, to 'assist in drafting the new Constitution'.[47] But three months later he was assuring Allenby that it 'is not the function of the mission to impose a constitution on Egypt', but merely to take preliminary soundings and offer proposals for reform.[48] Milner himself inclined to a comprehensive reading of his terms of reference and assumed, as is apparent from the early entries in his Egyptian diary, that the Mission under his presidency would enjoy wide powers of recommendation on the future government of the protectorate.

There was from the first, therefore, a degree of ambiguity not only about the political role of the Mission but also about the scope of its operations and the authority of its conclusions. In the event these ambiguities, combined with Milner's status as a senior Cabinet minister, with the widest experience of foreign and imperial affairs, allowed the Mission to proceed untrammelled by constraints imposed from either London or the Cairo Residency, and to achieve an independence from both which was later to have somewhat disconcerting consequences.

Milner was accompanied by five colleagues, three of whom were, like himself, either past or present servants of government. As his 'right-hand man'[49] Milner had chosen Sir Rennell Rodd, a career diplomat about to retire from the embassy at Rome, a choice partly inspired by Rodd's experience at the Cairo Residency under Cromer. Milner's second particular choice was Sir John Maxwell. Maxwell had served in Egypt and the Sudan from Tel el-Kebir until the Boer War, when, as a military commander and governor of Pretoria, his path and Milner's had crossed again. Subsequently Maxwell had returned to Egypt and had served there as Commander-in-Chief before and during the war. Milner believed that he was well-liked in Egypt and would help to break down suspicion and mistrust of the Mission.[50] The other official, Hurst, was intended to provide both legal expertise and a link with the Foreign Office as the responsible department. Of the two 'unofficials', J. A. Spender, an Asquithean and the editor of the *Westminster Gazette*, was by his own account the choice of Curzon;[51] while Sir Owen Thomas, the only member of the House of Commons in the party, was to represent the Labour opposition, if from a somewhat aristocratic and military standpoint. His energies seem largely to have been diverted towards an enquiry into agricultural conditions in Egypt, for which his experience well suited him.

This, then, was a commission whose chairman was pre-eminent in authority, influence and experience, not least because, with Cromer, Kitchener and Gorst in their graves, Milner's direct knowledge of Egyptian affairs was unique among ministers and politicians of his seniority. There was little doubt, therefore, that the Mission's approach to its task would lean heavily upon his analysis of the problem and his general ideas about the proper structure of British influence and authority in Egypt. Even before his arrival in the country, it is clear that Milner himself had reached certain broad conclusions which were to inform the whole policy of the Mission and determine its strategy. Despite his criticisms of Allenby, he did not believe that the protectorate could be preserved in its existing form merely by a display of resolution on the part of the High Commissioner. For Milner took as his model what he understood to be the guiding principles of Cromer's regime, and was inclined to attribute the difficulties which were being experienced in Egypt to neglect of Cromer's method. 'I am not sure', he told Robert Cecil in November 1919, 'that we have not got off the road since [Cromer's] day both to the right and to the left. . . .'[52] Writing to Curzon on his way to Egypt he made the same point more directly. 'A witch's cauldron', he said, 'had been brewing . . . as I now think, almost ever since Cromer left'; it was doubtful whether 'some such trouble as we have had was not bound to come owing to an agglomeration of disturbing influences some of very long standing'.[53]

This train of thought led Milner in the first instance to look for the causes of unrest not so much in the growth of a spontaneous nationalist sentiment as in those changes in British policy and practice which had provoked resentment. He was confident that 'we ought not in the future . . . to have any difficulty in securing the acquiescence of the fellahin in our presence and our authority always provided that they are assured of its permanence'.[54] But the susceptibilities of other Egyptians would have to be regarded: the representatives of the imperial presence should be 'most carefully selected, not too numerous . . . know the language, and be capable . . . of exercising great patience and tact'.[55] By comparison with the slimmer British presence in Cromer's time, it seemed to Milner that part at least of the recent trouble was due to the multiplication in the number of subordinate administrative posts held by expatriate British officials, a development which both lowered British prestige and disappointed aspiring Egyptians.[56] Part of the solution was to be found, therefore, in an administrative reorganisation which aimed at no more than a return to the conventions which had governed Britain's supervision of Egyptian affairs under Cromer. A few days later, in a further soliloquy, Milner extended the argument. Egyptian resentment, he reasoned, was directed at the British habit of keeping them 'too much on leading strings', a practice which bred bitterness and was undermining the confidence of British officials who were 'disheartened and on the defensive'.[57] The elaboration of British controls seemed self-defeating. 'Are we', Milner asked himself, 'trying to do too much for these people and getting ourselves disliked without materially benefitting them?'[58]

Milner lost no time in acquainting his colleagues with the main lines of his thinking. In a memorandum 'circulated to members of Mission soon after my arrival in Cairo', he sketched out a framework for the Mission's inquiries which explicitly recognised that the system which had obtained before 1914 had been obliterated. 'The "veiled protectorate"', he asserted, 'has definitely come to an end.'[59] The Mission's task was to consider in the light of this 'how much authority we ought to try and exercise in Egypt, what we should try to do and what we had better leave alone . . .'.[60] There was no question, he assumed, of resorting to Indian methods. 'I take it for granted that we are all agreed that wherever possible the indirect method of effecting our object by guidance and advice is preferable to the direct method of doing all the work ourselves or by direct orders.'[61] Once the future anatomy of the British presence had been identified, he continued, the Mission should seek consultation with the leaders of Egyptian society with a view to drawing up a new Anglo-Egyptian agreement to replace the shattered 'veiled protectorate'. Milner then went on to indicate the kind of settlement with which he thought it possible to replace the existing protectorate and in language which laid bare the assumptions that were to govern his approach throughout the Mission's life. Britain could not lay aside all her claims to exercise a protectorate over Egypt. 'We cannot', he said, 'give up the word altogether, for not only does it contain an absolutely necessary principle, viz. the exclusion from the affairs of Egypt of all foreign *political* influence except our own, but it is contained in the Peace Treaties . . . . But . . . there is evidently no use harping on it.'[62] Egypt's strategic importance would continue to dominate her relations with Britain, and set close limits on her freedom. But would this, discreetly clothed, stand in the way of Anglo-Egyptian partnership? Milner thought not. In a sentence which might, in retrospect, serve as the Mission's motto and epitaph, he suggested: 'It is quite possible that what *we* mean by "Protectorate" is not really incompatible with what they mean by "Independence".'[63]

From these premises, Milner began to devise a strategy for the restoration of imperial control and the recovery of political stability in Egypt. The central feature of the Anglo-Egyptian relationship was not to be the protectorate but a 'Contract . . . by which we should undertake to guarantee an agreed constitution for Egypt against foreign interference and internal disorder and Egypt, in return for that guarantee, would acknowledge our right to keep an Army of Occupation, and to retain certain posts in the Administration, and the control of the Sudan'.[64] The aberrations of the war years would be excised from British policy, and Britain's political role purified of its grosser accretions. The alternative to this, Milner argued, was 'the risk of perpetual agitation . . . a position of permanent discomfort, and even, having regard to the possible effects of political changes at home, of some danger'.[65] In this warning, designed, perhaps, to chasten his more conservative colleagues, could be heard an echo of the proconsular frustrations of another place and time.

The early circulation of this memorandum is further evidence of how little time was spent, once Milner and his colleagues arrived in Egypt, pondering 'the form of Constitution . . . under the Protectorate' which was best suited to British needs and Egyptian circumstances. The diagnosis of excessive British interference and involvement in internal administration which Milner had made became the watchword of the Mission's approach and recurred constantly in its report and in the authorised version which it produced of the origins of the uprising. Instead, the Mission's function became, almost immediately, one not of enquiry but of negotiation; its object not so much to produce a report on the situation as an informal agreement with the principal Egyptian politicians as to the distribution of powers under a revised form of the protectorate. What Milner hoped for was a public dialogue between the Mission and Egyptians of various allegiance which would promote the formation of a new consensus about the future relationship of Britain and Egypt. The Mission thus changed swiftly and almost imperceptibly from a detached observer of the Egyptian scene into a would-be political catalyst, dissolving previous loyalties and constructing fresh coalitions of interest. Like Montagu in India, Milner saw himself rallying the forces of goodwill and cooperation against the unreason of extreme nationalism. 'There are', he told Lloyd George, 'a lot of moderate men about who know that the present screaming agitation is folly . . . . But at present they are all terrorised and there is precious little backbone in any of them . . . .' What was needed was a programme around which these demoralised collaborators could gather. 'It is clear that if the Moderates are successfully to resist the Extremists, we must have something to give the Moderates; they must be able to hold out some attractive prospect of self-government. . . .'[66] And, at the very least, if no agreement emerged, the public debate which would have been generated would break down the barriers of resentment, suspicion and silence, and ease the tensions between the British and their wards. 'The more they talk', wrote Milner in the same letter to Lloyd George, 'the more they tend to differ among themselves . . . . It may very well end – I hope it will end – in their turning to us to show them a way out of the tangle into which they will get themselves.'[67]

This was written after three weeks of increasing frustration as the Mission strove to put its programme of political reconstruction into effect. Milner had proposed consultation with Egyptian leaders in his opening memorandum; but he found such a dialogue easier in prospect than in practice. The warnings from the Residency before the Mission's arrival that it would be boycotted by Egyptian politicians proved only too well founded. Instead of initiating, and refereeing, a wide public debate about Egypt's future, Milner found himself reduced to cajoling individual politicans to come to him by night and in secrecy. Far from stimulating a public discussion which might pave the way for a fresh consensus, he found it embarrassingly difficult to persuade what were thought of as influential Egyptians to commit themselves to any view at all, at least in public, which might expose them to local recrimination. These circumstances propelled Milner into a posture which increasingly resembled not that of an authoritative organ of British policy but rather that of a supplicant at the court of Egyptian opinion. In an effort to break the boycott he told Adly pasha, who was regarded by the British as the principal champion of the moderate party in Egypt, that the Mission did not require of those who approached it any expression of loyalty to the protectorate. In a phrase in which euphemism abounded, he told the pasha: 'We would welcome the absolutely unfettered expression of all honest opinion. . . .'[68] Indeed, so urgent was the Mission's desire to provoke an open discussion of some sort that Milner went further and made the remarkable suggestion that he would give 'any man who came before us . . . a certificate . . . to say that we should not regard him as having in any way compromised his future freedom of action by appearing before us'.[69] Consultation on these terms, it may be thought, was scarcely consultation at all.

But even an offer of this kind did not satisfy the anxiety of Milner's colleagues to establish contact with the elusive body politic of Egypt. Subject, perhaps, to the sense of impending dissolution which afflicts all transient authorities, they wished to make their presence felt as quickly as possible. Milner was pressed to *announce publicly* that the Mission would listen to all views – a concession which he had refused to Adly on the grounds that it would undermine the Mission's prestige.[70] Milner procrastinated, arguing that Allenby and the Egyptian ministers would have to be consulted. In the meantime, there was little improvement in the position of the Mission, increasingly a helpless onlooker rather than an active participant in Egyptian politics. Milner grew more and more irritated by what he saw as the malign influence of the Al-Azhar and its principal officials. In a private letter to Curzon, he gave vent to his sense of anger and frustration, even to the extent of doubting the value of the Mission's task:

> . . . how we are to frame or even suggest any form of constitution for this tumultuous and leaderless mob is indeed a problem. Any country less capable of 'self-determination' than the Egypt of today would be difficult to imagine.[71]

Rather than abandon the effort, however, Milner set out, in his own words, to 'make bricks without straw'.[72] Assuming that the process of open discussion had been blocked by Egyptian cynicism about the open-mindedness of the Mission, Milner now began to suggest that he and his colleagues would consider seriously even the most radical transformation of the British presence. 'Our determination to control the foreign affairs of Egypt was absolute,' he recorded of his conversation with Rushdy, the second pillar of the 'moderate' party, 'but subject to that . . . we were willing to discuss the whole future of Egypt with the Egyptians.'[73] Milner was even, he told Rushdy (who embraced the idea with enthusiasm), prepared to make an announcement on these lines in a further attempt to end the boycott.

By the end of December 1919, therefore, Milner had began to modify his original conception of the Mission's political role in two different ways. Firstly, he persuaded himself and, with some difficulty, Allenby, that the right course for the Mission was to issue a manifesto of the kind he had discussed with Rushdy. Allenby's fears were quietened by Milner's insistence that the essential character of the protectorate was in no way compromised by the terms of the manifesto.[74] Secondly, and perhaps more significantly, Milner gradually relinquished the hope that a settlement could be reached which excluded and isolated what he termed the Extreme party – the followers of Zaghlul's *Wafd* or 'delegation'. The reluctance of those whom the British thought of as powerful and influential to come forward, and the eagerness of the 'moderates' to involve the leader of the 'Extreme Nationalists', Zaghlul, in any negotiations,[75] slowly forced upon the Mission the realisation that it had failed to make contact with the real sources of power in Egyptian society, a realisation driven home by the way in which the boycott of the Mission had been enforced. A private note by Ingram, a member of the Mission's secretariat, to Thornton, Milner's private secretary at the Colonial Office, indicates that Milner and his colleagues were hoping that a public declaration of their readiness to range widely over the grievances of Egyptians would overcome the self-restraint of the Zaghlulists, and entice Zaghlul himself back from his retreat in Paris.[76] On 24 December 1919, when Milner showed Allenby the draft of the Mission's proposed manifesto, the two men discussed Zaghlul's return and agreed that he could not actually be invited back.[77] But four days later Milner overcame Allenby's caution and obtained the release from internment of a number of notables of Zaghlulist leanings, again to smooth the path for a general political dialogue, and tempt the *Wafd* into the deep waters of constitution making.

In the event, all these attempts to inveigle Zaghlul into a public discussion of the aims and objects of constitutional reform proved in vain. Zaghlul would not come, conscious, perhaps, of how little he stood to gain from a rapid political settlement which would allow the British, and the Sultan, to shore up their authority. Milner for his part grew steadily more pessimistic about the possibility of achieving 'that direct consultation with the leaders of native opinion which we always contemplated'.[78] Towards the end of January he told Curzon that the efforts of the 'moderates' to bring back Zaghlul and persuade him to participate in a negotiation with the Mission would fail; and that the Mission had virtually abandoned its search for a negotiated settlement in favour of the detailed study of the government and administration of the country, a more tranquil if less urgent undertaking.[79] By the middle of February, with no change in the political situation, Milner decided that no purpose would be served by remaining beyond the first week of March, and the last part of the Mission's stay in Egypt was devoted partly to a series of inconclusive interviews with the Sultan, and partly to drafting its report and the conclusions which its experience prompted. Early in March, Milner left Egypt for a short visit to Palestine and returned thence to Europe.

From first to last, judged by its chosen objective, the Mission's sojourn in Egypt had been a humiliating fiasco. But this failure did not alter Milner's convictions about the causes of imperial difficulty in Egypt or the correct solution to the problem. On 26 January, he had reported to Curzon on the collapse of his hopes for reaching an informal settlement, and proclaimed the futility of attempting to devise a new constitution until 'the Egyptians come to their senses'.[80] But from the turbulence of Egyptian politics he deduced not the impossibility of achieving an agreement between Britain and the recalcitrant local politicians but merely the necessity of postponing the attempt. '. . . I am convinced as I have been almost from my first day in the country', he told the Foreign Secretary, 'that the best remedy for the present intolerable state of affairs is to be found in something like a formal agreement call it a Treaty, Convention or what you will, between Great Britain and Egypt.'[81] Nor when he came to sketch the Mission's provisional recommendations, later embodied in the summary sent to Curzon in the middle of May 1920, did he retreat from this conclusion.

The core of the proposals which Milner eventually sent to Curzon was to be found in his insistence that the administrative changes which had accompanied the wartime expansion of the imperial presence should be scrapped. The protectorate which had become a symbol of British domination should be replaced by a treaty granting Egypt a substantial degree of internal autonomy – 'restricting the direct exercise of British authority [to the] narrowest possible limits'[82] – but retaining the direction of Egypt's foreign relations in British hands. In addition, Milner intended that the High Commissioner should keep general powers of supervision over the treatment of foreign communities and foreign interests to avert the danger of Egypt again becoming a focus of international dispute; and that his position should be suitably reinforced by a British garrison. But the central theme of Milner's new Egyptian order was the necessity of relying not upon the powers conferred by the assumption of sovereignty in 1914, but upon the willing cooperation of Egyptian politicians under a more flexible system of influence and control, and the definite reversal of any tendency towards incorporating Egypt into the British Empire on the model of India or tropical Africa. The hallmark of Anglo-Egyptian relations was to be the recognition of Egypt's independence in exchange for her acceptance of the obligation to remain in diplomatic and strategic terms a satellite of Britain.

That Milner should have advocated the partial retraction of imperial control, and even renounced privately the responsibilities of the 'civilising mission', may seem to mark a curious evolution in the career of one so closely identified with the imperial idea: the defender of helots and the apostle of anglicisation. This apparent contrast between the hammer of the Boers and the champion of Egyptian independence has even encouraged one historian to see in his justification for a wider Egyptian autonomy an embodiment of that 'failure of nerve' which supposedly permeated the guardians of empire after 1918.[83] To what extent such a collapse of morale occurred more generally is not easy to assess. But as an explanation for Milner's attitude to the future pattern of Anglo-Egyptian relations it is unsatisfactory. For Milner did not believe that the proper object of imperial policy was to impose a uniform system of close administration wherever Britain had established a foothold. Nor did he believe that the relationship between the mother-country and her dependencies should everywhere be the same. To deduce from Milner's policy in South Africa a monolithic theory of empire is to ignore Milner's own clear distinction between the importance to Britain of the colonies of settlement on the one hand and the tropical dependencies on the other. 'If I had to choose', he told the Royal Colonial Institute in 1908,

> between an effective union of the great self-governing states of the Empire without the dependent states, and the retention of the dependent states accompanied by complete separation from the distant communities of our own blood and language, I should choose the former.[84]

As this distinction implied, for Milner the closer integration of the colonies of settlement with Britain was vastly more important than the preservation of an intimate relationship with regions whose populations had little racial or cultural community with the mother-country. For this latter category different rules of association applied: rules which must take account of the absence of those sympathies and also of the limits on British power and resources, the deficiencies of which Milner had always been acutely conscious, and to the repair of which he had dedicated his career. In the alien dependencies, therefore, British policy had of necessity to be circumspect and calculating: achieving the objects of the imperial presence at the least cost; and mindful always, as Cromer had insisted, that while imperial control could aspire to a grudging tolerance, it could never be popular.[85]

With attitudes like these, formed well before 1914, it is clear that Milner was unlikely to regard the prime object of his Mission in Egypt as being to reinforce and entrench the most ambitious interpretation of imperial purpose implicit in the notion of the 'civilising mission', especially since Egypt, as Milner was to remind his Cabinet colleagues on several occasions, fell outside even the dependent empire. It was desirable that the imperial presence should be accompanied by useful or improving work but this, as Milner well knew from the concessions and compromises of the Cromer period, was scarcely the first priority of imperial control. Thus when he came to review the whole bent of British policy in Egypt, Milner laid stress upon the need to clarify exactly which tasks the British presence was directed towards and which objectives should most influence the shape of policy. Writing to Lloyd George in December 1919, he attacked the confusion which had reigned in this sphere. 'For some years past', he told the Prime Minister, 'we have really had no consistent policy at all. . . .'[86] It was necessary to establish a tighter control over the activity of the Residency and the British officials in the country since 'without a Cromer on the spot, we do absolutely need some better machinery at home to keep in touch with and supply intelligent guidance to the British element in the Egyptian administration'.[87] Such guidance and control should ensure that British policy in Egypt was 'directed in relation to what we are going to do in other parts of the Near East',[88] and was not allowed to acquire the kind of autonomy and internal preoccupation which characterised Indian administration.

This stress upon the subordination of Egyptian policy to the wider design of the British in the East was given added emphasis, in Milner's account to Lloyd George, by the likelihood that continued unrest in Egypt would react upon the stability of the imperial system elsewhere. 'It is evident', he declared, 'that till there is some change in the temper of the people, Egypt will continue to be a thorn in our side and will exercise a disturbing influence on our position in the whole of the Near East and to some extent also in India. This is a serious danger which we must try by hook or by crook to overcome.'[89] It followed that the yardstick of concession was to be the retention of essential strategic interests, not the attempt to preserve either the symbols or the substance of administrative authority where it was superfluous to this purpose. The keynote of the new clarity of thought which Milner promised the Prime Minister was to be an unsentimental and even machiavellian use of political concession to safeguard the original purposes of intervention in 1882.

It was in this calculating mood that the Treaty project was conceived. The problem it was intended to alleviate was the dissatisfaction of the Egyptians with their subjection to formal British rule. The difficulty, as Milner owned, was 'to find a way of making Egypt's relation to Great Britain appear a more independent and dignified one than it ever really can be without our abandoning the degree of control which . . . we are constrained to keep'.[90] The Treaty was to be a means of conceding the shadow and keeping the substance; of conciliating Egyptian pride. 'In dealing with an Oriental people', he proclaimed, 'the question of form is of capital importance.'[91] Indeed Milner was so convinced of the truth of this perception that he proceeded to make claims for his plan which later events would belie. An alteration in the form of the British connection would, he argued, restore Egyptian goodwill and regain that cooperation which was of 'paramount importance'.[92] British policy must regard the fact that

> the aspirations of educated and semi-educated Egyptians to become a 'nation', to invest their country with the dignity of an independent state will not die with the passing of the present turmoil. Indeed this aspiration is bound to grow constantly stronger as the number of educated and semi-educated increases. Our own action is, of necessity, always providing Nationalism with fresh recruits. We cannot hope to extinguish it even if we wished to; we can only seek to guide it into reasonable channels.[93]

This latter objective, Milner suggested, could be largely attained by a display of sympathy and sophistication in the British approach to Egyptian nationalism. Many nationalists, he asserted, 'condemned the methods of the present agitation [and] admitted their need of our future help . . . Men of this type are our natural allies. We need their co-operation as they realise they need ours. But such cooperation would be impossible if British policy were, or seemed to be, opposed to the attainment of their cherished aim.'[94]

The crux of Milner's argument now rested, as this implied, upon the compatibility of nationalism and imperial control, provided that such control was skilfully and discreetly exercised. For what Milner was anxious to demolish, especially, perhaps, in the mind of the Prime Minister, was the undiscriminating assumption that cooperation with those who demanded Egyptian independence was either impossible or unnecessary. The Mission had found the permeation of nationalist feeling within the native bureaucracy to be such that the High Commissioner's authority was becoming difficult to sustain. 'The situation', Milner remarked, 'was not one in which the plan of simply carrying on and taking no notice is a sufficient policy.'[95] And if the treaty project were not adopted, the only alternative would be not just the maintenance of the existing machinery of British control, but its drastic overhaul and expansion. But this, thought Milner, would not only face the 'great practical difficulty' of finding enough good men to carry it out, but would suffer all the disadvantages attendant upon 'a complete reversal of policy. . . . This is a prospect so unattractive that it can only be faced in the last resort.'[96] Indeed, as he told Curzon, even if the British strove by these means to root out Egyptian nationalism, there was no certainty that they would succeed. 'Further repressive measures, however necessary, will also supply fresh fuel for agitation and so we go round in the old vicious circle.'[97] And all this time the cost of preserving Britain's *essential* interests would grow higher and higher.

Thus the Mission's tour of Egypt and the boycott it had suffered served only to strengthen Milner's conviction, partially formed before he left England, that the experiment in closer administration which the war had encouraged had made the real purposes of a British presence in Egypt harder and not easier to achieve. The solution lay not in the precipitate abandonment of all British interest in the country, but in an intelligent separation of those powers which could be safely delegated to Egyptians from those which had to be retained in British hands so that the international status of Egypt and its contribution to imperial security would be unaffected. Milner did not believe that Egypt would rapidly become totally unamenable to British influence. His respect for Cromer's success in finding effective collaborators in Egyptian politics convinced him that a return to the more informal methods of control which he associated with Cromerian Egypt would yield a similar reward. What remained to be decided, even after the Mission had presented its 'General Conclusions' to Curzon in May 1920, were the precise powers which Egyptian politicians were to enjoy; and whether the division which the Mission proposed would satisfy enough of those whom it wished to appease. This contingency had troubled Milner at the time when the Mission's recommendations were first being drafted. Would 'any section of the Egyptian nationalists', he wondered, ' . . . be got to agree to such a "Treaty" . . .?'[98] When he returned to London, Milner set out in earnest to find the answer.

The Milner–Zaghlul Agreement

At the time when Milner returned to England from Palestine in late March 1920 and began the task of writing a full version of the Mission's report, there was little expectation either in the Foreign Office or in the wider circle of informed opinion that it would recommend any radical change in the established pattern of Anglo-Egyptian relations. Milner had told Curzon early on of his conviction that a treaty of alliance should become the mainstay of British influence and the instrument for the diplomatic and strategic control of Egypt; but he had remained vague about the fate of the protectorate under such an arrangement. Nor does Curzon seem to have asked for clarification of the views which Milner had indicated in his letters from Egypt, and, perhaps because of the press of business, appeared in the spring of 1920 to be untroubled by dark suspicions of the Mission's collective thoughts. Such public speculation as existed was, at best, under-informed. *The Times* suggested, as the Mission re-assembled to write its report, that its main recommendation was likely to be a reduction in the number of British civil servants in Egypt.[99] And in the Egyptian department of the Foreign Office, as late as 23 January, the expectation had been that Milner and his colleagues would propose a constitution 'similar to that proposed by Brunyate' with a strong contingent of advisers in the Upper Chamber.[100]

On 17 May 1920, Milner sent to Curzon a shortened version of the Mission's report embodying its 'General Conclusions', as a way of informing him officially of the direction its final report would take. In this document, Milner referred to the need to allow any negotiators 'great latitude' in settling the details of the new treaty relationship which the Mission favoured, but gave no indication as to who these negotiators – on either side – should be.[101] But even before making this suggestion, and sending the 'General Conclusions' to Curzon, Milner had initiated an attempt to draw Zaghlul to a conference with the Mission in London.

We have seen that while in Egypt Milner in his frustration had come to the view that if the Mission was to achieve what he took to be its prime function – a community of outlook with the leaders of opinion in Egypt – then it would be necessary to engage Zaghlul in a discussion of the future shape of Anglo-Egyptian relations. Thus Milner, in his own mind, did not regard the return of the Mission from Egypt as marking the end of its active participation in the making of British policy, despite the fact that a straightforward reading of its terms of reference scarcely envisaged that it should proceed to negotiate an Egyptian settlement independently of either the British or Egyptian governments. It is likely, however, that Milner regarded the apparent acquiescence of the Foreign Office in his efforts to negotiate with Egyptian politicians while actually in Egypt as confirmation of his own view of the Mission's task. At all events, without further consultation with the Foreign Secretary, Zaghlul and Adly were invited from Paris to confer with the Mission in London, since Milner was now convinced that they were both 'very anxious to come to terms'.[102] Milner's estimate was correct, perhaps because both Egyptian leaders feared that without some sign of their ability to influence the course of British policy, Allenby, the Sultan and their other enemies in Egypt would reconstruct Egyptian politics at their expense – indeed Allenby was about to make the attempt. On 11 May 1920, Milner telegraphed to Hurst in great secrecy instructing him to contact the two Egyptians discreetly through Osmond Walrond lest any premature publicity might frighten the pashas back into a public stance of non-cooperation.[103] The Egyptians, however, accepted the invitation without delay.

From the first, the Mission's negotiations with Zaghlul and Adly turned upon Egypt's international status and the reality of the independence which Milner was offering. At a meeting held at the Colonial Office on 21 June 1920, Milner told the Egyptian leaders that the Mission would not be able to recommend to the British government proposals which permitted the representatives of foreign powers full diplomatic status in Cairo or an Egyptian Foreign Office to maintain a diplomatic corps abroad free from British supervision. Egypt, he declared, must entrust her foreign affairs to Britain. The Egyptians replied that such controls were incompatible with independence.[104] The next day, when discussion was resumed, Zaghlul reiterated this demand for full diplomatic freedom, but offered that Egypt should bind herself not to ally with any other power. Milner was unwilling to make a concession on this point; but even more reluctant to break off the conversations. He agreed to keep the issue of diplomatic representation open, but insisted that the primacy of the High Commissioner in Cairo should not be compromised and that he should retain his title as a symbol of his extra-diplomatic powers.[105] Discussion then moved to the Mission's proposals for the reform of the Capitulations and the protection of the foreign communities. Hurst had suggested that the consular courts of the Capitulation powers should be abolished and their functions vested in the Mixed courts where European and Egyptian legal processes were combined. But as a guarantee against the mistreatment of the foreign colonies he had urged that the British should retain a veto on any change in the functions of the Mixed courts, that the department of Public Security within the Ministry of the Interior should be headed by a British official, and that a substantial element of the city police should be British.[106] These reservations were unpalatable to the Egyptians especially since they preserved British control over the police and strengthened Britain's power of intervention in disputes involving foreigners.[107] Milner, however, refused to set any term to British command of the police, adding at the next meeting, two days later, that 'we had always contemplated that a British officer of Public Security would, like a Financial Adviser, be permanently maintained'.[108]

Thus, as Milner himself had foreseen some months before, the substantial concessions to Egyptian *amour-propre* contained in the Mission's proposals to end the protectorate and reduce the powers of the British civil servants in the internal administration of the country did not satisfy the aspirations, real or affected, of those whom he regarded as the prime movers of Egyptian politics. He had been conscious all along of the reluctance of Zaghlul or Adly to identify themselves publicly with any proposals emanating from the British side. With this in mind, Milner resolved to concede, at the same meeting when he reaffirmed the permanence of British stewardship over the finances and foreign colonies of Egypt, what had hitherto been beyond concession – diplomatic representation for Egypt abroad.[109] This he coupled with the requirement that Egypt should make no international agreements incompatible with the projected treaty of alliance, and that the British High Commissioner should still conserve his special status. But if Milner thought that this major concession would create a breakthrough and produce a swift agreement, he was disappointed. For the remainder of July and on into August there ensued a desultory series of discussions as Zaghlul and Adly sought to widen the offer which Milner had made and erode the remaining constraints on Egyptian independence.[110]

By mid-August, with Milner refusing to yield to these fresh demands, mindful, no doubt, that those concessions he had already made were likely to cause trouble among his Cabinet colleagues, it was clear that the limits of flexibility had been reached. Yet neither side was eager to break off negotiation and leave the conference table empty-handed, or to admit publicly that their meetings had been fruitless. Milner was determined to modify Britain's Egyptian policy along the lines he had proposed to Curzon. For that he needed some convincing evidence that concessions of the kind the Mission were recommending could form the basis for cooperation with the leaders of Egyptian opinion.[111] Failure with Zaghlul and Adly would spell the total ruin of the Mission's policy. For their part, Zaghlul and Adly, while wary of committing themselves to anything less than a complete expulsion of British influence and authority, were reluctant to return to Egypt and face the inevitable accusation that they had been incapable of winning real concessions from the British. Such an outcome would contribute little to their standing or prestige. Moreover, by July 1920, they had an added reason for seeking some compromise with Milner since Allenby in Cairo was preparing to strike a bargain with the Sultan's faction that would result in the suppression of their following.[112]

Both sides had an interest, therefore, in cultivating the impression that they would soon be able to reach a satisfactory agreement on the terms of a new Anglo-Egyptian relationship. This community of interest produced the so-called Milner–Zaghlul Agreement which was drawn up in the middle of August. It was in actuality not an agreement at all but rather a communiqué or declaration of intent, meant to serve as the basis for formal negotiations between the properly accredited representatives of the British and Egyptian governments. The Mission and Zaghlul's 'Delegation' undertook to recommend its terms to the British government and the Egyptian people respectively. The agreement itself embodied the central argument of the Mission's 'General Conclusions' modified by the concessions made in the negotiations.[113] Egypt was to be recognised as an independent constitutional monarchy, bound by a treaty of alliance to Britain. Britain was to enjoy the right to station troops in the country, and to command Egyptian assistance even when Egypt's security was not directly involved. Britain was also to retain an ultimate control over the delicate international questions which might arise from the debt administration and the security of foreign interests; jointly appointed advisers at the Finance and Interior Ministries would supervise these sensitive sectors. As a further guarantee against foreign interference in Egypt, the British were to exercise a right of veto over laws affecting foreigners, a right hitherto reserved to the Capitulation powers. And, as Milner had constantly insisted, the British High Commissioner was to remain formally pre-eminent in Cairo.

These reservations made it clear that Egypt was not to be free to intrigue with Britain's imperial rivals, nor to allow any other power than Britain a foothold on her soil. As in the First World War, so in any future conflict, Egypt would make her facilities available to the British. What Milner had conceded in exchange fell into two parts. Firstly, he offered, in effect, to end all British interference in those matters which in no way affected foreign interests or Britain's defence requirements. The internal administration of Egypt was to be restored to the Egyptians; the encroachments of the war years and even before were to be rolled back; and the number of expatriate officials to be reduced. British intervention would be strictly confined to the reserved questions. Secondly, Milner, to entice the Egyptians into accepting freely and voluntarily the restraints on their international freedom of action, had eventually agreed that Egypt should have representatives abroad who held diplomatic status as a token of her independent nationhood, provided that her diplomacy was 'consistent' with the obligations of the treaty of alliance. And as a further evidence of British sincerity, he had been ready to limit the British garrison in Egypt to one cantonment away from the main cities, so as to reduce as far as possible the overt signs of Britain's ultimate supremacy in Egyptian affairs.

Milner was aware that this radical transformation of Anglo-Egyptian relations, which meant abolishing a protectorate declared no more than six years previously and recognising Egyptian independence, would arouse alarm and criticism in Britain and had no certainty of being accepted in Egypt. But his boldness seemed justified by what he judged as the favourable circumstances of Egyptian politics. For Milner was convinced, despite their apparent hesitation, that Adly and Zaghlul would support the terms of the August agreement loyally and secure their reception in Egypt: that they would be satisfied with the status and the concessions which the Milner–Zaghlul Agreement envisaged. And even if Zaghlul himself 'is too timid to back his own convictions which tell him that he has got an extremely good bargain',[114] Adly and Rushdy pashas, and the other leaders of the *Wafd*, 'would join forces and bind themselves to support the scheme and use all their influence to obtain the assent of the National Assembly. . .'.[115] (In this situation, Milner predicted, Zaghlul would retire from public life.) Thus the most effective political forces in Egypt, on Milner's reckoning, were ready to throw themselves behind the terms of the agreement, and should be given every inducement to do so. For it was upon the alliance of Adly and Zaghlul's following that the success of the Mission's policy now depended, or so it seemed. This calculation led Milner to view with apprehension and distaste the Residency's attempt to construct a party based upon the court which would oppose the Zaghlulists. At the end of June he was counselling the Foreign Office not to let Allenby 'form a "cave" in Cairo' or fall too much under the influence of the Sultan.[116] In mid-August, only a few days before the conclusion of the agreement, he vehemently denounced the suggestion of the Egyptian premier, relayed through the Cairo Residency, that the Zaghlulists should be suppressed if the negotiation broke down. Such a policy, he declared, would create a situation 'similar to that which exists in Ireland',[117] and he persuaded Curzon to veto 'any action which would exacerbate local situation by once more making Zaghlul and his followers our enemies and consolidate all sections of Egyptian nationalists against us'.[118] The Zaghlulists, he told the Foreign Secretary, ' . . . are now the pro-British wing of the Nationalist party, and, if we play our cards properly, the split between them and the extremists will be complete and irremediable'. It was 'vital that the Sultan and the Residency should not work against them'.[119]

Milner considered that the attitude he had taken up in negotiation with Adly and Zaghlul had been generous and imaginative, and had given the Egyptian nationalists all they could reasonably expect. But he also had no doubt that, as long as Adly and Zaghlul swung Egyptian opinion behind the August agreement, his policy would prove to have extricated Britain from a difficult and potentially dangerous situation in Egypt without reducing in any way the value of Egypt to Britain's system of imperial defence. This was how he justified to Curzon what he acknowledged to be the 'weak point' of his agreement – the concession of diplomatic representation abroad for Egypt – and the withdrawal of the British garrisons from the principal towns. A 'seductive offer' was necessary to obtain Egyptian consent, and the advantages thereof, to Britain's use of the country as a military base.[120] 'We want', Milner went on in language which revealed how little he contemplated Egypt's elevation, at that moment or in the foreseeable future, from the status of a British satellite,

> a strong foothold in Egypt as being a vital link in the chain of empire. That is the only reason why we ever went there. We could not let Egypt fall into other hands. And the link is more vital than ever now, when Wireless and Air Force, for both of which Egypt is a centre of the first importance, are bound to play an increasing part. What I want is the acknowledged right, conferred on us by Egypt herself in a treaty, to keep a military force on Egyptian soil to guard our communications . . . . At the same time the fact that we have such a force in Egypt at all, and that Egypt recognises our right to keep it there for our purposes, recognises, that is, her own permanent place in our Imperial system, will lend authority to the 'advice' of our representative in Cairo . . . . The presence of a military force, the High Commissioner's acknowledged position as the guardian of foreign interests, the two advisers, and, much more, the presence for years to come of a large number of British people in the Egyptian service . . . will, in my opinion, supply all and more than all we need for a policy of Influence as distinct from a policy of Domination. Especially as we keep the Sudan . . . .[121]

Cromer and Salisbury, so Milner might have said, could not have asked for more.

The Mission and British Policy: a Retrospect

The agreement of August 1920 proved to be the Mission's swansong. When Adly and Zaghlul returned to London in the autumn to resume negotiations, and to demand further concessions, Milner insisted that the Mission must make way for formal negotiations between the British government and representative Egyptians. By this stage it was already becoming clear that his recommendations were unlikely to be fully endorsed by the Cabinet.

The significance of the Milner Mission in British imperial policy lay in its attempt to impose on Britain's relations with Egypt a constitutional framework which, like that enshrined in the Montagu–Chelmsford reforms, would enforce a strict separation between those aspects of local administration which held no importance for the safety and smooth functioning of the imperial system, and would only draw Britain into sterile and self-defeating conflict with local politicians; and those which had to be supervised in the interests of Britain's political, military and commercial predominance in the eastern hemisphere. Whatever the unorthodoxy of its proceedings, or the eagerness with which it solicited local opinion, there could be no doubt that the Mission under Milner's guidance held firmly to this central distinction. Secondly, the Mission, like earlier essays in imperial policy, proposed to achieve its objective not merely by modifying the terms of Britain's supremacy. Milner's negotiations with Adly and Zaghlul, and his resistance to the Residency's tactics in Cairo, make it plain that he intended to preserve Britain's influence in Egypt by changing not only the mode of future collaboration, but the collaborators themselves. Milner, it is clear, had little patience with the Residency's intrigues and almost certainly agreed with Spender's view that 'there could not be a more rotten basis of British power in Egypt than alliance with Fu'ad'.[122] The treaty project, and the bargain with Zaghlul and Adly, was to be buttressed, therefore, by constitutional reform in Egypt: the creation of effective representative institutions that would place close limits on the Sultan's power. Collaboration was to have its proper reward.

What Milner's plans revealed, then, was a striking confidence in the *compatibility* of Egyptian nationalism and British imperialism: in the possibility of reconciling their demands. For he did not view his concessions as infringing what he conceived to be Britain's real interests. Nor did he accept that his readiness to treat Egyptian nationalism with sympathy was a sign of infirmity in his convictions. After the terms of the Milner–Zaghlul agreement became public, an anonymous correspondent, so Milner told his Cabinet colleagues, had reproached him: 'I fear, my Lord, you are getting old.'[123] This, said Milner, was 'unfortunately true. But I think that even in my hey-day I should have regarded the proposed concessions to Egyptian nationalism as just and politic and as calculated to strengthen and not to weaken our Imperial position.'[124] The alternative to offering independence, as he had defined it, was to proceed to annexation. The alternative to a flexible policy which preserved real imperial interests was to 'maintain our position . . . but we shall have to pay a very heavy price. I am not thinking merely or mainly of the cost of the Army of Occupation. More serious still is the prospect of the difficulties the Egyptian intelligentsia will create for us both in Egypt itself and throughout the world.' His proposals, Milner conceded, might look backwards, 'and in a sense they really are a step backwards, but to a more secure position than that which we now occupy'.[125]

But whatever the merits of Milner's enlightened imperialism, the programme he had laid down had to run the gauntlet both in England and in Egypt. Its success now depended upon the intrigues of politicians in Cairo and London who viewed the harmony of Anglo-Egyptian relations not as an abstract problem but as one aspect of their wider political struggles.

5 Egypt and the Cabinet

The Cabinet Considers

Up until the moment when his discussions in London with the pashas Adly and Zaghlul were broken off in the middle of August 1920, Milner had not revealed to his Cabinet colleagues either the objectives or the procedure of his enquiry into the Anglo-Egyptian relationship. And although he had indicated to the Foreign Secretary, as the responsible minister, the main lines of the Mission's approach, and had relayed through him terse reports of the London negotiations to Allenby, even Curzon had not been consulted about the extent to which the original project for a treaty of alliance should be modified in order to obtain the consent of Adly and Zaghlul. The reasons for Milner's reluctance to canvass the opinion of his colleagues before reaching his provisional agreement with Zaghlul are not difficult to understand. The Mission's proceedings in Egypt had been inconclusive, even disastrous. They could provide few arguments for the changes which Milner wished to bring about in British policy. Indeed his failure to draw the 'moderates' out into the open seemed, at this stage, powerful evidence that the solution which he propounded was neither safe nor feasible. There was, therefore, every reason for Milner to postpone his report to the Cabinet until such time as he could present an alternative policy with some claims to viability, and with some expectation that it would not only command support in Egypt, but also ease the difficulties under which the imperial presence was labouring. Only then could he hope to force a programme of change through a Cabinet already overwhelmed by urgencies and mistrustful of radical reform.

The result of this tactical delay, and of the eagerness with which the Egyptians communicated Milner's offer to the press, was that the Misson's proposals reached at least some members of the Cabinet, as Churchill later complained,[1] through the medium of the newspapers, in the first instance. Milner was placed at a disadvantage from the beginning in his attempts to prepare the ministry for a substantial change in the constitutional framework of imperial control in Egypt.

But even before this unfortunate breach of protocol, he had felt misgivings about the attitude which his colleagues would adopt towards a programme which, in Milner's hands, had been shaped by influences and considerations which it was difficult to lay completely bare – for example the Mission's mistrust of Allenby's expertise and intentions. These misgivings were reinforced by Curzon's warnings once he had focused properly upon the terms of the Milner–Zaghlul communiqué. Those provisions which related to the diplomatic representation of Egypt in foreign countries, the future role of the British advisers in the Egyptian government, and the garrison rights which Britain was to enjoy, attracted his particular attention; he told Milner, prophetically, 'I can't help thinking Cabinet will shy rather badly at this.'[2]

Milner's proposals were not, however, discussed by the Cabinet until Lloyd George convened a conference of ministers – an informal Cabinet meeting – on 1 November 1920. But prior to this a succession of memoranda had given warning of a rough passage ahead. The barrage was opened by Churchill, then Secretary of State for War, 'five hours', as he claimed, after reading press reports of the Milner–Zaghlul Agreement. He attacked Milner's recommendations on four grounds, all of which were likely to find an echo among his colleagues. Firstly, the Mission was denounced for concluding an agreement without seeking the approval of the government. This, said Churchill, combined with the effects of premature publicity, had placed ministers in a difficult and embarrassing position in any further negotiation. Secondly, Churchill questioned whether Milner's reforms would achieve their objects: was the independence of Egypt to be real, or was Milner's treaty designed to camouflage an essentially dependent relationship? If, as he suspected, it was the latter, was it likely that the nationalists would tolerate it? Thirdly, through the appended memoranda of his service chiefs, Churchill, as War and Air Minister, questioned the military aspects of Milner's projected agreement, and condemned the Mission's failure to consult the expert knowledge of the government's military advisers. Lastly, and perhaps with greatest effect, Churchill played upon the fears of those ministers who were already alarmed at the intransigence of nationalism in Ireland and India. 'One can easily see', he wrote, 'that these proposals will become immediately the goal of Indian nationalism.' The notion at the heart of Montagu's reforms, that India would eventually become a self-governing dominion within the British Empire, would be discarded in favour of independence on the Egyptian model, outside the imperial system.[3]

Because of his special departmental interest in Egypt as a vital sector of Britain's system of imperial defence, Churchill was fully entitled to comment upon any plans which might affect the disposition of military forces and the pattern of imperial security. And as a member of the Cabinet, bearing a collective responsibility for its decisions, he was justified in seeking to uphold its authority. But it is doubtful whether his rapid intervention was prompted solely by such considerations. His sweeping attack not just upon the detail of Milner's proposals but also against the thinking which lay behind them was intended, partly at least, to undermine Milner's authority in questions of imperial security, and to embarrass Curzon. For it was these two who, throughout the spring and summer of 1920, had thwarted Churchill's efforts to persuade the Cabinet to sanction the withdrawal of British troops from Persia and write off Curzon's cherished Anglo-Persian treaty.[4] Their combined influence had imposed on the Cabinet the view that a military foothold in Persia was vital to imperial security. The leaking of the Milner–Zaghlul Agreement, and the boldness of its terms, provided Churchill with a golden opportunity to destroy the combination which had so effectively checked the influence of his ideas, and which threatened him with political disaster if, as the Chief of the Imperial General Staff constantly warned, the inadequate British forces in north Persia were overwhelmed by the advancing Red army. For Churchill, his betrayal over the Dardanelles cast a long shadow.[5]

Churchill was followed into the ring some two months later by the Secretary of State for India, Montagu. In his memorandum,[6] largely based upon a minute by the permanent head of the India Office, Montagu also complained about the anomalous procedure of the Milner Mission. Like Churchill, he argued that concession in Egypt would encourage agitation elsewhere. But unlike Churchill, he went on to attack what he saw as the shrugging off of responsibility for the good government of Egypt, the failure, as Duke had expressed it, to provide 'protection for the fellaheen'.[7] He pointed to the contrast between this approach and that which had been adopted in the reform of the Indian constitution. But his most scathing and, as it was to prove, most damaging, criticism was reserved for the Mission's readiness to negotiate with the followers of Zaghlul, whom Montagu characterised as 'extremists'. Again he contrasted the method adopted in India: 'The extremists in India are ignored and I understand that nobody disputed the wisdom of doing so. In Egypt the treaty is made with extremists. I, like the Secretary of State for War, can find nothing which makes it possible to negotiate with Zaghlul, which does not, at least, point the way to negotiation with De Valera or Gandhi, and I have only to say that . . . the method of the Milner proposals has enormously increased our Indian difficulties.'

In some measure, Montagu's response was influenced by the special traditions and responsibilities of his department, by its almost instinctive association of political stability in Egypt with a continuation of British control in the localities. But his subsequent, and apparently painless, conversion to the principles of the Milner project suggest that, as in Churchill's case, considerations of personal influence helped to determine his conception of policy. For Montagu, too, was dissatisfied with the extent of his influence in the ministry, and felt, in particular, that his conduct of Indian affairs was insufficiently appreciated by his colleagues – a conviction which the tone of the recent Commons debate on the Hunter Committee Report had done little to shake.[8] His memorandum on the Milner proposals is better read as a justification of his and Chelmsford's proceedings in India, than as a specific commentary upon Egyptian policy, and as a reflex to the growing sense of frustration and failure which was to haunt him after the summer of 1920.

These two memoranda were intended to give a lead to ministerial opinion and to arouse controversy in the Cabinet. But their success in doing so was likely to depend upon the reaction of Lloyd George and the Unionist leader Bonar Law who, between them, decided which matters should be left to the discretion of individual ministers and which should be exposed to the uncertain fate of Cabinet discussion. For their part, Lloyd George and Bonar Law were keenly sensitive to the limits of their authority over the Cabinet and the two parliamentary parties upon whose support the coalition rested. Both were conscious that what they regarded as pragmatic and realistic policies at home and abroad were regarded with suspicion by one or other wing of their supporters; and they were in consequence unenthusiastic about making bold changes in the constitutional mechanisms of imperial control. Thus, when Curzon, as he later reported to Milner, informed the Prime Minister of Milner's 'general ideas', Lloyd George was, or affected to be, 'a good deal startled'.[9] Bonar Law's reaction, once Milner's concessions had been communicated to him by Curzon, was even sharper: 'The whole of these Egyptian proposals', he wrote back to Curzon, 'came to me as a great shock and I think that will be the effect on public opinion here when they are known.'[10] This mood of doubt and criticism continued,[11] while both men, and especially the Prime Minister, tested the mood of their Cabinet colleagues and tried to sense which aspects of Milner's plan would arouse real opposition. But, prior to the ministerial conference of early

November, Lloyd George, at least, seemed less concerned with the substance of Milner's ideas than with the mode of his proceedings. An exaggerated sensitivity to the dangers of being embarrassed by the activity of his colleagues – the occupational hazard of coalition government – was reinforced by Lloyd George's special loathing for any premature commitment, and, in this instance, by the sour memory of an earlier indiscretion of Milner's.[12] If Churchill remembered Gallipoli, Lloyd George was unlikely to forget General Maurice.

Dissension and mistrust within the Cabinet, occasioned by issues far removed from Egypt, thus created an unhappy atmosphere for the Cabinet's review of Milner's scheme, and denied him the easy acquiescence for which he might have hoped. As it was, when at last his recommendations were discussed by a majority of Cabinet ministers, it quickly became clear that the objections of Churchill and Montagu, aided perhaps by Beatty's reminder of the increased strategic significance of the Suez Canal with the rise of American and Japanese naval power,[13] commanded substantial support. Milner reiterated the case for substituting a treaty of alliance for the protectorate, and was at pains to deny Montagu's assertion that he had bargained with extremists. The discussion, however, centred upon the narrower diplomatic and strategic consequences of Egyptian independence. 'Considerable doubt was expressed as to how under the proposed scheme it would be possible to prevent the French or any other foreign power from intriguing in Egypt.'[14] At the same time, ministers were concerned lest Britain's responsibility for maintaining order in Egypt might impose, as Curzon had hinted,[15] a heavier burden upon her military resources than if the existing garrison rights, allowing immediate access to the major centres of population, were retained. In the second session of the conference, Allenby, who had been invited to attend, encouraged these fears and spoke strongly against the proposal to confine any British force to a single cantonment along the Canal.[16] Only Milner's insistence that, without some alteration to the shape of the imperial presence in Egypt, it would be impossible to maintain control 'otherwise than by martial law', brought about a reluctant acceptance of the need for change. 'The question for consideration', it was dourly recorded, 'was whether Lord Milner's proposed alternative was the best possible.'[17] But the conference reached no agreement on this. Seven weeks later, when the Egyptian question was, for the first time, discussed in a formal meeting of Cabinet, it proved no easier to find a middle way between Milner's conviction that any significant modification of his scheme would cause renewed unrest in Egypt and the determination of Churchill to amend the clauses which permitted Egypt diplomatic representation of her own abroad, and restricted the freedom of the British garrison to intervene effectively in the major cities. Chamberlain, Fisher, Addison, Lee, Munro and Montagu inclined towards Milner on this occasion; Geddes, Worthington-Evans, Churchill, Curzon and Lloyd George were 'decidedly against' him.[18] Bonar Law, significantly, in view of his earlier criticism, reserved judgment.[19]

With the entrenched opposition of senior ministers, there was, at this stage, little prospect of Milner being able to fulfil his part of the bargain struck in August 1920. For although the Cabinet had registered its desire to put forward proposals 'which . . . might . . . be acceptable to the Egyptian Nationalists' – a sign that Milner's warnings had made some impression – there seemed little evidence that it would be able to agree upon a formula while such disparities of view existed within its ranks. This impasse was partially resolved by Curzon, who, at the year's end, abruptly changed his tactics in Cabinet and began, with Allenby's help, and at his prompting, to assume a more positive role in the debate over Egypt than he had played in the opening phase of Cabinet deliberations.

The circulation of Milner's proposals to the Cabinet in August 1920, and his own departmental responsibility for supervising the affairs of Egypt, had necessarily imposed on the Foreign Secretary the obligation, not usually unwelcome, to express his opinion of the changes envisaged in the treaty project. Curzon had, of course, conveyed his doubts to Milner as soon as the latter had told him the detail of his agreement with Zaghlul, but had not defined his own attitude clearly. When he eventually did so in October,[20] after consultation with Milner, Allenby and General Congreve, the commander of the British garrison in Egypt, Curzon was well aware of the alarm expressed by Lloyd George and Bonar Law, and of the strenuous denunciations of Churchill. His own views were couched, therefore, in cautious language. The Milner scheme, he said, had been prepared 'quite independently of the Foreign Office'. He reminded the Cabinet that by their treatment of nationalism in Egypt they were ' . . . not merely solving a difficulty but creating a precedent'. He expressed his own objections to Milner's notion that a small garrison of under five thousand men, quartered on the Canal, would be enough to protect imperial communications and guard against a 'fanatical uprising' in the country, objections which, he claimed, were supported by Allenby. He condemned Milner's willingness to concede diplomatic autonomy, and the effects that this would have on the status and authority of the High Commissioner in Cairo. He raised the fearful prospect of French intrigue, and of a return to the tensions which had preceded the entente of 1904. But despite this heavy weight of criticism, which strengthened ministerial doubts about the scheme, Curzon nevertheless accepted the treaty of alliance as a solution to the problems of control in Egypt, and told his colleagues that nationalist opinion in Egypt had 'in general' welcomed the Milner proposals. 'There seems', he concluded with ambiguous intent, 'every reason to suppose that if it be endorsed by His Majesty's Government, it will be in the long run accepted in Egypt.'

From the overall tone of his memorandum, it might have been expected that Curzon would, in the ministerial discussions of November and December 1920, press for Cabinet support for the treaty principle while urging that its precise terms should be modified in any negotiation with Egyptian representatives. But there is little evidence that this is what he did. His remarks to Balfour were wholly critical,[21] while to Fisher he appeared united with Lloyd George and Churchill in opposition to Milner.[22] Curzon's reasons for this, and for his sudden conversion to the need for a favourable Cabinet decision, may have owed something to the lack of decision and drive which his biographer detects in the last phase of his career.[23] But it may also be that his reluctance to identify himself with Milner stemmed from the much fiercer controversy in the Cabinet over the future of Persia, and from the desire to maintain an appearance of consistency in his policies towards the British position in different parts of the Middle East. Curzon did not wish Churchill to become the arbiter of Britain's Eastern security. The same concern for his authority in the counsels of the Cabinet partially caused, it may be thought, Curzon's new-found enthusiasm for progress towards an Egyptian settlement in early 1921. Fresh tactics were required to limit the damage caused by Churchill's triumphs at the end of December, when it became clear that not only would British withdrawal from Persia be imposed by the Cabinet, but also that the responsibility for directing British policy in Mesopotamia, Trans-Jordan and Palestine would be vested in the Colonial Office, and the Colonial Office, after Milner's imminent resignation, in Churchill. To his old Persian ally, Curzon wrote mournfully in February 1921: 'I shall deeply deplore your absence from Cabinet. . . . Churchill is already spreading his wings over the entire universe.'[24]

Fear of Churchill's new authority in Middle Eastern affairs as the apostle of stability and retrenchment may, therefore, have encouraged Curzon to put a more positive face upon his misgivings about the ending of the Egyptian protectorate and the opening of negotiations with Egyptian nationalists on the terms indicated by Milner. But he was also under increasing pressure from Allenby who, while suspicious of the detail of Milner's proposed treaty, and resentful of his negotiations with Zaghlul, was yet convinced that publication of the August agreement had built up irresistible pressure for constitutional change in Egypt, and along Milner's lines.[25] By early February, Cairo was repeating these arguments with a new urgency. Zaghlul's influence, the Residency reported, was on the wane while that of the 'moderates' was growing.[26] But the price of a 'moderate' ministry, it emerged, was a declaration by the British government embodying the principles of the Milner–Zaghlul Agreement.[27] Without this, no official delegation could be formed in Egypt to negotiate with the British, and without a delegation, no moderate ministry under that favourite of the Residency's ministry-making, Adly pasha, would or could remain long in office. Once again, as so often before, Cairo begged London to strike while the iron of moderation was hot.

These considerations Curzon now chose to make the centre-piece of an appeal for a prompt Cabinet decision.[28] 'An early preliminary decision on the subject of Egypt', he told his colleagues, ' . . . cannot indeed either with honour or in safety be delayed.' Lord Allenby, who had his own reservations, was, nevertheless, very anxious to clear the way for a negotiated change in Egypt's status, and for this it was necessary for the Cabinet to authorise the eventual abolition of the protectorate. A failure to act quickly would vitiate any effort to settle Egypt's difficulties peacably and ' . . . we shall be back in the quick-sands'. Curzon then went on to discount just those fears which, partly with his encouragement, had dominated previous Cabinet discussion. There was, he said, an almost superstitious attachment in Egypt to the idea of abolishing the protectorate. If the Cabinet were to grant this whim, there was every chance of ensuring that almost every reservation to which they attached importance would be carried in the course of the detailed negotiations. But first it was necessary to make what Milner had called a 'seductive offer'.[29] Curzon then summoned precedent to his aid. 'Why worry about the rind,' he asked, 'if we can obtain the fruit? I take it that all we have in view is that Egypt would remain inside rather than outside the British Imperial system. If the best way to do this is to drop the word protectorate and conclude a treaty of alliance with her, as we did with the Indian princes a century or more ago . . . why not do it?'[30] Curzon declared his support for the substitution of the treaty for the protectorate and for the recognition of Egyptian independence. His advocacy and, perhaps more, the invocation of Allenby's wishes in the matter, secured a grudging victory in Cabinet over Churchill's desire for a postponement until the Imperial Conference met in June. But the Cabinet, while committing itself uneasily to formulating a new basis for Britain's authority in Egypt, declined to specify what that new basis should be; and the Cabinet declaration which Curzon obtained referred simply to the need for a fresh 'relationship' to replace the unsatisfactory status of protectorate.[31] With this uncertain mandate, Curzon began the task of renovating the tarnished heritage of Cromer.

The Negotiations

Curzon had assured his colleagues that, by agreeing to negotiate, they would be able to impose upon the politics of Egypt a more orderly and cooperative character, and, at the same time, secure for the imperial presence a less troubled existence. It remained to be seen how far the tactics of the Residency in Cairo, which had supplied these optimistic predictions, would give effect to such assurances. At first it seemed that their promises might be fulfilled, that the declared willingness of the British government to replace the protectorate by an arrangement more congenial to the Egyptian political nation, would generate a powerful party of 'moderates' committed to working in harness with the imperial power, and to reconciling Egyptian aspirations and British interests. Adly pasha, whom the Residency had consistently cast in the role of a willing and reliable collaborator, formed a ministry in March 1921 from which Zaghlul's followers were excluded.[32] The next step was for Adly to form with the approval of the Sultan, Fu'ad, an official delegation to settle the terms and conditions of Egypt's new status in London, an outcome which promised a substantial political reward for those of Adly's following. At this point, all the old tensions and conflicts in Egyptian politics, with which Cromer, Gorst and Kitchener had been so familiar, revived in full force; for Adly's gain was his rivals' loss. The Sultan, who had every reason to fear his triumph, summoned Churchill (then in Cairo for the Middle East Conference) to the Abdin palace and poured out his complaints about the direction of British policy. The imperial government's request for a delegation had, he said, upset such precarious tranquillity as had been achieved. He forecast that the negotiations would fail, and that the delegates would return to make trouble in Egypt. He filled Churchill's ears with imprecations against the selfishness and reactionary spirit of the pasha class.[33] But Fu'ad could make no impression on the Residency which was deeply committed to a conference along the lines set out by Curzon. Nor was he strong enough to act on his own. Instead it was Zaghlul who became the real obstacle to Adly's ambitions.

Since his conversations in London with Milner in the summer of 1920, and his abortive attempt later in the year to extract concessions from the Mission which went beyond those of the August agreement, Zaghlul had retired once more to France and the pleasures of Vichy. But the imminence of formal negotiation between the British and Egyptian governments, and the prospect of Adly stealing a long march, drew him back directly into Egyptian politics. On 21 March 1921, he addressed an open letter to Adly demanding that, before negotiations took place, the British government should accept the further demands of the *Wafd* which Milner had rejected in November 1920, and, in particular, that it should abolish the protectorate before any serious bargaining began. Zaghlul also demanded that the restraints imposed by censorship and martial law in Egypt should be lifted as a necessary prelude to free discussion between British and Egyptians.[34] But his real purpose was illustrated better by his insistence to Adly that his own followers should enjoy '*la précédence et la majorité*' in the official Egyptian delegation;[35] should therefore decide the terms and reap the benefits of constitutional change. Faced with this challenge to his fragile political authority in Egypt, Adly turned, as he had turned two years before, to the Residency. And not in vain. Allenby told him that Zaghlul would be unacceptable as the president of the Egyptian delegation, and that London would insist upon his, Adly's, '*précédence*'. The scene was now set for a political struggle in Egypt which threatened briefly to reproduce the upheavals of 1919.

For Zaghlul returned to Egypt to direct the campaign against Adly. An agreement patched up between them broke down over the vital issue of the membership and presidency of the delegation.[36] Both men manoeuvred for the support of the *Wafd* which, the Residency thought, was no longer united behind Zaghlul.[37] Adly declared his aims to be the same as the *Wafd*'s, but refused to accept as members of the delegation those who acknowledged the leadership of Zaghlul – a tactic designed to exploit Zaghlul's apparent loss of control over his former supporters. On 10 May, Adly's list of delegates was approved by the Sultan and forwarded, officially, to the British; but the departure of the delegates was delayed by an explosion of communal violence, worst in Alexandria, and ignited perhaps, by the friction between the rival factions of Adly and Zaghlul. That it failed to match the scope and intensity of the revolt of two years before may be attributed to the greater preparedness of the British, and also perhaps, to the greater caution of those who dominated the localities. But not until the beginning of July did Adly and his colleagues set out for the conference table in London.

If the uncertainties and confusions of Egyptian politics were hardening the attitude of the Residency's chosen moderates against any retreat from the full extent of the *Wafd*'s demands, there was little sign that those with whom they intended to bargain would receive their demands with greater cordiality than before. In the months that followed the Cabinet declaration of February 1921,[38] the critics of Milner's treaty project, and of Curzon's proposals for negotiation, remained suspicious of the Foreign Secretary's intentions, and subjected his management of Egyptian affairs to close scrutiny. Churchill in particular kept up a running fire against Curzon. The memorandum recording his conversation with the Sultan Fu'ad directly challenged the major premises of Curzon's policy by its suggestion that Adly and his following, the apple of the Residency's eye, and perforce of Curzon's, were no better, in effect, than those damned by official opinion as agitators and extremists. This drew a savage and scornful reply from Curzon in which he reflected upon the naivety and ignorance of the Colonial Secretary and reaffirmed Adly's credentials as 'unquestionably the ablest and most reliable of modern Egyptian statesmen'.[39] Curzon strove also to dispose of Churchill's contention, disguised as Fu'ad's opinion, that the nationalist movement in Egypt was merely the tool of the pasha class.

It was an ironic consequence of Cabinet politics that Curzon was to be found extolling the representative character of Egyptian nationalism. But neither this, nor his attempt to deride Churchill's claim to a Middle Eastern expertise, could free him from the restraints which Churchill's revolt had placed on him. For Churchill's doubts and denunciations were echoed, more mildly, by Balfour, Curzon's predecessor at the Foreign Office and still a major influence in the Conservative party in foreign and imperial affairs, and by Lloyd George. Both of them served notice, in the special forum of the Imperial Conference, that they expected Curzon to drive a hard bargain with the Egyptian nationalists.[40] Both emphasised the wide international interests at stake in Egypt; Lloyd George especially condemned as 'absolutely fatal' to Britain's imperial interests any proposal which might allow Egypt to recruit her expatriate civil servants freely. But again it was Churchill who stated the case against concession most vehemently; and in particular the case against permitting Egypt, as he saw it, to secede from the British Empire.[41] The right ideal for Egypt was, he argued, progress towards dominion status: internal autonomy while 'cooperating freely within the circle of the British Empire'. Churchill then took up a remark by Lloyd George and questioned whether Milner's proposed redeployment of British troops would not be a false economy. 'It would take more troops', he asserted, 'to protect the Canal, if they were quartered along the Canal, than it would take to keep order over the whole of Egypt and protect the Canal as well' – to which his successor at the War Office, Worthington-Evans, added: 'And more expense.' The solution to Britain's difficulties in Egypt, Churchill concluded, in diametric opposition to the whole burden of Milner's findings, was not to weaken British influence over the administration there, which would simply encourage a return to corruption and disorder; rather it lay in adherence to what he called, without definition, the 'Cromer System', combined with the maintenance of a large garrison. And, as a final cut at the premises of Curzon's policy, Churchill denounced the notion that a moderate party could survive any agreement with the imperial power short of complete independence: were Adly to do this, he declared, he would immediately be 'struck down' by Zaghlul.[42]

Time, it seemed, was not to be the cradle of concession. The Colonial Secretary's alternative version of political realities in Egypt found favour with the Prime Minister and Balfour; and their doubts frustrated Curzon's attempt to obtain from his Cabinet colleagues a real measure of authority in Egyptian affairs. Ministerial opinion, therefore, showed greater inflexibility than was compatible with the ebb and flow of Egyptian politics. The Cabinet which considered Curzon's draft treaty, drawn up in readiness for his conference with the Egyptian delegates, extracted from him an undertaking not to retreat from the reservations laid down in February: Egypt was to have consuls but not diplomats; there was to be no question of excluding the British garrison from the towns; and Britain was to retain a veto over the appointment of foreign officials and advisers.[43] Provided that these terms were acceded to, the Cabinet was prepared to allow the substitution of a treaty for the protectorate. But although the Cabinet's decision represented a modest advance upon the inscrutability of its earlier declaration, and a modest victory for Curzon over his critics, it also hammered home the potential difficulty of the situation in which the Foreign Secretary found himself. Chained down by a Cabinet upon whose fears Churchill and Lloyd George had played so successfully, he remained exposed to their jibes and sneers, even while he struggled to preserve the elements of British supremacy in Egypt. For Lloyd George and Churchill, badgering Curzon in this way over Egypt served partly to emphasise his personal responsibility for what might turn out an unpopular and dangerous policy; but it may also have been prompted by the imperatives of their Irish policy. Curzon was to meet Adly on 12 July; Lloyd George himself was to meet De Valera on the thirteenth. Although Curzon was very far indeed from being a die-hard in Irish matters, [44] there was clearly considerable advantage for the two leading Liberal ministers of the coalition in emphasising their reluctance to make concessions to every manifestation of recalcitrant nationalism. And, in addition, their Cabinet alliance with Balfour over Egypt may have been designed to ease the relations between this 'most irreconcilable Minister'[45] and a Prime Minister engaged in talks with the Irish rebels. Indeed Lloyd George, with one eye on the Conservative back benches, was eager to involve Balfour directly in the Irish negotiations.[46]

In imperial politics, therefore, the needs of Egypt took second place to the demands of Ireland: Adly was to be sacrificed that De Valera might be appeased. For Curzon, these exigencies in high policy imposed on him the unwelcome duty of conducting a conference which had little hope of success. This is not to say that, at this stage, he supported further concessions to Egyptians of whatever faction, even if he privately desired less restrictive instructions from Cabinet. But were he to fail in his reluctant efforts to square the circle of Egyptian politics, he risked the odium, already falling upon Montagu, which was reserved for those who sought without success to appease colonial nationalism.

The rigidities of British policy and the crosscurrents of Egyptian politics produced their inevitable result during the summer and autumn of 1921: neither Curzon nor Adly could find a compromise which satisfied their own requirements or those of their principals. In the six formal conferences with the Egyptian delegation which Curzon attended himself between 13 July and 17 August 1921, no progress was made upon the all-important issues of whether Egypt should enjoy the right of full diplomatic representation abroad, and whether Britain should, after granting independence, maintain her military occupation of Egypt upon the same terms as before. The delegation insisted that the British garrison be confined to the Canal zone and that it should enjoy unfettered access to military installations in the rest of Egypt only in wartime.[47] Curzon's offer to review the military clauses after ten years was rejected. The British side then shelved discussion of both these sensitive topics in the hope that agreement on the remaining issues would produce a more conciliatory mood among the Egyptians. But at the end of August, compromise was as far away as ever.[48]

Yet neither side showed any desire to break off these unproductive overtures. Curzon indeed had other preoccupations and delegated this unrewarding duty to an under-secretary, Lindsay, who, throughout September and October, carried on a desultory correspondence with Adly on matters of lesser importance. For Curzon the prolonging of the talks served several purposes. It postponed a return to the sterile sequence of events which had followed the collapse of Anglo-Egyptian cooperation in March 1919; it put off the day when he might have to go back, confessing failure, to his colleagues; it protected him from further intimidation by Allenby; and it offered the hope that a protracted series of discussions would erode the resolution of the Egyptians. Adly too had no wish, at this stage, to hasten his own return empty-handed to Egypt, to face there a Zaghlulist hurricane. On the other hand, like Curzon, he dared not accept any compromise on the two issues to which both sides attached the greatest importance. But for both, there was a limit to how long they would be allowed to preserve this comfortable if undignified posture.

For Curzon, the pressure to move forward came once again from the Residency and from Allenby in person. Since agreement could not be reached within the terms prescribed by the Cabinet, it was to the Cabinet that Curzon returned on 20 October 1921, to prepare the way for a modification in the British position. Blaming the activities of Zaghlul, and the effects of a visit by members of the parliamentary Labour party to Egypt for the 'very difficult stage' reached in the negotiations, he obtained from a reluctant Cabinet permission to circulate a paper showing what further concessions might be offered to the official moderate delegation. But such was the feeling among ministers that this remit to Curzon had to be coupled with the decision to set up, under his chairmanship, a Cabinet sub-committee to investigate the military requirements of imperial control should the negotiations break down.[49] Indeed it is not unlikely that this embodiment of ministerial pessimism was a deliberate and ingenious concession by Curzon to the mood of his colleagues; a defence against the charge that he favoured a settlement at all costs; and a device to focus attention upon the consequences of inflexibility.

In the weeks ahead, Curzon was to rely increasingly upon such byzantine tactics as he struggled to reconcile the demands of the Residency and the determination of the Cabinet. And, in the process, his relationship with Allenby became increasingly devious. For Curzon sought at one and the same time to control Allenby and also to use his intransigence to good effect among his Cabinet colleagues, thereby strengthening his own position and widening his discretionary power.

Allenby, however, was an unreliable instrument for this kind of trench warfare. His sibylline prophecies and pronouncements, especially on the subject of internal security, rarely had the effect on ministers which Curzon would have liked. These tactics and foibles of both the Foreign Secretary and the High Commissioner were amply displayed in the proceedings of Curzon's Cabinet sub-committee on the Egyptian situation which met for the first and only time on 24 October. Curzon opened discussion by arguing that, since there was little hope of securing an agreement with the Egyptians, the main priority was to manoeuvre into a position which would find favour at home as well as in Egypt; and that the British government's offer 'should be as generous as possible subject to the necessity of making sure of its refusal . . .'.[50] But if Curzon hoped that this curious argument for concessions would be supported by dire predictions from Allenby as to the consequences of refusing to alter the British terms, he was to be disappointed. For although the High Commissioner urged the unilateral abrogation of the protectorate even if no bargain were struck with Adly, he also asserted that a display of firmness by Britain would check any attempt by Zaghlul to make trouble; and, ignoring Curzon's hints, he appeared to substantiate directly Lloyd George's observation a few days earlier, that the repression of Zaghlul would achieve the same objects and with greater certainty, than the offer of larger concessions to Adly. To add to Curzon's embarrassment, Allenby went on to describe Adly as 'weak and timid',[51] and not at all the paragon on whose virtues Curzon had previously dwelt.

Despite this setback, Curzon continued to press the Cabinet for further concessions whether in hope of an agreement or as an insurance against failure with Adly. On 3 November 1921, he asked his colleagues to authorise a proposal which would withdraw British troops from Cairo and Alexandria after a year's tranquillity and place them in cantonments outside the two main cities.[52] He went on to argue that there must also be some easement over the question of diplomatic representation for Egypt, since it was clear that no agreement would otherwise be possible. Again, Curzon stated his belief that the Egyptian delegation would reject a settlement even if further concessions were made by the Cabinet, but claimed that an appearance of generosity was essential. The effect of this ploy he undermined, no doubt intentionally, by drawing a nightmarish picture of the reaction in Egypt should independence not result from the negotiations in progress. He feared, he said, 'a complete breakdown of the administration caused by a universal strike . . .'. The population would remain 'sullen and dangerous', even if cowed by the presence of a large military force, and a spirit of hatred would grow up. In the end, a future British government would be compelled either to annex Egypt, a course beset with difficulties, or to abandon imperial control altogether.[53]

Predictably, Curzon's appeal was countered by objections to further appeasement of the delegation and to any change in the disposition of British forces in Egypt. They were supported by Lloyd George who declared his belief that the government would be unable to carry 'any settlement except on the lines of the *status quo* through the House of Commons in existing conditions' and that consequently 'it was desirable to play for time'.[54] The Prime Minister then repeated the argument he had advanced in a conference of ministers a fortnight before. It was Zaghlul who was the author of discord, Zaghlul who was rousing Egypt against a reasonable settlement, Zaghlul who 'had created a very bad atmosphere in the House of Commons' where he was regarded as the true representative of Egyptian nationalism. Therefore, Zaghlul should be dealt with, if not for the sake of Egyptian tranquillity, then for the purpose of conciliating 'opinion in England hostile to any concessions'.[55]

Lloyd George had begun to show his hand. His real concern, it was clear, was less for imperial security than for domestic politics; his immediate anxiety was to create an atmosphere in Britain favourable to, or tolerant of, a more tempting offer to the Egyptians. This subtle change of emphasis, disguised as it was behind the denunciation of Zaghlul, may have been prompted by the advice which Philip Kerr, the Prime Minister's private secretary,[56] was now giving him. Kerr was convinced that Adly's collaboration was essential to British security in the Middle East and beyond, because, he thought, Adly was the only barrier to Zaghlul. And Zaghlul, in Kerr's eyes, assumed an almost demonic form; if Adly did not go back to Egypt and fight for a 'reasonable settlement', he told Lloyd George, 'Zaghlul will go Sinn Fein, and though we can put him down, Zaghlul will begin to create a Pan-Islamic Sinn Fein machine making mischief everywhere and linked up with Turks, Indians etc. all over the world'.[57] Even if Lloyd George remained unconvinced by this orgy of imperialist paranoia, he may have been influenced by the calmer and more rational note on which Kerr ended: 'As to occupation, if the charge is to be on the British budget, won't it be the House of Commons that will insist before many months on withdrawal?'[58]

When the Cabinet resumed its review of Egyptian policy on 4 November, Lloyd George immediately questioned Allenby, who had been invited to attend, about his views on the key issue of where British troops should be stationed. But the High Commissioner quickly enlarged his reply into a passionate appeal not to let the negotiations founder. It would be 'disastrous', he said, for him to return to Egypt and announce the failure of the conference; that would raise Zaghlul to the 'summit of power'. If negotiations could be prolonged, there might be disturbances, but they could be contained without any increase in British strength. Allenby emphasised, however, that reliance on military force would soon require more troops, since the Egyptian army, where all the young officers were Zaghlulists, could not be relied upon for internal security. He threw his weight, therefore, behind Curzon's request for a change of policy and added that it was essential to arrive at what he called 'an immediate decision as to our future in Egypt'.[59] This evidence changed the tone of Cabinet debate. The objections to Curzon's policy were stilled, and Lloyd George himself announced that the Cabinet would reluctantly agree to one further compromise, although, perhaps not without a conscious irony, he declared his distaste for 'making concessions that would have lasting bad effects in order to meet temporary difficulties'.[60] But no compromise was to whittle away Britain's military rights which were to remain untrammelled in peace and war. Instead, the Egyptians were to be offered full diplomatic autonomy provided that their foreign policy was consistent with British interests, and provided also that the pre-eminent position of the British representative in Cairo was assured – to be symbolised by his retention of the title of High Commissioner.

Curzon thus returned to the conference table armed with fresh weapons. On 10 November, Adly was handed a fresh draft embodying the Cabinet's latest proposals, but reaffirming that the original military clauses would remain unchanged. Five days later, Adly rejected these terms: Britain's military privileges, he told Curzon, would constitute '*l'occupation pur et simple qui détruit toute idée d'indépendance. . .*'.[61] Indeed, to set the seal upon this rebuttal, Adly proceeded to denounce Curzon's promise of diplomatic representation abroad as inadequate; and, contrary to his earlier willingness to acquiesce in an effective diminution of Egypt's control over the Sudan administration, he now complained that Egypt's rights there were not being properly safeguarded. This hardening of Adly's attitude at the very moment when he was extracting, after long delay, further concessions from the British, was prompted by the erosion of his position in Egypt where Zaghlul's influence appeared to be increasing rapidly. The Egyptian minister therefore abandoned his earlier tactics and prepared to disengage from the negotiation with the least possible embarrassment, and with his nationalist credentials unimpaired.

For Curzon, this was the end of the road, at least for the time being. No further offer to Adly was contemplated, and Curzon now concentrated upon persuading the Egyptian minister neither to publish the British terms nor to resign immediately.[62] It was, however, understood that he would resign once back in Cairo. To his colleagues Curzon spelt out the consequences of failure. 'It appeared likely', he told them, 'that we were on the verge of a serious new emergency in Egypt which might strain our available resources to the utmost.[63] He reminded them that he personally had favoured more extensive concessions in the military clauses and revealed the warnings of the British advisers in the Cairo government that administrative chaos would follow from the failure of negotiation.[64] But fortified perhaps by Allenby's confidence in his ability to check immediate disorder – a confidence which, in their collective memory, had become less qualified – the ministers did nothing beyond authorising Lloyd George and Curzon to draft a letter to the Sultan which would put the best face on British concessions. Not until Allenby re-opened the issue in early January by threatening resignation, did ministers turn their attention once more to the riddles of Egyptian politics.

The Residency Imposes

Curzon's efforts to draw the supposed moderates in Egypt out into the open, and to cajole them into an agreement which would leave Britain's power to intervene intact, had, like Milner's, come to nothing. Even the modest transfer of power which he contemplated had been enough to drive the factions of pasha politics into mutual antagonism, and to alarm the court. All this, however, left the Residency with the familiar problem of how to maintain some elements of administrative stability at a time when there was every prospect that the divided and embittered politicians would be bending all their energies to subverting the loyalties of the civil servants and clerks upon whom the government, and imperial control, depended. The Residency's main priority became, as always, the search for a ministry which would enable the hallowed tradition of indirect rule, and the fiction of British 'guidance', to be preserved. In this, it was instructed by the old orthodoxies of control which were adhered to, above all, by the British advisers in the Cairo government with whom Allenby was in constant touch, and by whom he was principally influenced. Their views were founded not upon any latter-day enthusiasm for self-determination, nor indeed upon an uncritical admiration of Egyptian nationalism. Clayton, Amos and Hayter had all commenced their Egyptian service during Cromer's time, and under that 'Cromer system' to which British ministers referred so nostalgically. But their understanding of that system was very different from Churchill's. In their eyes, it was the tradition of cooperation and partnership, of close and tactful collaboration, not the tradition of forceful British leadership, which was its principal feature; withdrawal of Egyptian consent, not the decline of administrative standards, its most dangerous challenge.[65] Thus in 1921, as in 1914, it was from British officials in Egypt, both in the Residency and in the ministries, that there came the most determined opposition to any policy which smacked of annexation or crown colony government. The old Egyptian hands were loyal, as they thought, to a structure of imperial control which the protectorate, left unmodified, threatened to undermine.

Curzon knew of, and perhaps even sympathised with, this outlook. Letters passed to him by Tyrrell[66] and Lindsay showed that Allenby's principal lieutenants in the Residency, Scott and Selby, were anxious about the consequences of a failure to re-enlist Egyptian political cooperation and doubtful of the readiness of British opinion to accept the military burdens which would be imposed by any attempt to dictate a settlement.[67] Both argued that the recognition of Egyptian independence and a military withdrawal to the Canal were the only alternatives to 'drastic action', and would, in any case, not seriously jeopardise imperial communications, guaranteed in reality by naval and military preponderance in the eastern Mediterranean. The advisers echoed this reasoning in more forthright language, unconstrained by the disciplines of hierarchy.[68] On 17 November 1921, just after the delegation's final rejection of the Cabinet offer, Allenby had telegraphed to Curzon a message from them which stated in the most explicit terms, that they expected the British government to pursue a 'liberal policy', and that their own influence with the Egyptian ministers and their subordinate bureaucracies was grounded upon an expectation of Egyptian independence in the near future.[69] And they forecast administrative chaos and a mutiny by the Egyptian police and army if 'substantial satisfaction' were not forthcoming.[70]

As we have seen, Curzon made use of this testimony in his report to ministers on 18 November, but it did not become, at this stage, the basis for a further discussion. Instead, the ministers' preoccupation with Irish affairs, and Allenby's return to Cairo, shifted the initiative in Egyptian policy away from the Cabinet and back to the Residency, which, in the aftermath of the breakdown, set about inveigling a fresh set of collaborators into the imperial embrace. Allenby's efforts in this direction, and the bargaining in which the Residency became engaged, provoked a series of messages back to the Foreign Office. Twice Allenby demanded the unilateral termination of the protectorate and the implementation of the proposals which Adly had rejected without requiring the Egyptians to enter into a treaty – a course of action which Adly himself had proposed to Curzon. Then for almost a month, Allenby fell silent as he grappled with the political crisis occasioned by Zaghlul's campaign. Then on 23 December 1921, Zaghlul was arrested and deported. With the British forewarned and forearmed, there was no repetition of the 1919 disturbances. But five days later, Allenby was forced to announce that the government would be conducted by the under-secretaries – mostly British officials – since no minister would take office. At last, on 8 January 1922, the Residency struck a bargain with Adly's former deputy Sarwat pasha, whereby he agreed to form a ministry provided that the British government agreed to recognise Egyptian independence without asking for a public renunciation by the ministers of their full demands. Convinced that without a ministry, even on these terms, British control in Egypt would collapse in a storm of disorder and non-cooperation, that the cost of rallying the moderates, though high, must be paid, Allenby, egged on by Clayton and Amos, turned once more to Curzon and to the Cabinet.

On the previous occasions when Allenby had urged a unilateral British declaration upon him, Curzon had refused – conscious, no doubt, of the furious reaction which this might produce among some of his colleagues, and anxious not to lose such remaining influence as he enjoyed over the Cabinet's Egyptian policy. But when Allenby asked again on 12 January, the Foreign Secretary decided to endorse his request and solicit the ministers for a greater concession than any they had granted hitherto. It was, on the face of it, a bold decision since it risked an outright defeat at Churchill's hands. But Curzon well knew how determined Allenby was to have his way.[71] And, despite the camouflage with which he had sought to conceal his true opinions from the Cabinet, it is likely that Curzon, by the end of his negotiations with Adly, had come to accept the argument of the officials that so long as Britain remained supreme in the eastern Mediterranean, and along the Canal, she had little to fear from an Egypt which, even if the Milner scheme were implemented to the full, would be no more independent than in the days of Cromer, Kitchener and Gorst. One further calculation may have weighed with him: the effect of Zaghul's arrest on his colleagues and especially upon the Prime Minister. For as Lloyd George had hinted in mid-November, dislike of Zaghlul, and reluctance to make concessions which might be attributed to his influence, were major stumbling-blocks to a more liberal attitude in Cabinet and outside it. By mid-January, Zaghlul was in custody in Aden, en route to the Seychelles. The beneficiaries of British goodwill would not, therefore, be his followers, but those of his enemies.

Curzon, then, circulated Allenby's request among the Cabinet, and, on 18 January, asked for its acceptance. He pointed once more to the danger of administrative chaos, and the necessity of Egyptian cooperation; Allenby's proposals, he said, represented the 'last chance' of forming a ministry and averting the distasteful alternatives of 'annexation or a disgraceful capitulation'.[72] Predictably Curzon was opposed by Churchill who had already signalled both his dislike of Allenby's project and his scepticism of the High Commissioner's judgment to Lloyd George.[73] Lloyd George's own unwillingness to support Curzon in the absence of Austen Chamberlain, whose function it was to interpret the feeling on the Unionist back benches, frustrated the Foreign Secretary's endeavour. Instead it was decided to summon home two of the advisers for consultation, a tactic designed both to put off decision and to test the veracity of Curzon's and Allenby's claim that all expert opinion was solidly in favour of this latest plan. But, as Curzon hinted to Allenby,[74] behind this non-committal attitude of the ministers lurked a fear of how the Conservative phalanx in the Commons, which was already watching apprehensively the implementation of Lloyd George's Irish treaty, would regard a policy of appeasement which, as Churchill remarked, would go further than anything conceded to Sinn Féin.[75]

But Allenby was not prepared to be the sacrifice on the Tory altar. The urgent need, as he saw it, to form a ministry in Cairo overrode all other considerations. On 23 January, the Cabinet was forced to contemplate his threat of resignation, and, to stave it off, authorised the senior ministers to offer him not the immediate abolition of the protectorate, but a parliamentary resolution which would formally concede independence on condition that Egyptian ministers agreed to respect Britain's reserved powers; a modest concession in the circumstances. Meanwhile Allenby again threatened to resign. On 26 January, Curzon told the Cabinet that Allenby's resignation would be followed by those of the four principal advisers in the Egyptian government – thus virtually decapitating the imperial presence in Egypt at a critical moment – and again recommended accepting Allenby's proposal.[76] But feeling against surrender remained strong. The next day, the ministers resolved to summon Allenby home and began to prepare for his resignation. They decided, however, to send him a telegram which, while containing Curzon's offer of a parliamentary resolution, would at the same time accuse the High Commissioner of having failed to explain Cabinet policy properly in Egypt, and of having failed to keep ministers informed of the political situation there.[77] This curious message well reflects the vacillations of ministerial opinion as they approached the confrontation: on the one hand their indignation at Allenby's metamorphosis from the agent to the author of policy, and their desire to discredit and remove him (for which purpose they proposed to draw up a statement for publication in case of need which, significantly, omitted their latest offer) and, on the other, their fear lest this extreme measure might provoke an explosion in Egypt and fierce criticism at home.

The inconsistencies and uncertainties of their management of Egyptian affairs ever since the March rising in 1919 aided, abetted and enforced as they had been by Allenby, were in the end, and ironically, a decisive factor in undermining Cabinet resistance when the crisis came. The legacy of the Milner Report, as Curzon had so often complained, hung round their necks like an albatross and challenged the credibility of any attempt by ministers to justify the removal of Allenby to a watchful press and a suspicious Commons. And a Lloyd George government had reason to fear the enmity of generals. Allenby's uncompromising attitude, once he arrived in London,[78] and his obvious resentment of ministerial strictures, made it plain that the treatment Lloyd George, Balfour and Curzon had meted out to Wingate could not be repeated, not least because Allenby, unlike Wingate, had access to the Upper House.[79] In these circumstances, Lloyd George came into his own. Following a hint from Curzon that Allenby was not eager to appear before the Cabinet again,[80] a meeting which could only have exacerbated the situation, Lloyd George decided that he and Curzon between them should find a way out. But when, after a preliminary interview between Curzon and Clayton,[81] the two ministers met Allenby on 15 February, they were unable to extract more than the most threadbare of face-saving clauses: that Allenby's proposed declaration should refer as explicitly to the reservations as to the concessions which Britain was prepared to make. Lloyd George's claim to the Cabinet the following day that the quarrel with the Residency had arisen not from genuine differences but from a misunderstanding, and, further, that Allenby had made a real concession to the Cabinet's views, went uncontested,[82] telling evidence of Lloyd George's personal authority at such moments, but also of the ministers' relief at having avoided an outcome which held such dangerous possibilities at home and in Egypt. In spite of all the objections which had gone before, there was now no opposition to the proposal that, even if Allenby failed to form a ministry on the terms he had extorted from the Cabinet, he should nevertheless continue to direct British policy in Cairo. Such plenitude of proconsular discretion could scarcely have been dreamt of by Curzon in his gilded youth.

Conclusions

By the terms of the British government declaration of 28 February 1922, often called the Allenby Declaration, the British conceded formal independence to Egypt and abandoned the experiment of 1914. Henceforth they pledged themselves only to intervene in Egyptian affairs when their imperial interests, or the interests of the foreign communities in the country, were called into question. The surveillance of Egypt's internal administration through the inspectors in the provinces and the advisers in the ministries was to end, except in so far as the obligations of Egypt towards the foreign communities and towards the Debt Administration were concerned. In these spheres, the British advisers were to retain their old rights to information and consultation. The appointment of British officials to the Egyptian Civil Service – a longstanding technique of imperial control – was now to be entirely in the hands, and at the discretion, of the Egyptian ministers, although no expatriates, other than those of British nationality, might be appointed without British consent. Finally, Egypt was to regain the right to conduct her own foreign policy, but only on the explicit condition that her diplomacy should not be at variance with Britain's own international policies.

These provisions reversed the wartime trend towards governing Egypt as a crown colony and marked the end of any systematic attempt to monitor, influence and manipulate the politics of the localities in the interests of Britain's overall supremacy on the Nile. But they did not of course signal any relaxation in Britain's claim to be the paramount foreign power in Egypt. The reserved points of the Allenby Declaration set close limits upon Egyptian sovereignty. For not only was the trusteeship of foreign interests to remain firmly in British hands, but Egypt herself was to remain unequivocally within the orbit of the British imperial system through London's supervision of her foreign policy and, above all, through the complete freedom of movement which British military formations continued to enjoy throughout the country. There was, in these circumstances, less real possibility of Egypt remaining neutral in any international conflict involving Britain than was open to the self-governing states which owed formal allegiance to the British Crown. This austere delineation of Egypt's international freedom was reinforced by the specific clause which affirmed the British intention to remain in full control of Egypt's former empire in the Sudan, as an essential buttress not only of their supremacy in Egypt but also of the security of their enlarged imperial commitments in East Africa.

The 1922 Declaration has commonly been treated as though it marked a climacteric in the relations between Britain and Egypt, a grudging acknowledgment by the weary Titan that the beginning of the end was in sight for its forty-year supremacy in Egypt. Indeed, in the most authoritative account of Anglo-Egyptian relations published between the wars, Lord Lloyd, whose own Egyptian proconsulship ended in humiliating dismissal in 1929, castigated the policy pursued between 1918 and 1922 as a surrender to the forces of disorder, a series of 'pathetic and futile endeavours' to appease Egyptian opinion,[83] and, overall, as a story 'of almost unbroken retreat'.[84] In the abandonment of Britain's internal role in Egypt, Lloyd detected a new spirit of demoralisation and defeatism and a sapping of the will to rule.[85] But the record of the private and collective opinions of policy-makers in Britain in no way supports the view that this was a wholesale retreat of imperialism before the forces of a new age. For what indeed had ministers agreed to sacrifice to the aspirations of the Egyptians? In effect, only those aspects of imperial control which they tacitly considered to be the least important and the most expendable – the mission to raise up the wretched, to protect the fellahin, to purify the administrative habits of Egypt. On the key issue of how far Egyptian politicians should be allowed to restrict British power to exploit Egypt in the interests of their world-wide security system, whether by inciting the intervention of other powers, or by threatening their control of the Sudan, British ministers remained adamant. Any concession which might obstruct Britain's ability to carry out her international obligation to protect the foreign colonies from disorder and violence, and expose her to the reproaches and interference of other Mediterranean powers, was firmly and consistently opposed, even if there existed some controversy over the extent to which the more 'liberal' policy envisaged by Milner, Curzon and the Residency might conduce to these evils.

If ministers were united in their determination not to permit Egyptian nationalism to disrupt the structure of imperial security which they had inherited, why was it that the Egyptian question provoked such heated controversy within the government? For, as Allenby and his successors at the Residency were to demonstrate, the ramifications of imperial and international interests in Egypt were such that, even under the terms of the declaration, there remained ample scope and every reason for British interference in Egyptian politics. The crises over the murder of Stack, over the control of the Egyptian army, and, above all, over Egypt's loyalty to Britain during the desert war of 1940–43, showed that the British could turn the course of Egypt's politics as effectually after 1922 as in Cromer's time. Part of the answer is to be found in the evident distaste of ministers for the method which Milner had adopted in his attempt to ease the difficulties of imperial control in Egypt, and in their high regard for propriety and prestige in the management of imperial policy. With an empire so largely dependent upon the myth of invincible power, rather than upon the reality of its exercise, it was natural that ministers should have reacted so sharply to the charge, propagated by Churchill and Montagu, that by bargaining with extremists, Milner was destroying the moral basis of imperial collaboration in other volatile dependencies. Ministers were ready enough to rally the moderates in Egypt; but what bred such division in their ranks was the apparent inability of Egyptian politics to produce a coherent party which would behave in the way in which they expected moderates to behave. For all Curzon's claims, it is clear that ministers suspected that neither Adly nor Sarwat pasha were really distinguishable from Zaghlul – a suspicion which Churchill had continually voiced.

The exacting criteria by which they proposed to judge the would-be moderates of Egypt dispose of any suggestion that ministers were unduly fearful of Egyptian nationalism, or that they had lost confidence in the ability of Britain to impose her will and satisfy her desires. Even to such moderates they were prepared to make only the most nugatory concessions to what Milner had called Egyptian 'amour-propre'. But regard for the continuities of imperial policy was not the sole determinant of ministers' attitudes, nor, perhaps, the prime motive of their thought and action. For from the very beginning their approach to the problems of imperial control in Egypt had become entangled with other issues which interlocked at the highest levels of policy-making. This aspect of imperial policy can be most clearly traced in the often tortuous manoeuvres of the main protagonists in the Cabinet for and against the implementation of Milner's proposals, whether in whole or in part.

Traditionally, it was the imperial ministers who, from their fastnesses in the Foreign Office, the Colonial and India Offices, the Admiralty and War Office, predominated in Cabinet discussion of imperial issues; while the close collaboration of the Prime Minister and Foreign Secretary and the watchful eye of the Treasury imposed close restraint on the wilder flights of departmental fancy. But in the coalition ministry of 1918 to 1922, the peculiar structure of power imposed by the party alliance, and the intensity of the multiple crises in foreign and imperial affairs, produced a more intricate pattern of conflict and rivalry inside the government. Thus Montagu, whose Indian policies made him both vulnerable and sensitive to criticism from the Conservative back benches in the Lords and Commons alike, was at first bitterly opposed to the relaxation of imperial control in Egypt, and anxious to highlight his own concern for the maintenance of political discipline in Britain's paramountcies. His conversion to Milner's new doctrine followed not so much from a desire to apply in Egypt the same, or similar, principles as had underlain his own policy in India, as from the extreme urgency, as he saw it, of conciliating Muslim opinion in India – inflamed by the Khilafat campaign – by a demonstration of British generosity in the Middle East. This overriding priority divided the Indian Secretary from his natural allies in the Cabinet and steadily undermined his position in the government. The position of Curzon, upon whom fell the unwelcome task of championing the claims of Egyptian nationalism, was, even more, the consequence of divergent and contradictory impulses. For, as his earliest reactions to unrest in Egypt demonstrated, he was not naturally inclined towards the more flexible approach to the problems of imperial control which characterised Montagu, even if his instincts were less viceregal than is often supposed. 'You and I agree', he had written to Milner in January 1920,

> that these Eastern peoples with whom we have to ride pillion, have different seats from Europeans, and it does not seem to me to matter much whether we put them on the saddle in front of us or whether they cling on behind and hold us round the waist. The great thing is that the firm seat in the saddle shall be ours. . . .[86]

But like Milner, Curzon had learned, amid the urgencies of war, to distinguish between the preoccupations of a proconsul and the priorities of a minister. The steady modification of his views on how best to solve the political problem in Egypt reflected, therefore, not the slow collapse of a once strenuous imperialism, nor even a decline into inconsistency and irresolution.[87] It was instead a function of his need to uphold his ministerial influence and authority in the Cabinet and in the Cairo Residency, in both of which it was, for reasons which have been described, under constant pressure. Once the necessity of modifying the protectorate had been forced home on him by Allenby at the end of 1920, Curzon pursued a policy which, at all important stages, was founded on the High Commissioner's advice, if only because his removal would have been difficult and dangerous. The Foreign Secretary's apparent vacillations, and his ingenious attempts to camouflage his own opinions, were sometimes a consequence of the ambiguous and erratic messages from Cairo, but more often flowed from his restless search for the widest possible freedom of manoeuvre in the conduct of policy both in Egypt and elsewhere in the Middle East. His variable relations with Lloyd George, and the lack of mutual trust between them, accentuated a tendency, necessarily pronounced in such a government and in such circumstances, towards duplicity and concealment.

The most serious threat to Curzon's control of imperial policy in Egypt was posed by Churchill, and, for wider political and personal reasons, by Churchill's friendship with the Prime Minister. Churchill, first as War Minister, and subsequently as Colonial Secretary, consistently presented himself as the most relentless and inflexible guardian of imperial security, in contrast with his earlier role as the champion of imperial devolution in South Africa. Since 1910, Churchill's attitudes had been modified by his revulsion against Bolshevism, and by his reaction to labour militancy in Britain. But the reasons for his criticism of Milner and Curzon cannot be attributed solely to a growing conservatism in foreign and imperial affairs, for he displayed in Irish matters just that readiness for conciliation which he condemned in Egyptian; and, in Persia and Mesopotamia, advocated a withdrawal of imperial control which, in 1920, had been vehemently opposed by the authors of concession in Egypt.

Churchill understood that politics were ruled by higher laws than consistency. Perhaps even more than Curzon, he was deeply conscious of the way in which the structure of the post-war coalition constricted his influence over its policies and threatened his political future. His departmental responsibilities at the War Office – undertaken in the shadow of mutiny – and his tarnished reputation as a minister, enjoined on him great caution in military affairs, and in his dealings with Unionist ministers of whose intentions towards him he was justifiably mistrustful. The carelessness which had marked Curzon's and Milner's early handling of Egyptian affairs in Cabinet, and the anxiety which this aroused among their fellow Unionists in the government, enabled

Churchill to strengthen his own defences, and enlarge his own influence in the ministry. But his criticisms were only partly inspired by ambition and insecurity. They were directed at the failure of British policy in Egypt to achieve what Churchill regarded as the indispensable conditions for any reduction of direct imperial control. He was convinced that it was both feasible and necessary for the concession of internal autonomy to be accompanied by an explicit undertaking on the part of its beneficiaries that they would remain, in external matters, a component of the British imperial system. Ideally, this should entail acknowledgment of the British Crown and acceptance of dominion status, as in the Irish case. At the very least, it would require the signature of a formal treaty of alliance, as in Iraq. Churchill believed that the inability of Curzon and Allenby to exact undertakings of this sort discredited their requests for a change in British policy, and arose from a mistaken choice of local allies. His precipitate memorandum of March 1921 argued, in effect, that in Egypt, as (at his prompting) elsewhere in the Middle East, British interests were best served by friendship and cooperation with the party of monarchy and tradition. Impatience with the labyrinth of Egyptian politics, and ignorance of the special traditions of imperial control there, reinforced, throughout 1921, Churchill's suspicions that the safeguards for which he had laboured in Iraq and Trans-Jordan, and for which he and Lloyd George had laboured long and thanklessly over Ireland, would be recklessly abandoned in Egypt, endangering in the process the parliamentary foundations of a coalition to the survival of which he was, necessarily, heavily committed.

While Churchill and Curzon competed for the favour of their colleagues, and sought ways of turning ministerial prejudices to their advantage, it was Lloyd George who, as the outcome showed, could sway the issue in Cabinet, prolong or cut short the arguments. The way in which he used this power depended heavily upon a variety of factors, few of which were susceptible of open discussion in Cabinet.

In the long debate over the reconstruction of imperial control in Egypt, Lloyd George's attitude was, almost until the last moment, marked by a rigidity and a dislike of concession which was at variance with his conduct of policy in most spheres of Cabinet responsibility. But it is unlikely that this apparently determined opposition to the appeasement of nationalism sprang from deep convictions about the dangers of an irresolute imperial policy, or from a special concern for the affairs of Egypt. As his intervention in the spring of 1919 might suggest, his primary consideration was that Egypt should cause the minimum of inconvenience and attract the minimum of public attention. It is surprising then, that the Prime Minister should have identified himself so consistently with Churchill's vehement criticisms of Milner's treaty project, and subsequently of Curzon and Allenby's attempts to reach agreement with a viable segment of Egyptian opinion. Surprising until the special methods and techniques which Lloyd George employed in policy-making are taken into account. For he had, as is a commonplace, an acute instinct of the personal and political advantage to be gained from issues of policy, a keen sense of how the balance of opinion might move, and how its movement might be turned to advantage. Lesser issues and their outcome were made to serve greater. Compromise and retreat in one sphere became the means to victory in another. A seeming inconsistency of policy and outlook was deployed to reassure doubters, drifters and critics. Supple and spurious distinctions between men and measures were drawn to delude the innocent, the ill-informed and the malevolent.[88]

Thus the rigidity of Lloyd George's declared views on Egyptian policy was the product of calculation not of conviction or obstinacy. Rigidity here was meant to indicate his ability to distinguish between those spheres of imperial control where a policy of concession was necessary (like Ireland), and those where appeasement was unnecessary or ill conceived; and thus to disarm those, whether in Cabinet or Parliament, who were tempted to portray the leader of the coalition as a man without respect for Britain's imperial interests, the old pro-Boer betraying the Empire from within. Lloyd George's commitment to an Anglo-Soviet rapprochement, and to the devolution of power in Ireland and India, exposed him to charges of this kind; Egypt offered the possibility of recouping his position by attacking a policy of concession, the principal architects of which were proconsular and Conservative. Whatever his private opinions, there was much to be said for staving off what might be an inevitable redeployment of the imperial factor in Egypt; and, at the very least, for exploiting the rift which had arisen between Curzon and others of the major partner in the coalition alliance of parties.

Thus the coalition's approach to Egyptian affairs was caught up in the toils of its difficulties elsewhere and buffeted by the play of ministerial rivalry. But for all the confusion that attended its debates, the Cabinet had moved gradually throughout 1920 and 1921 towards the conclusion that British interests were best served by the slackening of imperial control over Egypt's internal affairs so far as was compatible with the preservation of Britain's essential monopoly of foreign influence in the country. The same trend may be detected, with varying degrees of clarity, in the ministry's handling of Irish, Indian and Mesopotamian questions; and the same reservations were at work. Ministers were determined to defend the system of imperial power, upheld at such cost so recently. But they were undoubtedly oppressed by the burden of maintaining it in the face of hostility, violence and non-cooperation. Perhaps instinctively they moved towards solutions which would avoid recourse to indefinite repression or (in the case of Egypt) the extension of the apparatus of crown colony government; but which at the same time would have only the most limited effect on the diplomatic and strategic unity of the imperial system – with which both they and their parliamentary critics were chiefly preoccupied. In Egypt, indeed, the Allenby Declaration seemed to its champions in the Foreign Office to have produced not the decay of British influence but rather the revival of its flexibility and effectiveness. 'The policy of disentanglement', wrote the Foreign Office's principal expert on Egyptian affairs six years later, 'was not merely an attempt to divest ourselves of responsibilities which we were unable to discharge and which should properly have rested on the Egyptians; it also sought to place us in a position which would be unshaken by the absence of an Egyptian Government or by the existence of an openly hostile one.'[89] Interference in internal affairs, on this view, merely weakened the imperial factor by multiplying its enemies, and sapped the strength properly reserved for the guarding of purely imperial interests. It was to this doctrine that the Cabinet committed itself, not without hesitation, in 1922.

Part III

Problems of Imperial Expansion: the Middle East

The immediate background to the development of British imperial policy in the Middle East after 1918 is to be found in the various projects for the international partition of the Ottoman Empire to which the Entente powers committed themselves after 1914. In March 1915, by the Constantinople Agreement, Britain and France acknowledged the Tsar's claims to the Ottoman capital and laid aside their objections to the annexation of the Straits. In April 1915, the secret treaty of London guaranteed to Italy a share of any territorial gains which might be made from the German and Turkish Empires. The following March, the Sykes–Picot Agreement, ratified by the Russians, made a detailed provision for the partition of the Ottoman Empire. By its terms, the Russians were to gain control of the Armenian provinces of Anatolia, a region extending from the Black Sea to the northern boundary of the Mosul *vilayet*. The French were awarded the so-called 'Blue Zone' which comprised a coastal strip running north from Acre on the coast of Palestine, with an eastern boundary set some way to the west of Damascus and Aleppo, and widening into a more extensive area in south–east Anatolia. Here direct administration was not ruled out. As well as this 'Blue Zone', the French received as their sphere of influence area 'A', the remainder of what is now Syria, as well as the northern third of modern Iraq, the *vilayet* of Mosul. Here their control was to be exercised by indirect means. The British, for their part, gained rights of direct administration in the 'Red Zone', the valleys of the Tigris and Euphrates between Basra and a point to the north of Baghdad; and indirect supremacy in area 'B' which extended in a shallow arc from the Persian frontier north of Baghdad to the borders of Egypt in Sinai. The old Ottoman sanjaks in Palestine were to be internationalised.

During the remainder of the war, and in the first years of peace, these two agreements were supplemented by further pacts. By the treaty of St Jean de Maurienne in 1917, the Italians were granted zones of direct and indirect control in southern Anatolia from Mersina west to Smyrna and beyond. In 1919, however, this concession was unilaterally modified by the decision of France, Britain and the United States to allow the Greeks to occupy the region of Smyrna and administer it as a Greek enclave. Meanwhile the wartime agreements relating to Russia's projected share of the Turkish Empire had lapsed with the October Revolution and the formation of a Bolshevik government. At San Remo and Sèvres in 1920, the principal terms of the Sykes–Picot Agreement, excluding Russia and modified by territorial concessions to Britain over Palestine and Mosul (and with other revisions in favour of Greece and Italy) were endorsed by Britain, France and Italy and imposed upon the Turks.

A special feature of the partition of the Arab lands of the Ottoman Empire was that Britain and France were to act not as the suzerains of the provinces wrested from Turkish control but as trustees holding a mandate from the League of Nations for their administration. They were obliged to observe the principles of the Covenant as these applied to the government of mandates, and to submit draft constitutions of their mandates for the League's approval. As will be suggested below, it is very doubtful whether the invocation of this novel instrument of international supervision had much if any effect on the substance of British policy. But the necessity of submitting the constitutional arrangements for mandatory control to the Council of the League where they might be challenged by France or, through indirect pressure, by the United States, served, perhaps, to dissuade British ministers from policies which might cast doubt upon their willingness or ability to carry out the functions of a mandatory: and thus re-open international discussion of the way in which the Middle East mandates had been distributed. At a time when the cooperation of Arab politicians was already grudging and uncertain, this was a far from attractive prospect.

At San Remo, Britain secured a mandate to administer the three *vilayets* which made up Iraq and a mandate for Palestine, subsequently divided into Palestine proper and Trans-Jordan. In the chapters which follow, British policy in these two latter provinces is not traced systematically since, after the resolution of Anglo-French differences over Syria at the end of 1919, and before the dramatic inflow of Jewish settlers in the 1930s, the affairs of the two were very largely of local significance and the British presence in Palestine was strategically and politically a pendant of their operations elsewhere in the Near and Middle East. Palestine was of some value as an outwork for the defence of Egypt; and Trans-Jordan served as a convenient receptacle for the regal ambitions of Feisal's brother, Abdullah, once his candidacy for the throne at Baghdad had been rejected. But for British ministers before and after 1918 the main objects of imperial strategy and the real problems facing imperial expansion were to be found elsewhere.

6 War and Imperial Policy in the Middle East 1918–1919

Imperial Strategy and Imperial Expansion

The military occupation of the Middle East at the end of 1918 by British and Indian armies of nearly a million men marked the complete collapse there of the old international order, and heralded a revolution in British imperial policy. The dissolution of the Tsarist empire, and the defeat of Germany and Turkey, transformed the circumstances which had governed British policy in this region for a century and, all at once, made Britain the dominant political and military power in the lands between India in the east, the Caspian in the north, and Constantinople in the west.

Yet this vast new empire had not been acquired as the result of a long matured programme of imperial aggrandisement: its acquisition had been as unexpected as it had been sudden. Rather had it grown from small defensive beginnings: the seizure of Basra to secure the Persian oil fields which supplied the Royal Navy, and the approaches to the Persian Gulf;[1] and the operations of the Canal Defence Force on the Sinai frontier between Egypt and Ottoman Palestine. Both these campaigns had their roots in the Victorian strategies evolved by Palmerston, Gladstone and Salisbury for the defence of India and of the world-system of which India was so important a part. For it had been a cardinal doctrine of their diplomacy that no hostile power could be allowed to control either the Isthmus of Suez, or the upper reaches of the Persian Gulf whence India might be threatened. Traditionally these objects had been attained by means of a close but informal partnership with the Ottoman Empire, and by a strenuous resistance to any undermining of its political independence or its territorial integrity *in Asia*. But the entry of Turkey into the war as an ally of the Central Powers made necessary a more direct method and enforced a new approach to the longstanding problems of imperial strategy in the Middle East.

The need for a new long-term strategy in the Middle East arose primarily out of the recognition, which became more general and far-reaching as the war went on, that Turkey's willingness to act as the agent, in some sense, of German *Weltpolitik* would wreck the whole strategic conception which had underlain British power and influence in the East. For no longer could the route to India be guarded by the Navy and a few battalions of the British and Indian armies; and no longer would the Indian Empire be able to contribute positively to the security system which had been built up around it. Instead the terms upon which Britain had been able to protect the Canal and the Gulf would become far less favourable; for their defence, far from easing the strategic difficulties of the Eastern Empire, seemed likely to absorb almost all her energies. This unwelcome change in the economics of imperial defence had, of course, serious implications for those in Britain who understood the difficulty of reconciling the requirements of domestic politics with the preservation of a world empire – a difficulty which had obsessed the makers of foreign policy especially since the 1880s. But the conflict between the British and Ottoman empires had a second consequence which, to the official mind in both Britain and India, seemed no less dangerous. For it raised the prospect of a concerted effort by the Turks to subvert, on religious grounds, the loyalty of Britain's Muslim clients and subjects from Egypt to India itself, and thus destroy from within the fabric of the Eastern Empire. The delicacy of their relations as a Christian power with the Islamic societies which they dominated was never far (certainly after 1857) from the minds of those who directed Britain's affairs in the Eastern world.

As a result, the response of the British to the Middle Eastern war went beyond limited defensive operations in Egypt and Mesopotamia. They sought immediately to strengthen their political authority on the Nile by abrogating Turkish sovereignty over Egypt, a change which led, however, to no significant alteration, at this early stage of the war, in the substance of imperial control.[2] Elsewhere, at Basra, the need to ensure local cooperation in the struggle against the Turks gradually propelled the British towards an undertaking that Basra would not be returned to the Ottomans at the end of the war.[3] But on the wider issue of the future of the Ottoman system, ministers were more cautious and conservative. Asquith's declaration soon after the outbreak of hostilities that the Turkish Empire would be dissolved was slow to find its way into the working assumptions of ministers and their advisers. When the De

Bunsen Committee[4] was set up in 1915 to report on the kind of partition which would best suit Britain and satisfy her allies, it displayed a lingering solicitude for the old imperial principle in the Middle East, proffering, as an alternative to a real partition, a scheme for devolution: thus preserving the convenient fiction of Turkish suzerainty in Asia while reducing the control which the Constantinople government would exercise over the communities of Armenians, Greeks and Arabs in the Asian provinces.[5] This attempt to put off the day when Britain might have to confront the Russians on the Euphrates was short-lived. The need to conciliate the Russians in the interests of the wider war, the search for new allies in the Hejaz, and, above all, the implications of the Dardanelles expedition, enforced, by the end of 1915, a more fundamental revision of imperial strategy.

The results of this were embodied in the Tripartite Agreement concluded between Britain, France and Russia in March 1916. By its terms, the Ottoman Empire was to vanish. Its capital at Constantinople would at last become part of the Tsar's dominions. The Russians were also to extend their sway in eastern Anatolia, annexing the old region of Armenia.[6] For the British these large concessions to their greatest imperial rival in Asia seemed inevitable if the defeat of Turkey (a premature expectation) were not to destroy the unity of the victors, and if the overriding priority of the European war were not to suffer. But at the same time, they were anxious to limit the effects of Turkey's dissolution upon the security system of their own empire. Thus it became convenient not merely to compensate the third ally, France, but to ensure that the French sphere in the new Middle East should be both substantial and carefully drawn. In accordance with their long-standing distaste for a common land frontier with Russia, the British installed the French between their own projected zone in Mesopotamia and the projected boundary of Russian Armenia.[7]

For all that it represented a radical departure in the politics and diplomacy of the Middle East, the Tripartite Agreement, viewed in terms of British imperial policy, and the techniques of imperial control, reflected less the opportunism and expansionism of British policymakers than their conservatism and fear of innovation. The basic objective of British diplomatists remained the close limitation traditionally set upon Britain's military commitments on land. To satisfy this essential, the British were prepared to concede a substantial influence to the French, whose presence was normally regarded as so baneful, and to internationalise Ottoman Palestine. Thus the French, in a new Crimean system, were to perform the old function of the Turks in providing a front line against Russian advance. The British role, as in late Victorian times, would be confined to naval support and a lesser military presence. Such indications as did emerge of British policy towards that part of Turkey-in-Asia which was to fall under their influence – and in the absence of a clear agreement between the views of Sykes, of the India Office and the Government of India the future administration of the interior of Iraq remained at issue[8] – suggested that in London at least there was still a preference for no more than an indirect control over that part of Mesopotamia which lay outside the *vilayet* of Basra.[9]

In their care for the preservation of the most economical framework of imperial defence and in their enthusiasm for indirect rule in the frontier regions of the imperial system, the policy-makers of 1916 showed some regard for the pre-war traditions of Middle East policy. But, within little more than a year of its inception, this new imperial policy for the Middle East was in ruins; and the assumptions upon which it rested shattered, apparently beyond recall. To some historians it has seemed that the recourse to a different and more vigorous strategy in the Middle East thereafter was a by-product of the reconstruction that took place at the end of 1916 in the leadership and machinery of the British government: that Lloyd George's accession to the premiership witnessed the triumph of the proconsuls and the growth of a 'new imperialism'.[10] But while the downfall of Asquith may have enlarged the influence of those who felt a special concern for Britain's Eastern security, and may have increased the capacity of the British war machine for prompt and resolute action, it is doubtful whether political change at home played a decisive part in the major adjustment which took place after 1917 in Britain's Eastern policy. Far more significant were the new circumstances with which Lloyd George and his old proconsular warhorses had to grapple: the inability of a fully mobilised Britain to seize the initiative on the Western front; the resilience of Turkey in Palestine and Mesopotamia; and, above all, the increasingly rapid collapse of Russia's war effort.

These three factors were to consign the partition plans of 1916 to the scrapheap. Early in the career of the new ministry, Balfour as Foreign Secretary drew attention to the possibility that Germany's power would not be broken by the Allies and that her expansion from the North Sea to the Persian Gulf would present the gravest dangers to Britain.[11] This warning was taken up by Austen Chamberlain, Secretary of State for India, who insisted upon the 'vital importance' of frustrating Germany's drive into the Middle East.[12] A month later Curzon's Committee on Territorial Desiderata reported to the Imperial War Cabinet that, to preserve British security in the Middle East, the outright annexation of Palestine and Mesopotamia was essential.[13] But behind these re-affirmations of the strategic imperatives of the defence of India and of Amery's 'Southern British world', lay not so much the growth of new imperial appetites as an anxiety on the part of those ministers with express imperial or colonial responsibilities lest the review of war aims and priorities which began in the spring of 1917 should demote the claims of the Eastern Empire on Britain's war diplomacy, and (conceivably) clear the way for a negotiated peace which left the Ottoman Empire intact. In the event it was not until the end of 1917 that imperial policy in the Middle East began to shift significantly on its foundations.

The decline and dissolution of Russian power, and its corollary, the acceleration of Germany's *Drang nach Osten*, had already in 1917 induced some ministers to think in terms of a wider and more formal extension of imperial control in the Ottoman lands than had been envisaged by the Tripartite Agreement of 1916, should Germany escape defeat in Europe. But as the Tsar's armies disintegrated, it became apparent that the proposed annexations of Palestine and Mesopotamia were not sufficient by themselves to safeguard the British world-system against its enemies. For the war, in its new phase, began to affect directly parts of the Middle East which had hitherto claimed little attention from the policy-makers in London. Thus far the directors of the Eastern war had been absorbed by the need to protect Egypt and the Canal, and bar the way to the Persian Gulf. Now, however, it seemed that imperial policy should be refashioned as the Central Powers prepared to take the north circular route to the heart of the Eastern Empire – through Persia.

Ever since the beginning of the nineteenth century, policy-makers in Britain and India had recognised that the integrity and independence of Persia was crucial to the security both of the land frontiers of the Indian Empire and its seaward approaches from the west.[14] The Victorian period had seen a prolonged and uneven struggle between the Russians and the British over how far the southward thrust of Russian imperialism should be allowed to penetrate into Persia, and thus threaten the strategic interests of India. In 1907, the conflicting tendencies of the two empires had been regulated, though not resolved, by the Anglo-Russian Convention which divided Persia into three spheres of influence, one Russian, one British, and one, in central Persia, neutral. When war broke out, the mutual suspicions of the two imperial powers were overlaid, if not removed, by their common desire to root out German and Turkish influence, and their common interest in preventing the spread of pan-Turanian and pan-Islamic propaganda east of the Caspian. And although the British took advantage of the Tripartite Agreement of 1916 to extract Russian recognition of their primary interest in the neutral sphere in central Persia, they continued to rely, in effect, upon Russian military supremacy in north-west Persia to keep the pro-German and pro-Turkish elements in Persian politics in check,[15] and to stop the infiltration of enemy agents into southern Persia and Afghanistan. Thus, by an ironic twist of fortune, by 1916 it was the Russians who were guarding the gateway to India, and protecting the operations of the Anglo-Indian forces in southern Mesopotamia.

Russian decline and defeat towards the end of 1917 destroyed this partnership, so fruitful for Britain's imperial security, and made inevitable a revision of British policy in the Middle East. The pressure for such a revision came in the first instance from the Government of India, which was alarmed by the facility which Russian weakness gave to German and Turkish activity in Afghanistan and Turkestan, and wished to counteract the influence of the Central Powers in Persia by an appeal to Persian nationalism. In practice, this meant scrapping the 1907 Convention and allowing the Shah to maintain an autonomous army and to employ 'neutral' experts;[16] it meant also returning the South Persia Rifles, a gendarmerie set up under British command in 1916 to protect British interests and installations in the anarchic south of the Shah's dominions, to the control of the Persian government. The War Cabinet's Persia Committee,[17] encouraged by the India Office, discounted the alarmism of the Viceroy, and would sanction no new basis for Anglo-Persian relations. Both Balfour and Curzon, the moving spirits of the Committee, were dubious of the value of Persian goodwill upon which the Viceroy laid such emphasis; and both refused to consider the military concessions the Viceroy had urged, while the war lasted. They confined themselves instead to instructing the British envoy at Teheran to work for a more friendly ministry under Vossuq-ed-Dowleh.[18]

Curzon and Balfour's reluctance to institute a new policy in Persia reflected a lack of confidence in Britain's ability either to overawe or to conciliate Persian opinion, and an anxiety to cling to the tattered remnants of the system of 1907. They remained unmoved when the India Office, changing its tune with the new year, took up the Viceroy's call for a new policy to avoid what Shuckburgh saw as the 'dangerous isolation' which the 'complete reversal of Russian policy in Asia, emphasized by Bolshevist appeals to Moslems and to subject races in general has tended to place us . . .'.[19] For in Shuckburgh's eyes it was less the threat of German or Turkish invasion which endangered Britain's Eastern Empire than the fact that Britain now seemed to be the only Western power 'that adheres to the old "imperialistic" policy'.[20] Such an unlooked-for pre-eminence would, he thought, rouse a fierce propaganda throughout the East and steadily undermine British influence in Persia and Afghanistan, and even British control in India itself where opinion was 'already sufficiently agitated'.[21] Recognising the distaste of ministers for the Viceroy's proposals, Shuckburgh urged that France be taken into partnership in Persia. French financial influence had, he conceded, a 'dubious record', but 'the situation is so serious that risks of this kind must be taken'.[22] The political burdens of empire were, on this reckoning, already too great for the British on their own.

Shuckburgh's advice was rejected by his ministerial masters. In the following month they also declined a request from the British envoy at Teheran, Marling, for a military occupation of north-west Persia to strengthen British influence. This, the ministers thought, would discredit British policy in Persian eyes and 'bring on us odium of whole Moslem world'.[23] The politics of influence in the Islamic world still counselled caution and not a forward policy. The impetus for the abandonment of the 1907 system came not from the ministers and officials, but from their military advisers. The War Office was less mindful of the susceptibilities of Persian nationalism than of the need to find new allies among the Georgians and Armenians to hold the Turk at bay in the Caucasus and guard the flank of Marshall's army in Mesopotamia.[24] For this purpose secure communications through Persia were essential. Thus when the War Office's emissary to the Caucasus revealed how fragile these were, the reluctance and conservatism of the ministers were overcome. Milner, whose influence over military policy was, at this stage, second only to that of Lloyd George,[25] urged prompt action on Curzon. 'We must', he wrote,[26]

> stop the wave of German influence sweeping right into the heart of Asia . . . . In view of the condition of affairs in Trans-Caucasia, a move from the Baghdad side into Persia to block the Western border, wh. we have the power to make, seems necessary without delay.

At the beginning of March, the Chief of the Imperial General Staff descended upon the Persia Committee to ram home Milner's argument; having heard him, it resolved to embark upon the course it had so recently repudiated. North-west Persia was to be occupied to meet the requirements of the new strategic situation in the Middle East.[27] Henceforth, the British were to play an exaggerated version of the role against which Shuckburgh had warned. To Curzon, this seemed a step which a few years before he would have thought impossible 'by any government of which he was a member',[28] and a step to which, though inevitable, there attached grave risks. Balfour concurred.

The decision in which Balfour and Curzon had acquiesced without enthusiasm projected a vast forward movement in the strategic frontiers of the British world-system. Germany's triumph in the East, declared the Chief of the Imperial General Staff, required Britain to extend her efforts towards the Caspian, win over Armenia and 'make our influence predominate in the eastern ports of the Black Sea'.[29] It required also a further advance in Palestine and the despatch of a military mission to Turkestan.[30] For all these purposes, the paramountcy of British influence in Persia was essential. But despite the continued setbacks the British suffered in their attempts to carry out the strategy prescribed by Sir Henry Wilson, and despite the threat of a combined German and Turkish assault in northern Persia, a threat that grew greater as 1918 wore on, Curzon, through the new medium of the Eastern Committee, a sub-committee of the War Cabinet set up in March 1918 to coordinate British policy between Greece and Afghanistan, consistently opposed any proposal to bind Persia by formal ties to the British imperial system. He resisted Montagu's demands for a more vigorous military control of the country;[31] with Balfour's aid, he blocked the suggestion that Persia be offered a military alliance.[32] With the same objects in view, he denounced the notion of bringing the conduct of Persian affairs, civil and military, within the sphere of the Government of India.[33] Instead the political strategy he propounded was 'to set up a Moslem nexus of states to stop the German and Turkish advance',[34] a strategy which required the greatest delicacy in the handling of Moslem opinion.

The revolution which the War Office had instigated in British relations with Persia was, therefore, tempered by Curzon's anxiety, while the war continued, to set a close limit on the acceptance of new political responsibilities there. Elsewhere, in the Ottoman lands, the political and military circumstances of 1918 had gradually modified the assumptions upon which imperial policy had rested since March 1916. In the spring, the possibility of peace with Germany undefeated led Curzon to talk in terms of an Anglo-Ottoman condominium in Mesopotamia on the Sudanese model as the best protection for Britain's interests, although Basra, he insisted, would remain British come what may.[35] But by the summer, Allenby's successes were imposing a different perspective on British policy-makers in their search for the most viable means of imperial control. For with the rapid expansion of the area under British occupation in Palestine and Syria, the issue of France's future role in the Middle East, dormant since 1916, revived. The French were anxious to implement the partition with the least delay before the politics of the conquered Turkish provinces hardened into new and inflexible moulds. To the British, however, the promises made to the French in 1916 became more and more of an embarrassment. Allenby and his military superiors in London insisted that the orderly administration of the occupied territories, and the necessary recruitment of local allies, could not be jeopardised by French interference: the efficacy of imperial control depended upon the untrammelled partnership of the British and their Arab collaborators.[36] With this Curzon had much sympathy. His instinct was to emasculate the Sykes–Picot Agreement. His favoured instrument was none other than the Wilsonian doctrine of self-determination. Britain, he argued, should reaffirm her desire to secure Arab independence and declare that 'His Majesty's Government will countenance no permanent foreign or European occupation of Palestine, Iraq (except the province of Basra) or Syria after the war'.[37] The defeat of Turkey and the decline of Russia had not only rendered the French dispensable, but had transformed them into a menace. For Curzon and his colleagues now thought they had found, in the Arab and indigenous elites of Asiatic Turkey, collaborators more suited to the purposes of imperial policy, but collaborators whose loyalty and compliance could only be assured by the promise of a largely unfettered autonomy in Syria and Iraq. And, as the Peace Conference grew nearer, such a loose system of imperial control came to seem especially suited to the wider international circumstances with which imperial diplomacy now had to reckon.

The Grand Design, October–December 1918

While Ottoman Turkey continued to fight, the devices and desires of ministers in London remained overshadowed by the more immediate and importunate demands of military strategy; and their plans for the Middle East were, of necessity, provisional and conditional, liable to a further turn of fortune's wheel. But with the signature of the Turkish armistice at Mudros on 30 October 1918, followed by the German armistice twelve days later, the future security of Britain's imperial interests in the Middle East in peacetime, hitherto an almost academic issue, became of immediate and practical significance. For by the terms of the Mudros armistice the Turks were bound to evacuate their former

Arab provinces as well as Cilicia and the territories which they had occupied in Persia and the Caucasus, and thus to abandon the last vestiges of their pre-war imperial system.[38] The turbulence of the war-torn regions of the Middle East was one factor which impelled the directors of British policy in London to seek a rapid conclusion to the complicated issues of power and sovereignty in the wake of Ottoman withdrawal. But no less pressing was the need to prepare a statement of British desiderata in the Middle East as an up-to-date basis for negotiation between the victorious Western allies, since it was widely assumed in British official circles that the forthcoming Peace Conference would set about constructing a Turkish treaty no later than the spring of 1919.

It was for these reasons, therefore, that the Eastern Committee at the end of October began the task of defining British purposes in the Middle East with greater precision than before, and in the expectation that its conclusions would exercise a decisive influence on the future shape of British power and authority in the East; and, by implication, on the workings of the British world-system as a whole. As a result, its members quickly found themselves wrestling with issues that lay at the heart of the controversy (which had raged intermittently since the 1880s) over the character and function of British imperialism.

In its attempt to draw up recommendations about the disposition of the conquered territories of the Middle East, the Committee did not question, and scarcely discussed, the assumption that Ottoman Turkey would cease to be an imperial power. For this, the shock of Turkish hostility in 1914, and, even more, the durability of the Ottoman armies, was, perhaps, partly responsible. Bitterness over a prolonged, expensive and often humiliating struggle with a hitherto despised military power did much to eradicate the sympathy for Turkey which had existed before the war. Revulsion against the atrocities committed against Christian populations in Anatolia, and a realisation that further collaboration with the Turks was neither possible nor necessary did the rest: *Carthago delenda est*. But if the policy-makers were all convinced that any resurrection of Turkish power would risk a repetition of the Middle Eastern war – a conviction which uncertainty about how Germany would emerge from the Peace Conference helped to harden – they remained unclear about what kind of Turkish state would be set up to replace the doomed empire; and, as a result, they largely failed to consider at this stage the vital issue of how the survival of Turkey in any form could be reconciled with the projected partition and with the security of the successor states to the south and east of Anatolia. Instead the question of Turkey's future became entangled almost immediately with the obsessions of Indian politics. Curzon wished to evict the Sultan from Constantinople and drive the Turks 'back into the highlands of Asia' because he believed that this would shatter the influence of the Sultan-Caliph in the Islamic world and destroy his pretensions to international authority.[39] Montagu opposed him on the grounds that such a policy would alienate Britain's millions of Muslim clients and subjects, and endanger as a result the prospects for political reform in the Indian Empire.[40] For both ministers it was the menace of pan-Islamic agitation, rather than the threat of Turkish nationalist irredentism, which was at this moment the real challenge to Britain's imperial interests. Their differences remained unsettled, since it proved impossible in December 1918 to reach agreement upon the appropriate regime to replace the Turks in Constantinople and at the Straits.

Imperial policy in the Middle East thus suffered, even at this early stage, from confusions about the proper management of the defeated power. There was, however, a second difficulty which was increasingly to vitiate the calculations of the policy-makers. Since early in 1918, their plans had been framed on the assumption that Russia would cease to play, for an indefinite period, any active part in the affairs of the Ottoman Empire and Persia, and that Britain's strategic frontiers in these lands, even in peacetime, would not be the same as those of the pre-war era. Acceptance of this assumption was implicit in Curzon's newfound enthusiasm for a much enhanced British role in Persia and, more explicitly, in his declaration, endorsed by the Eastern Committee as a whole, that Britain desired 'to see strong independent states – offshoots of the former Russian empire – in the Caucasus'.[41] At no stage in these discussions was the possibility of a Russian imperial revival seriously considered, and the survival of powerful elements of pro-Russian and pro-Soviet sentiment in the 'offshoots' went unnoticed.[42] Partly this reluctance to anticipate a return to the old pattern of imperial rivalries in the East may be explained by the immediacy of the problems which the British faced in the aftermath of the war; but even more, perhaps, it derived from the extreme difficulty of predicting the course of Russian internal politics, the probable outcome of the civil war, and the kind of state which would ultimately be formed. The rapidly changing fortunes of the Bolsheviks and their opponents on the battlefield prolonged these uncertainties until almost the end of 1919.[43]

The sudden relaxation of the pressure which, throughout the nineteenth century, had been exerted by the Russians upon the frontiers of the Anglo-Indian imperial system, combined with the plenitude of physical power which the British temporarily enjoyed all over the Middle East, lent the deliberations of the Eastern Committee an almost euphoric atmosphere, and encouraged hopes that Britain would at last be able to break out from the international straitjacket which had constricted imperial diplomacy since the 1880s. But the millennium of total security, envisaged by Amery and those who shared his eagerness for British domination of the Cape to Cairo route and the Middle East in order to protect the 'Southern British world',[44] seemed threatened in the Middle East by the rejuvenated imperialism of another great power, France. Thus Curzon and his colleagues, as soon as they grasped the possibility of a post-war Middle East liberated from Russian and Turkish imperialism alike, became instinctively mistrustful of both the short- and the long-term effects of conceding to the French the territorial gains they had been promised under the wartime agreements. The Eastern Committee, declared Curzon on 18 October, had for long assumed that the Sykes–Picot Agreement was defunct. The new circumstances obtaining in Syria required that the French abandon their 'monopoly interest' in the Mediterranean ports of Alexandretta and Mersina, their 'special rights' in the Tigris and Euphrates valleys, and their claim to a preponderant influence in the northern part of Palestine.[45] Britain's imperial interests required that France should be confined to the narrowest possible limits in the Arab lands, preferably in the region of Beirut, to avoid the probability of friction and conflict in the future, and to protect the eastern approaches to Egypt and the Canal.[46] The economics of imperial defence were no more sympathetic to a land frontier with the French in the eastern Mediterranean than they had been to a military confrontation with the Russians on the Euphrates.

Fear that Britain would be robbed of the long-run strategic benefits of her dearly-bought Eastern conquests lay behind this apparent enthusiasm for a vast accretion to Britain's informal empire, just as in Salisbury's day the partition of Africa, and the extension of formal political controls, had seemed preferable to the enlargement of naval and military commitments in the eastern hemisphere to combat French and German ambitions. The need to create a local substitute for the political and administrative institutions of the Ottomans pushed ministers, as we have seen, in the same expansive direction, for in Syria the stability and effectiveness of British over-rule in the confused aftermath of victory appeared to rest upon the cooperation of the Sherifian dynasty and its local allies; and the price of Sherifian cooperation, reiterated to the Eastern Committee by T. E. Lawrence, was the widest autonomy under British, but not French supervision. The Sherifians were deeply suspicious of French intentions and feared the imposition of direct rule wherever French influence was supreme.[47]

Curzon's instinct was to accept the logic of collaboration with the dynasty of Hussein. 'For the safety of our Eastern Empire,' he remarked, 'I would sooner come to a satisfactory agreement with the Arabs than I would with the French.'[48] Balfour, Montagu and Cecil were in broad agreement. They shared his preference for the conveniences of political monopoly. But both Balfour and Cecil, as Foreign Office ministers, cast doubt upon the likelihood of French acquiescence, and Balfour particularly warned against the danger of giving the French, or the Italians, the impression that Britain intended to evade the secret agreements of the war.[49] The need for French cooperation in Europe was too great to risk a serious conflict of aims in the Middle East.

Two supreme objectives: the need to preserve the system of local collaboration established by the British occupying armies, especially in Syria, and the desire to secure a lasting strategic advantage from the Anglo-Ottoman war by excluding any imperial rival from the land approaches to Egypt or the Persian Gulf, thus dictated the kind of political settlement which British ministers thought best suited to the liberated provinces of the Turkish Empire. Indeed it was this second objective which lent a special urgency to the first. On both grounds it seemed essential that British influence in the Arab Middle East should be as self-effacing as possible and discreetly veiled by a façade of self-determination. This policy had first been suggested by Curzon in July 1918, and had already, before December, found expression in the joint Anglo-French Declaration assuring the peoples of the Arab lands of a wide measure of political freedom. For British ministers this display of liberalism in their imperial thinking marked no conversion to the national principle nor any access of enthusiasm for the ideals of a relaxed and kindly trusteeship. It derived most directly from a dispassionate calculation as to how best the new balance of power between the victorious allies could be exploited for the traditional requirements of imperial security.

The entry of the United States into the European war as the ally of Britain and France had already awakened British official circles, by the end of 1917, to the importance of accommodating Britain's declared colonial war aims to the language and values of the administration in Washington. Lloyd George's famous declaration in January 1918 reflected the anxiety of ministers to secure American support or acquiescence for the destruction of Germany's colonial empire, and also for the frustration of France's imperial ambitions.[50] The price of American support was well understood: there should be no annexations; and no imposition of alien rule without a specific commitment to the principle of trusteeship. Wherever possible, the institution of alien rule should be accompanied by evidence of local consent. It was to these notions that the directors of British policy in the Middle East decided to appeal. Their intentions were expressed most succinctly by Robert Cecil. It was, he said, 'most important' that the French should not be allowed to annex any part of the Blue Zone that they had been awarded under the Sykes–Picot Agreement. 'We wished to secure the cooperation of the Americans in settling the future of the occupied territories, and in order to do this we must declare against annexation.'[51] Curzon, Balfour and Smuts felt that such a tactic formed the best chance of escaping from the engagement with France without dangerous repercussions in Europe.[52] 'There was a great chance', opined Balfour, that President Wilson would denounce the secret agreements, and with them the claims of France in the Middle East.[53] The British case for informal paramountcy in Syria and Mesopotamia alike must rest not upon the fact of conquest, nor upon the imperatives of imperial communications, but upon the apparent readiness of the local political élites to accept the tutelage of their liberators.

Thus the Eastern Committee's resolution that 'no foreign influence other than that of Great Britain should be predominant in areas A and B'[54] (modern Syria and Iraq), had as its corollary the pledge that there should be no annexation, but rather the creation of an Arab government, or governments. But there was little doubt in the minds of ministers that, whatever form the local administration might take, British control in matters of imperial concern would be real and effective. Two months earlier, Montagu had urged a renunciation of any intent to annex by arguing that 'we could maintain an Arab façade and yet ensure British paramountcy',[55] while Balfour with felicitous brevity concluded: 'we will have a Protectorate but not declare it.'[56] The imperial ministers were in general agreement, therefore, that British supremacy in the Arab Middle East both permitted and required a system of political control approximating more to the model successfully developed in Egypt than to that which characterised the provinces of British India. Only over Palestine was there a reluctance to ride with so loose a rein, a reluctance in which Curzon's desire to exclude any foreign influence from this 'strategical buffer of Egypt' joined forces with Balfour's anxiety lest a slackening of imperial control should endanger the Zionist settlers and the creation of a Jewish national home.[57]

The traditional strategic significance for Britain of Turkey's former Arab provinces, combined with what seemed in December 1918 a position of invulnerable military supremacy in Syria, Palestine and Mesopotamia, produced among ministers who attended the Eastern Committee a remarkable convergence of aim, limited only by doubts about the diplomatic side-effects of so vast an increase in Britain's spheres of influence. But when the Committee turned its attention to the desiderata of British policy further to the east, this unanimity showed signs of strain, and eventually, over the issue of imperial control in the Caucasus and beyond the Caspian, of breaking down altogether. For Curzon, however, it was Persia's future that was of the greatest importance.

At the time of Britain's military intervention in north-west Persia no decision had been taken to alter the relations between the Shah's government and the British. Curzon had steadily resisted for the remaining period of the Middle East war any move to extend Britain's political control over the country, or to draw Persia into a formal alliance, largely, it may be thought, because he calculated that any bargain struck before Britain had won the war in the East would commit the imperial power to the defence of Persian interests without compensating advantages. The elevation of Vossugh-ed-Dowleh to the premiership in August 1918 fulfilled, in Curzon's view, all Britain's political requirements at that stage.[58] But if Curzon had reckoned that the withdrawal of Russia and the defeat of Turkey would prove an adequate guarantee of Britain's primacy in Persian affairs, the attitude of the Persian government was soon to disillusion him. In late October, he told the Eastern Committee that Britain would act as Persia's trustee at the Peace Conference.[59] But, little more than a week later, it was clear that Persia's readiness to adopt such a position of clientage could not be assumed so easily; and Curzon warned his colleagues of the danger that a Persian delegation, let loose in Paris, would play off the powers one against the other,[60] throwing off at a stroke Britain's informal and undeclared status as the protecting power. This eventuality it became Curzon's chief purpose to avert. His method was to seek to commit his ministerial colleagues to the proposition that Britain had both a special need and a special responsibility for the regeneration of the Persian state, and that this required formal tokens of British paramountcy.

The crux of Curzon's argument lay firstly in his assertion that without continued British support the cooperative ministry of Vossugh would collapse; and secondly in his insistence that Britain's move into Mesopotamia had created a situation for which the policy pursued by Britain in Persia before the war was ill-adapted. 'You have the situation now', he proclaimed,[61]

> that Persia, instead of being a solitary figure moving about in a state of chronic disorder on the glacis of the Indian fortress, has the Indian frontier on one side of her and what is tantamount to a British frontier on the other.

This, allied with the 'enormous importance' attached by the Admiralty to secure supplies of oil from the Persian Gulf, pointed 'to the conclusion which I venture to place before the Committee that our stake in Persia is a greater and not a less one in consequence of the war'.[62] It followed that 'we must insist on maintaining there in whatever form . . . the general political predominance which is justified and demanded by the interests I have described'.[63] This, in turn, required the continuation of Britain's military presence for a further period, and the imposition of a British army commander and a British financial adviser to put the Shah's house in order.

To clothe the bare bones of his strategic argument, Curzon had recourse to two props designed to win over his colleagues and ultimately, perhaps, Britain's mistrustful allies. Firstly, he laid emphasis upon the constructive role which Britain would play in reconstituting the tattered fabric of the Persian state in order 'to fortify the integrity and independence of Persia'.[64] Trusteeship, not annexation, was, as further to the west, to be the order of the day. At the same time, Curzon conjured up the nightmare prospect of a Bolshevik invasion, of a complete relapse into anarchy, or even of a dictatorship by Starosselski, the Russian commander of the Cossack brigade. Despite all this, the expansionist plans of the former Viceroy evoked neither enthusiasm nor indeed much opposition among ministers. Cecil and Montagu were doubtful about staying in Persia and sceptical of Curzon's fears. Balfour was absent. The only real opposition to Curzon came from the Foreign Secretary to the Government of India, Sir Hamilton Grant. Since 1917, New Delhi had been apprehensive of the effects on India's Muslim politics of any further territorial aggrandisement by Britain in south-west Asia, and eager to conciliate Persian opinion by abrogating the Anglo-Russian convention of 1907. This formed an implicit part of Grant's attitude towards the plans that Curzon put forward, but it was not the sole reason for the Indian Government's opposition. For Grant, while recognising that Indian security required that 'we must exclude any other power from obtaining a dominant position or indeed . . . a political position at all in Persia', spelt out the constraints upon Indian participation in the commitments of the imperial system. The Government of India, he declared, had been prompted

> by a desire to regulate our policy in accordance with the military force at our disposal, and, since the war, to avoid involving ourselves in diversions and commitments of an indefinite character, involving very heavy expenditure, which would fall upon the people to a considerable extent, and involve us also in the continuous possibility of military operations in Persia. . . .[65]

What New Delhi wanted at the end of the war was substantially the same as it had urged earlier in the year. In the era of the Lucknow pact and with constitutional reform impending, India, so Grant seemed to say, could no longer be treated as the barrack of the Empire, an evolution not lost on Montagu who, with the ending of hostilities, appeared to lose much of his enthusiasm for the closer control of Persia and to draw nearer the policy of the Indian Government.[66] But at the penultimate meeting of the Eastern Committee, Curzon, the only minister present, swept aside all criticism and declared the Committee to be in accord with his views.[67] As Montagu tartly commented a few days later, 'the Chairman . . . not unnaturally agreed with the Chairman'.[68]

Over Persia, Curzon was able to exploit his ministerial seniority and his special expertise in Eastern affairs to overcome or evade criticism or opposition. When he directed the Committee's attention to the issue of imperial control east and west of the Caspian Sea, these advantages were largely neutralised by the vigorous intervention of Balfour. For although the Foreign Secretary was, at bottom, as eager as Curzon to liquidate the strategic weaknesses of the pre-war British Empire in the East, he lacked Curzon's confidence that this could be accomplished by extending the sphere of British supremacy, however informal, over ever-widening regions of the world. Curzon was as anxious as over Persia that British intervention in the Caucasus and Trans-Caspia should yield enduring benefits to the security of India. He was keen to exploit the new freedom of the southern marches of the Tsarist empire to build buffers against a resurgence of Russian imperialism. But in December 1918 the major threat to these objectives appeared to come less from the instability of the local politics of these regions than from the likelihood that the Peace Conference would, at least in the case of the Caucasus, hand over the 'rising nationalities' to the care of another great power. It was this fear of foreign intervention which, as in the case of Persia, spurred Curzon, aided and abetted by the General Staff, to insist that Britain should contemplate a post-war commitment in the Caucasus to prevent the French from establishing themselves, as heirs to the Turks and Russians, on the north-west approaches to Persia in the event that the Americans should refuse to act as the protecting power.[69] Here again, Curzon sought to shroud the real purposes of intervention with the suggestion that Britain should act as the trustee of the Caucasus states until such time as they could guard their own interests – a proposal which drew nothing but cynicism and sarcasm from Lord Robert Cecil and his cousin Balfour. Such a policy, said Cecil, would simply produce a second Egypt – Britain would never withdraw. Balfour was even more brutal: 'We are not going to spend all our money and men in civilizing a few people who do not want to be civilized. . . .'[70] To Curzon's protest that the populations could not be left to cut each other's throats, Balfour replied, 'I am in favour of that.'[71]

The issues of trusteeship and the civilising mission were, however, entirely subsidiary in the minds of British ministers. The real question revolved around the strategic relationship of the Caucasus to India and the future defence of the *Raj*. 'You ask', said Curzon, 'why should England do this? Why should Great Britain push herself out in these directions? Of course the answer is obvious – India. You may say that we are going too far, but your remedy is that others should be allowed to go farther.'[72] But Curzon's delineation of the strategic frontier of India was sharply criticised by Balfour, Cecil and Montagu. The gateways to India, Balfour remarked ironically, were 'getting further and further from India, and I do not know how far west they are going to be brought by the General Staff'.[73] Curzon's counter that the course of the war had 'proved that . . . the defence of India, so far from being confined to that narrow corner [i.e. south-east Persia] has spread out to Hamadan, Tehran, Resht, and right away to Baku',[74] won no hearts. At an Imperial War Cabinet three days later, he was instructed to reconsider his proposals; and when the Caucasus next came before the Eastern Committee, he adopted a more conciliatory line: Britain should accept a mandate for the Caucasus only in the 'last resort'.[75] At the end of the month, in deference to the feelings of his colleagues, he made much of his own determination to prevent General Thomson, the British commander in the Caucasus, from extending his role beyond the protection of the railway and pipeline that ran from Baku to Batum on the Black

Sea.[76] In the absence of any definite information as to the attitude of the Americans, or of the Italian government, towards assuming a mandate for the area, and with the Paris Conference now imminent, there the matter rested.

The discussions within the Eastern Committee reveal much of the spirit of ministerial imperialism in this the immediate aftermath of the war. What is plain is that there was no lack of determination that, wherever possible, Britain's imperial interests should be safeguarded against a repetition of the severe crisis which had been occasioned by Turkey's entry into the European war. The imperialism of the ministers was essentially a continuation of the 'war imperialism' which had so expanded the range of Britain's territorial responsibilities over the preceding four years. And it was an imperialism devoid of any concern for either the civilising mission or the economic exploitation of captured territories – the discussions of November and December 1918 seem little influenced by Hankey's zeal to control the Middle East oil reserves, or by Lloyd George's vision of Mesopotamia as the granary of the Empire. Instead the dominant theme of discussion and debate was the necessity of excluding by one means or another any potential rival from the Middle East: and in the wake of revolution in first Russia and then Germany this rival was generally thought to be France, with her long-standing ambitions in the Levant.[77] All the ministers were agreed upon the *desirability* of assuring to Britain a preponderant influence in the former Arab provinces of Turkey; and no minister opposed the extension of this logic to Persia. Only in the Caucasus and Trans-Caspia did such a role appear to exceed the furthest limits of Britain's far-flung Asian interests, although not to Curzon. Where ministers differed was over the means whereby such an advantageous position could be reached.

Underlying the eagerness of Curzon to use British power to reshape the Middle East in the interests of Indian security, and the scepticism of Balfour and Cecil as to the feasibility of his plans, were different assumptions about not only Britain's diplomatic priorities but also the political and strategic relationship between Britain and her Indian Empire.[78] As the difficulties of reaching agreement on the European settlement began to reveal themselves in the course of 1919, and as the consequences of the Indian reforms became clearer, the incompatibility of these assumptions became more and more marked. Meanwhile, political change in the Middle East and in Britain itself cast a longer and longer shadow over the hopes and expectations of the policy-makers.

Decisions deferred, January to June 1919

The resolutions and recommendations of the Eastern Committee had been drawn up in the expectation that Middle Eastern affairs would reach the agenda of the Peace Conference in the spring of 1919. But the fall of three empires in central and eastern Europe left a wreckage too complicated for swift repair, and relegated the problems of the Middle East to the background except in so far as they impinged directly upon the cordiality of inter-allied relations. The tendency to neglect the conduct of Eastern policy at the highest levels of authority was increased by the division of power and responsibility in the British government which followed from the decision that the Prime Minister should lead the British delegation to Paris – a decision which, it should be said, was probably unavoidable given the dependence of Allied cooperation in the later stages of the war upon close personal relations between the heads of government. The passage of imperial policy from the drawing boards of the Eastern Committee to the corridors of diplomacy became, as a result, hazardous and uncertain. Lloyd George, as the principal British delegate, was naturally unwilling to tie his hands in advance by encouraging his colleagues to formulate too precise a statement of policy. Perhaps for that reason, the Eastern Committee resolutions were not formally endorsed by the War Cabinet, merely discussed in the Imperial War Cabinet – a larger body of ambiguous and ill-defined constitutional powers soon to be transformed into the British Empire Delegation. Certainly in Hankey's view, the role of this gathering was no more than 'to take note of these resolutions and to give a free hand to the Prime Minister and Foreign Secretary to do the best they can. . . .'[79]

This formula accorded well with Lloyd George's own instincts and was vital if he were to negotiate authoritatively with Wilson and Clemenceau. Hankey's memorandum had also recognised the need for the abrogation of the Sykes–Picot Agreement to gain the consent of both the parties to it, and referred implicitly to the interlocking of European and Eastern issues which was to bedevil the Middle East settlement. But the price of this diplomatic flexibility was a growing confusion about the aims and priorities of imperial policy, and a volatility of apparent purpose which together encouraged a wide diversity of approach among ministers and their departments to the problems of expansion and control in the Middle East. Thus Curzon, who held day-to-day responsibility for the supervision of policy in the East, was soon complaining that he was not sufficiently informed of Lloyd George's and Balfour's proceedings in Paris.[80] And

Montagu, who had fiercely opposed the Eastern Committee's resolve to evict the Turks from Constantinople, waged a vigorous campaign to persuade Lloyd George to abandon, for reasons largely internal to India, this important aspect of Curzon's proposals. Departmental differences in London, the special needs of conference diplomacy and the local consequences of political revolution in the Middle East made the prompt adjudication of claims a quite unrealistic prospect by early 1919.

The consequences of this were most clearly evident in the prolonged struggle over the future of Syria, the fate of which was, in the view of the Eastern Committee, one key to the whole structure of British imperial control in the Middle East. Lloyd George had played no direct part in framing the territorial desiderata of December 1918. Even before the Committee had held its first full discussion of Syria, Lloyd George had reached a provisional understanding with the French premier by which France was to concede amendments to the Sykes–Picot Agreement: the *vilayet* of Mosul was to fall under British influence and the boundaries of Palestine were to be extended northward to Dan.[81] At the same time, contrary to the policy which Curzon had pressed upon his colleagues, the fundamental principle of a French sphere of influence in the Syrian hinterland was to be respected. It seems likely that Lloyd George and Balfour were sceptical about the chances of forcing through a root and branch revision of the 1916 agreement against French opposition, but that, rather than engage in controversy with Curzon, they chose to veil their intentions and preserve their freedom of manoeuvre. Both the Prime Minister and Foreign Secretary were anxious to keep the oil-rich region of Mosul (in 1919 these riches were being anticipated rather than enjoyed) within the British sector; and for strategic and economic reasons to enlarge Palestine. But they did not share Curzon's apparent conviction that British domination of the Arab Middle East as a whole should be an overriding priority of Britain's foreign and imperial policy.

Lloyd George did not, however, pursue a consistent approach to the problem of Syria. For British policy still hung upon two connected uncertainties: the role which the Americans would play, and their attitude towards the Sykes–Picot Agreement; and the reaction of Feisal and his supporters to French control of Syria in any of the various forms that it might take. The prospect of American pressure on the French to rein in their Eastern ambitions and the increasing intransigence of the Arabs probably encouraged Lloyd George, egged on by his military and naval advisers, to press Clemenceau in February for further concessions – the addition of much of the south-east quarter of the French sphere under the 1916 agreement to the proposed British zone B in Mesopotamia.[82] This demand, and Curzon's reiteration to Cambon, the French ambassador, four days later that, in the British view, the 1916 agreement could not be adhered to,[83] increased French irritation and suspicion. Early in March, Lloyd George again assured Clemenceau that Britain wished France to take the mandate for Syria, but again asked for further territorial concessions.[84] The American proposal for a commission to discover the wishes of the population and the return of Feisal to Syria annoyed and alarmed the French. In May Anglo–French differences over Syria produced a fierce altercation between the two prime ministers; no further progress was made in the dispute until after the signature of the German peace treaty.

It is likely that in Lloyd George's diplomacy the Syrian question was a useful counter in his bargaining with the French over the more immediate issues of the European settlement, and that, in pragmatic fashion, imperial policy was subordinated to greater needs closer to home.[85] It was on the European treaties after all that the eyes of the coalition's parliamentary supporters were most intently fixed. Syria offered the possibility for applying pressure on the French, or for displaying British sympathy and goodwill. But to those of his ministerial colleagues who were anxious to stabilise British commitments in the Middle East, this subtle approach came to appear increasingly dangerous and costly. Milner had told the Prime Minister early in March that he was 'totally opposed to the idea of trying to diddle the French out of Syria . . . ', although he was anxious that French control over Feisal should take a mild form.[86] Balfour told Curzon that Middle East policy was in Lloyd George's hands but was doubtful whether 'he has thought the question out as a whole'.[87] Curzon himself, for all his instinctive desire to throw over the Sykes–Picot Agreement, became more and more nervous about the effects of delay in reaching a decision over the disposal of the Turkish Empire. In his memorandum, 'A Note of Warning about the Middle East', he questioned whether it was safe to assume Turkish acquiescence in Allied plans, and claimed that the old party of Enver and Djemal was 'everywhere active in the background'. Meanwhile, on all sides, there were 'manifest symptoms of Allied weakness and disunion'.[88] A month later, Curzon pressed upon Balfour the necessity of settling Anglo-French differences before Allied power in the East dwindled to nothing. 'Time', he warned, 'is being given to Moslem sentiment throughout the world to consolidate and concentrate on a supreme effort for the recovery of Islam.'[89] For Curzon, therefore, the desirability of excluding the French from Syria had been overtaken by what he saw as the urgent need to prevent the revival of Turkish-inspired pan-Islamic feeling – an event which, in his view, would wreck the major achievement of the Middle East war: the destruction of that many-headed hydra which was the principal threat to British power throughout the Islamic world.

The urgency of Curzon's tone was partly the result of his fear, which seemed at one stage well-founded, that the commission set up at the instigation of the American President[90] would widen its scope by investigating the political preferences not just of the inhabitants of Syria but of those of Mesopotamia and Palestine as well. This would have served to embarrass the British administration in both places at a time when every report from Allenby's subordinates in the Occupied Enemy Territory Administration in Syria spoke of the growing intensity of Arab feeling.[91] At the end of May, Allenby, who continued to direct the military government of Syria and Palestine, warned Balfour that insurrection in Syria would spill over into Palestine and Egypt.[92] It also seemed likely to challenge British control in Mesopotamia.

Fear that a delay in checking the aspirations of Feisal and his supporters would stimulate the growth of a pan-Arab nationalism, and thus render the pacification of the Middle East more difficult, was instrumental in persuading the India Office that there should be no hesitation in coming to terms with the French. Hirtzel,[93] who expressed this view at an early stage, added a further reason for preserving Anglo-French amity. 'It will not be many years', he predicted, 'before there is a great revival of German power and France and we will have to bear the brunt of it.'[94] Imperial reasons, therefore, in both the long and the short term, required that active collaboration with Feisal in Syria should cease, although the military administration in Syria, conscious of the fragility of its rule, vigorously opposed this conclusion. But while the dispute remained unsettled, and until the character and extent of French influence in Syria was known, it proved impossible, even leaving aside the future limits of the Turkish state, to define the terms of imperial control in the Arab lands.

Further east this enforced delay in the evolution of policy was less marked since the affairs of Persia and the borderlands of the Caucasus and Trans-Caspia were less intimately entangled with the peace diplomacy at Paris. Hence Curzon retained an authority over the direction of policy for these places through his presidency of the reconstituted Eastern Committee[95] and his duties as acting Foreign Secretary, which he had yielded to Lloyd George in the case of Syria.

This did not mean, however, that his design went unchallenged. For although Balfour's opposition to keeping British troops in the Caucasus had not been decisive in December 1918, and although he had then been translated to Paris, Curzon found it difficult to sustain his own policy of extending an informal protectorate over the infant Caucasian republics so as to protect the route to India and Persia from either the French or marauding Bolsheviks. Montagu remained determined that the wartime extension of India's strategic frontiers should not be prolonged into the peace; and in January he was joined by a new ally more forceful and persistent than Balfour. The demobilisation crisis in the new year had led to Churchill's replacing Milner at the War Office, ostensibly to bring fresh energy to bear on the problems of transition from war to peace in the politically sensitive field of manpower and labour.[96]

This change was of some consequence to the fate of Curzon's Eastern policies, for Milner had been deeply sympathetic to the needs of imperial security in Persia and the Caspian.[97] Twice in December 1918, from his key position at the War Office, he had defended Curzon's desire to keep troops in the Caucasus.[98] Churchill, however, was far more concerned to protect the army and his own delicate reputation against any charge of recklessness or mismanagement. He was more amenable, in this respect, than Milner might have been to the new mood of caution in his military advisers. Early in March 1919, he proposed to the War Cabinet that the Caucasus be evacuated.[99] Curzon succeeded in referring this request to the Eastern Committee, but here again he was confronted by Churchill and Montagu. Curzon was forced to accept the gradual withdrawal of the British contingent along the line westward from Baku to Batum on the Black Sea,[100] a decision reported to the War Cabinet on 6 March.[101] The timetable of evacuation was not precisely defined and subsequent concern about the fate of the Armenians at the hands of the Turks which spread to Balfour and Lloyd George gave Curzon a useful opportunity for delaying action.

Curzon was even less successful in his attempt to prolong the wartime military presence established during 1918 in Trans-Caspia where it had been feared that German and Turkish propaganda would threaten British and Indian interests. His suggestion that General Malleson's military mission should devote itself after the armistice to keeping at bay the 'hordes of triumphant Bolsheviks' who were demolishing the short-lived independence of the central Asian republics[102] found no place in the recommendations of the Eastern Committee, probably because Curzon was unwilling to call attention to the isolated detachment. Pressure from the Government of India, however, quickly brought the future of the Malleson Mission into question, since Malleson's operations were financially and militarily a call upon Indian resources.[103] Montagu passed on the demand for prompt withdrawal and endorsed the Viceroy's claim that there was no necessity to remain in Trans-Caspia.[104] At the Eastern Committee, Curzon exploited the War Office's reservations[105] to postpone a decision while General Milne, commander of the British army of the Black Sea, prepared an appreciation.[106] Milne's report was damning. Malleson's position was only tenable if he were substantially reinforced from the Caucasus – a proposal the War Office would not consider. Politically too, it was clear that the prospects for an effective Turkoman regime to resist the Bolsheviks were slight, and that if Malleson stayed on he would be driven to assume the functions of government. Curzon gave way, and agreed to Malleson's retreat to Meshed in north-east Persia.[107] By the beginning of April, Britain's brief intervention in the politics of central Asia had ended.[108]

Curzon's struggle to postpone the hour of British military withdrawal from the borderlands of the old Tsarist empire was not inspired by any irrational zeal to widen the bounds of imperial power, nor primarily by a desire to hasten the disintegration of imperial Russia, although it is true that, unlike Churchill, he was suspicious of the long-term aims of White generals like Denikin, whom he described as 'an Old Russian and an Imperialist . . .'.[109] Least of all was he influenced by visions of the economic exploitation of the Caspian by British commerce. Throughout the first half of 1919, all his efforts in this eastern sphere of imperial policy were geared to the achievement of an informal protectorate over Persia. It was on these grounds that he resisted the abandonment of the Caucasus and pleaded for the retention of the Batum-Baku line; on these grounds that he insisted that Malleson remain at Meshed to guard the frontier of Persia and vehemently opposed the Indian government's attempt to pull Malleson further back to Duzdap.[110] The same preoccupation led him to argue against the reduction of the Anglo-Indian expeditionary force in south Persia in March and April.[111] On each occasion Curzon produced the same argument: precipitate British retirement would weaken the hand of Sir Percy Cox who was negotiating for an Anglo-Persian agreement in Teheran, an argument which relied heavily on Cox's reputation as a proconsul.

In all this Curzon was greatly assisted by the fact that among his ministerial colleagues there was a qualified sympathy for the aims behind his Persian project and an ignorance, perhaps, of its likely implications, financial and military. Montagu, who had denounced any suggestion of political interference in the Caucasus or Trans-Caspia after the war, laid aside his earlier reservations and became strongly in favour of Curzon's proposals for Persia so long as genuine Persian consent manifested itself.[112] Even Churchill, who was later to become so telling a critic of Curzon's Persian policies, confessed to a desire to annex the Caspian 'if there was any prospect of keeping it permanently',[113] and thus confirm British primacy in Persia. The only serious opposition to Curzon came from New Delhi, where the arguments deployed by Grant at the Eastern Committee still found favour. To combat these, Curzon and Montagu leaned upon Cox's skill to demonstrate the eagerness of the Persian government for British help and guidance.[114] By the early summer of 1919, Cox had succeeded in drafting an agreement broadly acceptable to the ministry of Vossugh-ed-Dowleh whose friendly attitude to Britain Curzon was so anxious to build into the future fabric of Anglo-Persian relations.

Between the October armistice and the end of June 1919, the terms on which Britain had enjoyed power and influence in the Middle East at the end of the hostilities were strikingly transformed. The refusal of the Americans to embroil themselves in the region had by midsummer largely shattered the British hope that they could be used to fend off Britain's traditional Mediterranean rivals from the Levant. In these circumstances, the stubborn determination of the French to hold Lloyd George to the main terms of the Sykes–Picot Agreement could not be overcome without risking grave damage to the structure of Allied cooperation in Europe. President Wilson's reluctance to act the part, in which Curzon, Balfour and Cecil had fondly cast him, of a *deus ex machina* who would tear up the now superfluous and embarrassing secret treaties, had a further ruinous consequence. The projection of Mediterranean rivalries into Anatolia destroyed all hope of coming quickly to terms with the Turks and establishing a friendly and reliable successor state. By June, the shadow of a Turkish imperialist revival, basing itself upon a general Muslim discontent and anxiety and regenerating the pan-Islamic sentiments that Curzon was so anxious to eliminate, was beginning to obsess the acting Foreign Secretary.

Thus, from a position where the British had hoped to exploit the political revolution in the Middle East to exclude all foreign influence but their own, certainly from the Arab hinterland, they were being driven, on Curzon's reckoning, to seek a rapid accommodation with their principal imperial rival in order to quell the rising force of indigenous nationalism which, in the Ottoman Empire at least, threatened to overthrow the precarious structure of imperial control altogether, and restore the worst features of the pre-war years. With the overt challenge to British authority in Egypt and Afghanistan, and with growing signs of restlessness in Mesopotamia, it seemed the more necessary to exploit the favourable circumstances in Persia so that here at least the defence of India, the primary purpose of the war effort in the East, should be placed on a secure footing. To Curzon this seemed elementary. He had, he told the Eastern Committee in April,

> no confidence in the ability of the Peace Conference to solve the intricate problems of the Middle East. He asked himself what was the duty of a British politician in these circumstances, and was convinced that it was to build up the bastions of India, which had always been and must always be the pivot and focus of British interests in the East.[115]

But even as Curzon's plans for Persia reached fruition, new forces at home, in the Middle East and in the wider international sphere, arose to further weaken the short-lived British supremacy in the East.

7 The Search for Security, 1919–1920

The delay in the taking of essential decisions about Britain's future role in the Middle East was an almost inevitable consequence of the extreme concentration of power which the structure of inter-allied cooperation and diplomacy had produced, and the vast scale, scope and complexity of the European issues which had first call on the attention of the Allied leaders and their electorates. Neither Curzon nor Montagu, for all their agitation about British power and influence in the East, was able to arouse, at this stage, much interest in Lloyd George, in whose hands (and those of his entourage) lay all those aspects of peace diplomacy which required Allied agreement. Only over Persia, where the British appeared for the moment unchallengeable, was Curzon left to plough his own furrow undelayed and undisturbed. As a result, the exercise of British authority in the Middle East during an interval of some seven months was shaped more by local circumstance than by the dictates of a coordinated strategy, except in Syria where Balfour's repeated insistence on the temporary and provisional nature of the British presence checked the tendency of Allenby's military administration towards the creation of a veiled or informal British protectorate.[1]

This hiatus came to an end with the signing of the German treaty on 28 June 1919, and the gradual revival of Cabinet government in Britain. Two important factors thrust Middle Eastern affairs upon the ministers: the growing strength of the nationalist reaction in Turkey against a widening sphere of Greek occupation which made a pressing case for a prompt peace settlement; and the threats of Churchill, the War Minister, that without economies in the huge garrisons which Britain still maintained in the Middle East, there would be no reserves for what the Chief of the Imperial General Staff termed the 'storm centres' of Ireland, Egypt, Mesopotamia and India.[2] Against this background and in the second half of August 1919, the principal ministers in the coalition held their first collective discussion of Britain's revised requirements in the Middle East.

The Containment of Turkey

The result of these ministerial deliberations was to reveal a general unity of feeling with regard to the disposition of Turkey's former provinces in the Arab lands. Ministers were 'all agreed that we should go as far as we legitimately can, without breaking our pledges, to help the French in respect of Syria'.[3] And 'as a *sine qua non* of course Mesopotamia, including Mosul must be entrusted to us'.[4] The question of Palestine, and its development as a Jewish homeland, commanded a less general enthusiasm. Curzon and Montagu would both have preferred, although for different reasons, to decline any British responsibility for promoting the Zionist colonisation in a territory whose frontier with a French-dominated Syria was not yet delimitated, and whose politics were unlikely to be harmonious. But both feared, no doubt, to go against the Prime Minister, 'who talks about Jerusalem with the same enthusiasm as about his native hills',[5] and Balfour who had displayed an apparently unyielding commitment to his wartime declaration.

These broad conclusions represented a significant modification of the ambitious programme laid down by the Eastern Committee nine months before for the Arab lands. Three influences may be held responsible for this. The most important was undoubtedly the conviction of Lloyd George, Balfour and Milner, all of whom had had close dealings with the French at Versailles, that any attempt to subvert the main outlines of the Sykes–Picot Agreement would have general and disastrous repercussions elsewhere.[6] The signing of the German treaty did not diminish in any way the value of French cooperation in the remaking of Europe. Even Curzon, the main advocate among the ministers of a British Syria, came to grasp the necessity of French friendship, less, perhaps, through his observation of the European as of the wider Near Eastern scene.[7] By the early summer of 1919, he was eager to concede Syria to the French to secure a Turkish settlement without further delay. The third quarter whence came counsel of caution and restraint was the War Office which had, like Curzon, undergone a considerable change of heart since the euphoric discussions at the end of 1918. The warnings of Allenby and his subordinates in the military administration of Syria against the dangers of French activity there were ignored by Churchill and Wilson, the Chief of the Imperial General Staff, who were determined that, wherever possible, the army's strength in the Middle East should be drastically reduced. And it was their repeated demands for realism in military policy which overshadowed the Cabinet's view of the Middle East in August 1919. Complaining to

Balfour of the general inconclusiveness of the meetings of 19–20 August, Curzon nevertheless remarked:

> But this fact did emerge: the burden of maintaining an English and Indian army of 320,000 men in various parts of the Turkish Empire and in Egypt, or of 225,000 men excluding Egypt, with its overwhelming cost, is one that cannot any longer be sustained.[8]

Curzon used this latter argument to press upon Balfour, yet again, the need for energetic peacemaking in the East. 'The examination and settlement of the Eastern Question' could not, he claimed, be postponed until President Wilson gained his Senate's approval for a Turkish mandate, nor until the Paris Peace Conference could be re-assembled.[9] But while ministers were broadly united on the necessity for Britain to concede Syria and retain control over Mesopotamia and Palestine, they were at loggerheads over the other crucial issues of any Eastern settlement: the territorial extent and political independence of the reduced Turkish state, and its political relationship with Britain, in her new imperial role in the Middle East. For, by this stage, it seemed increasingly unlikely that the United States would undertake the supervisory role in Turkish affairs which British policy-makers had tended to expect.[10]

The wide range of opinions expressed in Cabinet on these questions was indicative of the havoc wrought in the old canons of imperial policy by the Anglo-Turkish war. The controversy centred upon the enduring focus of Britain's Eastern policies: Constantinople, capital of the defeated empire. A strong party in the Cabinet – Barnes, Long, the Geddes brothers and Montagu – wished Constantinople to remain Turkish but under a British mandate, although their reasons varied widely. Curzon dismissed Long and the Geddes brothers as 'stout tories . . . who revel in the thought of the British flag flying over Constantinople, who think that the Turk is not such a bad fellow after all, and who are firmly convinced that the only people who can solve this or any other problem are the British'.[11] Montagu, however, was scarcely of this school. His alignment with Long, Barnes and the Geddes brothers was a mark of his anxiety to find some way of frustrating the declared zeal of Curzon and the known preference of Balfour for the eviction of the Turks from their capital, a measure which, Montagu was convinced, would destroy the political credibility of his reforms programme in India.[12] Thus the Indian dimension of his thinking led him towards a policy of benevolent protection over the surviving elements of the Ottoman Empire in Europe and Asia Minor, the 'advanced and imperialistic line' which Curzon in his letter to Balfour contrasted with the caution of Milner, Chamberlain and himself, and their hesitancy about assuming further imperial responsibilities. The opponents of a British mandate in Constantinople were similarly inspired by a variety of motives. Fisher believed that 'going to Constantinople' would have undesirable consequences for 'our relations with Russia'.[13] Milner was as anxious as Montagu to keep the Turks in Constantinople,[14] but rejected the proposal that Britain should govern the city. Bonar Law and Chamberlain were probably most influenced by a reluctance to extend Britain's fixed financial and military commitments except where ministerial opinion was unshakeable. But the most interesting and articulate critic of the proposal was the doyen of proconsuls, Curzon himself.

Curzon was convinced that the great object of British Eastern policy in the aftermath of the war must be the systematic destruction of the far-flung influence and pretensions of the Turkish Empire. He did not believe that the military defeat of Turkey was alone sufficient to root out the prestige and moral authority that the Ottomans had enjoyed before the war in the Islamic world, and which still remained as a deadly threat to Britain's imperial security in the Middle East and India. Turkey must be reduced not only in her own eyes but in the eyes of the Islamic world from her former status as a great imperial power and the champion of the Muslim faith to that befitting a nation state of, at best, the second rank. The pan-Islamic and pan-Turanian ambitions which had inspired Turkey's war strategy, and so endangered Britain's security, must be destroyed once and for all. To this end, the Sultan, in his dual capacity as the Commander of the Faithful and the head of the Ottoman state, must be excluded from Constantinople, the great historic symbol of triumphant Ottoman imperialism and of the pre-eminence of Turkey among the Muslim peoples. Once deprived of the mystique which possession of Constantinople conferred, the destructive power of the Sultan-Caliph and his advisers would be healthily constrained; and a Turkish state in Asia Minor, enjoying a wide autonomy, could join the other successor states of the old empire.[15]

It was this policy, combining the ruthless suppression of Turkey's lingering supra-national claims and a generous treatment of the Anatolian heartland, which Curzon urged upon his colleagues. Any other combination, he argued, would expose Britain's new imperial stance in the Middle East to great risks and endanger the fruits of military victory. It was just this preoccupation with the viability of

Britain's new commitments in the East which dictated his vehement opposition either to a British mandate in Constantinople or to the survival there under any circumstances of Turkish sovereignty. 'I cannot bring myself to think', he told Balfour,

> that a British mandate for Constantinople will not fatally disturb the true orientation of our Eastern policy in future, and land us in endless trouble: we should have the opposition of the French; we should presently become entangled in the cockpit of the Balkans; and we might later on have to face the resentment of a resuscitated Russia.[16]

Britain's real strategic interests, so Curzon's argument ran, lay east and south of the Straits; she could not afford to be embroiled in the Balkans as well. By the same token, she dare not leave the Turks at the Straits where they would be poised to exploit their old powers of intrigue among the European states to regain their lost paramountcy in the East. But if Curzon could not contemplate a British mandate at the Straits, neither would he consider a French mandate over Asia Minor and Constantinople which Lloyd George, in 'one of those large deals which appeal to his kind of mind', had proposed as an alternative to their control of Syria and Cilicia. Once again, the most powerful argument to Curzon's mind was the fear that France would 'split Islam into two sections and . . . become the head of a great Moslem movement' in opposition to Britain.[17]

The general tenor of Cabinet discussion suggested that virtually all the ministers were keen to exclude Italy, Greece or any other power from Asia Minor, both to avoid the diplomatic complications and the Turkish backlash which Curzon and Montagu were agreed in forecasting; that most ministers preferred an international control in the Straits if it were feasible; that some were prepared to see a British mandate there while others bitterly opposed it; that only Balfour and Curzon were utterly committed to ending the political connection of the Turks with their capital. In these circumstances, the attitude of the Prime Minister became of considerable significance. Had his influence been thrown against Curzon on this issue, it is unlikely that divisions within the Cabinet would have been serious or lasting. But Lloyd George was determined not to give way to those of his colleagues who wished to see Asia Minor handed over to the Turks in its entirety without a partition or the imposition of mandates. His support for the creation of a Greater Greece in the eastern Mediterranean guarding the Straits as the ally of

Britain (a policy which commanded much wider and stronger backing in British political and official circles than it later became fashionable to admit), enjoined on him some strategem to evade the opinion of his colleagues. The solution lay in division and delay: Curzon and Balfour were encouraged to ignore the majority view over Constantinople; and to Curzon was entrusted the task of negotiating the preliminaries to a Turkish treaty. A collective decision on the disputed issues was postponed *sine die*.[18]

Both Lloyd George and Curzon harboured ambitious plans for the re-ordering of the Middle East which, for all their differences over the enhancement of Greek power, depended alike upon the close containment of the Turks. Both were faced, however, with the same difficulty: most of their colleagues either did not understand or were antagonistic to a policy which would impose territorial losses on the Turks still more severe than those laid down in the armistice; and which seemed likely to require a strong military presence to enforce it. Both men were thrust, therefore, into a reluctant alliance, aimed at preserving the subtleties of Eastern policy from the scrutiny of the Cabinet as a whole. The fuller implications of their plans, and the assumptions upon which they rested, were jealously guarded from open debate.

The Cabinet's attempt to formulate a policy for the Ottoman Middle East as a whole cleared the way for Lloyd George and Balfour to reach an accommodation with the French over the Arab provinces and end the long confrontation over Syria.[19] But there had been no agreement on the terms for the settlement of Asia Minor and European Turkey, upon the success of which the stability of Anglo-French control in the Arab lands was to become more and more obviously dependent. Nevertheless, Curzon set about the task of constructing a treaty which would meet the specifications of Lloyd George, Balfour and himself. The first step was to reach an understanding with the French who had watched British diplomacy in the East with suspicion, and who had sustained before 1914 a very large financial investment in Constantinople and Anatolia.[20] In early December 1919, the easing of tensions over Syria, which the British had agreed to evacuate, smoothed the path for Anglo-French cooperation. Clemenceau came to London to confer with Lloyd George and Curzon, who found him reluctant to evict the Sultan from Constantinople and eager for a closer financial control over the new Turkish state than Curzon wanted.[21] These differences were, however, resolved between Curzon and Berthelot, the permanent head of the Quai d'Orsay, Curzon accepting financial controls in exchange for French consent to the creation of an international state embracing Constantinople and the Straits, and the annexation by Greece of most of Thrace.[22]

The success of Curzon's diplomacy was soon devalued. The opposition in Cabinet to his Constantinople policy, overridden in August and ignored in December,[23] prepared its overthrow. The moving spirits were Montagu and Milner, who argued that the eviction of the Sultan would aggravate Muslim suspicions of Britain not only in India but in Egypt and the Middle East.[24] At the end of December, Milner was, of course, far away, lost in the political labyrinth of Egypt; but his place among Curzon's critics was taken by another well-fitted by temperament and vantage-point to confront the Foreign Secretary. This minister was Churchill, aided and abetted by a professional adviser, the Chief of the Imperial General Staff, whose preoccupation with the internal security of the Home Islands and whose contempt for the military judgment of civilian ministers found vent in his attack on the continued dispersal of British detachments across the Middle East from Constantinople through the Caucasus to Persia.[25] At the end of December the influence of this adviser was explicitly promised to Montagu's struggle against Balfour, Curzon and Lloyd George.[26]

This reinforcement proved fatal to Curzon's design. At the Cabinet meeting on 6 January 1920, summoned to ratify the joint Anglo-French approach to Turkey, and at the informal Cabinet the day before, he encountered the familiar proposition advanced by Montagu that a Turkish treaty along the lines of the Curzon–Berthelot Agreement would create a reaction in India 'comparable to the Sinn Fein movement'.[27] But it was Wilson who delivered the most punishing blows. First of all, he pointed to the general military situation in the Middle East, the possibility that Denikin's[28] collapse would open the Bolshevik road to Persia, and the danger of a general uprising along India's far-flung defence lines. Defending India (and, of course, Persia) along the Batum-Baku line, to which Curzon was committed, 'would only be possible if the Turks were friendly to us', while 'all military opinion was opposed to ejecting the Turk from Constantinople'.[29] Wilson went on the next day to deliver the *coup de grâce*. Questioned by Lloyd George on the relative military commitments involved in either expelling or maintaining the Sultan, he replied that were Turkey's political capital to be removed to Asia Minor, 'the whole military position would be altered to our disadvantage . . .'.[30] Once out of the range of Allied guns, the Turks would become a more dangerous and unpredictable enemy; and the security of the Straits would require a far more elaborate defence and 'a much larger garrison'.[31] All this was calculated to alarm ministers unconvinced by Montagu's Indian arguments. The point was hammered home by a swift *tour d'horizon*. Attention was drawn, Hankey's minutes record,

> to the already very great military commitments assumed by the British Empire in Mesopotamia, Palestine, Persia etc. This was recognised as a strong argument against the adoption of any system that would increase the burden of forces to be maintained for Constantinople and the Straits.[32]

In the vote which followed, only Auckland Geddes and Addison supported Curzon and the Prime Minister,[33] since Balfour 'was playing golf on the North Berwick links, and was . . . unable to confuse the issue'.[34]

The Cabinet decision that Constantinople should be left in Turkish hands by the peace treaty was a striking revolt against the combined authority of the Prime Minister, Foreign Secretary and an absent Balfour, and on an issue of prime importance. But although Curzon and Lloyd George did not dare on this occasion to ignore the unmistakable feeling of their colleagues, the revolt over Constantinople did not widen into a general rejection of their Eastern policy. The dissenting ministers, with the solitary and ineffective exception of Montagu, had in mind no alternative approach to the problem of controlling Turkey. Their vote was a gesture of anxiety and mistrust at the management of imperial policy in the Middle East; and particularly at the prospect of an uncontrolled expansion of Britain's commitments in pursuit of aims which, in this instance, were neither properly explained nor properly understood. Thus when Churchill and Wilson attempted to exploit ministerial feeling to pull the army out of the Caucasus and north Persia, they found that it was easier to refuse fresh obligations than to shrug off those that already existed. On 14 January, Wilson's request for authority to withdraw the six British battalions from Batum went to the Cabinet, where in a depleted meeting and without Lloyd George and Curzon, it was granted.[35] But this decision, stigmatised by Amery, the acting Colonial Secretary, as a 'policy of scuttle' and blamed by him on Churchill's pique at the rejection of his plans for helping Denikin,[36] was simply not acted upon. And despite the approach of the budget and the sensitivity of ministers to the need to reduce the high level of military spending, Curzon, with the implicit approval of Lloyd George, was able, throughout the first half of 1920, to veto any withdrawal of the contingents in the Caucasus and Persia, on the grounds that to do so would be to jeopardise not only the achievement of the Anglo-Persian Agreement, but also the moral authority that was needed to carry through a Turkish treaty.

For all their humiliation, therefore, over the future of Constantinople, Lloyd George and Curzon, it is clear, retained control of Britain's Turkish policy, and used it to press for a settlement that would shackle Turkish irridentism. At the first Conference of London (February to April 1920), the British and French agreed upon the principal terms to be presented to Turkey: the cession of almost all of Thrace to Greece; international control over the Straits and an international force to maintain it; close financial supervision of the Turkish government; the cession of Smyrna to Greece with only residual Turkish sovereignty; and the creation to the east of Anatolia of independent states in Armenia and Kurdistan.[37] These terms were in broad conformity with Curzon's desire to root out Turkish imperialism, but the instrument for putting them into effect was the hitherto compliant Ottoman government at Constantinople, the only Turkish government recognised by the Allies. Its cooperation in applying the peace treaty in the Turkish hinterland (and suppressing the Kemalist regime at Angora) was essential if the Allies were to avoid fresh military operations. But in the spring of 1920, this cooperation became more and more uncertain as the British began to fear the growing influence of Kemalist sympathisers in the city. In early February the bellicosity of the Kemalists and the arrival of prominent nationalists in Constantinople for the opening of the Turkish parliament seemed to augur the collapse of Allied authority in the capital.[38]

Churchill and Wilson were quick to warn Curzon that the reinforcement of Constantinople would require the abandonment of Batum and the British position on the Caspian.[39] But although in the absence of Lloyd George the Cabinet endorsed the War Office's view, Curzon successfully resisted Churchill's demand that British policy choose between Constantinople and Teheran. But, as the crisis of authority at the Straits grew worse, he was forced to modify more and more those assumptions about Britain's relations with Turkey upon which the whole edifice of his Eastern policy had been constructed.

The problem (familiar enough to the British) which the Allies faced was that of persuading reluctant, timid or hostile politicians to sustain a client-government increasingly discredited in the eyes of their own countrymen. In March, with the downfall of another Turkish ministry, this problem reached an acute phase. Lloyd George and Curzon were alike determined that there should be no concessions to Turkish nationalist feeling and that the terms hammered out at the London Conference should be applied in their full rigour. To adopt the proposals of the British and French High Commissioners who urged the return of Thrace to the Turks, and the expulsion of the Greek army from Smyrna, Curzon told the Conference, would be unacceptable. 'Lenient terms would destroy all hope of a reconstituted Armenia and it would mean a Turkish Kurdistan. In other words it would mean an absolute reversal of the policy the Allies had decided to adopt.'[40] But the alternative to concession was coercion, a logic that Curzon fully recognised. While deprecating Lloyd George's enthusiasm for partnership with Greece,[41] he joined the Prime Minister in advocating the military occupation of Constantinople by the Allies as the only means whereby his grand scheme for the containment of Turkey's Eastern ambitions could be realised. At the same time, he continued to block Churchill's attempts to recall the Batum garrison, arguing that evacuation would encourage the Kemalists in their Eastern designs and that Batum 'was a symbol of the British and Allied interest in the Middle East'.[42]

The elements of stability in the Middle East continued, however, to be elusive. Allied occupation of Constantinople and the despatch of some leading nationalists to that way-station of Eastern malcontents, Malta, failed to check the tide of Turkish nationalist reaction or weaken the Kemalists. No sooner had the Allied peace terms been handed to the purged Turkish government than the British High Commissioner reported the demoralisation of the ministry and a further loss in its authority in Asia Minor.[43] By early June, its ability to keep order even in the adjacent Ismid peninsula was in doubt. On 15 June, de Robeck reported that nationalist forces had attacked British outposts in the peninsula and he appealed for immediate reinforcements.[44] His request reached ministers at a moment when the apparent deterioration of Britain's position not only at the Straits but also in northern Mesopotamia and Persia was causing considerable alarm, and seemed to justify a review of her Middle Eastern commitments.[45] At a ministerial meeting extending over 17 and 18 June, the problem of reconciling the overall military weakness between Thrace and Persia depicted by Churchill with the new emergency at Constantinople again threatened Lloyd George's and Curzon's Turkish strategy. But an expedient was found. Ministers approved the reinforcement of Constantinople from Palestine and made a gesture towards Churchill's anxieties. But their real decision was to accept, at Lloyd George's prompting, Venizelos' offer of Greek military support against the

Kemalists, and to agree to throw Britain's weight behind the Greek struggle against the Turks in western Anatolia as the only means of destroying the canker of Turkish nationalism.[46] Two days later at Hythe, Lloyd George obtained French consent to the unleashing of a Greek offensive in Thrace and Anatolia;[47] and in the respite that followed, the Sultan's government at Constantinople was persuaded to sign the Treaty of Sèvres.[48]

The Treaty of Sèvres marked the culmination of Curzon's efforts, with the assistance of Lloyd George, to construct a general settlement of the Middle East which, by means of an informal partnership with a new Turkish state, would allow the creation in the Caucasus, Armenia and Kurdistan of buffer states that would in their turn facilitate a relatively loose and economical control over Persia and Mesopotamia in the interests of Anglo-Indian security. To obtain this, Curzon had been willing to acquiesce in Lloyd George's policy towards Greece and the denial of Smyrna to the Turks; and subsequently to approve an informal alliance with the Greeks to suppress the Kemalist movement in Anatolia. In all this despite the protests of Churchill and Montagu, Curzon and Lloyd George had carried the Cabinet with them, helped no doubt by Milner's readiness, once Constantinople had been promised to the Turks, to support Curzon's position. Churchill's efforts to subject Middle Eastern policy as a whole to critical review were blunted by the device of allotting the task of defeating Kemal in the field to Greek not British armies, a proposal which apparently satisfied those ministers who, in January, had opposed new commitments at Constantinople. Nevertheless, as will be seen, the failure to set up in Turkey a stable and effective client-regime – a failure compounded by French hostility and Lloyd George's relations with Venizelos – was to exercise a decisive influence over the pattern of British imperial policies in the Middle East.

Neither at this stage, nor by the end of 1920, was there much sign that ministers anticipated that collapse in the façade as well as the fabric of allied unity which by the autumn of 1921 was to provide such significant encouragement to Kemalist resistance and to make the task of constructing a pliable but effective Turkish government at Constantinople hopeless beyond recall. Yet even before 1920 was out the divergence of Allied interests was already ominously visible. Thus the Italians, for whom the Adriatic was the central preoccupation, showed a steadily diminishing enthusiasm for the coercion of Turkey. They had, moreover, some grounds for resentment at the direction which the Turkish settlement had already taken since the region around Smyrna originally designated as Italy's sphere in Asia Minor had been summarily transferred to the Greeks in the spring of 1919. By the early months of 1920 Italian reservations about the drift of Allied policy came to the surface over the question of occupying Constantinople. Subsequently, Italian disillusionment with the rewards of their military presence in southern Anatolia was strongly reinforced by the financial and domestic anxieties of the Nitti government and by a military setback at Konya at the hands of Kemalist forces. Perhaps the shadow of Adowa was enough. Italian troops were steadily withdrawn from Anatolia and Nitti, while reserving Italy's claim to an economic sphere, renounced all territorial ambitions in Asia Minor.

The Nitti government, therefore, began the process of detaching Italy from the struggle to impose in Turkey a regime that would perform the requirements of the Entente powers. Under Giolitti, who succeeded Nitti in mid-1920, this tendency in Italian policy was carried a stage further. The new foreign minister, Count Sforza, abruptly terminated the Tittoni–Venizelos Agreement of July 1919 whereby Italy had acquiesced in Greek control of Smyrna and the Dodecanese (the latter were still in Italian hands). By this gesture Italy dissociated herself from the Greek struggle for Ionia. By November this dissociation was showing some signs of being transformed into a positive preference for good relations with Kemal.[49] The reason for Sforza's more definite departure from the approach favoured especially by Curzon and Lloyd George may in part have been a shrewd and prophetic appraisal of the balance of military power in Asia Minor.[50] But other considerations were almost certainly at work. Sforza himself told Buchanan, the British ambassador in Rome, that the abrogation of the agreement with Greece and the retention of the Dodecanese was the obverse of his policy of seeking better relations with Yugoslavia and settling the sensitive question of the Adriatic. No minister, said Sforza, could remain popular who renounced everything: Italy had renounced her position in Albania; the Dodecanese must be held.[51] It is likely, however, that the cooling of Italy's relations with Greece was not purely a political convenience. Italy did not regard the Near East and Asia Minor as a region of only peripheral importance to her. Before 1914 Italian governments had displayed considerable interest in the eastward expansion of Italy's commercial and financial influence and had exploited Turkey's military and political weakness to seize Ottoman territory in north Africa and to demand concessions in Anatolia.[52] But in the circumstances prevailing by mid-1920 it seemed clear that Italy was unlikely to benefit from the triumph of Greek armies in Asia Minor; and the creation of a Greater Greece extending from the Adriatic to central Anatolia was an uninviting prospect on economic and strategic grounds alike. The penetration of Italian influence in the eastern Mediterranean would be halted. The balance of power in the Balkans would be altered almost certainly to Italy's disadvantage. And Italian commercial enterprise had little hope of prospering in an Anatolia governed by a Greece that was financially dependent on London. Little wonder then that Italian support for the coercion of Turkish nationalism fell away once the aftermath of the crisis of June 1920 revealed how much Greece stood to gain from a confrontation with Kemal. What restrained the Italians from an open disavowal of the Sèvres Treaty and its enforcement was a reluctance to quarrel directly with Britain and perhaps an uncertainty as to whether such a course would really strengthen Italian influence and interests in Turkey.

But if British ministers could afford to overlook Italian disaffection, French discontent with the course of events in the Middle East posed a far more serious threat to the chances of enforcing the terms of the Sèvres Treaty. French goodwill was essential to British hopes of stabilising central Europe. France was a military power of far greater consequence in the Near East than Italy, and her determination to play a leading role in the East had not been worn down by the strains which had led to Italy's withdrawal from Asia Minor. Moreover, France's influence in Turkey, based upon a long-established financial presence, was much greater than Italy's and was reflected in the cultural orientation of the Turkish elite.

From the beginning the prospect of Anglo-French cooperation in the post-war Middle East had been clouded by mutual distrust and hostility. French suspicion that Lloyd George and Curzon meditated their exclusion from the Arab Middle East had led, as we have seen, to bitter exchanges in the summer of 1919. Even after the principle of French control in Syria had been admitted, the local representatives of France remained convinced that British intrigue was compounding the difficulty of establishing a French mandate in Syria. Anglo-French relations at Constantinople were not immune from the ill-will bred by such suspicions, but the safeguarding of French financial and commercial interests and the desire to find a Turkish administration that would serve them ensured a greater convergence of aim than elsewhere in the Middle East. But after the middle of 1920 a number of factors conspired to overthrow this comparative harmony and propel French policy gradually towards a separate accommodation with Mustapha Kemal.

Of these none was more important than the persistence of French difficulties in Syria. France's authority in Syria as mandatory designate was resisted locally by the supporters of Feisal but also by Kemalist military activity along the northern border of the mandate in Cilicia. In July 1920, while the French were intent on the repression of Feisal and the nationalists of the Syrian Congress, Turkish irregulars destroyed a French garrison only fifty miles from Aleppo.[53] Even after Feisal's expulsion from Syria, internal disturbances and Turkish pressure delayed progress towards a settled administration, compelling France to maintain a garrison of some 50 000 (mainly colonial) troops on into 1921.[54] As enthusiasm for the financial burden of the *mission civilisatrice* waned in the French Assembly,[55] stability in Syria appeared more and more dependent on some adjustment in French relations with Kemal. The alternative was a military solution that would eliminate the Kemalist nuisance but such a solution could not but increase the insecurity of France's Middle Eastern position in the long term. For no less than Italy, France viewed with distrust and even fear the aggrandisement of Greece; indeed she had more to lose from it. The expansion of Greek power in Asia Minor would inflict a permanent barrier to the recovery of her financial influence. The supremacy of British naval power in the eastern Mediterranean, supplemented by a grateful client, would become yet more overweening. France's hard-won mandates in Syria and the Lebanon and her stake in the prospective oil wealth of Mosul would be menaced by the conjunction of Greek and British expansion. For the French did not believe that British acknowledgment of their mandatory rights in Syria was sincere; long into 1921 the suspicion remained that the eviction of French rule by the fomentation of local discontent was a standing object of Britain's Arab policy. Hence the outright defeat of Kemal to which Lloyd George and Curzon looked forward as the first step to the permanent settlement of Turkey's political status and the stabilising of Britain's commitments in the Middle East took on a far more baleful aspect when seen from Paris. Far from promising security, it threatened the slow but steady constriction of France's narrow bridgehead of influence and power in the Levant and at Constantinople, the revival of British designs on Syria and a further stimulus to unrest in the mandate.[56] When, therefore, the prospects for Kemal's resistance began to look less forlorn, and when political upheaval in Greece installed a regime whose hostility to France seemed beyond doubt, it was to be expected that far from rallying to Britain's side both France and Italy would be encouraged to undermine still further the purposes on which both London and Athens had set their hearts. And so it turned out.

British Policy in Persia, 1919–1920

For Curzon the containment of Turkey and the destruction of Ottoman imperialism formed the first great precondition for the solution of the acute problems which the political instability of the Middle East had posed for Anglo-Indian security since 1914. The second precondition was the reconstruction of Persia. By the middle of 1920, as we have seen, the pursuit of the first had led to increasingly desperate expedients, and seemed further from attainment than at any time since the Mudros armistice. At the same time the omens for Curzon's treasured project in Persia began to look increasingly gloomy.

In August 1919, by contrast, Curzon's Persian policy had appeared a marked success. Sir Percy Cox, the British minister at Teheran, had negotiated an agreement by which, as Curzon told his Cabinet colleagues,

> without assuming a direct control over Persian administration or involving ourselves in continued financial responsibilities on a large scale, we should yet be able to provide Persia with the expert assistance and advice which will enable the State to be rebuilt.[57]

This extension of British responsibilities Curzon justified in the same terms as those he had earlier employed in the deliberations of the Eastern Committee. The 'magnitude of our interests in the country, and the future safety of our Eastern Empire' made it impossible for Britain to be indifferent to Persia's fate, above all at a moment when Britain was about to assume the mandate for Mesopotamia.[58] To bolster these arguments, Curzon deployed once more the emotive spectre of marauding Bolshevism, and the more material attractions of a secure source of oil for the Royal Navy. But behind these generalised assertions there lay, perhaps, in Curzon's mind more detailed calculations about the benefits of a political monopoly in Persia for Britain's position in the Middle East as a whole. For Curzon's plans for Persia had been framed, as his memorandum hinted, with an eye to the future of the Ottoman Empire; and his proposals for Persia, for Turkey, for Armenia and Kurdistan, and, as we shall see, for Mesopotamia, were in his conception to be mutually supporting and closely integrated.

At the heart of Curzon's thinking lay the notion which he had put forward at the Eastern Committee in June 1918 of a 'Moslem nexus of states' which would act as a shield or buffer against any future attack on the Anglo-Indian defence system in the Middle East. Since he had first adumbrated it, this notion had become more refined and complex. It is clear that by 1919 Curzon intended that this 'nexus' should include a reorganised Turkish state, chastened but friendly; Persia bound by an agreement with Britain; a Christian Armenia barring the way to any revival of pan-Turanian activity; and a fringe of states in the Caucasus and Trans-Caspia released from the Tsarist empire. Just as Turkey was the key to the achievement of this design on one side of the Middle East, so Persia was the key to its success on the other. A disorganised and chaotic Persia would wreck the delicate balance by which Curzon hoped to nudge the competing political forces of the Middle East into their proper place, and would threaten a renewal of the difficulties which, in the past, had seemed likely to follow from its disintegration.

Up until the end of the Middle Eastern war in October 1918, Curzon does not seem to have pondered very fully the means whereby Persia could be brought to play such a role. He had tended to argue that the instalment of a friendly prime minister in Persia – Vossugh-ed-Dowleh – would of itself guarantee Persian cooperation. But the danger that Persia would not consent to become Britain's diplomatic ward at the Peace Conference, and might disrupt his grand strategy by intriguing with France or the United States, propelled Curzon towards seeking a more formal influence in Persian affairs.[59] Thus although the Anglo-Persian agreement made no reference to any such convention,[60] Curzon on successive occasions made it clear to the Persian government that he expected Persia's foreign policy to be in conformity with that of Britain, and that any attempt to pursue an independent diplomacy, whether at the Peace Conference, with the Soviet regime in Russia, or with the intransigent Afghans, would incur grave displeasure.[61] Political monopoly of this kind – a 'veiled protectorate' – was to be one pillar of the new relationship between Britain and Persia. But it would not by itself ensure that Persia contributed to Britain's imperial security.

In his Cabinet memorandum Curzon had emphasised that the Anglo-Persian Agreement did not signal the assumption by Britain of any formal suzerainty or trusteeship over the country. The agreement meant 'not that we have received or are about to receive a mandate for Persia . . . not that Persia has handed over to us any part of her liberties; not that we are assuming fresh and costly obligations . . .'.[62] Yet in this same memorandum Curzon had stressed the need for the 'rehabilitation' of Persia, and the nearness of the Persian state to disintegration. The political conflicts of the constitutional era before 1914, the bitter divisions produced by the war itself, the existence of rival armies outside the control of the central government, the centrifugal tendencies of the great tribes, the political convulsions on Persia's borders, east and north, with the former Tsarist empire, and the uncertainties generated by the military occupations of the Russians and the British, had all done little to strengthen a regime the fragility of which had preoccupied Anglo-Persian relations since the 1860s.[63] Curzon proposed to tackle the weaknesses of the Persian state by a programme of financial and military reform, to be imposed on Persia through the time-honoured device of British advisers, dangling, as the reward for cooperation, a loan of two million pounds and the further prospect of British economic assistance with the development of communications. The creation of a single national army and the construction of an efficient system of revenues were intended to provide the basis for that revival of central authority which, together with the expansion of British trade through the Gulf ports, would both enable and encourage Persia to play her part in Curzon's grand strategy, and reverse the processes of decline and subjection to Russia which Curzon himself had forseen in the 1890s.[64]

The reforms that Curzon had in mind held a double significance for British policy. For they were designed not only to make Persia a more effective component of a new Anglo-Indian system of defence, but also to strengthen the position of those at the centre of Persian politics whom Curzon regarded as Britain's friends and partners. He had told the Eastern Committee that without British aid this group of politicians could not sustain themselves.[65] The raising up of central government was, however, a new departure in British policy which required its agents to find allies very different from those with whom they had worked before 1914 and through much of the war – the autonomous and refractory tribal chiefs and provincial governors of south and east Persia whose resistance to the claims of Teheran had needed little British encouragement.[66] Curzon's conviction, first glimpsed in the summer of 1918, that Britain should work with national rather than local politicians threw the established principles of collaboration into reverse and discarded the techniques of regional predominance in the Anglo-Russian Convention of 1907.

Curzon's chosen allies at Teheran were the group which had formed round Vossugh-ed-Dowleh and the so-called Triumvirate. Vossugh had been regarded since 1916 as a friend of Britain but his description by unsympathetic observers as variously 'a former Russophile'[67] and a 'professional Anglophile'[68] suggests that his motives were less transparently simple. He was himself part of the administrative elite of the Persian Empire, and it is likely that his approach to Anglo-Persian relations was dominated less by a desire to serve as Curzon's Achates than by an eagerness to exploit Britain's interest in Persia to fortify the fraying bounds of Persian unity and enhance in the process the power of his own supporters.[69] The collapse of central authority, and above all of its revenues,[70] made the agreement with Britain attractive, even imperative, for those in Vossugh's following who hoped to build their fortunes on the revival of central government.

Here then were the makings of a successful experiment in informal empire along classic Palmerstonian lines, using British resources not to control Persia but to stimulate modernisation and its *Doppelgänger*, centralisation. The first signs were encouraging; the agreement had been favourably received except among quarters predictably hostile to Vossugh.[71] But before long the difficulties began to mount up. Even before August was out, Cox was urging Curzon to concede a time limit to the agreement and a date for renewal, modifications for which Vossugh had asked.[72] A few days later Cox reported that although support for the agreement was growing there was still much intrigue in Teheran, adding somewhat ingenuously that the main feeling was not against Curzon's agreement but against Vossugh's cabinet[73] – as if the two could be so easily dissociated. In mid-September, Vossugh, to Cox's approval, suppressed the opposition to the agreement, but did not still what the British minister described as 'unreasoning impatience' in the provinces 'for signs of its taking effect'.[74] Vossugh's opponents started rumours that the agreement would mean the abolition of the religious courts, while his own faction began to show signs of strain and difficulty, and a hunger for further British concessions with which to impress Persian opinion – support for frontier 'rectification' in Persia's favour, a larger loan, and an end to the Capitulations and to interference by Britain's provincial consuls.[75]

These hints and nods, relayed by Cox, were the early traces of a syndrome depressingly familiar to British policy-makers, especially, perhaps, in Egypt – the inability of those politicians in whom they had trusted to stand up to local rivals without doing violence to their relations with Britain. Curzon for his part was unwilling or unable, for domestic and international reasons, to make further concessions. Above all, he was not prepared to compromise on what swiftly became the central issue between Vossugh and the British: the ratification of the Anglo-Persian Agreement by the Persian parliament or *Majlis*. Evidence of popular consent in Persia was for Curzon an essential support of his diplomatic defence of Britain's predominance in Persia against French and American criticism, and of great importance to the credibility of his policy among his Cabinet colleagues. It constituted also an acid test of

Vossugh's ability to act the role in which the British had cast him. In the new year, however, Vossugh's difficulties multiplied. His relations with the Shah – legatee of a once powerful autocracy – worsened;[76] resentment against the appointment of his favourites in central and provincial administration increased;[77] and, worst of all, the penetrations of the Bolsheviks on Persia's north-eastern and north-western borders weakened his political authority and encouraged those who had watched his earlier triumphs with alarm. Time and again through the agency of Cox, Vossugh pressed Curzon to hold off the Bolsheviks in the Caucasus, to reinforce the British garrison at Kazvin, to provide more money, to postpone the withdrawal of the British force in east Persia.[78] The Persian government, wrote Curzon at an early stage, was 'disposed both to ask and to complain overmuch'.[79]

The logic of Vossugh's weakness was driving the British steadily towards the solutions which Cromer had deployed so effectively in Egypt in the 1880s. But Curzon, however much he might privately sympathise with Cox's advice, was unable to repeat the achievement of Gladstone and Salisbury. British policy towards Persia was already embarrassed by the failure to come to terms with the Turks, and by the strain which the long period of uncertainty all over the Middle East imposed upon British military resources. It was difficult to press for reinforcements to north Persia when other places, traditionally enjoying a higher priority in British foreign policy, seemed at risk. Curzon found it hard enough to resist the demands of the War Office that the British detachments at Batum and in east Persia should be withdrawn. Perhaps as an earnest of good faith, he gracefully accepted the Cabinet Finance Committee's decision that the British force in the southern province of Fars should be stood down and disavowed Cox's appeal for its retention.[80] But he stubbornly opposed the simultaneous decision to pull Malleson's force out of Khorasan where it confronted the triumphant Bolsheviks in Russian Turkestan, arguing that to do so would jeopardise the Anglo-Persian Agreement.[81] Here, however, Curzon was faced not only with Churchill's determination to relieve the Army estimates,[82] but with the refusal of the Government of India to contribute financially to the upkeep of the troops in south and east Persia.[83] The maintenance of British influence – the main function of the east Persia force – was not an Indian affair, remarked the Viceroy.[84] Not surprisingly, Curzon vehemently denounced this view of Indian interests,[85] but the alliance of the War Office and New Delhi was too much for him. On 5 May 1920 the Cabinet authorised the earliest withdrawal of Malleson's men.[86]

British evacuation of the southern and eastern periphery of Persia can have given little comfort to Vossugh and his followers in Teheran. But, by the early summer of 1920, they were faced with a more dangerous threat much closer to home as the southward drive of the Red Army against the remaining pockets of White Russian resistance brought them to the borders of Persian Azerbaijan and, with the capture of Baku, easy access to the Caspian. On 14 May, Vossugh pleaded with Curzon for an addition to the British force in north-west Persia – Norperforce[87] – on the grounds that if the Bolshevik armies occupied Persian Azerbaijan his government would fall and with it the agreement.[88] Cox followed this appeal with an account of panic in Teheran and of the growing chorus against the British.[89] Curzon, however, was fully engaged with the struggle not to reinforce Norperforce but to prevent its abolition at Churchill's hands. Churchill's military advisers were uneasy at the exposed position of the force, with its far-flung detachments, lying as it did at the end of a long and vulnerable line of communications.[90] For them, the arrival of Soviet troops on Persia's frontiers was substantiation of their fears. For Churchill himself it was the urgency of making economies in defence spending, especially in the inflated garrisons in Mesopotamia, of which Norperforce was operationally and financially a component, which acted as the keenest spur; and over north Persia he found, perhaps, least resistance in the General Staff to the prospect of those 'arbitrary reductions of garrisons' against which Wilson, the Chief of the Imperial General Staff, registered a private protest.[91]

Throughout May and June, Churchill launched repeated attacks upon the retention of any British troops in north Persia. But despite the declining credibility of Curzon's 'rehabilitation' of Persia, despite the pressure for public economies, and despite the humiliating British evacuation of Enzeli on the Caspian in the face of Soviet troops,[92] Curzon succeeded in keeping a British force at Kazvin to preserve British influence in north Persia and British prestige in Teheran. Even amid the crisis of mid-June, he was able to beat off Churchill's demand for the military evacuation of Persia.[93] The strength of Curzon's position lay partly in the influence and standing of Cox whom he deployed at an important meeting of the Cabinet Finance Committee in the middle of August,[94] and partly in the support he could muster in Cabinet. Here his principal ally was Milner[95] who had on several previous occasions displayed a close sympathy for the overall shape of Curzon's Eastern policies while differing over some of the details. Milner sought to mollify Churchill, and take the wind from his sails, by agreeing that the level of military spending in Mesopotamia and Persia was far too high – as a permanent commitment.[96] But, he insisted, conditions in the Middle East were too unstable to permit an early withdrawal without lasting damage to British interests. Time was needed to reach an agreement with Russia, and to decide the future of Turkey-in-Asia. And for Britain's plans in the Middle East, a cooperative and orderly Persia was essential: it was better to hold on 'temporarily' in north Persia rather than see a collapse into anarchy, for 'a chaotic or, worse still, a hostile Persia', would render Britain's position in Mesopotamia 'untenable, or only tenable at such a cost that we should certainly end by giving it up'.[97]

Milner and Curzon backed these arguments, according to Montagu, with the threat of resignation if they were overruled and were supported by Austen Chamberlain, a former Secretary of State for India.[98] Lloyd George, although much importuned by Churchill, was unwilling to take serious issue with Curzon,[99] perhaps because he was anxious to carry the Foreign Secretary with his policy of negotiation with Soviet Russia. But both Milner and Curzon were aware that retaining a military presence in Persia was no more than a temporary palliative, and that unless British diplomacy at Teheran could yield some positive results the pressure for troop withdrawals would become irresistible.[100] The crux of the matter was the continuing inability of successive Persian ministries to contemplate summoning the *Majlis* and presenting the agreement for ratification, thus clearing the way for financial and military reform and enabling Curzon to claim that a genuine local power base existed for his policy. But although the presence of British troops secured a succession of pliant ministers after the fall of Vossugh in June 1920, and although it allowed the vigorous new commander of Norperforce, Ironside, to dispose of the old White Russian officer corps of the Cossack brigade who were considered a major obstacle to army reform and British influence alike,[101] it could not solve the deeper difficulties of Vossugh's successors. They remained chronically incapable of exerting the critical degree of control required to produce a compliant assembly of notables. For Curzon, after his brave talk in Cabinet, the embarrassment was unwelcome and his ill-feeling was vented on Norman, Cox's unfortunate replacement at Teheran.[102] By early November, with renewed demands for military economies after the end of the Iraq rebellion, it was clear that the old justifications for retaining a garrison and paying a subsidy to the Persian government would no longer suffice. Parliament, Curzon told Norman, was unlikely to allow the troops to stay beyond the spring when the passes re-opened,[103] an attitude with which, by this time, Curzon himself seemed in sympathy. A fortnight later, Norman returned the despairing but accurate prediction that there was no prospect of ratification by the end of the year – the time limit set by the British Cabinet if the troops and subsidy were to continue.[104]

By the end of 1920, Curzon's grand scheme for a rejuvenated Persia under an informal but vigorous British influence had come to nothing, overwhelmed less by the force of Bolshevik arms or the resilience of Persian nationalism than by the stimulus which Russian aid had given to provincial particularism in north Persia, and to the opposition of those at Teheran who stood to gain little from administrative reform under British auspices. Yet what is striking is not the eagerness of Curzon's Cabinet colleagues to abandon a policy which had brought military embarrassment and political failure, but their apparent willingness to go on endorsing his attempt to extract ratification of the agreement from a Persian parliament. Not until a full fifteen months after the first signature of the agreement did the Cabinet finally lose patience and set a firm date on the recall of Norperforce and the suspension of the subsidy. And that decision was probably taken for reasons relating less to Persia in itself than to tactics within the Cabinet.[105] For almost all of 1920, however, Curzon and Milner were able, in the face of Churchill's fulminations, the muted grumblings of the Prime Minister,[106] the doubts of Fisher, and the (for Curzon) irritating scepticism of the Government of India, to win Cabinet acquiescence for their proposition that a compliant regime at Teheran was vital to Britain's interests in the Middle East.

Imperial Control in Iraq 1919–1920

In 1919, as the high tide of her wartime military occupations began to recede from Trans-Caspia, the Caucasus and Syria, the defence of Britain's imperial interests in the Middle East, outside Egypt, came to hinge more and more upon three great centres and the political systems they were expected to control. These three centres were Constantinople, Teheran and Baghdad, which the British had made, for their own purposes, the administrative headquarters of the occupied Turkish *vilayets* of Basra, Baghdad and Mosul. In Turkey and Persia, British policy had attempted to work through existing political institutions, suitably modified, to create a climate congenial to Britain's longstanding strategic interests. In the occupied *vilayets*, called collectively

Mesopotamia or Iraq, these institutions had first of all to be created, and the terms of British control defined. In both these tasks, the British had, necessarily, to bear in mind the part that Baghdad would play in the overall pattern of their new Middle Eastern policy.

In the year which followed the Mudros armistice there had been little controversy among ministers over the future of Mesopotamia and, until August 1919, no discussion of its affairs outside the confines of the Eastern Committee. Then, when the Cabinet came to consider Britain's desiderata for the forthcoming Turkish peace negotiations, the presumption that Britain would control Mesopotamia went through on the nod, at the same moment when the future of Constantinople was furiously and inconclusively debated. The reasons for this apparently uncritical acceptance of a major new territorial responsibility may be found partly, perhaps, in the emotions aroused by the protracted and costly struggle there against the Turks; partly also in the fact that a British presence of some kind had been envisaged since the early days of the war; and partly in the anxiety of some quarters of the government to preserve a British monopoly in the exploitation of Mesopotamia's oil resources. But, it may be suspected, this unanimity of ministerial feeling was only possible because, at this stage, the full meaning and implications of the commitment had been neither grasped nor weighed.

In fact, the bare commitment to control Mesopotamia left unanswered a whole catechism of fundamental questions. No orthodoxy existed within the Cabinet in regard to the degree of direct control which Britain should exercise, nor the mode of administration which would be employed. This was not surprising since there had been no decision as to the precise function which Mesopotamia as a whole (rather than Basra) was expected to serve in Britain's Eastern security system; nor over the related issue of whether the three *vilayets* were to form a unitary state or a loose confederation under varying degrees of British domination. It had not been decided whether the substantial Kurdish population in the Mosul *vilayet* should be accommodated within a territory predominantly Arab, nor whether the Arab notables of the three *vilayets* could be harnessed together in a central administration. All these questions were to perplex British policy-makers throughout the life of the Lloyd George coalition largely because their solution depended upon Britain's relations with France, Persia and above all with Turkey. British policy in Mesopotamia was thus the creature of more far-reaching calculations about the shape of Britain's power and influence in the East.

Since the summer of 1918, the civil administration of the occupied territories had been in the hands of A. T. Wilson who had been nominated as Cox's deputy on the latter's appointment to Teheran. Theoretically, the political framework for the administration had been laid down firstly by the Anglo-French Declaration of November 1918, and subsequently by the gloss which the Eastern Committee and the India Office had added. These additions had referred to the undesirability of annexation or the creation of a formal protectorate, and to the need to make some show of consulting the population.[107] In February, Montagu had told Wilson that 'our objective should be a flexible constitution . . . such as will provide for Arab participation as time goes on in the actual government and administration of the country . . .'.[108] At a meeting of the Eastern Committee in mid-April, when Wilson was authorised to set up six provinces, including an Arab province in Mosul, with a fringe of autonomous Kurdish states, Curzon reiterated Montagu's call for a flexible constitution 'which should . . . prevent Arab nationalism being drawn into permanent opposition to British rule'.[109] In practice, however, Wilson was left the widest discretion in interpreting these sybylline instructions for much of 1919.

Wilson's approach was, perhaps, most influenced by the peculiar administrative conditions prevailing in the conquered *vilayets* at the end of the war. For in many areas British control had only been established in the most tenuous form and depended upon fragile bargains struck with tribal sheikhs. At the same time the civil administration in Mesopotamia, as in Egypt, had to serve as the handmaiden to a war machine with a voracious appetite for labour, food, fuel, transport animals, and building materials.[110] Since well over 200 000 men of the British and Indian armies remained in Mesopotamia for many months after the armistice, this appetite, and the burden it placed upon the administration, was slow to diminish.[111] For these reasons, Wilson was reluctant to contemplate any major political changes which would lessen British authority, not least because he feared that their result would be to jeopardise the collection of the land revenue, and thus the solvency of government.[112] Still less was he ready to consider any proposal which would introduce members of the Sharifian dynasty into positions of power and influence. To London's desire for evidence of Arab 'participation' in the government – a stratagem devised to embarrass French claims to Syria – he was unsympathetic. What he offered the Eastern Committee in April 1919, and thought they had accepted, was no more than consultative councils at a local level, and the appointment of selected Arabs as district governors[113] – a scheme which had the obvious merit of retaining full control over the central government and the pace of devolution firmly in his own hands.

What Wilson presented in 1919 was an uncompromising case for a unitary Mesopotamia, a British protectorate in all but name, with a 'steel frame' of British officials who would retain an overall executive control in the districts. It might have been expected that his ideas would find favour in those quarters of the coalition where the defence of British interests on the western marches of the Indian Empire was regarded as of dominating importance. Yet Curzon, the greatest champion of those interests in the government, gave Wilson's scheme no support, and became indeed his severest critic in the ministry.

Curzon was initially reluctant to intervene directly in the running of Mesopotamia, responsibility for which was shared between the India Office and the War Office (for civil and military affairs respectively), but he was hostile from the first to any grand project that would extend the sway of the Baghdad government into Kurdish khanates north and east of Mosul; and cautious of any scheme which appeared to entrench the wartime recourse to direct rule in the post-war politics of Mesopotamia. In August 1919 he spoke against any forward movement into Kurdistan, and warned that Mesopotamia could not be treated as a second India.[114] In November he attacked Wilson's regime for being too expensive and for running counter to the Anglo-French Declaration of 1918. Again he urged that the more northerly parts of Kurdistan should be left out of the new Mesopotamian state. 'The northern boundary of Mesopotamia', he told the Eastern Committee, 'should be brought down as far south as possible.'[115] For a time Curzon's attempts to interfere in Mesopotamia by goading the India Office were frustrated by the refusal of Sir Percy Cox, to whose judgment the Eastern Committee was asked constantly to defer, to make any criticism of Wilson's policy.[116] But in the spring of 1920, the imminence of the San Remo conference where the prospective French and British mandates in the Middle East were to be discussed, gave him a further opportunity and an immediate incentive. He made a fresh assault on the direction in which Wilson's constitutional preferences seemed to be taking him. 'He did not', he announced to the Committee, 'like the idea of Sir Percy Cox[117] sitting in Council surrounded by ten so-called Arab ministers. He wished to avoid starting Mesopotamia on Egyptian lines.'[118] He rehearsed his objections to Wilson's desire for the absorption of the Kurds into the new state. The Committee had to decide, he concluded, between that school which favoured direct administration and the 'Native State school'.[119] When Wilson reported the proposal of the

Bonham-Carter Committee[120] that Mesopotamia be governed broadly on Egyptian lines, Curzon insisted that he be prevented from publishing the Committee's recommendations.[121] When Wilson ignored this advice from London, and opined that no significant devolution could be carried through within two years, Curzon pressed relentlessly for his immediate recall and replacement by Cox.[122] Probably only the outbreak of the rebellion saved Wilson from this humiliation.

Curzon's repeated demands for a rapid devolution of power, and for a swift contraction of Britain's political and military role in the far north of Mesopotamia, are at variance with his common reputation as an imperialist of the first water. Yet it would be reckless to suppose that the leopard had changed his spots or that his thinking had been compromised by a sudden passion for liberalism in imperial policy. He had, after all, proclaimed that Baghdad was to be the pivot of Britain's position in relation to Persia and the Persian Gulf.[123] In fact, Curzon's utterances on Mesopotamia were conditioned by his view of the wider context of British policy in the East. A clue to his thinking is to be found in his distaste for any British involvement in Kurdistan which, he said, must not be allowed to become the North-West Frontier of Mesopotamia and an intolerable strain on its finances.[124] Kurdistan must be autonomous but a barrier to pressure from the north. 'We had to contemplate', he had observed in November 1919, 'the possibility of a resuscitated Turkey, and it was advisable for us to consider whether the provision of a little help towards the establishment of the Kurds as an independent nation would not repay us a hundred times over.'[125] But the problem, as Montagu pointed out and as Curzon well knew, was to keep the Turks out of Kurdistan. This task Curzon intended to perform not by licensing the costly sub-imperialism of Wilson, but through the terms of the general peace settlement with Turkey. A forceful diplomacy at the Straits, not Indian methods on the Zab, were to secure the British position in Iraq, a choice of method which, as we have seen, pushed Curzon towards a confrontation with the Kemalists and a reluctant partnership with the Greeks.

Curzon chose, therefore, to seek Britain's objectives by action at the centre and not the periphery of Turkey's defunct imperial system. His inclination was reinforced by the pressure of other considerations: the hope that the French might be persuaded to impose a control in Syria not more rigorous than that applied by the British in Mesopotamia, thus softening the political and strategic impact of France's unwelcome irruption into the Arab lands; and the desire to avoid further heavy expenditure in the East. Wilson's schemes were, according to Curzon's plans for the Middle East, not only unnecessary but counter-productive, causing distortions in British policy and in the allocation of defensive resources. Curzon himself had no special passion for the extension of close administration on the model of British India and his ironic comment on its Supreme Government is well known. The alternative, where feasible, of indirect control on the model of the Indian States had attracted him in the past[126] and found an echo, perhaps, in his expressed belief that only the Hashemite prince Abdullah could hold the disparate provinces of Iraq together.[127]

For Curzon, then, the strategic benefits of the conquest of Mesopotamia could be secured by the economical method of setting up a 'native state' which would look south and east to India, not north and west to Turkey. But as crisis followed crisis in Constantinople, this attractive and convenient prospect began to fade. In the meantime, despite his criticism of Wilson, Curzon was unwilling to sanction any specific constitutional announcement in Iraq before the terms of the mandates had been settled between Britain and France, and in advance of a Turkish peace.[128] This timetable was overtaken by the outbreak of the Iraq rebellion in June 1920, but, even before that, the indecisive management of Mesopotamian affairs between Curzon, Montagu and Wilson had been attacked by Churchill. Churchill's feelings are not difficult to understand. He had been enjoined by the Cabinet early in 1920 to achieve drastic savings in the costs of occupation in Mesopotamia. By the summer the crisis at the Straits, the worsening situation in Ireland, and the threat of widespread industrial unrest at home were inflicting great strains on an army still struggling to recover from the upheavals of demobilisation and the return to a peacetime footing. As a departmental minister Churchill was determined to exercise close control over the distribution of the army's strength and bitterly resented the Foreign Office's 'directing impulse' in Mesopotamian policy which, he claimed, resulted in an extravagant use of army manpower in remote districts of the country.[129] The deployment of the garrison must be brought back, he insisted, under the effective supervision of the War Office which had to pay for it, and limits set to the demands of the civil administration, even if this meant abandoning parts of Mesopotamia for a period.[130] But although he pressed his attack in Cabinet and by direct appeal to the Prime Minister, Churchill made little headway against the opposition of Curzon and Milner who stood together over Mesopotamia as over Persia, arguing that while Turkey's future was uncertain Britain's military grip could not be relaxed.[131] Their opposition and the unwillingness of Lloyd George to intervene, took strength from the reservations of the General Staff over any withdrawal to the railheads, a policy which, they argued, would only weaken the military position further and generate a flood of refugees.[132]

Churchill undoubtedly feared that in the event of a military disaster in Mesopotamia, or a violent public outcry against the high level of military spending there, he would become the scapegoat for decisions in the making of which, as he complained to Curzon, he had had no share.[133] Churchill was haunted by the personal catastrophe which his public, solitary and unjust identification with the failure at Gallipoli had brought upon him. It may be the radicalism of his proposals in May was primarily intended to force the real authors of policy out into the open and require his colleagues to share publicly the burden of responsibility. Certainly Churchill was insistent that his defence of Mesopotamian expenditure to the House of Commons in June should enjoy the personal support of the Prime Minister.[134] But clearly his demand for the evacuation of large parts of Iraq did not persuade the Cabinet, nor, perhaps, was intended to. When the scattered and bloody uprisings in the territory threatened Britain's control, ministers resolved 'to plough through this dismal country'[135] and suppress the rebellion. Reinforcements were brought from India, the reduction of military expenditure halted and the dominions canvassed for contingents.[136]

For while ministers had been arguing over how British authority in Iraq should be redeployed, the foundations on which it rested were crumbling rapidly. By the spring of 1920, some parts of Mesopotamia had been under British military occupation for nearly six years and everywhere the administration retained many of the characteristics of a military government careless of custom and imbued with the belief that order and discipline were the supreme requirements of the moment. But however firm the grip which Wilson and his cohort of political officers sought to keep on the conquered territories, there were, inevitably, potent causes of unrest and uncertainty at work among those who had lost the privileges and benefits which Ottoman rule had conferred on its collaborators and those whose hopes of an enlarged power and influence had received little encouragement from the kind of regime over which Wilson presided. The permanence of British rule, its ultimate form, the success of the nationalist revival in Turkey, the fate of Feisal and Hashemite aspirations in Syria, the influence of Wilsonian ideals on the great powers, the political future of the Kurds, all had remained in doubt while the Allies turned gradually from their European preoccupations to decide upon the political settlement of the Middle East. Fear and uncertainty, hope and expectation necessarily flourished among those in the three *vilayets* who were concerned to protect and promote the interests of their family, tribe, community, religion, business or political network.

Wilson's achievement had been to maintain an uneasy stability while the political future of Mesopotamia remained in limbo. But after the spring of 1920 there were increasing signs that the containment of its multifarious discontents was becoming steadily more difficult. As the fate of Turkey and Syria moved towards a crisis the danger that the pent-up frustrations of the heterogeneous communities of Iraq would burst the dam impressed itself upon the Civil Commissioner in Baghdad. Both in Mesopotamia and in the East generally, he told Hirtzel, 'we have got the wolf by the ears . . . if we let go any position we hold we are done for, or at best committed to hostilities with the wolf'.[137] One cause of Wilson's anxiety was the resentment provoked by the army of occupation and the political insensitivity of its commanders over whom he had no authority.[138] But he regarded the supporters of Feisal as the greatest threat to imperial control in Mesopotamia and remarked bitterly on the patronage which the home government had bestowed on Feisal's cause in the past. The turbulence of Feisal's followers along the unregulated border with Syria, and the intrigues of his admirers in Baghdad and the Mesopotamian towns[139] seemed indeed the most visible political opposition to British rule – although not, as it turned out, the real source of Wilson's difficulties in the months to come. Moreover, the existence of groups of armed men, loyal to Feisal and beyond the reach of the civil administration, appeared a dangerous challenge to a government such as Wilson's whose authority derived largely from the myth that its power was omnipotent and irresistible.

Three connected events gave the signal for the outbreak of widespread disorders in Iraq. The distribution of mandates at the San Remo conference placed it beyond doubt that the fading dream of a free Arab confederacy under Feisal would be substituted by the harsh reality of a partition of the Fertile Crescent between France and Britain and the perpetuation of their influence over Syria and the Iraq *vilayets*. Then, as the French set out to establish an effective authority over the hinterland of Syria and over Feisal's political headquarters in Damascus, the opposition of his supporters erupted into an open conflict with the French army and generated great excitement among those who may have thought that the hour of liberation had struck. Thirdly, the publication of the terms which the Allies intended to enforce in the Turkish peace settlement lent colour to the belief – widespread in the Islamic world – that the Western powers were determined to destroy the authority of the Caliph, fracture the unity of Islam and open the way for the disintegration of the true faith. The effect of these events, disseminated among populations whose suspicion of alien rule was already considerable, and whose credulous reception of rumour, propaganda and religious xenophobia was heightened by the disturbed conditions already created by the aftermath of conquest and the presence of a foreign garrison, was explosive. After the scattering of an army detachment by disaffected tribesmen near Rumaitha on the Euphrates in late June 1920, there were outbreaks of violent disorder over a wide area of the country and in many districts the British officials who supervised the financial and judicial administration – Wilson's eyes and ears – were driven out or, in some cases, murdered.[140]

The breakdown of British authority was prolonged and severe. By the end of July, after a month of spreading revolt, Wilson was predicting British withdrawal from the Euphrates valley – much of the southern half of Iraq – 'because our military weakness is so extreme'.[141] A fortnight later, he warned that the Mosul *vilayet* might have to be evacuated.[142] British control, had Wilson's fears been realised, would have been reduced to the area around Basra, Baghdad city and whatever towns British garrisons were able to defend. In fact, while risings occurred in different parts of Iraq, on the upper Euphrates, at Samarra on the upper Tigris, at Kifri and Erbil in the north-east, the revolt against British rule did not become general. On the lower Tigris, around Basra and in the Mosul region no rebellion took place. The heart of the revolt lay among the tribal communities of the lower Euphrates south of Baghdad where resistance to British rule derived in part from the new revenue burdens which the British had placed on the notables and the reaction which these notables encountered when they attempted to enforce a wider influence in their localities.[143] The close proximity of the holy centres of the Shi'ites, the predominant Muslim sect in Iraq, and the loathing of the priests for foreign Christian rule, probably intensified, in the special conditions of 1920, local antagonism against the government in Baghdad. Nor, in Wilson's jaundiced view, were British efforts to suppress the rebellion in its early stages assisted by the poor quality of the garrison troops and the vacillations of their commander-in-chief.[144]

Yet, despite the severity of the uprising which took more than three months to subdue, which cut off Baghdad's rail communications to Basra and which required substantial military reinforcements to be sent (mainly from India) at short notice,[145] the disorders in Iraq failed to generate or to sustain a political movement comparable with the *Wafd* in Egypt. No 'national' leaders emerged to bargain for constitutional concessions or with any claim to control the rebels at large. The lack of any concerted protest in the towns and the absence of any figurehead capable of weaving diffuse local grievances into a rudimentary political programme gave the revolt the character not so much of an outburst of national feeling as of a rural backlash against the age-old oppressions of government and town, a tribal *jacquerie* innocent of any large political ideas. Certainly Wilson himself believed that the Shi'ite tribesmen 'are out against all government as such',[146] that the rebels had no notion of what they were fighting for,[147] and (by mid-August 1920) that the 'revolutionary movement has for some time past ceased to have any political aspect and has become entirely anarchic'.[148] No one, he went on, 'appears more anxious than the leading mujtahids [learned elders] and many of the leading people in Baghdad to put an end to the disturbances they themselves have created . . .'.[149] 'What we are up against', he told another correspondent, 'is anarchy plus fanaticism. There is little or no Nationalism.'[150] Wilson's analysis was not disputed by the imperial government. No question arose of allaying the revolt by conciliation. Instead order was restored by the time-honoured methods of the Indian frontier: the punitive expedition and the show of force to overawe the tribes. Nevertheless, from the débâcle which had overtaken his model government, Wilson drew a sorrowful conclusion. 'Our policy has failed', he confessed, 'and we must find a way out.'[151]

The effect of the rebellion was not, therefore, to shake the determination of the ministers that Iraq should remain a part of Britain's security system in the Middle East, whatever form its internal administration might take. But the shock of an open revolt and the costs of pacification gave weight to Churchill's demand that the Cabinet should formulate a policy which would define the political objectives of the military occupation and relieve the War Office of what he saw as an open-ended and embarrassing commitment. When the extent and seriousness of the revolt became obvious, a meeting of the Cabinet Finance Committee was convened. Its recommendation was that Cox should be placed in charge at Baghdad as soon as possible. Beyond this touching demonstration of confidence the Committee would not go, although it noted in passing that Wilson's suggestion that Feisal be considered as head of an Arab administration would antagonise the French; and speculated whether it might still be necessary to create more than one state in the occupied territory.[152] This was not to carry matters very far. A few days later, Montagu in classic fashion called for a rallying of the moderates in Mesopotamia – the 'pro-British nationalists' – under one head, either Feisal or Sayyid Talib, the political 'boss' in

Basra.[153] But when the Cabinet next considered its policy, it confined itself to authorising Cox to assume full powers for a political reconstruction even while military operations continued.[154]

Thus, all the ministers could agree upon at this stage was that Cox should be trusted to set up an Arab government which, without a weakening of Britain's overall control, would, as he himself had claimed,[155] take the heat out of the agitation and clear the way for a vast saving of military resources. Cox went to work with a will, recruiting Arab ministers and appointing Arab replacements to the British political officers in the districts.[156] Beyond these immediate steps to place the rod of political discipline in part at least in Arab hands, his plans were opaque. In London, continuing uncertainties about the consequences of remaining in Iraq began to build up fresh pressures within the Cabinet. Montagu, who was still responsible for civil administration in the country, was alarmed by the terms of the British mandate for Iraq which the Foreign Office had drafted. 'It launches us', he wrote, 'upon liabilities the force and expenditure to fulfil which nobody can forecast.' It would be 'intensely unpopular in this country' and would appear in the public mind to contradict the purposes of Cox's appointment – the careful limitation of Britain's commitment. For his part, Montagu declared, if the mandate were to mean more expenditure and a larger garrison, he would support Churchill's call for evacuation.[157] The Indian Secretary, whose management of the Amritsar affair had already made him an object of loathing to a section of the ministry's supporters in the Commons, had no taste for the odium which a protracted military and financial burden might bring – especially since Churchill was so determined to emphasise that the War Office was the servant and not the fountainhead of policy. His attempt to gain a wider backing for his fears was frustrated by Cox's prompt declaration of approval for the terms of the draft mandate,[158] but within a few weeks Churchill re-entered the fray.

Churchill's discontent had been re-awakened by the warning of his commander in Mesopotamia that there could be no hope of reducing its existing garrison strength before April 1921, and no certainty even then of a rapid return to the troop levels of June 1920; let alone the kind of economies the Cabinet had called for early in the year.[159] This would mean a large supplementary estimate since the War Office vote had made no provision for so great a force; and it again called into question the promise of financial and military relief implicit in Cox's appointment. Churchill was plainly reluctant to go before the Commons clothed only in such half-knit strands of policy as had yet emerged. At the beginning of December, he carried his grievances to a conference of ministers. The War Office, he complained, was being asked to finance the policies of other departments: a large part of its additional requirement would go to pay for the services of its fellow departments in the Middle East, and for the use of the Indian army.[160] And it was well known that the Commons would be very hostile to further expenditure unless a convincing programme for bringing it under control were presented. All Churchill obtained, however, was the inevitable promise to consult Cox about troop levels.[161] A week later he tried again without success for an ampler definition of policy.[162]

As the date of the Commons debate on his estimates drew nearer, Churchill revived the tactic he had employed in May. He demanded a change of policy sufficiently drastic that the Cabinet would be forced to take account of his objections and frame some kind of answer. In May Churchill had urged the evacuation of the remoter districts; in December he pressed for a military withdrawal to a line covering Basra and the Persian oil fields, abandoning two thirds of Mesopotamia – a step which, he claimed, would reduce the cost of military control from some thirty million pounds to the more modest figure of eight.[163] For this proposal Churchill claimed the support of the General Staff. As he had no doubt calculated, it produced a vehement response. To add fuel to the flame, he told the Cabinet that the General Staff no longer believed that Mesopotamia was an appropriate point from which to try to defend the approaches to India.[164] Churchill's case was challenged (almost certainly by Curzon) on both military and political grounds: withdrawal to the Basra line would not achieve the promised economies because of the disorder that would follow; while the political consequence of withdrawal would be the abortion of the mandate and the entry of the Turks, 'possibly in collusion with the Bolsheviks', into the vacuum created.[165] In the afternoon the debate continued. A. T. Wilson, recalled from Baghdad, added his witness against the feasibility of a retreat to Basra, and predicted that Turkish rule would replace British control in Mosul and Baghdad. The Cabinet reached no decision: but Wilson's support for Churchill's critics had touched a raw nerve. 'The Cabinet generally felt', the minutes recorded, 'that the re-establishment of Turkish rule would be a most deplorable sequel to a great and successful campaign. . . .'[166]

This left Churchill to face the Commons without stronger props of policy than had already been vouchsafed: the promised transition to an undefined Arab government. He secured once again the rhetorical support of the Prime Minister. But two days after the debate, on 17

December, the Cabinet was persuaded to instruct Cox and Haldane, the army commander, to prepare plans for a withdrawal to the Basra line once the force in Persia had returned to Baghdad in the spring.[167] This coup of Churchill's brought an end to the stalemate in the Cabinet. The opposition to the War Minister was mobilised. Montagu reiterated the arguments against the 'Basra solution': Britain, he wrote, would be breaking her pledges, without any certainty of savings, by such a policy.[168] Cox's warning that Churchill's proposal was 'fundamentally incompatible' with the acceptance of the mandate was circulated.[169] Curzon expressed solidarity with Montagu.[170] But Churchill, buoyed up, perhaps, by the irritation of those ministers with primarily domestic responsibilities at the management of affairs in Iraq, was able to extract a price for his acquiescence in the continued military occupation of Mosul and Baghdad *vilayets*. Henceforth, the Cabinet decided, responsibility for Britain's policy in Mesopotamia would no longer be shared between the War Office and the India Office; and the coordinating role of the Eastern Committee, which allowed Curzon so much influence, would become superfluous. Instead, the full responsibility for the political control and internal security of Mesopotamia, as of Palestine, would fall upon a Middle Eastern department to be created within the Colonial Office. The framing of policy and the raising of all funds which that policy might require were at last to be centralised within one department. And that department was itself to come under the authority not, as Curzon wished, of the Foreign Office, but, as Churchill had long urged, of the Colonial Office,[171] whose record of parsimonious but trouble-free administration in Africa may, in ministers' minds, have been contrasted favourably with the Foreign Office's expensive ventures in Persia and the Caucasus, and its continuing difficulties in Egypt.

This compromise ended the acute phase of the ministerial crisis over Mesopotamia, and its terms are revealing. They suggest that despite the desultory discussion of Feisal's merits as a ruler, propagated by Churchill's opponents to lend credibility to their case for remaining in all three *vilayets*, and despite Churchill's ability to exploit a strong undercurrent of discontent within the Cabinet, the real issue between the senior ministers was not whether Britain should control Iraq, which was implicit in the draft mandate; nor how Iraq was to be governed, which remained undecided; nor the objects of Britain's continued presence there, which were not discussed. Rather it was the more immediate question of who was to bear the burden of defending what was recognised as a necessary but unpopular policy against the kicks and curses of members of all parties in Parliament, and at a moment when the tensions of coalition politics were being aggravated by political and economic difficulties in many parts of the imperial system. Churchill, Montagu and Milner all wished to avoid the poisoned chalice. Curzon would probably have liked to retain the system against which Churchill had railed, but, in the last resort, struggled to keep the strings of Eastern policy in his hands. But whatever their past differences over the direction of policy, Curzon, Milner, Montagu, Churchill and Lloyd George were all prepared, in December 1920, to stand firm in Mesopotamia until Cox's efforts bore fruit, and to contemplate the diplomatic risks of employing Feisal as an agent of British policy if the High Commissioner in Baghdad could demonstrate his utility. It was left to Christopher Addison to complain in Cabinet that the creation of a new department did nothing to reduce the burdens imposed by the policy of control.[172]

British Policy in 1920: a Retrospect

Since early in 1919, at the bidding principally of Lloyd George and Curzon, British ministers had taken as their objective in Eastern policy the preservation of the extraordinary supremacy in the Middle East which their armies had won for them and which was symbolised in the Mudros armistice, concluded not between Turkey and the Western Allies but between Turkey and Britain only. To preserve a monopoly of influence in the region, they had been prepared to subscribe to the Wilsonian doctrine of self-determination, to talk the language of trusts and mandates, and to repudiate the spirit of the wartime agreements with France over the partition of Turkey. When the prospect unfolded at Mudros appeared threatened by French intransigence and military and financial stringency, the ministers had cut their losses by conceding the French a limited presence in Syria (countered by the demand for an enlarged British Palestine), and by abandoning the outworks of their overweening supremacy in the Caucasus and Trans-Caspia. But despite their revolt against the expulsion of the Turks from Constantinople, and the intermittent complaints of Montagu and Churchill, ministers had remained committed to the overall strategy laid down (for all their mutual misunderstandings, resentments and criticisms) by Lloyd George and Curzon: the strict containment of the new Turkish state in Anatolia; the securing of a dominating influence in the international aspects of Persian affairs; and the maintenance of an economical but effective British control over the strategic plains of the Tigris and

Euphrates. To sustain this grand strategy, the Cabinet had acquiesced in a continued confrontation with Turkish nationalism, the unleashing of Greek imperialism in Asia Minor, and the retention of a large and expensive British and Indian garrison in Persia and Mesopotamia.

By the autumn of 1920, however, the unity and coherence of this great programme of defensive imperialism was beginning to break down into piecemeal and conflicting expedients to meet the pressure of local emergencies. The pivot of British policy, on which the viability of the ministers' plans depended, was the construction of a moderate, pacific and compliant Turkish state, purged of its colonial aspirations, at peace with the stripling successor states which were to surround it to the south and east. To the achievement of such a state both Lloyd George and Curzon, though with differing emotions, were dedicated; but their efforts had thus far been in vain. The Turkish 'moderates' at Constantinople, despite British support, were incapable of subduing the 'extremists' at Angora, or indeed of exercising real authority over any part of the Anatolian hinterland. Without an army or a proper revenue, their credibility declined as time went on.[173] The British, however, continued to pin their hopes on the triumph of Constantinople over Angora, and, in the first instance, on the fortunes of the Greek army on whom, for want of any other force, had fallen the task of destroying the pretensions of the Kemalist regime. Throughout the latter half of 1920, in face of growing French and Italian opposition, and despite the fall of Venizelos and the Kemalist conquest of Armenia, Lloyd George and Curzon clung to their policy of applying the Sèvres Treaty without modification, and obtained the acquiescence, if no more, of their colleagues in this endeavour.[174]

The difficulties encountered in Turkey and the decision to make no concessions to Turkish nationalism (justified partly by the implicit analogy between Kemal and the discredited triumvirate of Turkish war leaders and partly by the prospect of a decisive Greek victory) reacted, however, upon the rest of the dispositions which Curzon especially had in view in the Middle East. For ministers were undoubtedly alarmed by the danger of Britain's involvement in a war at the Straits and by the strain which the threat of a Kemalist attack already imposed on the army's manpower and resources. Churchill from the War Office had pressed Lloyd George to deal with a 'really representative Turkish governing authority' as early as March 1920,[175] and in December renewed his appeal for a wholesale re-ordering of British policy to end the conflict between Britain and the Turkish nationalists.[176] His arguments were supported by the General Staff's appreciation of the strategic burden which the necessary assumption of Turkish hostility imposed, not least in Mesopotamia.[177] Churchill claimed in December that his call for friendship with Turkey was supported by Bonar Law, Chamberlain, Montagu and Milner, although they would seem to have expressed their views less forcefully than he.[178]

It is possible, though the evidence is at best circumstantial, that the decision to abandon Curzon's search for a secure client-regime in Persia and to end Britain's military presence there when the passes to Baghdad re-opened in the spring of 1921, was in part intended to meet Churchill's case that Britain was trying to do too much in the Middle East, and to forestall a Cabinet revolt such as that which had stopped Lloyd George and Curzon in their tracks in January. There were other grounds too for treating Teheran as of lesser moment than Constantinople or Baghdad. For the commitment to extend Britain's interest in Persia to embrace the north and centre of the country which was contained in Curzon's Anglo-Persian Agreement had been a by-product of the military crisis in the Middle East in 1918. It went well beyond the accepted limits of British involvement as these had been understood before 1914 – though not in Curzon's mind. The failure of Curzon's policy at Teheran seemed to justify those who shared Grey's view of the limits of British strength. But the core of the matter was the fact that north Persia, so it appeared, could be abandoned without inflicting immediate damage on Britain's position in the Persian Gulf or on the security of India's frontiers. The ungovernability of Persia, its vast distances and primitive communications turned, in this new situation, to Britain's advantage. For they made possible an alternative policy of concentrating British influence and activity along the Gulf littoral and in the old British sphere of influence: a return in effect to the strategy of local alliances which had obtained before the war.[179]

But in Mesopotamia no such alternative policy of a limited military and political commitment seemed viable. No mountain barrier guarded the approaches to Basra at the head of the Persian Gulf. Nor at the end of 1920 did there appear any possibility of setting up in Mosul or Baghdad successor states which could protect Britain's stake in the security of the Gulf. Ministers accepted the estimate of Cox and A. T. Wilson that pulling back to Basra would mean the return of the Turks to Baghdad, and that no reduction of the geographical scope of Britain's military and political presence would produce real savings unless the loss of the whole of Mesopotamia could be faced. Such an outcome the ministers dared not risk for domestic and international reasons alike.

Thus the deterioration of Britain's influence in Turkey and the growth of Kemalist power in eastern Anatolia produced a hardening of resolve towards the future of Mesopotamia, despite the internal dissensions which the costs of its garrisoning had generated within the government and the ranks of its supporters. The easy talk of creating an Arab façade and running down the administrative framework the British had created gave place to more realistic discussions about the ability of any Arab ruler to hold the gimcrack state together. This movement of opinion was most marked in Curzon whose earlier passion for a 'native state' was transformed by the failures and disasters of 1920 into a recognition that the expenditure against which he had fulminated must be borne until a suitable ruler could be found; and a determination that Britain should prevent at all costs the recrudescence of Turkish imperialism in Iraq. It was in this uncomfortable posture that the Cabinet's Eastern policy rested at the end of 1920. Not for the first time in Britain's imperial policy the failure of diplomacy at the Straits had led to the prolongation of a temporary occupation in a province of the Ottoman Empire.

8 The Limits of Imperial Power

The Decline of War Imperialism

For two years after the German and Turkish armistices, the formation of British imperial policy, especially in the Middle East, remained profoundly influenced by the ideas, the preconceptions and the priorities instilled by four years of war government. The continuation of this wartime mentality was reflected at home in the very high levels of army manpower and military spending which were tolerated, although grudgingly, long after January 1919 when demobilisation had begun; in the continuing interest which ministers displayed in the closer military integration of the Empire;[1] and in the formulation of plans designed to retain British manpower within the Empire through government participation in a programme of Empire settlement.[2] In the Middle East, the legacy of wartime strategic thinking showed itself in the willingness of ministers to endorse proposals which were aimed at excluding Britain's imperial rivals from political influence in the region. Moreover, the attainment of a costly military victory had encouraged a belief not only in the necessity of reconstructing the Ottoman and Persian Empires in ways which would buttress Britain's imperial security; but also in the practicability of such a venture. Thus for long after November 1918, few doubts had been entertained about the ultimate feasibility of British attempts to bend Persia and Turkey to their imperial design, even if there were differences about the right method to employ.

Towards the end of 1920, however, the flaws in this optimistic vision became more and more apparent, despite the reluctance of the directors of policy to admit that they had encountered more than transitory reactions against the side-effects of political change in the volatile societies of the Middle East. Thus in the last weeks of the old year, at the same time as departmental reorganisation was emerging as a palliative for ministerial disagreements over Mesopotamia, Lloyd George and Curzon, who had trenchantly opposed any modification of the Treaty of

Sèvres, at last acknowledged that concessions to Turkish feeling might be necessary to end the conflict between Greek and Turk in Anatolia, and to avoid the total collapse of their strategy for containing the Turkish state closely within ethnic boundaries. This was in part a gesture towards Churchill, whose insistence that their overall strategy in Turkey, Persia and Mesopotamia was dangerously unrealistic seemed to carry weight with senior members of the Cabinet. But it was also a recognition that the overthrow of Venizelos at the Greek polls in November 1920 and the probable restoration of Constantine to the throne would rupture such Anglo-French cooperation as still existed over the enforcement of the Sèvres Treaty, since it was well known that the French, at whose instance Constantine had been exiled and dethroned in 1917 for his pro-German sympathies, regarded his exclusion from the monarchy as 'imperative'.[3] The British attitude was ambiguous. Venizelos was regarded by Lloyd George and the Foreign Office alike as Britain's staunchest friend in the Middle East. Yet an attempt to lever his return to power by denying financial, military and diplomatic aid to his royalist opponents might precipitate a Kemalist triumph in Asia Minor, and expose the weak Allied garrisons at the Straits to disaster. In that eventuality, there would be no question of revising the Sèvres Treaty; only one of how best to bury it.[4]

For these reasons Curzon would have preferred to allow Constantine to resume the Greek throne under strict guarantees. But anxiety about French reaction dictated caution.[5] Early in 1921, therefore, the Cabinet was asked to approve fresh negotiations with the Turks; and at Paris later in the month Britain, France, Italy and Japan agreed to summon a peace conference to which the Kemalist regime would be allowed to send representatives.[6] But the conciliation of Turkey and the appeasement of French hostility to the prospect of a Greater Greece dominating, under Britain's aegis, the eastern Mediterranean, was not to extend very far. Curzon was prepared to make concessions over the increasingly uncertain future of Armenia, to concede Turkish 'supervision' in an autonomous Kurdistan, 'owing to our present position in Mesopotamia', and to offer Turkish suzerainty but not control in the Smyrna *vilayet*. But over Thrace, the administration of Constantinople, the demilitarised zone along the Straits and the internationalisation of the Straits themselves – all those facets of Ottoman power which had drawn Turkey into European politics before 1914 – no compromise was possible. And even these modest concessions were vigorously criticised by Lloyd George and Balfour as likely to encourage Kemalist intransigence and 'bring . . . fresh trouble in the East'.[7]

Lloyd George's reservations dominated British policy at the peace conference which met in London in mid-February.[8] For, while urging the Greeks to yield suzerainty over Smyrna to Turkey, and make other concessions, he vetoed any proposal to prohibit them from continuing their Anatolian campaign and tried to embarrass the French by arguing that any revision of the Sèvres Treaty should extend to the Arab lands as well, and that Feisal should present the Arab case.[9] When the conference broke down after a month, Lloyd George gave a veiled approval to Greek plans for a fresh offensive and authorised discussions between the Greek government and the Treasury regarding a new loan on the British market.[10]

The course and outcome of the London conference suggests that Lloyd George certainly, and Curzon probably, were not wholly convinced that their original plan for the containment of Turkey had failed, and that the war in Anatolia might not end after all in the destruction of Kemalism. The prospect of a successful Greek offensive in late March seemed to encourage Lloyd George to adopt a more uncompromising attitude towards the Angora government; while the unpredictable pattern of victory and defeat in Asia Minor seemed, not for the last time, to justify an informal partnership with Greece. Nevertheless, the conference was a turning-point in the evolution of policy towards Turkey: it signalled a grudging recognition that Kemal could no longer be treated merely as a rebel against the legitimate government in Constantinople; that unless the Greeks could gain an outright victory, it was he, and not the docile ministers of the Sultan who would control the new Turkey. The elaboration of Kemal's diplomacy, and his treaties with the Russians and the Afghans, reinforced this impression.

If the fate of Lloyd George and Curzon's grand strategy in Turkey was still unresolved in March 1921, the complete failure of the Foreign Secretary's plans for a reinvigorated Persia under British tutelage seemed manifest. Amid signs of an imminent disintegration of the Persian regime in the face of a Bolshevik advance on Teheran, Curzon confirmed to his minister there the Cabinet's resolve that, come what may, the British troops of Norperforce covering the Persian capital would be withdrawn in April.[11] In the meantime, Curzon confined himself to impressing upon Norman the importance of the Shah's not leaving the country as he wished; and urging upon the Treasury the necessity of preserving the South Persia Rifles as a disciplined force at least until the moment of British withdrawal.[12]

As he contemplated the ruin of his policy, two rival strategies were urged upon Curzon for the defence of those imperial interests which had once been used to justify intervention in the affairs of Persia. The first of these proposed, in effect, to abandon northern Persia to its fate, but to protect Britain's interest in the oil field and in the security of the Persian Gulf by setting up a new and more viable client-state in southern and central Persia with its capital at Isfahan or Shiraz. This idea had been broached within the Foreign Office towards the end of December 1920,[13] and clearly attracted Curzon. In early January he sought Norman's view as to the practicability of reaching an agreement with the Bakhtiari chieftains to protect the approaches to the oil fields and the Gulf. At the end of the month Cox, who as a former Political Resident in the Gulf and a former minister at Teheran disposed of considerable experience in Persian affairs, raised this possibility in a telegram to the Indian Secretary which was subsequently circulated to the Cabinet. With characteristic suppleness, Cox counselled against any hasty abandonment of Teheran, arguing that Bolshevism would not thrive in Persia, and that the Bolsheviks themselves were beset with difficulties. But were all attempts to 'rally our adherents' in the Persian capital to fail, then the alternative lay in encouraging an independent regime among the Bakhtiari and Kashgai of the south-west.[14]

This, the 'southern policy', was proselytised with more single-minded vigour by Armitage-Smith, veteran of a brief and frustrating term as Financial Adviser to the Persian government under the abortive Anglo-Persian Agreement. Britain could not afford, he argued, to let Persia relapse into anarchy. 'The North is lost at least for the moment. The South is not yet lost. . . .'[15] But to save the south, even if a subsidy from the Anglo-Persian Oil Company were forthcoming, would require a proper financial administration and the maintenance of order. Neither of these, observed the discarded adviser, could be promised north of Isfahan. The object of British policy, therefore, should be to move the Persian government to Isfahan; to replace the Shah with a more compliant Qajar princeling; to enlarge the South Persia Rifles; and to push through, in this more favourable setting, the measures of military and financial reform which the old agreement had envisaged.[16]

The geographical modification of his earlier design held some appeal for Curzon, who was severely embarrassed by the failure of his diplomacy at Teheran, and under some pressure to guarantee the safety of the Royal Navy's fuel supplies.[17] But the implications of such a policy were strongly criticised by the Indian Viceroy. Urging, like Cox, that Teheran should not be written off prematurely, Chelmsford passed to his main objection. Splitting up Persia 'into a Soviet government in the north and a Shah government, supported or dominated by Britain in the south' would not restore good relations between Britain and her Muslim subjects and allies. And only by 'working back to our old role of champions of Islam against the Russian Ogre', and regaining Muslim confidence and trust, could imperial security in south-west Asia be assured. This, of course, was no more than a Persian variation on the Government of India's Turkish theme, familiar and tuneless to Curzon's ear. But New Delhi could influence Persian policy more effectively than it could Lloyd George's and Curzon's treatment of the Turks: there was no question, Chelmsford concluded his message, of India's accepting any share of the financial and military burden of setting up a new client-state in south Persia.[18] These reservations were echoed by Norman at Teheran. An alliance between the British and the rapacious Bakhtiari tribes would, he thought, drive the rest of Persia into the arms of the Bolsheviks;[19] while the feasibility of creating a new state in south Persia would depend heavily on the financial assistance that London could provide.[20]

In the event, any decision by Curzon on this issue was precluded by political developments in Persia. On 21 February 1921, Reza Khan, an officer in the Persian Cossacks, staged a military coup in Teheran, ostensibly to secure a ministry capable of decisive action against the threat of a Bolshevik advance. The government formed at his instigation under Seyyid Zia ed-Din soon attracted enthusiastic comment from Norman. The new premier was the 'first who has ever seriously attempted to introduce reforms . . .' and had won the hearts of the British community in Teheran.[21] He was eager for British friendship, for British money and for the loan of British officers. But Curzon was irritated by the new government's insistence on the formal repudiation of the Anglo-Persian Agreement, and cynical of Norman's judgment. Nevertheless, the faint hope which the emergence of a new ministry held out could not be overlooked. Curzon therefore persuaded a reluctant War Office to sanction the loan of officers and wheedled a further subsidy from the Treasury to help with the reorganisation (or facilitate the disbandment) of the South Persia Rifles. But there was no question of a fresh British loan to Persia.[22]

The apparent but unpredictable improvement in Persian affairs put off for the moment serious consideration of the 'southern policy': probably, given the distaste of his Cabinet colleagues for further commitments in the East, to Curzon's real relief. At the same time, there appeared encouraging signs that the southward drive of Bolshevik revolutionary activity had halted. Indeed, at the beginning of January, in a secret telegram considerably at variance with his oft-stated fears of a Bolshevik take-over in Persia, Curzon confided to Norman his hopes of a mutual withdrawal of both British and Russian forces as a result of a Soviet-Persian agreement. To advance this cause he instructed Norman to make it known that 'we should be prepared to give . . . a definite undertaking that we harbour no aggressive designs against Bolsheviks through Persia'.[23] Privately, he began to adopt the optimism of the Indian government that all was not lost in north Persia,[24] although relapsing at times into despondency and self-pity. Such hopes were nourished by Norman's reports on the progress of Soviet-Persian negotiations in Moscow; by the seeming resilience of the new Persian government; and by the possibility, towards which he was beginning to look with some confidence, that the terms of an Anglo-Russian trade agreement would include a mutual recognition of interests in the East and the abandonment by the Bolsheviks of a strategy of subversion against the Indian Empire.[25] The contents of the Soviet-Persian Treaty of 26 February, which promised complete non-interference in Persian affairs by the Soviet government, except in the event of a third party using Persia as a base for an attack on Russia, came therefore as a relief to the directors of imperial policy. But how successfully the Persian government would stand up to the pressures of an active Soviet diplomacy at Teheran, as opposed to revolutionary particularism in Gilan, remained, in March 1921, uncertain.

The limited concessions which Lloyd George and Curzon had been prepared to make to Turkish nationalism and their reluctance to abandon Greece and all hope of Greek victory over Kemal seemed to suggest that both were still largely committed to the Sèvres Treaty as the centrepiece of the coalition's imperial policy in the Middle East. Yet it also seems clear that during the first quarter of 1921 there occurred a sea-change in the hopes and expectations of all those ministers with a direct responsibility for Britain's interests in the Middle East. After the Third Conference of London, and especially after the failure of the Greek offensive that followed it, it was difficult to build with any confidence on the assumption that Turkey would ever peacefully submit to the Sèvres Treaty in its pristine form. Turkish nationalism was a force which would have to be given far greater weight than hitherto in the calculations of imperial strategy. At the same time, the coalition ministers had come to acknowledge the hopelessness of trying to establish Britain as the paramount power in Persia on the old (pre-1914) Egyptian model, and the necessity of taking a more realistic view of Britain's military strength in the hinterland of south-west Asia. Above all, perhaps, there had been an important change in the attitude of British ministers towards Russia. The Anglo-Soviet Trade Agreement of March 1921 marked a grudging acceptance that Bolshevik control over the former Russian empire was almost complete and that the international activity of the new Soviet state, even in those territories 'liberated' from Russian control after 1917, would have to be accommodated within the ordinary conventions of great power diplomacy.[26]

The revival of Russian power and influence in Afghanistan, central Asia, Persia and on the eastern borders of Turkey seemed at first sight and to some observers to augur a seismic change in the terms on which Britain could guard the routes to India and the Indian frontier itself. In November 1920, Curzon had claimed that 'the Russian menace in the East is incomparably greater than anything else that has happened in my time to the British Empire'.[27] But it is doubtful whether that menace was as serious or as novel as Curzon wished it to seem. The official mind in London exaggerated the sinister capacities of the Bolsheviks by failing to grasp that Bolshevism was not just anarchism; that its ability to exploit the nationalist ferment in Asia was limited by exigencies of colonial policy no less tormenting than those faced by London. To throw Russian power behind pan-Islamic or pan-Turanian movements might unsettle the British; but it was certain to endanger in the process Soviet control over the southern Caucasus, Turkestan and Central Asia.[28] The substance of Soviet diplomacy in early 1921 showed how clearly this was understood in Moscow.[29] The achievement of Russian policy in Persia, Afghanistan and the Caucasus was not to build launching platforms for an assault on the British Empire. Rather it was to serve notice that the brief interval during which the nineteenth-century pattern of Anglo-Russian rivalry had been suspended was now over. Curzon's angry reaction to this development, like his opposition to any compromise which might allow Turkey to become once again a European as well as an Asian power, was a mark of his deep commitment to an important but unstated war aim: that victory in 1918 should lead to the permanent abolition of great power rivalries in the unstable polities of south-west Asia, where, since the 1880s, they had constantly threatened the security of Britain's Eastern Empire.

The spring of 1921 saw, therefore, the beginnings of a return to something like the pre-war pattern of diplomacy in the Middle East and the end of the euphoric period during which the total recasting of the geopolitics of the region had seemed possible. This sobering experience was parallelled by changes at a different level of imperial policy. For as the pressure for economy at home grew more intense, and as the internal difficulties of the imperial system in Ireland, India and Egypt grew more intractable, London became increasingly anxious to lessen its direct involvement in the internal government of Britain's dependencies. The dismantling of the war economy and the reaction against more rigorous imperial control in the subject territories argued for a return to the looser supervision which had been practised before 1914 but which the pressures of war administration had outmoded. The difficulty lay in combining this old fondness for indirect controls with the apparent requirements of strategy, security and stability in the troubled aftermath of the war. In few places at the end of 1920 did the rival demands of economy, defence and political convenience seem more in conflict than in Iraq.

Devolution in Iraq

In fashioning a new imperial policy in Iraq, the Lloyd George coalition was compelled to take account of two separate considerations which were, nonetheless, closely interlocked. The first of these was the recognised necessity to open up the Iraq administration to Arab aspirations and ambitions in order to avoid further unrest. The force of this argument owed something, perhaps, to Milner's insistence that the frustration of ambition in Egypt had played a large part in the difficulties which confronted the British there. The second consideration derived not so much from the local circumstances of Iraq as from its place in the wider framework of imperial strategy in the Middle East: the need to ensure that any scheme for devolving power should be compatible with the preservation of Iraq as a unitary state and one which would remain healthily independent of Turkish influence, and a reliable buttress to British security in the Persian Gulf.

By the time of the Cabinet's resolution to transfer responsibility for Iraq to the Colonial Office, and of Lloyd George's almost simultaneous decision to place Churchill at the head of that department, some progress had already been made towards the first of these requirements. The recall of Cox from Teheran to his old post at Baghdad had been specifically intended to mark the introduction of a policy of associating Arabs more closely with the administration – a policy which Cox himself had predicted would remove much of the unrest in the country. The new High Commissioner devoted his early months in Iraq first of all to creating a provisional government in which the various portfolios were entrusted to selected Arab ministers under the presidency of the chief notable of Baghdad, the Naqib. At the same time, the British administrative cadres in Iraq were substantially reduced in number while their functions became advisory rather than executive.[30] All this had a familiar ring: it bore a marked resemblance to the Cromerian methods for managing Egypt to which the Milner Report had, in effect, urged a return. And, like Cromer, Cox continued to wield an authority over the native ministry which was no less real for being more discreet, and which was based upon the physical power of the imperial garrison.

How much further or faster Cox himself wished to go towards a devolution of powers is unclear. In his philippic against Wilson in mid-1920, Curzon had asserted that Cox had shared many of Wilson's preconceptions about how Iraq should be governed.[31] This was perhaps natural in that Wilson had been Cox's protégé; but it followed that the purpose of summoning Cox to London prior to his official return to Baghdad was not so much to consult him as to educate him in London's views. Once in Iraq, therefore, Cox abruptly abandoned the experiment in direct rule which the rising had seemed to condemn and successfully solicited local allies. But his efforts to establish a 'national' government which could hold Iraq together by its own authority were less convincing. The prospect of a new constitution rapidly revealed major differences in the communities of the three *vilayets*: the hostility of the tribes to a centralised authority; the antipathy of the large landholders to the idea of a substantial tribal representation in the projected national assembly;[32] the resentments of the old Ottoman official class; the anger of the Shi'ites at the apparent monopoly of patronage and power by the Sunni élite.[33] Gertrude Bell, whose function as Cox's Oriental Secretary at the High Commission in Baghdad was to monitor unofficial opinion and collect the gossip of the salons, concluded in February 1921 (although not perhaps entirely disinterestedly) that 'the present Government has got no hold in the provinces . . . ', even if it was 'gaining ground' in Baghdad itself.[34]

As we have seen, Cox himself proclaimed a belief that without the steel frame provided by the imperial garrison the new regime in Iraq would rapidly collapse, and the way would be open for a return to Turkish rule. Nor did he believe that a partial withdrawal of that garrison to Basra would yield a less disastrous result. Thus, by December 1920, it was clear that the real problem facing the British was not the conciliation of nationalist feeling in the three *vilayets*, nor the satisfaction of local ambitions, but rather the familiar colonial problem of constructing a successor state which could survive the change from the formal to the informal mode of imperial control while continuing to serve the purposes of the imperial power. It is possible that Cox himself might have preferred to continue for some time the temporary system he had introduced in October 1920 and postpone more constitutional innovation. But two pressures pushed him relentlessly forward. The first was the necessity to devise a constitution which would fulfil the terms of the mandate and equip Iraq with such representative institutions as would satisfy the League of Nations, and also home opinion, that the new state was being built upon firm political foundations. The second was the gathering strength of London's commitment to economy, above all in defence spending and the deployment of the army. As a former minister to Persia, Cox could hardly have failed to appreciate the significance (for his own work in Iraq) of the Cabinet's decision to withdraw militarily from Persia. Nor was he likely after the Cabinet discussions of December 1920 to underestimate the resentment of Churchill, his new ministerial master, at the apparent delay in making Iraq self-sufficient financially and militarily.

Even before Churchill had entered, with some show of reluctance,[35] upon his new administrative inheritance, anxieties of this kind had led Cox to revive the old scheme to nominate a member of the Sherifian dynasty as amir or king of the Iraq state which had been abandoned during the period of acute Anglo-French tension over Syria and Feisal's attempt to resist the establishment of a French mandate in Damascus by armed force. The candidacy of Feisal himself had actually been canvassed by A. T. Wilson during his last months at Baghdad. The conversion of this hitherto implacable opponent of Sherifian pretensions anticipated, indeed, the dilemma in which Cox found himself: how to preserve, after the concession of local autonomy, the unity and cohesion of the new state. Only Feisal, the doomed proconsul had remarked, 'has any idea of practical difficulties of running a civilised state on Arab lines'.[36] Cox, however, dwelt upon arguments which were likely to chime in with the new mood of ministers and overcome their reluctance to give offence to the French who still regarded Feisal as a dangerous influence in the Arab lands and an agent of British imperialism. In a telegram to Montagu (while the Indian Secretary still retained responsibility for the civil administration in Iraq), which was rapidly circulated to the Cabinet, he spelt out Feisal's supreme virtue: 'he would be in a position to raise National Army quicker than any candidate [for head of state] from Irak' and thus cement the country together.[37] Two days later the Cabinet instructed Montagu to seek more details from Cox, and in particular to establish whether Feisal would be acceptable to the Iraq notables.[38]

Thus when Churchill took control of Mesopotamian affairs early in January 1921, the bare bones of the new policy had already begun to emerge. Nor was Churchill slow to decide that the selection of Feisal held out the best hope of a solution to the Iraq problem. On 10 January he sought Cox's opinion of Feisal's qualities and of the feasibility of arranging for him to be chosen locally; and in a tone which conveyed his own sympathy for the proposal.[39] Two days later, he told Curzon that he had a 'strong feeling' that Feisal was the best man.[40] Churchill himself had good reasons for reaching a rapid decision on the future of Iraq. He was undoubtedly anxious that a new and plausible political framework should be constructed before new estimates had to be presented to Parliament, and so that immediate reductions in the imperial garrison could be announced. But at the same time, he dared not risk a policy which might lead to the dismemberment of Iraq and its reoccupation by the Turks, an outcome against which the Cabinet had firmly set its face, and which would have been enormously damaging to Churchill's own reputation. The pressures to which Churchill felt himself subject are revealed in the asperity of his early messages to Cox, who at first appeared to think that Churchill's appointment presaged the withdrawal to Basra that had been debated in December, and was roundly rebuked for his presumption.[41] Cox for his part was clearly nervous lest Churchill's enthusiasm for reductions in the garrison might lead to precipitate action before the ground could be prepared for the new policy, and warned of the growing support in Iraq for a Turkish prince and the rejection of a British mandate.[42]

By the time that Churchill set out for the Cairo Conference in March, the notion of making Feisal king of Iraq already commanded the support of his own department[43] and that of the War Office, a department with a material interest in the outcome of his policy.[44] Churchill's own status as the supreme director of British policy in Iraq, Palestine and the Arabian peninsula had been confirmed by the Cabinet and grudgingly accepted by a resentful Curzon;[45] and Churchill had formally succeeded Milner at the Colonial Office. His prime object in summoning a conference of the principal administrative and military officers in the Middle East – of whom Cox, Sir Herbert Samuel (High Commissioner in Palestine) and the garrison commanders were the most important – was, perhaps, to establish authority over men who had served different masters and who like Cox were impatient of London's commands. It was moreover part of Churchill's style to visit his subordinates on the spot. But there was a second purpose no less important: Churchill was determined to achieve the largest savings in money and men compatible with the security of Iraq in particular, and wished to reach agreement on this with the indispensable Cox by a means less vulnerable to procrastination and misunderstanding than telegraphic correspondence. The Cairo Conference was therefore an assembly of officials and technicians who were to perform the dramatic function of acclaiming the choice of Feisal for Iraq, and of his brother Abdullah as ruler of a separate Arab province in Trans-Jordanian Palestine; and a more businesslike task in drawing up under Churchill's eye and at his prompting an agreed timetable of military withdrawal and financial contraction.

The first four days of the conference were devoted almost entirely to the affairs of Iraq. On the second day, Churchill reported to Lloyd George that there was an unanimous view in favour of selecting Feisal.[46] But the real work of deciding the pace of withdrawal was less quickly accomplished. It was soon agreed that the existing garrison should be reduced by one third to 23 battalions as soon as possible, but the disposal of the remaining force caused controversy. The proposal of General Haldane, General Officer Commanding in Iraq, that the army should hold the three stations of Mosul, Baghdad and Basra, saving money and men by pulling back from outlying districts, was strongly opposed by Cox who was supported by Congreve of the Egypt–Palestine command.[47] Trenchard, the Chief of Air Staff whom Churchill had brought with him to press the case for controlling Iraq by surveillance from the air, was forced to admit that no scheme for air control could be operational in less than a year. And neither the more rapid embarkation of troops awaiting transport home at Basra, nor economies in staffing and stores yielded Churchill as dramatic a saving as he wanted, although reducing the estimate for Iraq from £30 million to some £25 million for 1921–2.[48] Churchill's solution increased the already heavy dependence of his policy on the successful installation of Feisal as ruler. The conference had decided, he told Lloyd George, to impose a second round of troop reductions in October 1921, by which time the new regime under Feisal would have been established at Baghdad, bringing the imperial garrison down to twelve battalions costing £6 million *per annum* by the end of the financial year.[49]

Churchill himself had no illusions about the total reliance of his imperial policy in Iraq on the selection of Feisal, and on Feisal's willingness and ability to establish a cooperative regime in Baghdad. On 22 March the Cabinet accepted his proposals as they were conveyed through Lloyd George and approved arrangements to be made by Cox to stage an election and disseminate informally British approval of Feisal's candidacy as ruler.[50] 'Decide to invite Feisal to take over', Fisher recorded with laconic candour.[51] The Cabinet's only reservations were prompted by Curzon's worries about the reaction of the French and the need to extract from Feisal firm assurances that he did not contemplate trying to reverse his military overthrow at French hands in July 1920. At the end of May, the Cabinet expressed satisfaction with the progress of Churchill's plans, while the Colonial Secretary's defence of his policy in the House of Commons, with its promise of substantial and steady reductions in cost and manpower, appeared to end the long period during which the coalition's Middle East policy caused resentment and anxiety among its parliamentary supporters.[52] A month later, on 14 July, Asquith, a persistent critic of the Government's Eastern policies, gave Churchill's proposals a cautious welcome, although he was sceptical as to whether the oft-repeated promises of reduced estimates could be sustained, and jibed at the ministry 'who have given [Feisal] a coupon'.[53]

Meanwhile the arrangements for Feisal's 'emergence' as the popularly chosen ruler of Iraq – a device which ministers felt was essential if French and American opinion were to be reconciled to their policy – were pushed forward by Cox. In the five months which elapsed between the Cairo Conference and the formal elevation of Feisal to the throne in Iraq, the British were forced more and more to abandon their initial posture of detachment and display an open partisanship on behalf of Feisal and his party. In mid-April, Sayyid Talib, the Minister of the Interior and the only considerable Iraqi politician who resisted Cox's blandishments and spoke openly against the nomination of Feisal, was summarily deported to Ceylon.[54] On 17 June, five days after Feisal began his journey to Iraq to announce his candidature, Cox announced that the British Government had no objection to his election as ruler.[55] On 11 July, as Feisal's triumphal progress from Basra to Baghdad received a somewhat mixed reaction except among those who looked with eager anticipation upon the prospect of a prince of the Sunni sect (more than half of Iraq's population, especially in the south, belonged to the rival Shi'ite sect),[56] the ministers of Cox's provisional government declared their support for Feisal as king, and, at Cox's direction, set in train a referendum to test popular opinion. The official result of this referendum showed that more than 96 per cent of those who voted favoured the Hashemite prince,[57] who was installed without delay as king of Iraq in August 1921.

The pattern of devolution in Iraq revealed not the weakness and timidity of British imperial policy in a period of contracting military power but rather the ruthlessness of its drive to accomplish the classic objectives of Victorian imperialism: the creation of a compliant local regime which would preserve Britain's political and strategic interests while relieving her of the trouble and expense of ruling directly over an alien and unpredictable society. It was for this advantageous position that successive British governments had striven in vain in Egypt in the thirty years which followed the occupation of 1882. The smoothness of Feisal's installation as king of Iraq was not, however, simply the product of a defter and subtler statecraft than Cromer's; still less the reward for a greater sensitivity to the aspirations of colonial nationalism than had characterised imperial policy before the war. Rather was it the consequence of the special circumstances which shaped the politics of the three *vilayets* cobbled together by the British as a single state at the end of 1918.

British support for the nomination of Feisal had seemed justified, even necessitated, by the acute divisions within the new state – geographical, economic, political and religious. British policy-makers believed that no other candidate could surmount the regional jealousies of the three *vilayets*, could command the loyalty of the small but important clique of Sunni army officers in Baghdad – the nucleus of any future defence force – or had the expertise in state-building which Feisal had already demonstrated in Syria. Above all, no other candidate could show such credentials as an enemy of Ottoman imperialism. But once they had decided upon Feisal, the disunity of Iraq became of crucial assistance to the British in their efforts to secure his election as ruler. No opposing candidate could mobilise support which transcended differences of regional loyalty and sectarian affiliation. Talib's summary exile to Ceylon aroused no such demonstrations as those which had overturned British policy in Egypt after Zaghlul's deportation in 1919. The humiliating failure of Talib's démarche was indicative of the character of Iraq politics. There existed no nationalist movement comparable with that which plagued the British in Egypt. 'A spirit of nationality may probably be relegated to a very low seat among the factors which have led up to the rising,' wrote a British political officer in evidence submitted to the Cabinet in London on the causes of the rebellion of 1920.[58] This view was shared fully by Churchill and Montagu[59] and passed unchallenged in the Cabinet. It is not surprising that this conclusion was drawn for there existed in 1920 and 1921 scarcely any mechanism which might have allowed the ragged chorus of local grievances to assume a national or nationalist character. The novelty of Iraq's political unity meant that the linkages which bound the districts to the new capital at Baghdad were either too rudimentary to be effective or were under British control.[60] Following Cox's administrative changes in the autumn of 1920, these same linkages, in so far as they were no longer in British hands, were dominated by newly appointed Sunni officials who saw in Feisal's election their best security against the power of the tribes or of the Shi'ite majority. Moreover, the hand of the British still lay heavily in many districts following the suppression of the disturbances. The effect of all this was to ensure that the notables who constituted the referendum electorate were acutely anxious that their opinions should not conflict with the voice of authority[61] – an anxiety which the form of the ballot (which required the names of those opposed to Feisal to be listed alongside those who supported him) can have done nothing to alleviate[62] – lest, in familiar fashion, retribution would be visited upon the enemies of government.

For a brief moment, therefore, British policy in Iraq achieved the triumph which had eluded Milner in Egypt: 'Sir Percy and Feisal between them are making a new Sherifian party composed of all the solid moderate people,' wrote Gertrude Bell in July 1921.[63] And that party won. But its victory was not intended to remove Iraq from British control. Feisal's authority inside Iraq was meant to be real enough and was buttressed by Britain's military power. But where, as in Kurdistan, it was expected that Arab rule, even under British auspices, would place too great a strain on political allegiance, and redound to Turkish advantage, the writ of the new king was expressly excluded, and the British retained their former powers. In questions of defence and external affairs Feisal was expected to conform to the instructions of the British.

In all this, it was plain that the logic of British policy had little to do with any concern for the good government of Iraq except in so far as it impinged upon the ability of the new state to hold together and pay for its own defence; and even less with the preferences of the various communities whose desire for a unitary Iraq state was never properly tested.[64] Wider imperial concerns decreed that Iraq should be unified and centralised; just as they decreed that the Palestine mandate should be partitioned, on grounds of political convenience and military economy, into an Arab state and Palestine proper, to which Jewish settlement would be restricted and where the fulfilment of the Balfour Declaration ruled out early recourse to indirect rule.[65] It remained to be seen, however, whether Churchill's reconciliations of ends and means in Iraq through the agency of Feisal could withstand the stresses of political change, external pressure and Britain's military withdrawal.

Iraq and the Turkish Problem

After March 1921, all the major debates between ministers and in the Cabinet over the management of policy in the Middle East revolved around two great residual problems which together had dominated the making of Britain's Eastern policy for a century. For, as Russia's revival in the Caucasus and Central Asia, and the Cabinet's decision to abandon the Anglo-Persian Agreement, stripped away the accretions of war imperialism, Britain's imperial policy in the Middle East resolved itself into a familiar preoccupation with the two strategic zones which guarded the exit from the Black Sea and the landward approach to the Persian Gulf. The defence of the embryonic Iraq state and of the Dardanelles, although the responsibility of different ministers, were nevertheless two facets of a single political and strategic task. For in both, the protection of British interests appeared to depend upon resistance to, or an accommodation with, a vigorous and resilient Turkish national movement dedicated to the recovery not only of Thrace, but of a substantial part of the new Arab state – the former *vilayet* of Mosul.[66] In particular, the success of the Iraq experiment in devolution, of which Feisal's enthronement in Baghdad was only the beginning, turned upon the outcome of the struggle in Asia Minor between Greek and Turk, and on the extent to which their anxiety about the Straits hindered the readiness of British ministers to contemplate the appeasement of Turkish nationalism.

Churchill, the principal author of British policy in Iraq, had no doubt about the vulnerability of his political settlement there to the effects of a continued confrontation with the Kemalist regime at Angora. Long before he assumed responsibility for Iraq, he had recognised that the search for stability and economy in its administration would make little progress until a general framework for peace in the Middle East had been established.[67] This conviction seems to have been powerfully reinforced by what he learned from Cox at the Cairo Conference. Cox, who had been responsible for devising an administration to replace that of the Turks during the Mesopotamian War, and who, more than anyone, was the founder of the Iraq state, was well placed to know the fragility of his creation. He was, perhaps as a result of his earlier experience, acutely conscious of the surviving ties of loyalty and self-interest binding the old official class in the *vilayets* to the Turkish connection. Churchill therefore stressed in his messages to Lloyd George, that the selection of Feisal and the run-down of the imperial garrison – the essence of the new policy – were only feasible if there were no interference from outside, that is, from Turkey.[68] At the Cabinet which approved the Cairo Conference recommendations on Iraq, ministers were reminded of this condition in Lloyd George's summary of the Colonial Secretary's telegrams.[69] On his return home, Churchill reiterated this point to his colleagues,[70] and to the House of Commons;[71] while a stream of telegrams from Cox, the tone of which grew more urgent as the year wore on, repeated this theme with minor variations over and over again.

Like Montagu, then, Churchill had powerful reasons for insisting that Britain and her allies come to terms with the Kemalist regime without delay. But to a greater extent than the Indian Secretary, he was prepared to recognise that a wider view of imperial security pulled the makers of policy in a contrary direction. At the end of May 1921 the dilemmas of the Cabinet's Middle Eastern policy became manifest as the deterioration of military security in Ireland, and the necessity to send more troops to Silesia to quell disturbances there, produced what the Chief of the Imperial General Staff regarded as intolerable strains on the army's manpower.[72] Wilson was convinced (not perhaps for entirely professional reasons) that either the garrison in Ireland should be substantially reinforced or that the attempt at repression there should be abandoned. The new Secretary of State for War, Worthington-Evans, 'impressed and frightened'[73] by Wilson and Macready's[74] arguments, proposed to his ministerial colleagues the withdrawal of the six battalions stationed at Constantinople, to furnish more troops for Ireland in a supreme effort 'to break the back of the rebellion'.[75] This brought the whole issue of the Government's Turkish policy to a head. Curzon, drawing upon the arguments of Eyre Crowe, permanent under-secretary at the Foreign Office, vehemently denounced the abandonment of Constantinople. With Crowe's prophecy that this would lead to 'little short of the complete restoration of the Turkish empire as it stood before the war' and to a 'perpetual threat to our position in Mesopotamia, in Palestine, and probably in Egypt',[76] he had much sympathy. To allow Kemal such a triumph would undermine British authority and prestige all over the Islamic world. Churchill agreed that withdrawal would damage Britain's position in Mesopotamia and

Palestine unless it formed part of a general peace.[77] Lloyd George insisted that even if Constantinople were to be evacuated the Dardanelles should be held.

This inconclusive debate between ministers was continued in smaller meetings on 1 and 2 June. Churchill, while acknowledging the need to keep a firm military presence in Constantinople, now pressed for an approach to Kemal to avoid an expensive confrontation in Iraq; and urged that the Greek army be pulled back from the Anatolian hinterland as a first step towards fresh negotiations. But Lloyd George, and almost certainly Curzon as well, threw their weight against this.[78] On 9 June, a committee of senior ministers again discussed Constantinople and on this occasion agreed that a further Allied attempt at a settlement should be made.[79] The garrison meanwhile was to stay. Churchill, who had sought to use the debate to hammer home an awareness of the contingent nature of his policy in Iraq, was deeply irritated with Lloyd George's apparent lack of sympathy for his difficulties. When Lloyd George facetiously suggested that Britain's burdens in the Middle East might be lightened by handing over Iraq and Palestine to the United States, Churchill responded angrily to this repudiation of the value of his efforts to retain imperial control in these regions. He called the Prime Minister's bluff by proposing to make his suggestion public. Lloyd George quickly recanted.[80]

Churchill's great anxiety, brought out in this episode, was lest the defence of Asia Minor against the Kemalists should be purchased at the expense of his own public commitment to drastic military economies in Iraq; and especially lest, in the resultant uproar, Lloyd George would deftly transfer the whole responsibility for the decision for remaining in that country on to his shoulders. Although the Cabinet now veered towards making further concessions to the Angora government over the defence of Turkey's European frontiers, and over the treatment of the Muslim population in what had become Greek Thrace, there was as yet no proper reconciliation in British policy between what Churchill conceived to be the requirements of imperial security in Iraq and what Lloyd George conceived to be those of imperial security at the Dardanelles. Churchill wished to restrain the Greek army while Lloyd George hoped it might yet win a decisive victory.[81] Meanwhile all Curzon's advisers both at Constantinople and in the Foreign Office warned of the intractability of the Kemalists and the folly of undermining the Greek war effort before the Kemalists had signed a peace treaty. In the event, the third attempt at a Turkish settlement was abortive.[82] But further conflict in the Cabinet was staved off for the rest of the summer by the apparent success of the Greek offensive in Anatolia which seemed for a while to justify Lloyd George's faith in the quality of the Greek army;[83] and also by the Cabinet's decision not to escalate their policy of repression in Ireland, but rather to seek a truce with the Irish rebels.[84] These developments eased the strains on the army's manpower, and put off for the time being the necessity of reaching a fresh agreement on an overall British strategy in the Middle East.

In the late autumn of 1921, however, pressure for another attempt at mediation between Greece and Turkey built up once more inside the Cabinet as the collapse of the Greek offensive at the Sakarya – in retrospect the decisive watershed of the war in Asia Minor[85] – challenged Lloyd George's claim that Britain's imperial interests in the Middle East were best served by licensing Greek expansion, and could be entrusted to the Greek armies. Churchill feared that a Kemalist military victory in Asia Minor would allow the Angora government to turn its attentions to Iraq's northern frontier at the moment when the untried Arab levies were taking over the burden of its defence.[86] Curzon expressed sympathy for Churchill's views and was undoubtedly eager to try for a settlement before an outright Kemalist victory removed all his bargaining power at the Straits; but he remained unconvinced that a fourth intervention by the Allies to define the boundaries of the new Turkish state would be more successful than its predecessors.[87] And he was unwilling, as he had been earlier, to consider coercing the Greeks into accepting terms which might prove attractive to Kemal.[88] In early November, however, a Cabinet preoccupied with the search for accommodations with Irish and Egyptian nationalists approved a fresh initiative and Curzon set about persuading the French and Italians to join in a combined approach to the Greeks and Turks. After lengthy delays, caused partly by a change of government in both France and Italy, and partly by French suspicions of British motives, the three powers assembled in Paris to revise once more the terms of the Sèvres Treaty in the latter part of March 1922.

The readiness of the ministers to sanction further concessions to the Turkish nationalists, especially with regard to the administration of Smyrna, the European frontier of Turkey and the Allied surveillance of Constantinople,[89] and their commitment to the view that the Greeks must evacuate Asia Minor militarily after a peace settlement, were a mark of Lloyd George's inability to sustain any longer the old strategy of open collaboration with Greece, and of a general awareness that the diplomatic relations of Kemal with France and Russia made any effective coercion of the Angora regime out of the question.[90] But this did not mean that by the spring of 1922 ministers had given up their belief that imperial security in the Middle East required the containment of Turkish power within the southern and western limits of Asia Minor. In his proposals to the Cabinet,[91] and in his dealings with the Turks and the Allied powers,[92] Curzon insisted that, whatever else might be conceded to the Turks, they were not to be allowed to control both shores of the Dardanelles. The Straits were to be internationalised; but as a final guarantee of free passage Turkey's European frontiers were to be drawn so that the Gallipoli peninsula remained in Greek Thrace. To this there was no trace of opposition within the Cabinet. It was axiomatic that, after the ruinous consequences of Turkish control of the Straits during the war, and with great uncertainties hanging over the future course of a Kemalist state, to surrender the Dardanelles entirely to Turkish control was incompatible not only with the demands of imperial prestige but with the imperatives of imperial safety. The concealed expansion of British power implicit in the opening of the Straits to the Royal Navy was, in Curzon's view, a yet more valuable fruit of victory than any gained, and lost, in Persia and the Caucasus. For it denied to Turkey the opportunity of repeating the tactics of 1914, and manipulating European conflicts for her own purposes. 'Is no attempt to be made in the Treaty to avoid a repetition of the Turkish game of playing off one country against another?' Curzon had demanded of Montagu in June 1921.[93] Significantly, even the most effective critic in the Cabinet of the failure to come to terms promptly with Kemal echoed this feeling. Denouncing the policy which had led to the alignment of Kemal and the Bolsheviks, and which risked the expulsion of the British from Iraq, Churchill nevertheless conceded that he would rather 'have a continuance of a state of war, at any rate of disturbance, even involving the evacuation of Mesopotamia, than to return the mastery of the Straits to the Turks'.[94]

The convergence in the views of Lloyd George, Curzon and Churchill over the Dardanelles thus enabled Curzon to preserve largely intact what was perhaps the most important plank in the platform he had constructed in 1918 for imperial policy in the Middle East – the sundering of Turkey's old links with the power politics of Europe so as to restrict her opportunities for interference in Britain's strategic nerve-centres in south-west Asia. Churchill, whose task it was to anchor the British presence in Iraq both cheaply and flexibly, was less well fortified, as we have seen, against attempts to reduce the level of Britain's commitment there below that required for the exercise of a paramount influence. Lloyd George at times seemed impatient with the timetable for military withdrawal that Churchill had laid down, and ready to leave Feisal to his fate.[95] Churchill for his part seemed torn between claiming on the one hand that Britain's position in Iraq was on a firm basis as a result of his policy, and on the other that the success of the Iraq experiment was endangered by factors and influences beyond his direct departmental control.

Churchill might have hoped that the installation of Feisal would clear the way for a smooth progress towards a new treaty relationship that would incorporate Britain's mandate over Iraq, and towards the substantial economies in military spending he had promised. Both were essential if his policy were to be presented as a model of successful devolution which yet preserved Iraq, diplomatically and strategically, as a part of Britain's wider imperial system. Instead the viability of Churchill's policy continued to arouse controversy within the ministry for two main reasons. The first was the refusal of the War Office and the General Staff to admit the practicability of the means whereby Churchill proposed to defend Iraq's frontiers against attack and maintain internal order. The second was the unexpected and unwelcome reluctance of Feisal once crowned to play the cooperative role in which Churchill and his advisers had cast him.

Even before Feisal had been formally elected to the Iraq throne, Churchill was in a hurry to move on to the second phase of the programme of military withdrawal that he had set out in March, and to obtain formal Cabinet sanction for the introduction of Trenchard's scheme for air control in Iraq in October 1922. Under this scheme eight squadrons of aircraft were to replace ground forces in the routine tasks of patrolling Iraq's hinterland and imposing a prompt retribution on tribes and communities which flouted the authority of the central government in Baghdad.[96] By these means, and with four battalions of infantry, two British, two Indian, stationed at Baghdad, the stability of Iraq could be ensured, so Churchill claimed, for an outlay of a little over £4 million a year from the British exchequer.[97] Any other scheme more expensive in manpower would breach his commitment to Parliament, and would impose a crippling burden of defence spending on the infant state.[98]

Churchill's haste was not merely the product of his characteristically energetic methods in administration. It was also prompted by a desire to keep ahead of the new wave of economies which became politically necessary in the summer of 1921 and which led to the appointment of the Geddes Committee on Public Expenditure in

August.[99] But Churchill's route to political safety was barred by the War Office which still retained operational control over the deployment of imperial troops in Iraq and which continued to deny right through 1921 that Churchill's military policy was workable unless Kemal was bought off. Worthington-Evans and the General Staff employed the tactics learned from Churchill. In May the Staff declared that either the Mosul *vilayet* should be abandoned or troop reductions would have to be suspended.[100] 'We are back to the withdrawal from Mosul stunt,' commented Montagu sardonically.[101] Five months later Worthington-Evans was painting a grim picture of the British garrison of Baghdad being cut off by a Turkish invasion, and advocated the old remedy of a withdrawal to Basra to cover the Persian oil fields.[102] The General Staff denounced the air scheme as unworkable and the local Arab defence forces as 'unreliable'.[103] Churchill complained to Worthington-Evans,[104] to Lloyd George,[105] and to the Cabinet[106] that the War Office was cramping his style and demanding unrealistic garrison levels.

In part the War Office's attitude was justified by a legitimate concern for the safety of the perilously small garrison of four battalions which Churchill wanted at Baghdad. For in an era before large-scale troop reinforcements by air were practicable, Baghdad's remoteness from the nearest seaport at Basra was a real consideration; and memories of Khartoum still haunted British military planners. But it is likely that War Office calculations were informed, especially after the summer of 1921, by considerations not simply of logistics. The appointment of the Geddes Committee threatened the Army and Navy alike with drastic and unwelcome reductions in manpower and finance. In a new and more intense phase of the struggle for resources, the War Office was determined that Britain's commitment in Iraq should be used to strengthen its departmental claim.[107] Thus, in a furious reaction to the Geddes proposals for army reductions, Wilson, as Chief of the Imperial General Staff, insisted that the defence of Iraq required no less than two divisions of infantry to be held in readiness as reinforcements.[108] Churchill's proposal to base the defence of Iraq upon the capability of the Royal Air Force added, in this context, insult to injury, since the Geddes Committee praised the efficiency of the air arm and opposed the War Office's desire to bring the Air Ministry under its control.[109] Thus, as in December 1920, arguments about the viability of imperial control in Iraq were caught up in the internal quarrels of the ministers, which derived in reality from issues more domestic than imperial. But, as in December 1920, these quarrels were not allowed to subvert the Cabinet's determination to maintain a British presence in northern and central Iraq. Neither Lloyd George, nor any of the other senior ministers, was prepared to let Worthington-Evans obstruct Churchill and thus reopen the whole issue of Iraq's future. Hence Churchill's air scheme was given Cabinet sanction in August 1921, and again, after the Geddes report, in the following February.[110] The War Office's stated desire to pull back from Mosul if the reductions took effect was overborne.[111] And it was Churchill who chaired the Cabinet's review of the effects of the Geddes cuts on the armed forces.[112]

Churchill was able to rely, therefore, on strong support in the Cabinet, especially from Curzon, for his security policy of 'hot air, aeroplanes and Arabs'.[113] But his attempts to come to terms with Feisal in a treaty which embodied Britain's control over external aspects of Iraqi affairs were less warmly received by his colleagues. Churchill himself seemed unprepared for the slow and difficult progress of the negotiations, perhaps because he had not properly considered the political role that Feisal would play once installed as king; or because he had assumed that, as a constitutional monarch, Feisal's interests would be identical with those of the British. Thus the Colonial Office had instructed Cox to obtain from Feisal at his coronation a public statement of his acceptance of Britain's ultimate authority over him,[114] a demand which Feisal rebutted, with Cox's support, on the grounds that if his authority was so obviously circumscribed 'he can't hold his extremists . . .'.[115] This was an early warning that Feisal would be less easily managed than had been supposed.

Once they embarked upon the making of a treaty, the British found themselves checked and thwarted by the side-effects of an internal competition for power in the same way as, though to a lesser extent than, they had been in Egypt. Feisal was naturally anxious to entrench his position; and he was eager to settle the terms of the treaty before the projected constituent assembly began work on the organic law, or constitution, of the new state.[116] This would have enabled him to acquire a prior control over the instruments of power delegated by the British and thus to strengthen greatly his hand against any attempt by the native Iraq notables to reduce him to a cipher. But to achieve this advantageous position, Feisal was bound to raise the price of his cooperation to the British, and also to adopt a public stance that would enable him to compete with the notables for the support of the political nation. To Churchill the evidence of Feisal's refractoriness was merely irritating. When Feisal's demands for his sovereign status were passed on by Cox, he minuted sourly:

> I am getting tired of all these lengthy telegrams about Feisal and his state of mind. There is too much of it. Six months ago we were paying his hotel bills in London, and now I am forced to read day after day 800 word messages on questions on his status and his relations with foreign Powers. Has he not got some wives to keep him quiet?[117]

Feisal, however, would not remain quiet. Already by early November, Churchill, under pressure from Cox, had extracted from a reluctant Cabinet permission for Feisal to make contact with Mustapha Kemal, a proposal justified as an exercise in information-gathering but with obvious internal implications for Feisal's position with regard to the surviving elements of pro-Turkish feeling in Iraq.[118] Then at the beginning of the new year, the Colonial Office began to modify the desiderata for the Iraq treaty that it had laid down in November.[119] In particular, Churchill now proposed to concede the principle of independent diplomatic representation for Iraq in foreign states subject to the consent of the British Government.[120] No sooner had this been rejected by the Cabinet at the instance of Curzon, Balfour and Lloyd George,[121] than new and more far-reaching demands arrived at the Colonial Office. Feisal and his prime minister, the Naqib of Baghdad – the leading notable in the capital — had united to call for the abrogation of the British mandate over Iraq and the substitution of a simple treaty relationship, unencumbered by the extensive and ill-defined powers which Britain would otherwise enjoy as the agent of the League of Nations.[122]

Feisal's object in pressing for this large concession was plainly to enhance his authority within Iraq as the real architect of independence; and, coincidentally, to increase the value of his cooperation and goodwill to the British. His request was supported by Cox who advanced the well-worn argument that only by strengthening the prestige of their friends could the British stave off the triumph of extremist nationalism. The 'moderate and pro-British party will find it very difficult to run counter to the expressed opinion of the Naqib',[123] he warned, and urged that regard for the 'fresh experience' of colonial nationalism in Ireland and elsewhere should sway ministers towards acquiescing in the scrapping of the mandate. If they did not, he argued, there was little hope of the projected national assembly ratifying a treaty.[124] But Churchill, although he had little sympathy for the 'obsolescent rigmarole' of the mandate system,[125] and, by the spring of 1922, was cautiously championing Cox's views in the interests of 'strengthening the Arab system against the Turkish system',[126] found difficulty in persuading his Cabinet colleagues to adopt a generous attitude towards Feisal's *amour propre*. The opposition of Curzon and Balfour to abandoning the mandate and their mistrust of the proposal to widen Feisal's diplomatic status was born less of any fear that Feisal would use concessions of this kind to throw off British controls, than of an anxiety lest the re-emergence of Feisal as an international figure would alarm the French in Syria at a moment when French cooperation in the search for peace in Anatolia was vital; and lest the surrender of the mandate would encourage both the French and the Americans to reopen the whole question of British influence in Iraq.[127] Thus the first reaction of ministers was to insist that Feisal accept both treaty and mandate together.[128] But this display of firmness, which Churchill reinforced by a threat, intended for Feisal, that Britain might withdraw altogether if he were obdurate, yielded no result while the internal balance of authority in Iraq remained undecided.

Chanak and the Iraq Treaty

Ever since their first serious discussions of the terms of the peace for Asia Minor and European Turkey in August 1919, it had been a cardinal assumption of British ministers that the sea passages between the Mediterranean and the Black Sea – the Dardanelles and the Bosphorus – would not again fall under Turkish control. The Cabinet revolt in January 1920 against the eviction of the Sultan from Constantinople had expressed a fear that the task of controlling Turkey and safeguarding the Straits would be made harder, not easier, if the Turkish capital were to be established in the Anatolian hinterland.[129] The decision in June 1920 to permit a Greek offensive in western Asia Minor sprang from the desire to prevent the Kemalist forces from reaching the Asian shores of the Straits, but at the same time to avoid committing British troops to their defence.[130] Indeed, throughout the period of Lloyd George's open sympathy for Greek aims in Asia Minor, it had been the contribution of the Greek armies to the security of the Straits and Constantinople which had blunted the force of Montagu's and Churchill's criticism, and of Curzon's soft-voiced doubts. Reliance upon the Greeks had an additional consequence in that it had spared the coalition from a serious and detailed analysis of Britain's real interest in the Straits and the lengths to which Britain alone would be prepared to go to defend them.

In the autumn of 1922, however, the British were at long last compelled to reckon the costs of extending their power and influence into this strategic zone, to assess the value of this fruit of victory in the Middle East. Curzon's attempt in March 1922 to induce Kemal to a peace conference by offering in concert with France and Italy further territorial concessions in Eastern Thrace and a relaxation of the financial and military clauses of the Sèvres Treaty, came to nothing.[131] Curzon believed that the Allied offer had been sabotaged by secret promises from the French to Kemal that they would not enforce its terms;[132] and that the French and Italians were both willing to see the Kemalists in control of the European and Asian shores of the Straits.[133] But he remained convinced that some form of international supervision must prevent Kemal 'from marching to the Dardanelles and again blocking the Straits'.[134] Balfour, who acted as Foreign Secretary during Curzon's long illness from June to August, shared the latter's hope that this could be achieved eventually by cooperation between the Allies; but added that, in the last resort, the defence of the Straits and of Constantinople might require once again an open partnership with Greece. In either event, a British military presence at the Ottoman capital was still essential.[135]

The strategy at the Foreign Office, therefore, continued to rely upon the summoning of a peace conference and the defence of the Straits by diplomacy. When Curzon returned to harness he set in train a proposal for such a conference at Venice. Meanwhile the overriding importance of preserving some shreds of Allied unity had led Balfour to warn the Greek government against occupying Constantinople in anticipation of a Kemalist *coup de main* there.[136] In the late summer of 1922, however, all these diplomatic calculations were thrown into confusion by the sudden and final collapse of the Greek armies in Asia Minor and the appeal of the Greek government to the British to arrange an armistice.[137] In the early days of September British ministers had for the first time to consider how the supposed requirements of imperial strategy in the Near East could be guaranteed by British power and British diplomacy without benefit of the Greek shield.

The record of ministerial deliberations in the anxious month which followed until the signature of the Mudania convention on 11 October reveals a fixity of purpose which can only be explained in the light of the frequent reaffirmations of Britain's interest in the Straits zone which had been made since August 1919. At the outset of the crisis, the Cabinet committed itself to the defence of the Paris terms of the previous March, and the exclusion of the Kemalists from the neutral zone (defined in the Sèvres Treaty) which ringed the Straits on both shores.[138] Curzon at this stage still hoped that Kemal would accept a peace conference and stop short of an armed confrontation. But as Kemal's march towards the neutral zone continued, the Cabinet made preparations for its defence resolving to use force if necessary.[139] From this moment, the imminence of conflict began to narrow the Cabinet's options, since it became apparent that their original intention to repel any Kemalist attack along the whole eastern shore from Chanak to the Black Sea was militarily impossible, especially when the attitude of the French and Italian troops in the Straits zone was unpredictable. On 19 September, as the French and Italians withdrew from Chanak and the Ismid peninsula opposite Constantinople, the committee of senior ministers, formed to cope with the day-to-day direction of policy, moved towards a decision to concentrate British strength at Chanak on the Dardanelles so as to protect the Gallipoli peninsula from the Turks, whilst leaving the defence of Constantinople to the Allies.[140] The next day, while Curzon went to Paris to rally French support for a conference, the committee decided to instruct General Harington, who commanded the Allied forces in the Straits zone, that it was Chanak that was of 'the highest importance' to British policy since it was the key to the control of the Gallipoli channel and hence of the Straits as a whole.[141].

The full implications of this decision were concealed for some days while Curzon's efforts in Paris seemed likely to avert fighting between the British and the Turks. Curzon believed that he had persuaded Poincaré to check Kemal's advance and bring him to the conference table.[142] On 23 September, a joint Allied note was sent to Kemal promising Turkish control in Thrace included the disputed city of Adrianople. But on the twenty-seventh Kemal's apparent refusal to leave the neutral zone and the intensification of his pressure on the British garrison at Chanak produced a fresh crisis. That evening, a committee of ministers comprising Lloyd George, Austen Chamberlain, Horne, Churchill, Birkenhead, Curzon, Worthington-Evans and Lee, met to decide whether they were prepared to contemplate war in defence of Chanak and the Dardanelles. Both Churchill and Chamberlain, who together had coordinated ministerial discussions on what policy to pursue, believed that Britain's limited military capacity and her special interest in access to the Straits dictated a stand at Chanak. To withdraw from Chanak, Chamberlain had declared earlier in the day, would seriously undermine Britain's international authority.[143]

This conclusion was resisted by Curzon who had fretted throughout the crisis at the constraints which military considerations and the judgment of his colleagues had imposed on his freedom of diplomatic manoeuvre. But in questioning the wisdom of making the defence of Chanak a *casus belli*, Curzon was in no sense advocating a capitulation to Kemal, or the abandonment of the Straits to the Turks. With his eyes still fixed on the ultimate objective of a peace conference at which the Allies would together impose international control of the Straits, so as to guarantee free passage through them, and a delimitation of Turkey's European frontier, the Foreign Secretary stressed the political importance of Constantinople. To withdraw the British garrison from Constantinople to hold Chanak would mean an open breach with France and Italy and destroy all hope of Allied cooperation in the making of a new treaty. It would surrender the Ottoman capital to Kemal – a political prize of the utmost importance – and clear the way for the swift and unilateral re-establishment of Turkish rule in Thrace and beyond, while the British remained in their 'second Gibraltar' at Gallipoli, powerless to influence the real issue: the auspices under which Kemal would be allowed to reconstitute a Turkish state in the Middle East.[144] To treat Chanak and Gallipoli as Britain's *supreme* interest, so Curzon seemed to say, would require the sacrifice of the very objects which gave them their value. It was Constantinople, if anywhere, which should be defended.[145]

These arguments had force. Other ministers almost certainly shared Curzon's doubts over the acceptability of Chanak as a *casus belli* to Parliament and the country.[146] Lloyd George himself expressed sympathy for Curzon's views. But these reservations were overborne by Chamberlain. Was it possible, he inquired of Lord Beatty, the First Sea Lord, to reinforce and supply Constantinople if Chanak fell into Turkish hands? Beatty's reply settled the matter. Constantinople could not be held without Chanak. All the ministers were agreed that something must be held. Therefore it must be Chanak. The die was cast.[147]

Everything now depended upon the actions of Kemal. On 29 September, alarmed by a telegram from Harington, that the Turks had penetrated so closely to the British lines at Chanak that the position of the garrison had become impossible, ministers decided on the explicit recommendation of the Chiefs of Staff, and without apparently much further discussion, to instruct Harington to issue the notorious abortive ultimatum.[148] This instruction Harington ignored, but the next day he persuaded Kemal to forbid any attack; and subsequently to enter into negotiations at Mudania as a preliminary to a peace conference. At

Mudania Harington demanded, on the Cabinet's instructions, Turkish withdrawal from the neutral zone and a delay before Turkish control replaced that of Greece in Eastern Thrace, as preconditions for the summoning of a conference. Not without difficulty, [149] and only after Curzon had visited Poincaré to appeal for an end to French obstruction, Kemal was brought to agree. These terms were embodied in the Mudania Convention of 11 October 1922, and served as a foundation for Curzon's subsequent diplomacy at Lausanne.

The strategy pursued by the Lloyd George coalition in this, the last great Near Eastern crisis, has been portrayed as erratic and irresponsible brinkmanship; the consequence of Lloyd George's eagerness to divert attention from his domestic difficulties, and of Churchill's addiction to military adventure.[150] Yet the evidence shows ministers united at every stage in the belief that the preservation of free access through the Straits was an imperial interest of the first order (even if minor differences existed over how best to defend that interest); and that the Kemalists should not be allowed to overthrow the verdict of victory in 1918 without a struggle. Nor is this surprising. All the senior ministers saw in Kemal the shade of Enver Pasha and his confederates. And in 1922 the shadow of the Gallipoli expedition still lay long and deep. Withdrawal in the face of the Kemalist forces appeared to lead inexorably to the re-establishment at Constantinople of the regime of 1914, and, still worse, to the restoration of the position of vantage which had allowed that regime to threaten Britain's Middle Eastern lifelines by exploiting European conflicts.[151] Inclined as they were to equate Britain's interest in the Straits with the defence of Gallipoli, ministers grasped instinctively that this was the real issue. In a memorandum written in preparation for the Lausanne Conference, Harold Nicolson described with characteristic insight what seemed to ministers the real significance of the Chanak crisis for imperial policy. The conflict, he wrote,

> appeared, and still remains, one between the continental or military system, and the oceanic, or naval system. Put in another way, the question was whether the Straits were to form a territorial bridge between Europe and Asia, or whether they were to constitute a blue water line separating these two continents.[152]

The Chanak crisis demonstrates with telling force the determination of the coalition to defend what appeared to be the most fundamental political and strategic benefit which painful victory in 1918 had yielded to Britain's system of imperial defence in the Mediterranean and the Middle East, and therefore to the safety of the imperial system as a whole. It reveals too the significant limits of ministerial sympathy for the claims of Asian nationalism and for the principle of national self-determination where imperial interests as they conceived them were at stake. In their search for an Iraq treaty, ministers showed the same vigorous discrimination between those forms of nationalism which they thought compatible with Britain's imperial policy and those which seemed to conflict with the essential purposes of imperial control.

All through the spring and summer of 1922 Feisal and his ministers continued to resist the efforts of the British to inveigle them into a treaty that would entail public acceptance on their part of Britain's mandate, and therefore of her ultimate international control over the government of the Iraq state. Feisal remained determined that the British and the Iraq notables should not between them reduce him to a constitutional figurehead, without power or patronage; and sought constantly to enlarge the scope of his authority and the extent of his political base. Thus early in April, and without consulting Cox, he dismissed four of his ministers on the grounds that they had been negligent in defending Iraq against Saudi incursions. Later in the month, he sought, and appeared to reach, a concordat with the leading Shi'ite dignitaries at Kerbela,[153] an implicit challenge to the Sunni élite who dominated the Baghdad administration. Meanwhile, he continued to bid for the support of the 'young Iraqis, the newspapers and the articulate elements in the towns' whom Cox believed to be opposed to the mandate, by pressing for changes in the wording of the treaty so as to veil its references to the mandate,[154] and shroud in ambiguity his obligation to accept the advice of the High Commissioner especially in financial questions.[155]

The effect of Feisal's tactics was to destroy the semblance of political discipline under British auspices which Cox had so carefully stage-managed at the time of the referendum.[156] At the goading of the king, the prime minister, the Naqib, and his ministers also began to oppose the inclusion of the mandate in the projected treaty. While Cox begged Churchill for a treaty formula that would 'sterilise present campaign of anti-Mandate propaganda',[157] rumours of a British evacuation began to circulate and the loyalty of the Euphrates tribes, measured by the sensitive barometer of revenue collection, started to fray.[158] Feisal, however, was wary of pushing matters too far, or of risking a personal confrontation with Cox which might lead to his abrupt removal by the British. Fears of this kind, Cox believed, prevented Feisal from coming to London in August.[159] Nevertheless, in late June, despite Cox's hopes that he would accept the treaty and the mandate after changes in the wording of the treaty,[160] Feisal at the last moment drew back and demanded that he should be allowed to reserve his position on the mandate while agreeing to the rest of the treaty – a demand soon echoed by the council of ministers.[161] Such a concession would leave the king free to denounce the mandate in the forthcoming elections to the constituent assembly at which the Iraq constitution was to be drawn up, and would lead, Cox thought, to 'armed turmoil'.[162] The most that might be conceded, the High Commissioner suggested, was that a resolution setting out Feisal's and the ministers' objections to the mandate be appended to the treaty when it was published. But if Feisal went on after this to allow agitation against the mandate, then his own position as High Commissioner would become impossible. The tension, Cox told Churchill in mid-August, had reached 'breaking point'.[163]

Churchill's reaction to these difficulties, while often clothed in strong language, was cautious, even hesitant. In April, when Feisal and his ministers had pressed for the abolition of the mandate, and when Cox was asking for some concession to be made, he had extracted at the second attempt from an unwilling Cabinet, and against the wishes of Curzon, the principle that Iraq should have the right to independent diplomatic representation although only in places to which London agreed.[164] But his proposal that the League be approached for a modification of the mandate was blocked by Lloyd George on the grounds that it would cause friction with France, and by Fisher[165] because it would alienate the United States.[166] Instead Churchill was instructed to tell Cox that rather than abrogate or modify the mandate, Britain would leave Iraq altogether.[167] Churchill knew therefore that he had little to offer in the way of propaganda concessions to Feisal; and that any attempt to retreat from the mandate would be disavowed by Lloyd George, Balfour, Curzon and Fisher who between them were responsible for Britain's international diplomacy. The most he dared offer was British support for Iraq's admission into the League of Nations before the treaty expired, thus automatically terminating the mandate.[168]

But if appeasement was difficult, no less so was the coercion of Feisal. When Cox suggested that Arab opinion in Baghdad might be chastened by the announcement that Britain would, if need be, retire to Basra, thus fracturing the unity of the Iraq state, Churchill declined his advice, ostensibly because he himself had said too often in the past that to hold Basra would be as expensive as holding Baghdad;[169] but in reality, perhaps, because such a threat would gravely compromise his resistance to the War Office's attack on his military policy. Churchill was extremely loth to admit the failure of his partnership with Feisal on which he had staked so much publicly and privately. He feared that any public announcement of the differences over the mandate would revive demands for a complete evacuation of Iraq in Parliament,[170] and reopen the whole issue of his policy in Cabinet. Moreover, to discipline Feisal by suppressing the political forces he claimed to represent opened the dangerous possibility that the reduction of the imperial garrison would be delayed if not reversed. Even in June, therefore, Churchill held out no prospect to Cox that a recourse to repression on his part would be endorsed in London.[171]

This paralysis in the Colonial Office's policy left Cox in a position of considerable discomfort. In the late summer and early autumn of 1922, it appeared to be leading directly towards a major crisis. For, as anti-British feeling grew in Baghdad, and the evidence of tribal unrest in central Iraq accumulated, the added threat of a Turkish attack in the north-east under cover of a Kurdish uprising[172] delivered a further blow against the frail edifice Churchill and Cox had constructed. In Kurdistan, the reluctance of the military command at Baghdad to sanction an effective deployment of ground forces[173] – a local reflection of the War Office's attitude – increased the likelihood that a prolonged guerrilla war, and the erosion of British influence over the Kurdish tribes, would make what Curzon had called Iraq's 'north-west frontier' the graveyard of Churchill's hopes. In Baghdad meanwhile, the political crisis reached its height when Cox adroitly took advantage of a hostile demonstration staged against him in the grounds of the king's palace to insist on an apology from Feisal for this open challenge (as Cox insisted it was) to his authority.[174] Feisal promptly took to his bed with appendicitis,[175] while Cox seized the opportunity, as acting head of the government, to arrest a number of the leading critics of the mandate. Everything now depended on whether Feisal, on resuming his constitutional functions, would endorse Cox's actions or whether he would attempt to rally an opposition against this forcible adjustment of the political balance in the country.

In London, Churchill watched this dual crisis with apprehension. 'The Turkish menace has got worse,' he wrote to Lloyd George, 'Feisal is playing the fool if not the knave.' Keeping the Turks out of northern Iraq would once again impose a heavy military burden. 'I do not see', he went on,

> what political strength there is to face a disaster of any kind, and certainly I cannot believe that in any circumstances any large

> reinforcements would be sent from here or from India. There is not one newspaper which is not consistently hostile to our remaining in this country . . . .[176]

Once more, as so often in the past, Churchill declared that sooner than take responsibility for an impossible policy, he would favour a total evacuation, and demanded 'definite guidance'[177] from the Prime Minister. Lloyd George responded to this appeal with an equivocal promise of support. 'On general principles', he said, 'I am against a policy of scuttle in Iraq as elsewhere', and he counselled Churchill to lay all the alternatives before the Cabinet.[178] Before this could take place, however, the crisis at Baghdad had passed as Feisal caved in to Cox's demand that he endorse the High Commissioner's policy of repression; perhaps, as Cox believed, because he had been impressed by the ease with which the arrests had been carried out and with the weakness of the anti-mandate party.[179] Thereafter, progress towards the acceptance of the treaty and the mandate was relatively smooth with only one last flicker of non-cooperation from Feisal; the treaty was signed on 10 October 1922. The easing of the internal situation, moreover, saved Churchill's scheme for air control from renewed debate; and the arrival of Sir John Salmond as Air Officer Commanding – and therefore garrison commander – at the beginning of October brought a more vigorous response to Turkish incursions in Kurdistan.[180] By the end of October, the danger of a serious Turkish attack in the north had passed.

Cox's skill and Feisal's surrender saved Churchill from the necessity of seeking a new basis for the policy of imperial control in Iraq. Yet despite the tone of Churchill's letter to Lloyd George on 1 September, and the threat of evacuation he had transmitted to Feisal from the Cabinet earlier in the year, it is unlikely that continued intransigence by the king would have resulted in the abandonment of the mandate and the renunciation of all British influence over the newly constituted Arab state. The considerations which had turned ministers against such a course in December 1920 applied with yet greater force two years later at the height of the confrontation with what appeared an aggressive and expansionist Turkish nationalism. It is improbable that the continued hostility of the press to the Iraq commitment would alone have deterred ministers who were ready to contemplate war over Chanak, so long as remaining in Iraq did not require a drastic reversal of the garrison reductions to which Churchill had pledged the Government. The ease and speed of Cox's repression in August, for which Churchill gained the prompt and unquestioning approval of senior ministers,[181] suggested that even had Feisal continued to obstruct the treaty, the will and the means to discipline him were not lacking. The most likely outcome of further difficulties with the king was his relegation to constitutional impotence, and the construction of a new partnership between Britain and the notables: a task which, on Cox's showing, would not have taxed Britain's military resources. Nor, ultimately, as the example of Egypt suggested, was failure to agree upon a treaty an obstacle to the retention of imperial controls in matters of foreign policy and defence.

Conclusion

When the Lloyd George coalition fell in October 1922, the work of delineating Britain's imperial posture in the post-war Middle East was still incomplete. The status of the Straits and the attitude of the Kemalists towards the incorporation of the Mosul *vilayet* into Iraq were still unresolved.

Nevertheless the coalition had presided over the gradual reduction of the vast territorial responsibilities, and even vaster geopolitical ambitions, which had overwhelmed ministers and their advisers at the end of the war, to a size and scope more in keeping with the peacetime strength of Britain as a land power. The short-lived bridgeheads in the interior of south-west Asia had been abandoned to a revived Russian empire with few real regrets. In Persia, where the political involvement of Britain had a long history, the pangs of abandoning Curzon's great project for a veiled protectorate had been eased by the emergence of a government hostile alike to British and Russian dominance, while Loraine, the British minister at Teheran, settled down to the diplomatic trench warfare that would have been familiar to his predecessor before 1914.[182] The course of Anglo-Persian relations still waited, however, upon the durability and success of the regime created by Reza Khan – a question on which there continued to be differences of opinion among British diplomats in Persia.[183] The last traces of the 'southern policy' had yet to be eradicated from British policy.

Elsewhere in the Middle East, the development of policy, especially after March 1921, reflected above all else the influence of strategic concepts that would have been familiar to policy-makers in the later nineteenth century but which had been adapted to the new circumstances which prevailed after the disintegration of the Ottoman Empire in 1918. With the exception of Palestine, where special considerations imposed a commitment alien to the traditions of imperial policy, the last phase of the coalition's Middle Eastern policies demonstrated its belief that it was British influence at the Straits and at the landward approaches to the Persian Gulf which mattered most. The resolution displayed by ministers in the defence of an imperial control in some form of these strategic zones contrasts vividly with their readiness to write off the Caucasus, central Asia and northern Persia. Neither at the Straits nor in Iraq were ministers concerned with Britain's economic interests or the close ordering of local politics. But they were determined to prevent the construction of regimes that might turn these vital regions once again into a cockpit of international rivalries and thus recreate the conditions of military crisis that had beset them in the Middle East between 1914 and 1918.

It was, therefore, the old pursuit of security along the route to India which drove the coalition, in a period of contracting military power, shrinking finances and nationalist upheaval, to seek strange bed-fellows, to espouse superficially novel doctrines of trusteeship and to risk armed conflict over Chanak. Fear of Turkish imperialism led them to champion Arab nationalism and tolerate its exponents. Failure to shackle Kemalism by international controls, coupled with logistical constraints, enforced unseemly bargains with febrile political movements thrown up by the war and the fall of the Ottoman Empire. But in all the expedients to which the coalition had recourse, there is little to suggest that the management of imperial policy was informed by novel conceptions of imperial rule; still less by any loss of confidence in the future of the British world-system.

Part IV

Consequences

9 Indian Policy and the Oil Question

It was only to be expected that the great expansion of British power in the Middle East after 1918, which seemed one of the principal consequences of the Great War, and the expedients adopted by British ministers to conserve the main fruits of victory there, would have repercussions on the rest of the British imperial system. The problems of imperial policy provided something like a test case for the post-war relationship between Britain and the self-governing states of the Empire, which the dominions resolved, at the time of the Mesopotamian uprising and subsequently of the Chanak crisis, by showing that the military and political integration of the Empire in wartime would not be prolonged into the peace. Perhaps more significantly, the reconstruction of the Middle East brought into focus the latent strains and tensions between the imperial government in London and its administrative agents in British India, increasingly sensitive to the special anxieties of communities and electorates in India, and increasingly unhappy at their involuntary association with British imperial policies elsewhere in the world. Lastly it remains to be considered whether Britain's policy in the Middle East reflected to any real extent the growth of new economic preoccupations; in particular, the question of how the actual and potential oil resources of Iraq and Persia influenced the makers of policy, and to what degree their dispositions revealed a demotion of the old strategic priorities of Palmerston, Salisbury and Grey in favour of a new economic imperialism.

Britain, India and the Middle East

India's wartime contribution to imperial defence and the sensitivity ministers had displayed over her security during the war made it inevitable that British desiderata for a peace settlement in the Middle East should be strongly influenced by a desire to safeguard the *Raj* against the external dangers that had threatened it. The difficulties which faced ministers in this task were formidable enough in the Middle East; but after the middle of 1918 the extent of Indian involvement in the region, coupled with the imminence of constitutional reform in India herself, made the task of coordinating foreign policy between London and New Delhi both more necessary and more difficult. Indeed, no sooner had the discussion of Britain's desiderata in the East got under way at the war's end than the divergent tendencies of British and Indian foreign policy began to reveal themselves.

To Curzon it was axiomatic that the foundation of imperial policy in the Middle East was the need to defend India. On the fate of the territories in the Middle East, he declared, 'will depend not only the future of the territories themselves, but also the fate of the British Empire in the East'.[1] It was the defence of India that made necessary a British presence in north-west Persia and even in the Caucasus.[2] For Mesopotamia the argument was the same. The rescue of the inhabitants from Turkish misrule might justify, but it was Indian security that demanded, the acceptance of administrative responsibility by Great Britain.[3] Faced with these large claims on India's behalf, the reaction of the Viceroy and the India Office was equivocal. Montagu believed certainly that Indian prestige required the outright defeat of Turkey and the conquest of Mesopotamia.[4] But the Government of India was less confident. Throughout the war it had been haunted by the fear that British and Indian military occupation of the Islamic empires would spark off an explosion of anti-Christian and anti-British sentiment among Indian Muslims.[5] At the end of 1918, this anxiety led the Viceroy to oppose the policies which Curzon had formulated for the future of Persia and the remnants of the Ottoman Empire in Anatolia and Thrace.

What roused the apprehension of the Indian government was Curzon's insistence that the only possible basis for Anglo-Persian cooperation was an agreement which, so New Delhi feared, would be denounced by Indian Muslims as a veiled annexation. India's interest in Persia, declared the Indian foreign secretary, was simply that no foreign power should be allowed to hold there 'a dominant position or indeed a position at all'.[6] Disciplining the Persian tribes held no attraction for a government with tribes enough of its own. If Persian goodwill was desired, it could best be cultivated by denouncing the agreement of 1907 and by continuing the wartime subsidy.[7] Political caution and a suspicion that Curzonian expansion in Persia would become a charge on Indian resources, argued against a forward policy in any shape. But Montagu was won over to Curzon's plan by the assurance that Persian politicians were eager for British help;[8] so the Government of India confined itself to insisting on the withdrawal of its contingents in north, east and south Persia.

Over the future of Turkey, however, the Indian Secretary joined the Viceroy in a far more resolute opposition. If Muslim opinion seemed likely to jib at a veiled protectorate over Persia, the prospect of its reaction to the dismemberment of the Ottoman Empire was daunting indeed. And when Curzon revealed his proposal for the eviction of the Sultan from the old Ottoman capital at Constantinople, the Indian government's worst fears were realised. For the Sultan's status in the Islamic world was not founded only on his sovereignty over the most powerful Mohammedan state. He also enjoyed as Caliph a unique authority over millions of Muslims living outside the Ottoman Empire. As Commander of the Faithful, he was the recognised (if rarely active) leader of the Islamic world. His humiliation and maltreatment by the Christian powers of the Entente, and particularly by Britain, seemed certain to react on the relations between the *Raj* and its Muslim subjects, whose loyalty, Montagu told the Eastern Committee, had already been subjected to 'continuous strains'.[9] 'It is not really Constantinople I am afraid of,' he declared. 'It is the idea that this country has become an anti-Mohammedan state.'[10]

Balfour and Curzon were unsympathetic. Montagu, fearful that a swift Allied declaration on the principles of the Turkish peace would present India with a *fait accompli*, appealed directly to Lloyd George. Indeed, by the spring of 1919, the conciliation of Muslim sentiment seemed more urgent than ever. The emergence of the Khilafat movement in India as a vehicle for the rival claims of Muslim politicians to provincial power under the projected reforms,[11] the eruption of unrest in the Punjab in March 1919, and the outbreak of the third Afghan war at the same moment, all seemed to betoken a dangerous and unpredictable Muslim reaction against British influence and authority. To Montagu they held the additional threat that the delicate balance of Indian politics, upon which the success of his reforms scheme depended, would be disastrously upset.[12] 'The Viceroy', he told Lloyd George, 'tells me that Mohammedan unrest is at the root of the troubles in India at the present moment . . . and he assures me that a just peace with Turkey would go far to remedy the situation.'[13]

This strident appeal anticipated three years of vain but constant protest against the determination of Lloyd George and Curzon to contain Turkish power within close geographical limits and stifle any recrudescence of Turkish aspirations to a supranational influence in the

Islamic world. Montagu's resentment, and the alarm of the Government of India, were sharpened by what seemed the progressive deterioration of Anglo-Turkish relations as the installation of the Greeks in Smyrna and Thrace, Allied occupation of Constantinople, and the open sympathy of the British for the Greek attack on Kemal after June 1920, denied the possibility of a settlement that might appease at least some section of Indian Muslim opinion. For as Anglo-Turkish relations declined towards open conflict, Montagu's hopes for a harmonious partnership between imperial rule and Indian politicians in the working of the reforms steadily evaporated. By September 1919, the Khilafat movement's campaign for a restitution of the Caliph's full dignity and the preservation of the holy places in Muslim hands appeared, with the gathering of an All-India Khilafat Conference at Lucknow, to be widening and deepening its political base. Moreover, the leadership of the movement was passing increasingly from the hands of established Muslim politicians into the control of the ulama, who were less susceptible to the attractions of place, profit and patronage which were the lubricants of constitutional politics.[14] With the passing of the Government of India Act in December 1919, and the preparations for the inauguration of the reformed constitution in 1921, the problem of Muslim unrest and agitation, and the danger that it would be exploited by Hindu 'extremists',[15] bulked larger and larger in the calculations of the Viceroy and the Indian Secretary. In March 1920, the Central Khilafat Committee pronounced against participation in the new constitution. 'Educated moderate minded Mahommedans', wrote Chelmsford comfortingly to Montagu, ' . . . are not very greatly concerned with details of Turkish Peace Settlement'.[16] But, in reality, the political initiative within the Khilafat movement was shifting more and more to Muslims who were neither educated (Chelmsford meant in the Western manner) nor moderate.[17] Worst of all, by the late summer of 1920, the Khilafat movement was providing Gandhi with a political base from which to challenge the established leaders of Hindu nationalism and propel the predominantly Hindu Congress party away from cooperation with the reformed constitution and towards an open confrontation with the government.[18]

With Gandhi's triumph at the Nagpur Congress in December 1920, and the launching of the campaign for *swaraj in one year*, the Government of India faced not only the embarrassment of a rejection by Hindus and Muslims alike of its new constitution,[19] but also the likelihood that the boycott of its courts and councils by the educated would encourage violence and disorder among the rural and urban masses.[20] The Viceroy and his advisers believed, however, that non-cooperation would fizzle out if left to itself and instructed the provinces in January 1921 to adhere to the Supreme Government's policy 'of abstaining as far as possible from interference in order to avoid making martyrs of fanatical leaders or precipitating disorders'.[21] This cautious strategy depended heavily, however, upon Government's success in rallying support for cooperation among 'moderate' Indian politicians. As non-cooperation got under way, therefore, Chelmsford repeated his appeal to London: 'only by a real modification' of the Turkish treaty could Muslim excitement be allayed and the Muslim 'moderates' detached from the 'extremists'.[22] In late February 1921, Chelmsford told Montagu that he had received a Muslim delegation – a further political tactic aimed at the seduction of moderation. Montagu, in turn, continued to press these opinions especially upon Curzon[23] and the Prime Minister.

Indeed, throughout 1921 and into 1922, he pestered his colleagues with appeals for concessions to Turkish nationalism; for an early peace with Turkey; citing the opinions of Reading, who had replaced Chelmsford as Viceroy but who adopted the same approach to non-cooperation; of George Lloyd, Governor of Bombay; and of administrative subordinates in the Indian districts: all to show that if there was an acceptable Turkish peace non-cooperation 'would collapse like a house of cards'.[24] But despite Montagu's brave words to the Viceroys in moments of optimism, there is no evidence that at any stage his attempt to modify imperial policy in the Middle East to ease the pressures of agitational politics in India influenced his ministerial colleagues. For this failure three reasons may be advanced. Firstly, as has been suggested in an earlier chapter, the most senior ministers in the coalition were convinced that concessions to Kemalist nationalism, especially where these involved liberating the Angora regime from Greek military pressure in advance of a properly ratified treaty, or readmitting the Turks to Europe, were incompatible with their fundamental purpose of destroying Turkey's ability to play the international role which she had played in October 1914. No considerations of Indian politics, nor ultimately of domestic British politics, were sufficient to outweigh their attachment to this object. Secondly, perhaps because of the strength of this commitment, none of the senior ministers was disposed to take seriously Montagu's claim that the treatment of the Caliph was a real political issue in India. When, in December 1918, Indian Muslim sentiment had been adduced as a reason against evicting the Turks from Constantinople, Curzon had poured scorn on the Indian government's fears. The Muslim nationalists in India, he declared, were pro-Turk because they were anti-British, not because they were fellow Muslims. 'I do not think', he added, 'that Pan-Islamism has any substantial hold in India at all.'[25] And although this confident judgment was undermined by the events of the following months and years, Curzon's fear and loathing of pan-Islamic sentiment was too great, it may be thought, for him to admit any compromise with its political manifestations, least of all within the imperial system. Both Balfour and Lloyd George broadly shared Curzon's prejudice. Even Milner, who had supported Montagu's call for the retention of Constantinople as the Sultan's capital, believed that Muslim agitation over the Caliphate was 'largely factitious and certainly very extravagant'.[26] Lastly, Montagu's attempts to modify Cabinet policy suffered from his own lack of personal and political authority among ministers, partly in consequence of his temperament, but increasingly – especially after his disastrous speech in the Commons debate on the Amritsar report – because of the strong resentment against him among Conservative backbenchers. Lloyd George, with whom for a brief period Montagu had enjoyed close political relations, mistrusted his political judgment. The Prime Minister, Montagu told Reading despairingly in July 1921, 'has, as you know, little or no faith in me'.[27] Awareness of his impotence within the Cabinet pushed Montagu more and more towards attempts to influence it from outside by direct pressure from the Viceroy, and ultimately by a breach of constitutional convention which ended in his enforced resignation in circumstances of irreparable personal humiliation.

India in the Imperial System

The critical or uncooperative attitude adopted by the Government of India towards the efforts of the Home Government to safeguard imperial interests, whether in Turkey, Persia or Afghanistan[28] (where, once more for internal reasons, the Indian government rejected the Cabinet's advice that it should insist upon the exclusion of Russian diplomacy from Afghanistan before agreeing to a new treaty), was generally regarded by ministers in London with irritation and resentment. Even Austen Chamberlain, who had served at the India Office and under whose auspices the proposals for constitutional reconstruction in India had assumed their original pristine form, expressed an incomprehension of Indian policy towards the Middle East. 'They disclaim all interest and all responsibility', he complained of the Indian government, and refuse financial help. I do not know that this represents their permanent state of mind, but Heaven knows, we have burdens enough on our shoulders here and India cannot expect us to pay the whole cost of what I may call her external frontiers. I know that the financial difficulties of the Government of India are as great as ours but I cannot understand their assumed attitude of perfect indifference to the peace of Persia and the Arab countries.[29]

The impatience of ministers at home may well have arisen from the sense of financial strain to which Chamberlain alluded and from a feeling that, compared with the mother-country, India's burdens were light. The volume of work imposed on senior ministers and the concatenation of foreign and domestic crises at frequent intervals between 1918 and 1922 did not encourage a tolerance for the trials of lesser men. These circumstances, however, provide only part of the answer. For behind the quarrels of London and New Delhi and periodically illuminated by the twists of imperial policy in the Middle East, lay deeper disagreements about the implications of constitutional change for the political relations of Britain and India and for the structure of the imperial system in the Eastern hemisphere.

During the nineteenth century, the relations between the Home Government and the Government of India had been marked by a steady increase in the degree of control exercised over the Viceroy by the Secretary of State in London,[30] just as within the Indian Empire itself the autonomy of the provinces became more and more circumscribed by the growth of the Supreme Government's regulatory powers.[31] While London was conceding responsible government to Britain's colonies in Canada, South Africa and Australasia, legislation on India which passed through Parliament constantly reaffirmed the supremacy of the Secretary of State and (as recently as the consolidating act of 1915) his power to 'superintend, direct and control all acts, operations and concerns relating to the government or revenues of India'.[32] Indeed the only formal constraints upon the wide discretion of the Indian Secretary were contained in the advisory functions of the Council of India – a body of retired administrators – and in the right which Parliament reserved to scrutinise the purposes for which the military resources of India might be used.[33]

In practice, of course, the stark clarity of the Home Government's supremacy was modified by the reliance it was often forced to place upon information and advice provided by the Viceroy. The Home Government, remarked Balfour in a lapidary phrase, 'did not issue any instruction without first consulting India, just as India took no initiative without first referring home'.[34] What Balfour had in mind, primarily, was the conduct of Indian foreign policy and the deployment of the Indian army, for, as we have seen, it was control over these and access to the resources which sustained them that gave India a special significance in British eyes. And in questions such as these, as Balfour's silky formula implied, while New Delhi might propose, it was London that disposed. Nor at the time of Balfour's pronouncement was it intended that constitutional reform in India should diminish ultimate British control over those aspects of Indian administration which affected her contribution to imperial defence. At the heart of the Montagu–Chelmsford scheme lay a careful distinction between those subjects over which authority would generally lie with the representatives of Indian electorates, and those which would continue to be the ultimate responsibility of the British Parliament; a distinction broadly similar to that which had been observed previously when the settlement colonies had been granted responsible government. Thus the Reform Act of 1919 which arose out of the Montagu–Chelmsford Report prohibited the elected members of the Central Legislative Assembly from discussing expenditure classified by the Viceroy as relating to political (i.e. relations with foreign powers or the Indian states) or defence matters.[35] The thinking behind this distinction was bluntly stated by Lionel Curtis, whose hand was widely seen in the reform proposals, and to whose influence Montagu himself paid a cautious tribute.[36] India's foreign affairs, wrote Curtis, 'are those of the whole commonwealth. She can never therefore control them apart. . . . If India were now inhabited', he went on,

> by a people already as fitted and practised in self-government as those of England herself, it would not be possible, so long as they remain part of the British Commonwealth, to place the Indian frontier under the control of a Government responsible only to the people of India.[37]

'The defence of India', remarked the Montagu–Chelmsford Report more tersely, 'is an imperial question.'[38]

But whatever the intentions of ministers and officials in London and New Delhi, the politics of reform did not permit so rigid a separation of the local and the imperial sphere. Montagu himself was anxious to demonstrate that the *Raj* was responsive to Indian opinion and solicitous of Indian interests. The Government of India, he said, 'must learn to be politicians, they must learn to defend themselves . . .'.[39] It was essential to develop 'that political instinct which would enable them to carry with them public opinion'.[40] For Montagu, this 'political' role meant, in part, the identification of the Government of India with the particular interests of Indians within the imperial system even though Indian politicians were to be excluded from all questions of defence and foreign policy. He was determined therefore to build upon the decision of the Imperial War Conference in 1917 which, by conceding full representation to India at future imperial conferences, appeared to give India broadly the same international standing as the white dominions.[41] In consequence, India, like the dominions, was granted separate representation within the British Empire Delegation at the Paris Peace Conference, with Montagu, leader of the Indian delegation, enjoying plenipotentiary rank. It was on the basis of this formal enhancement of India's international status that Montagu pressed his demand for India's special interests to be accommodated within imperial policy. In February 1919, he sought Lloyd George's permission for the Indian delegation to put forward its own distinctive view on the treatment of Turkey. 'Separate Representation has been given,' he told the Prime Minister. 'It must be used.'[42] Montagu was also anxious to show that the *Raj* in its new incarnation could improve the lot of Indian emigrants overseas, especially in East Africa.[43] And most spectacularly of all, he wished to press India's claim to the trusteeship under mandate of German East Africa, as proof of her growing status among the self-governing states of the Empire.[44]

The quarrels between the Home Government and New Delhi over imperial policy in Turkey, Persia and Afghanistan took place, therefore, in a wider context of debate about how far India as a dependency of the Crown should be allowed to frame a foreign policy which challenged or, at the very least inconvenienced, the directors of policy in London. Montagu's conception of India's elevated place in the imperial system did not attract much support among his colleagues, least of all among senior ministers who were unlikely to favour the growth of colonial particularism or Montagu's willingness to adopt a local rather than an imperial perspective. 'Your attitude has often struck me', Lloyd George once reproved the Indian Secretary, 'as being not so much that of a member of the British Cabinet but of a successor on the throne of Aurungzeb.'[45]

The general lack of sympathy and understanding displayed by ministers towards the efforts of the India Office and the Government of India to ingratiate themselves with domestic Indian opinion was no less marked in the controversies that arose after 1919 over the use and control of the Indian army proper, and the maintenance of the British contingents stationed in India at Indian expense.[46] Significantly, at the moment when the Cabinet had authorised the Montagu–Chelmsford reform scheme conceding a measure of power in the provinces to Indian politicians, it had also accepted the report of the Esher Committee, set up to review the organisation of the Army in India in the light of the Mesopotamia Commission's strictures.[47] This committee declared roundly that 'we cannot consider the administration of the Army in India otherwise than as part of the total armed forces of the Empire . . .'.[48] Indeed, the Esher Report, while claiming to take account of impending political changes, in India,[49] was largely devoted to recommending ways in which the influence of the professional head of the *British* Army might be exerted more strongly on the administration of both the British and the Indian elements of the Army in India 'so as to develop the military resources of India in a manner suited to imperial necessities'.[50] In order to achieve this central objective, the Committee was prepared to see 'an increase in the annual cost of the Army in India',[51] to be borne on Indian revenues, at a time when Britain's own military budget was being steadily reduced. Nor did it conceal the assumptions that lay behind this desire to impose a yet heavier military burden on the Indian taxpayer. 'Just as the security of India demands the presence of . . . British troops,' it reasoned, 'so the fresh military obligations devolving on the Empire as a result of the war necessitates the employment overseas of considerable numbers of Indian troops.'[52]

The clear implication of the Esher Report was, therefore, that the extension of British commitments in the Middle East would require the maintenance of a larger standing army in India than before the war, the cost of which, except when on active service overseas, would be carried on the Indian exchequer. Such a proposal was scarcely calculated to commend itself to political opinion in India nor indeed to an Indian government casting round for moderates who might be rallied against Gandhi and the Khilafatists. Thus, when in September 1920 the Home Government, its appeals to the dominion governments for troops having been coldly received, directed the Indian Government to send reinforcements to help quell the Mesopotamian rebellion, the Viceroy, while complying, took the opportunity to challenge the assumptions upon which the Esher Report and the Home Government's instruction both rested. 'We have evidence to show', he told Montagu,

> that the great bulk of educated opinion in India is opposed to our undertaking extensive obligations in regard to overseas garrisons . . . moderate opinion considers India is being exploited in being asked to provide for service outside India an unreasonably large proportion of troops now employed for imperial purposes. . . .[53]

Montagu, with his mind fixed on the working of the new constitution, took up the Viceroy's arguments in a frontal attack on the Esher Report at the end of 1920. India, he showed, was spending more and more on the upkeep of the Army in India, and, as depression bit into revenue receipts, defence expenditure would become proportionately a yet heavier burden.[54] The political consequences of this were not hard to predict:

> In India where taxation is not imposed by the representatives of the people, a high level of taxation maintained for purposes which India strongly argues are not in India's best interests, form a ready weapon for the extremist agitator in his campaign for fomenting racial hatred, and can only form a grave political danger.[55]

This argument Montagu reinforced by claiming that any attempt to raise fresh taxation to meet military expenditure 'may have the disastrous result of driving the moderate party on whose strength the future of the reformed constitution depends, into the arms of the extremists'.[56] The new political conditions in India set close limits on the scale of India's military forces; and it was 'definitely impossible for us to make any contribution to Imperial Defence'. The 'grandiose schemes' of the Esher Committee for military expansion in India would have to be scrapped, and with them 'all idea of initiating as a normal peace measure a scheme whereby [India] is to become the base for vast military operations in the Middle and Far East. . . .[57] In short,' Montagu concluded, 'we must definitely get out of our heads the vague idea, too often entertained, that India is an inexhaustible reservoir from which men and money may be drawn towards the support of imperial resources or in pursuance of Imperial strategy.'[58]

Montagu's onslaught provoked little immediate reaction among his ministerial colleagues although Churchill sought to challenge his claim that India's defence burden was inequitably heavy.[59] Probably this reticence derived from a feeling that the Esher Report, which had originally been framed in the expectation of a general integration of the military resources of Britain, India and the dominions, was not worth defending; and also from a reluctance to be found championing the retention of large imperial forces in the Middle East. Meanwhile in India the new Indian Legislative Assembly, devised as a representative element in India's central government, denounced at its first session the propositions of the Esher Committee as they related to the development of the Indian Army for imperial purposes;[60] and Chelmsford, to appease moderate opinion, set up under the Commander-in-Chief in India a committee to examine the implications of the Esher Report.[61] This manoeuvre, and the steady reduction during 1921 of the imperial garrisons in the Middle East, allowed the issue to be shelved for a time, until at the end of the year the Government of India's proposals for a revision of military arrangements began to be considered by ministers in London.

By the early weeks of 1922, however, differences between London and Simla over defence and foreign policy had become partially submerged by more immediate issues. As non-cooperation seemed to reach a climax of violence and disorder, ministers became gravely embarrassed at the prospect of the visit of the Prince of Wales to India which might reveal in the full glare of publicity the shortcomings of their Indian policy. Reading's proposal for a conference to parley with the leaders of non-cooperation was denounced by Churchill, Curzon and Austen Chamberlain as appeasement of sedition.[62] Instead the Cabinet pressed Reading to arrest and prosecute Gandhi without delay and grew increasingly angry at his reluctance to do so.[63] Chamberlain, in particular, was anxious to check the growth of anti-coalition sentiment in his party and to outflank the die-hards by a display of firmness in imperial policy. In late January he urged Montagu to lay down clear guidelines of policy, 'primarily for the Government of India but probably also, and later of Parliament'.[64]

It was, therefore, in a mood of vexation with the Viceroy that ministers turned to inspect the plans of the Government of India for the future of the Army in India. For the Viceroy, faced with the task of steering a budget through the Indian Legislative Assembly, and of enlisting the cooperation of its members in a visible demonstration of the virtues of the new constitution, was determined that the gap between expenditure and Government's depressed revenues should be narrowed as much as possible by public economies, and as little as possible by new taxation.[65] To ease India's military spending and conciliate Indian opinion he proposed to reduce the British contingents quartered in India at Indian expense, and to begin a major programme for 'Indianising' the officer corps of the Indian army.[66]

Predictably, senior ministers rejected this package entirely, mainly on the grounds that both the Viceroy's proposals would weaken British control in India, but also, perhaps, because, as the War Minister pointed out, to bring home part of the British component of the Army in India would throw a further burden on the Treasury at an inconvenient time.[67] India was not to be permitted to alter unilaterally the military system which had underpinned the defence economy of the Empire for so long, however urgent the need to conciliate moderate opinion in the sub-continent. Moreover, this firm reassertion of India's subordinate place in the British world-system was soon to be matched in the sphere of imperial foreign policy. For as renewed pressure was brought to bear on the Viceroy to arrest Gandhi, Reading and Montagu cast round for some device to balance this recourse to coercion and flatter the Indian moderates. Montagu's solution was to by-pass the Cabinet and authorise the publication of the notorious telegram in which the Indian Government protested once again against the coalition's Turkish policy, to demonstrate thereby a sympathy for Indian Muslim anxieties.[68] But this attempt to challenge London's supremacy in a question affecting the external relations of the imperial system ended in disaster and destroyed Montagu's career. Curzon forced his resignation and triumphantly upheld the principle of metropolitan control over India's foreign policy. India's request for a separate voice in matters affecting Britain's relations with Islam, he told Chamberlain, 'is not only inconsistent with any theory of sound imperial policy but is inconsistent with the position of India in the Empire'.[69]

As matters turned out, the Viceroy chose to avoid the use of his reserved powers to force through new taxation to cover increases in expenditure; and evaded a confrontation with either the Cabinet or the Indian Legislative Assembly by setting up a committee (along the lines of the Geddes Committee) to review public spending and reduce the deficits outstanding from previous years and anticipated for 1922–3.[70] And in the milder political climate (in India at least) of August 1922, the Home Government eventually rejected the pretensions of the Esher Report.[71] But the Cabinet's refusal in February and March to give the Indian Government a free hand in questions of internal security, to allow it to alter the structure of its military commitments, or to overlook its assertion of a minimal independence in international affairs, all show how reluctant ministers were to concede that the strains of Britain's expansion in the Middle East could impose changes of policy elsewhere in the imperial system; and how rigid a conception they still preserved, in the era of post-war reform, of India's traditionally subordinate status in all questions affecting the international security of the Empire.

British Policy and the Question of Oil

In the course of the first half of the twentieth century, the Middle East came to hold a dual significance in the minds of those responsible for the conduct of Britain's foreign and imperial policy. It remained, of course, a vital strategic zone where the outer defences of the British imperial system had to be guarded against Russian or German encroachment. But it also became a major source for a fuel increasingly important to the efficient functioning of an advanced industrial economy and crucial to the waging of mechanised war on land and sea or in the air. Access to the oil fields of Iraq and Persia, and their denial to the enemy, became in the Second World War strategic objectives of a high order.

This special economic position which the Middle East came to hold in the calculations of the great powers particularly after 1939 should not, however, impose a dogmatic view of the motives and objects of British imperial policy in the region between 1918 and 1922. In a period when Middle East oil – in reality oil from Persia alone – accounted for only a tiny fraction of the world's production,[72] and when the colossal growth in its output by the 1960s was beyond all reasonable prediction, there is room for scepticism as to how far 'oil imperialism'[73] can explain the twists and turns of British policy described in previous chapters. Indeed, it is argued here that while British ministers were not indifferent to the enchanting prospect of a great Middle East oil industry controlled by British enterprise, in the everyday management of policy it was the larger and more immediate problem of constructing stable and friendly regimes in Turkey, Iraq and Persia which preoccupied them to the exclusion of almost every other consideration; that in so far as they anticipated at all the creation of an empire of oil, it was only as an agreeable consequence of policies pursued for other and more pressing reasons.

The experience of the First World War undoubtedly produced a transformation in the thinking of British governments about access to supplies of fuel oil. Even before the war, the decision to convert the Royal Navy from coal-burning to oil-burning, and alarm at the violent fluctuations of oil prices, had persuaded a reluctant Admiralty to press for a majority shareholding by the government in the Anglo-Persian Oil Company – an offshoot of Burmah Oil – whose production was geared primarily to the Navy's needs.[74] The war itself stimulated a dramatic increase in Britain's consumption of oil. Between 1914 and 1918, the declared value of oil imports rose from under £13 million to almost £64 million *per annum*.[75] 'In no other sector of our imports', announced the War Cabinet Report for 1917, 'has the demand increased to such an extent.'[76] In August 1917, to coordinate the supply and distribution of what had become a precious strategic material, the War Cabinet set up the Petroleum Executive under the direction of Sir John Cadman, a leading British oil expert.[77]

Although the Petroleum Executive's primary function may have been to advise on the management of Britain's large imports of oil, its responsibilities were soon extended as a result of the War Cabinet's drive for a greater self-sufficiency in all essential materials, both within Britain and within the imperial system as a whole.[78] In 1918, when the costs of importing oil were running at almost double the figure even for the previous year,[79] and when the overwhelming dependence of Britain and France on American oil – which furnished some 80 per cent of their requirements[80] – was manifest, the need to develop independent British supplies both to safeguard Britain's naval supremacy and also, perhaps, to relieve her huge trading deficit with the United States,[81] became more urgent than before. Thus in July 1918, Admiral Slade, principal oil adviser to the Admiralty, urged that the development of the fields in Persia and of the anticipated reserves in Mesopotamia should be kept under purely British control after the war, and that the British oil companies should be prevented from falling under the influence of foreign investors.[82] Later in the year a government committee under Lord Harcourt, a former Colonial Secretary, sought ways of asserting greater British control over the important Anglo-Dutch concern Royal Dutch Shell; and Anglo-Persian, as the Navy's main all-British supplier, was encouraged to prospect more widely in the British Empire in Canada, Australia and Papua.[83]

There is thus little doubt that at the time when the war unexpectedly ground to a halt the quest for all kinds of war supplies which might be produced under imperial control and for imperial purposes formed an important part of the coalition's overall strategy for winning the war. There was, moreover, in the immediate aftermath of the war, a certain eagerness to build upon the autarchic tendencies of wartime economic planning to eradicate the economic weaknesses which the war had revealed in the imperial system and to bind the Empire together as a powerful, cohesive and self-sufficient bloc.[84] More particularly, the vast enlargement of British power in the Middle East, the accelerating demand for oil on the world market, and the expectation that American oil reserves would soon be depleted,[85] encouraged hopes in Britain that the fuller exploitation of new sources under British control would allow the tables to be turned and make America's industrial economy dependent upon British oil suppliers.[86] It would be reckless, however, to conclude from such evidence that the framing of imperial policy in the Middle East between 1918 and 1922 was undertaken wholly, or even primarily, in the light of a long-term strategy for bringing its known and anticipated oil wealth under exclusive British control in the interests of enhancing Britain's world economic power.

In 1918 the only significant supplies of oil in the Middle East, leaving aside the rich and important fields round Baku in the Russian Caucasus, were to be found in Persia in the concessions held by the Anglo-Persian Oil Company. The security of the fields and of the refinery at Abadan on the Shatt al-Arab, no more than eighty miles from Basra, had been of concern to British policy-makers both before and during the First World War. For the most part, however, the protection of the oil installations and the pipeline had depended upon a small contingent of the Indian Army and upon the friendship and cooperation of the local rulers of the region, especially the Sheikh of Mohammerah, who were remote from the influence of the imperial capital at Teheran, nearly five hundred miles away by the primitive communications of the Persian Empire. As we have seen, when the British decided in March 1918 to intervene militarily and politically in north-west Persia, it was the need to forestall a German and Turkish advance on Teheran and to prevent an attack on the flank of the British army in Mesopotamia which swayed a reluctant Eastern Committee. And Curzon's eventual conversion to the idea of prolonging the British presence in northern Persia after the war to effect a reconstruction of Persian administration owed much to his fear of Persian intrigue at the Peace Conference and to his determination to establish stable Muslim polities along India's northernmost strategic frontiers; but little if anything to a belief that the local and regional interests of the Anglo-Persian Oil Company could only be protected or promoted by the establishment of a predominant British influence at Teheran.

Thus although Curzon cited the protection of Britain's oil interests in Persia against Bolshevik interference from the north as one justification for the Anglo-Persian Agreement and the formal statement of Britain's deep interest in Persia (relying perhaps on the erratic geography of his colleagues), the terms in which he discussed Persian affairs both with his subordinates and his fellow-ministers suggest strongly that his vision extended far beyond the narrow promotion of an oil industry centred in the deep south-west of the country. Indeed, in the task of reconstructing Persia's administration and binding the Persian Empire more closely to Britain's international system, the importance of the Anglo-Persian Oil Company lay in its role not as the focus of imperial policy but as one instrument for its successful realisation. Persia's commercial orientation towards Russia which had dominated her import and export trade before 1914,[87] and through which lay her main access to Europe,[88] had long been a major stumbling-block for British diplomacy at Teheran. In the aftermath of the war, however, when Russia's economic life collapsed, the Anglo-Persian Oil Company represented the single most powerful channel of foreign investment and commercial influence in Persia, and a channel which Curzon wished to use for wider imperial purposes, especially to encourage closer trading links between the heart of the Persian Empire and the British-dominated Persian Gulf.[89]

In the brief period of active British intervention in north Persia between 1918 and 1920, Curzon appeared to take the same lofty view of the oil company's role as that which had inspired Lord Salisbury's attempts to use the great chartered companies to bolster British diplomacy in the east, south and west of Africa before 1900.[90] The rapid expansion of Anglo-Persian's oil production after 1918 would help to rectify Persia's shattered finances and fortify her connections with Britain at the same time. And even after the failure of the Anglo-Persian agreement, it was to the revenues of the oil company that Armitage-Smith had looked when the project for a British-controlled state in south-central Persia had been briefly considered in early 1921.[91] Later still, in May 1921, the Foreign Office was instrumental in arranging a loan to the Teheran government from Anglo-Persian, a loan which the company was only willing to make 'if . . . Lord Curzon felt that politically it would be desirable'.[92] But perhaps the firmest evidence for the subordinate role played by oil interests in the Cabinet's Persian policy is to be found in the implicit recognition by ministers that the abandonment of the Anglo-Persian agreement at the end of 1920 would have little if any detrimental effect upon the viability of the oil company's operations; that the safety of Britain's most important stake in the international oil industry had only the most tenuous connection with the attempt to regenerate Persia under British auspices.

The argument that British policy in the Middle East after 1918 was guided by the quest for a permanent and exclusive control over its potential resources has, however, been more usually and more strenuously maintained in the case of Iraq, where imperial control was more thorough and longer-lived than in Persia.

Although by 1918 in none of the three *vilayets* of Mesopotamia was oil being produced in commercial quantities,[93] geological similarities with the oil-bearing zones in Persia had seemed to provide convincing evidence of potentially large reserves of oil in the Mosul *vilayet* and had encouraged a competition for concessions before 1914. Under an agreement setting up the Turkish Petroleum Company in 1914 to prospect and exploit the oil fields, British interests and their nominees were to control half the shares of the company while the remainder were to be divided between the German *Deutsche Bank* and Royal Dutch Shell.[94] For the British Government this agreement represented a suitable recognition of the part already played by British enterprise in the development of an oil industry in the Middle East; and a satisfactory continuation of a policy aimed at preventing the commercial life of the three *vilayets* from being too markedly oriented towards German influence.

At the end of the war, when the international circumstances in which the Turkish Petroleum Company had been set up had undergone a radical transformation, the question of the future control of the oil concessions in Mosul revived as an important factor in the attitude of the British and French governments towards the partition of the Arab Middle East.[95] But despite Lloyd George's keen sensitivity to commercial considerations in international diplomacy,[96] and the new awareness among British ministers of the need to secure supplies of oil which would be controlled by British entrepreneurs in the event of another war, it is unlikely that the Prime Minister's notorious arrangement with Clemenceau in December 1918 under which the French conceded British paramountcy in the Mosul *vilayet*, hitherto reserved for France by the Sykes–Picot Agreement, was motivated solely or principally by a desire to bring its expected oil reserves under British sway. For, as we have seen, both Balfour and Curzon had favoured for some months past the reduction of French influence in the 'Blue' zone – and elsewhere in the Middle East – to the narrowest possible limits on broad political and strategic grounds.[97] The oil resources of Mosul supplied useful buttresses to their arguments, just as Curzon sought later to exploit ministers' interest in Persian oil to win acceptance for his large schemes for Anglo-Persian cooperation. Moreover, to obtain French acquiescence in the dismantling of the Sykes–Picot Agreement, British ministers were prepared to concede to France a quarter share in the output of the projected fields in Mosul, while insisting, in conformity with the stress placed by the Admiralty on the Navy's need for guaranteed supplies of fuel, that the commercial apparatus of a Mosul oil industry would remain under 'permanent British control'.[98]

By this device, certainly, ministers sought to protect and strengthen the primacy of British commercial interests in the event of Mosul's becoming an important centre of oil production, and to build upon the advantageous position conferred by the pre-war concession. But having imposed a close limit on the extent of any foreign involvement in the area of the concession, ministers displayed thereafter little interest in the exploitation of Iraq's oil resources. Thus Curzon had been anxious to exclude French influence from the Mosul *vilayet*, and had been as conscious as any senior minister of the strategic importance of oil.[99] But he showed no sign of wishing to tailor the shape of the British presence in Iraq to the supposed requirements of a putative oil industry, or of an ambitious programme for achieving an imperial self-sufficiency in oil. His critique of the Indianising tendencies of Wilson's administration in 1920 revealed no special concern for the security of the oil-bearing zones of the country. Nor did his eagerness for the northern boundary of the Arab state to be brought as far south as possible, leaving much of northern and eastern Mosul to an autonomous Kurdistan, imply that the rapid discovery and exploitation of the region's oil under imperial supervision occupied a position of special importance in his strategic thinking. Moreover, neither he, nor the Cabinet as a whole, appeared to have been influenced during 1920 by the pleas of Long, then First Lord of the Admiralty, or Kellaway, a junior minister with a special concern for petroleum affairs, for the swift development of the Mesopotamian fields to counter the rapacity of the American oil companies and protect the Navy's fuel supplies.[100]

Still more revealing, perhaps, of the relative significance which ministers in general attached to the control of Mosul's oil resources was their reaction in December 1920 to Churchill's demand for a military withdrawal to Basra. For Churchill's arguments were resisted and ultimately overborne not on the grounds that abandoning Mosul would endanger a valuable economic interest of the imperial system, but on the wider grounds that a retreat to Basra would pave the way for a Turkish reconquest of all Iraq wiping out the strategic benefits which, it was believed, had been gained by wresting the three *vilayets* from Ottoman control. That is not to say that ministers were indifferent to the safety of the Navy's oil supplies. Indeed, even Churchill proposed to provide for their protection. For Churchill and his colleagues were at one in identifying Britain's real oil interests not with the operations of the embryonic Turkish Petroleum Company in northern Iraq, but with those of the Anglo-Persian Oil Company with its vulnerable pipeline and its refinery at Abadan in south-west Persia. Had the Iraq concessions begun to fulfil by 1920 their promise of a rich return, and had there been a substantial British investment in what became the Kirkuk fields, the terms of ministerial debate might have been different; as it was, the prospect of an oil bonanza seemed too remote to exercise a real influence over the thinking of those ministers most concerned with the conduct of policy in the Middle East.

The failure to make progress in finding large deposits of oil in Mesopotamia (compounded by the disturbed condition of the country), and the slackening of the demand for oil after 1920,[101] contributed, perhaps, to the absence of any general ministerial sympathy for the urgings of Long and Kellaway even after the question of Iraq's frontiers had been resolved by the Cabinet's acceptance of Churchill's Cairo policy. At much the same time, the project for establishing an exclusive British control over the exploitation of Iraq's reserves came to be regarded with increasing disfavour in the Foreign Office where there was a growing conviction that it would inflict great damage on Anglo-American relations and would cause particular difficulty with a Republican administration in Washington.[102] In the course of 1921, fears of this kind appear to have become more widely shared among ministers, and with them the realisation that American cooperation in passing the draft mandates for Palestine and Iraq through the council of the League of Nations[103] was more important than the preservation of the terms of the Cadman–Berthelot Agreement.[104] In reaching this conclusion they were, perhaps, helped by the gradual acceptance among the government's petroleum advisers, representative as they were of far-flung British investment in the major centres of oil production, that the oil industry was too international in character, too interdependent in its operations in different regions of the world, for the pursuit of self-sufficiency and exclusive British control as cardinal objectives of an imperial oil policy to be either practicable or desirable.[105]

Ministers then were brought without real debate to the necessity of admitting American oil interests to participation in the Iraq oil concessions by a revision of the Cadman–Berthelot Agreement. But one element of the oil strategy which had been mapped out towards the end of the war continued to attract them. Having abandoned the dream of empire self-sufficiency, they were still keen to strengthen the participation of British enterprise in the international oil industry by an amalgamation of those firms wholly controlled by British capital with Royal Dutch Shell, which alone could compete with the major American concerns in the scale of its operations, and which was already partly

British in composition. But once again, when ministers tried their hand at arranging such a marriage, it proved impossible to find terms which would satisfy the Admiralty – which wished to preserve government control over Anglo-Persian – and the companies, and which would also meet the Foreign Office's anxiety about American reaction.[106] Even on this limited front, therefore, little real progress was made under the coalition towards devising ways in which Britain's dependence on foreign suppliers for her oil might be reduced.

The evidence of ministerial discussion and debate and the actual course of British oil policy after 1920 suggest that the search for an oil monopoly is of doubtful value as a key to the strategy of the Lloyd George coalition in the Middle East. Plainly ministers hoped that the discovery of profitable oil fields in northern Iraq would be turned to Britain's commercial advantage and would help to finance the penurious Iraq state and ensure its survival as an economic unit. But it is unlikely that the absence of a prospective oil field in the Mosul *vilayet* would have materially altered the course of British policy, since the importance of Mosul to Britain's imperial interests in the Middle East was based on much more than its looked-for mineral assets. Mosul, the British believed, was essential to the security and viability of the Iraq state because the alternative to its incorporation in a British-protected Iraq was re-absorption within a Kemalist Turkey. Baghdad itself lay only sixty miles from the southern border of the Mosul *vilayet*, with no defensible barrier between.[107] A Turkish army in Mosul would have the fragile Arab state at its mercy and could wreck the calculations which underlay Britain's policy of informal rule and military disengagement.[108] For British ministers, amid the political upheavals of 1920 to 1922, it was the certainty that the abandonment of Mosul would bring the Turks back by stages to the Persian Gulf, in circumstances of unimaginable humiliation for their post-war imperial policy, which governed their actions; and even the promise of a British share in the oil wealth to come could do little to sweeten the bitter pill of this unwelcome military and diplomatic burden.

10 Conclusion

In the four years which immediately followed the end of the war in 1918, the directors of imperial policy grappled with a variety of problems which tested some of their most fundamental assumptions and expectations about Britain's imperial power, and about the imperial system which they had inherited from the late Victorians. In Egypt, in India and in Ireland they faced challenges to British authority which were longer lasting and more widely supported than almost any previous expression of dissidence since the Indian Mutiny, even if they fell short of the intensity of the Transvaal's great rebellion against British paramountcy. In all three places, the ability of British rule to maintain order and to obtain the collaboration or acquiescence of the local population in the continuation of British supremacy in some form was called into question by the success of local politicians in rallying mass support against cooperation with the agencies of British power. Civil disobedience in India, disorder and non-cooperation in Egypt, and open insurrection – apparently condoned by the majority of the population – in Ireland, all came as warnings that the permanence of British over-rule, and the capacity of the imperial system for meeting the aspirations (or quelling the indiscipline) of subject populations, could not be regarded as settled, certain or inevitable. Resistance to the exercise of British influence in Turkey, Persia and Iraq seemed to confirm the existence of a new fragility in the structure of British world power.

To many contemporaries the fractiousness of so many colonial or non-European societies in the aftermath of the Great War, and the attacks launched upon European political authority or economic influence as far afield as China, seemed evidence of a coming era of revolution, or at least of radical change, in the relations between the European colonial powers and the indigenous peoples of Africa and Asia. The deference long shown towards the representatives of more advanced, or wealthier, civilisations was breaking down; the moral authority and self-confidence of the European was deserting him; the societies over which he had once exercised sway were becoming resentful and rebellious. Instead the 'determination to get rid of white rule',[1] and the 'world revolt against Europe',[2] had flung the processes of European expansion into reverse and had set a term on the old imperial order. 'Imperialism as it was known in the nineteenth century is no longer possible,' remarked Leonard Woolf in 1928.[3] If Britain was to retain any influence over her dependencies, or maintain some shreds of authority over their affairs, a fresh basis for the exercise of paramountcy would have to be found, and a closer attention paid to the needs and opinions of the governed. 'We must swim with the new tide which is set towards education and not towards the government of what used to be called the subject peoples,' Hirtzel warned Arnold Wilson in 1919.[4] The old type of imperial rule, he declared, was 'dying in India and decomposing in Egypt'.[5]

These new symptoms of imperial weakness were variously attributed to the debilitating effects of the Great War on Europe, to the diffusion of the political ideas associated particularly with Woodrow Wilson, and to the influence of Bolshevism. But however cogent this interpretation of the international landscape of the immediate post-war years, it is not clear how far imperial policy-makers in Britain accepted its premises or acted upon its logic. In Egypt and the Middle East, they encountered resistance to imperial control and a reluctance to work with the agencies of British influence. Yet there is little evidence that they deduced from these difficulties that the structure of their imperial system had become unsafe; or that they would have been right to draw such a conclusion.

In Egypt after March 1919, the British were opposed by the classic pattern of nationalist unrest against the perpetuation of alien rule. Dissidence among notables and politicians was followed by a brief but general insurrection; and then by strikes of public servants. The politicians refused to act as the instruments of an indirect imperial control and embarrassed the British by making overt the fact of their supremacy. By doing this, they faced the British with the awkward choice either of resorting indefinitely to direct administration, with all the risks of a headlong confrontation with every element in Egyptian society, or of offering terms which would gravely compromise imperial control in the vital spheres of diplomacy and defence.

As we have seen, ministers eventually accepted the argument that some relief had to be found for the embattled Residency. They took refuge in a policy designed to enlist Egyptian cooperation at the minimum risk to imperial interests and they were helped, in the event, by the decline in the tempo of popular unrest by the autumn of 1921. What they sanctioned was not a revolution in Anglo-Egyptian relations but an adjustment; not a general withdrawal of imperial influence but rather its rationalisation: the shrugging off of commitments that had become over-extended during the war and which, as Milner had argued, were undermining the real purpose of the British presence. In so far as domestic considerations influenced ministerial thinking, their effect was not to jostle the policy-makers into abdication but to reinforce the arguments of those who insisted that an indefinite recourse to repression in order to sustain the wartime expansion of British authority in Egypt's internal affairs would constitute a profound innovation in the character of British over-rule and commit Britain to a political experiment the costs of which would bear little relation to its likely benefits. Ministers, in fact, felt themselves confronted not so much by the necessity to retreat as by the danger that, without the renunciation of those more novel aspects of administrative supervision which were recognised as superfluous to *imperial* requirements, the political burden of guarding their strategic interest in Egypt would grow steadily greater. And while it was doubtful whether the climate of domestic opinion was propitious for the conciliation of colonial nationalism,[6] there could be little dispute that it was positively unsympathetic to the enlargement of Britain's imperial commitments.

Thus British policy in Egypt was the product of two conflicting pressures: the refusal of the Egyptian politicians to work the protectorate and the conservatism of British ministers, unwilling to contemplate the coercion of Egypt by methods which had failed in Ireland and yet resolute that Egypt should not be allowed to drift out of the imperial system and endanger Britain's monopoly over her strategic benefits. The concessions to which the Cabinet were brought with such reluctance by Allenby conferred on Egypt an independence which fell far short of the status which the dominions enjoyed inside the British Empire even prior to 1926. Yet, perhaps unexpectedly, they proved sufficient to entice Egyptian politicians back into cooperation with the Residency. While over the fourteen years during which the '1922 system' defined the terms of imperial control there were repeated confrontations between the Residency and the different factions in Egyptian politics, there was no recurrence of the general instability that had threatened imperial interests in 1919–21. As late as 1935, despite the failure to obtain an Anglo-Egyptian treaty (for which the Allenby Declaration was intended to clear the way) the policy-makers in London were well satisfied with the results of the experiment which the coalition and Allenby had embarked upon.

There was some reason for this satisfaction. Despite the turbulence of the aftermath and the rise of the *Wafd*, the British were not confronted after 1922 with a nationalist movement capable of imposing increasingly drastic constraints on the occupying power or of driving it out altogether. The leaders of the *Wafd* were too conservative to risk repeating their first experience of mass agitation. Moreover, for much of the inter-war period, they were preoccupied with the struggle not against the influence of the British but against the power of the Palace and the dynasty. Before 1922 it had been the divisions in Egyptian politics that had frustrated Milner and Curzon in their search for an Anglo-Egyptian agreement since neither of the principal factions would tolerate the prospect of a lasting partnership between the British and their rivals. After 1922 these same divisions protected British influence against a general campaign for real independence. In the curious triangle of Egyptian politics, neither the *Wafd* nor the Palace could govern securely without the tacit support of the Residency – the promise that London would not use its reserved rights and the physical power of its garrison on behalf of the rival faction. The Residency was able, as a result, to use the *Wafd* to check the king and the king to check the *Wafd*. In these conditions, even Zaghlul lost much of his demonic quality. In 1924 Allenby humiliated him over the Stack crisis. Two years later, after the *Wafd* had triumphed at the polls, an interview with Lloyd was sufficient to deter the old man from forming a government.[7] The machinations of the Palace were no less rigorously supervised. The Egyptian prime minister, complained Fu'ad thirteen years after London had declared Egypt independent, 'dared not move a pencil on his desk without Residency advice'.[8]

In the longer view, therefore, the crisis in Anglo-Egyptian relations which faced the coalition government had less ominous consequences than many ministers had feared. The *Wafd* with its reservoir of popular support in the towns and among the students had come to stay. But the more dangerous symptoms of political upheaval proved less enduring as the effects of the war and its aftermath died away. Hence the Allenby Declaration did not turn out to be the prelude to the irreversible decline in the strength of Britain's grip in Egypt. Rather it embodied a stalemate in the struggle for Egyptian independence which persisted so long as the British remained powerful enough to exclude their imperial rivals from a direct voice in Egypt's affairs, and so long as the creation of a single focus of power – through the processes of revolution – eluded Egyptian politicians. In 1922 the disappearance of either of these fundamental conditions of British power and control seemed so remote as to be almost inconceivable.

If imperial policy in Egypt demonstrated the confidence of the policy-makers in the future of the imperial system, and their conviction that a monopoly of British influence could and should be maintained in its strategic centres, Britain's actions in the Middle East showed no less effectively that the old objectives of pre-war imperial policy kept pride of place in the calculations of post-war policy-makers. It had been axiomatic before 1914 that control over the approaches to the Persian Gulf and to India's frontiers could not be allowed to fall into hands actually or potentially hostile. What changed after 1914 was not this cardinal objective but the method by which it was to be attained, since reliance upon the Ottoman Empire and the defence of its integrity in Asia no longer seemed useful to, or even compatible with, the aims of Britain's diplomacy in the region.

After the first flush of military victory in the Middle East had passed, British policy came to be concerned primarily with the control of three vital strategic zones whose political future appeared of the greatest importance to the security of the imperial system. In Persia, at the head of the Persian Gulf, and at the Dardanelles the British were determined to establish regimes upon whose loyalty they could rely; or, at the very least, regimes whose capacity to threaten their Empire would be negligible. In Turkey, Persia and Iraq, the whole drive of British policy was to construct political settlements which would strengthen and enhance the safety of the British world-system. Far from sensing the coming dissolution of their world power, the policy-makers set themselves the task of digging its foundations yet more deeply by a series of bold interventions in those regions where the pre-war structure of imperial defence had been most vulnerable.

But, as in Egypt, this attempt to exercise political control encountered resistance and hostility among those whose cooperation was necessary to its success. By the end of 1920, the coalition had found in Turkey, Persia and Iraq alike that the installation of pliable satellite regimes was far more difficult than they had anticipated; that local politics would not flow into the moulds which the official mind had prepared. The coalition's difficulties were most acute in Turkey where their power to shape events in the hinterland was feebler than in Persia or Iraq. There the effect of social and economic change in the war years, and of racial and religious cleavages in Ottoman society, had carried the political system further and faster towards national revolution than similar internal tensions had carried the other polities of the Middle East. Yet the British believed that in the proper adjustment of Turkish politics lay the key to their security in the Middle East. They saw the early development of Kemalism not as a healthy revival of the Turkish body politic but as a warning that the Turks would attempt to restore the Ottoman Empire at the first opportunity. Whereas both Milner and Curzon were to claim that Egyptian nationalism was not inimical to Britain's real imperial interests, no influential member of the government consistently favoured a programme of concession and conciliation towards the rebel regime at Angora. Coexistence with Turkish nationalism seemed impossible. As a result, its containment and suppression became the centre-piece of imperial policy in the Middle East; and the possibility of Turkey re-establishing herself as a Eurasian power – coupling the intrigues of Europe to her designs in Asia – the greatest threat to the hard-won victory on the strategic frontiers of the British Empire.

This identification of post-war Turkish nationalism with wartime Ottoman imperialism largely explains the course of British policy both in Turkey and in Iraq after 1918. It explains why, even after the destruction of Kemal had become an unlikely prospect as Russia revived as a Middle East power, Lloyd George, Curzon and the senior ministers of the coalition clung to the hope that Greek military success would force Kemal to come meekly to the conference table and renounce Turkey's old role in the Near and Middle East. Had war broken out over Chanak, it would have been fought to reduce Turkey to a second-class Asian power. In the event, and after the period with which we are concerned, the British reached an informal accommodation with Kemal which seemed to satisfy their central objective. Kemal created a regime which was less prone to European intrigue and infiltration than the Ottoman; and which abandoned the dream of empire in the interests of internal consolidation. But between 1918 and 1922, when this future evolution of Turkey seemed only the most optimistic of speculations, confrontation between the British and Kemal, far from signalling a new and erratic twist in Britain's foreign policy, was no more than a logical working out of the old themes of Palmerston's and Salisbury's diplomacy amid the chaos and uncertainty of the war and its aftermath.[9]

Whereas British policy in the former Ottoman Empire came to depend after 1918 upon a partition of its provinces and for a while on close international control over its old Turkish core, in Persia imperial interests seemed to dictate a programme of vigorous rehabilitation for the Qajar empire under British auspices. This, as we have seen, was a far more ambitious enterprise than British policy-makers had dared to contemplate in Persia at any time before 1914. For Curzon and his advisers proposed to advance the frontiers of British influence far beyond their old lines in south-east Persia and along the Persian Gulf. Above all, they proposed to reverse the pre-war tendency towards the decentralisation (not to say dissolution) of the Persian Empire by its division into rival spheres of influence; instead the authority of the central government in Teheran was to be supreme and the financial and military resources of Britain were to help to make it so. Thus, with its finances and its army transformed by British expertise, and with its rulers looking gratefully to Britain for aid and advice, Persia would no longer be the zone of weakness and instability which had perplexed London and Calcutta before 1914. Henceforth, it was to serve as a solid buttress, a powerful outwork, of the imperial system.

That so grandiose a programme found backing in London at the end of the war is a reminder of how influential still were the ideas and assumptions that had guided the Cromerian regime in Egypt in its heyday. But the pursuit of a Cromerian policy in Persia was doomed to failure. The huge extent of the Shah's dominions, their regional diversity, the strength of local particularisms and the absence of communications rendered the task of unification and centralisation far beyond the means of Britain's local allies in Teheran. And the British for their part were poorly placed to help their friends. The weight of British commercial and political influence outside the south and south-east of the country had never been very great. Much of Persia was inaccessible to British trade and British ideas. There was no substantial class of would-be collaborators in the north and centre of the empire. In default of this, Britain's ability to attract loyalty and support in Teheran and the provinces rested heavily upon the retention of her wartime garrisons in southern, eastern and northern Persia. But by the end of 1920 it was plain that these garrisons would not stay unless Britain's friends in Teheran could demonstrate a real authority in the provinces; and that Britain's friends could not do this if the garrisons left.

The unwillingness of British ministers to postpone military withdrawal beyond the spring of 1921 reflected their general distaste for *novel* imperial commitments that extended beyond the limits of imperial influence laid down before 1914. Ministerial and public opinion resisted Curzon's argument that holding *northern* Persia was vital to imperial security. However, the consequences of British withdrawal and the resurgence of Russian influence at Teheran proved much less damaging than at first appeared. Russian expansionism was more cautious than before 1914; and, paradoxically, it helped rather than hindered the centralising policies which Reza Shah set in train in Persia and Kemal in Turkey. Moreover, not until Reza Shah's capacity to resist Russian and

British domination alike became clear did the old contingency plans for securing a regional predominance along the Gulf gradually fade from the thinking of the policy-makers in London. Hence the evolution of the coalition's Persian policy reflected not so much a growing lassitude in British imperialism as the effects of a gradual, and grudging, recognition that the acquisition of new spheres of informal empire was incompatible with a return to pre-war levels of expenditure in imperial defence – except where local conditions were more favourable, or the strategic arguments more compelling, than in Persia. In Iraq both factors combined to impose a quite different pattern on British policy.

In both Turkey and Persia in the four years after 1918 the British had found themselves struggling to control political systems which had been plunged into crisis by the multiple effects of pre-war constitutional upheaval and the far-reaching political changes which the war had imposed on them. In Iraq the problem confronting imperial policy was, perhaps, even more fundamental. Here it was not a question of bending an existing system to the imperial design but of constructing a new regime in a region which lacked almost all the attributes of political, social, economic or religious unity. Indeed, the internal coherence of the territorial unit which became the Iraq state derived not from any nation-building tendencies at work in its diverse communities but from the conviction of British policy-makers that the three *vilayets* of Mosul, Baghdad and Basra should fall within Britain's sphere of influence; and that only if they were combined within a single political framework could that influence be effectively exercised.

Even in this different political setting, the British encountered considerable difficulty in imposing a paramount influence and in creating a unitary political system which would be a suitable vehicle for their strategic needs. As elsewhere, the after-effects of the war aroused political feelings which were hostile to the permeation of European influences, and which accentuated distrust of alien interference. Awareness of this, combined with financial constraints on imperial policy, forced the British to make the construction of a strong autonomous regime their real objective. Even this proved far from easy, but in Iraq, as opposed to Turkey or Persia, the directors of policy enjoyed three advantages of enormous value. Firstly, the experience of the war had convinced most ministers of the crucial importance of Iraq to imperial security and made them far less willing than in the Persian case to contemplate a withdrawal. Secondly, the inchoate state of the social fabric of the future Iraq state prevented the development of a nationalist movement capable of frustrating their plans. But thirdly, and most important of all, the military conquest and subsequent administrative control of all three *vilayets* gave the British what they lacked in Turkey and Persia: a direct influence in the localities; and a real control over the representatives of local opinion. By this latter means, it was possible to ensure the selection of a ruler who would ultimately prove amenable to the requirements of imperial defence, and whose concern to resist especially Turkish influence was no less marked than Britain's.

Between 1918 and 1922, when the future orientation of Turkey, Persia and Iraq was in doubt, no other part of the Middle East outside Egypt assumed a comparable importance in the minds of British policy-makers. Because the whole position of Britain in the Middle East appeared to depend upon the outcome of the struggle in these places, the policies which were adopted in Palestine and the Arabian peninsula were, essentially, of secondary importance and aroused little interest among ministers. Subsequently, of course, the decisions taken in Palestine in this initial period – the licensing of Jewish settlement and the creation of Trans-Jordan – came to assume a critical significance as the Arab reaction to the Jewish immigration of the 1930s undermined the basis of post-war Anglo-Arab cooperation and weakened British influence at a vital moment. But in the early 1920s, the considerations governing British policy in Palestine, Trans-Jordan and Arabia were less intimately linked to ministerial thinking about the wider structure of imperial defence. And once the danger of Anglo-French competition in the Middle East receded after 1920, the main external discipline upon administrative arrangements in Palestine was the need to avoid any disruption of the understanding whereby French control had been established in Syria. Meanwhile, the official mind continued to hope that no serious incompatibility existed between the interests of Arab and Jew in the new mandate.

If in Egypt, Turkey, Persia and Iraq, the motives behind imperial policy were fundamentally the same as those which had prompted policy-makers before the war, how are we to interpret the seemingly contradictory tendencies of policy in the various theatres of the Middle East: the move towards conceding more internal autonomy in Egypt; the relentless hostility to Turkish nationalism until the Lausanne agreements; the making and breaking of the Anglo-Persian Agreement; and the vigorous programme of state-building in Iraq? At one level, each of these represented the attempts of the policy-makers to safeguard the outworks of the imperial system as best they could in a variety of circumstances. But at a deeper level, perhaps, the apparent inconsistencies of method arose out of the variable impact of the war and its aftermath in the different sectors of British involvement in Egypt and the Middle East. Everywhere the struggle to win the war had forced the British to interfere more widely and intensively than ever before in the society and economy of the whole region, whether directly or through the use of proxies. But this great expansion of the imperial presence provoked, as soon as the war was over, local responses which varied greatly in their character and tempo. At the same time, the British themselves were being compelled, by political and financial pressures at home, to reduce the scope of their political and military dominance in the Middle East, and to rely upon local support rather than the deployment of a vastly expensive army and administration. These two factors worked in conjunction, not to achieve an absolute reduction in British power and influence, but rather to force a retreat from the extravagant pretensions of what might be termed 'war imperialism'; and a return to the methods and constraints which had characterised policy before 1914. It is the gradual and selective casting off of the temporary additions to imperial power in a world which had grown less dangerous and more parsimonious, not a nerveless collapse in the face of insurgent nationalism, which best describes the spirit of the Lloyd George coalition's imperial policy after 1918.

It is for this reason unsatisfactory to portray the thinking behind imperial policy in 1922 as marked by a general pessimism not apparent in 1914. Certainly, abundant expression of anxiety and alarm may be found among those who watched events in Ireland, Egypt and India with fear and astonishment. No imperial power, it might be added, can be free from a certain anxiety about the loyalty of its subjects; all empires seem plagued – at every phase of their existence – by periodic sensations of incipient decline. It was inevitable, after an exhausting war and with intractable political difficulties at home and abroad in the aftermath, that the long-term future of the imperial system should sometimes appear in doubt; and that the years before 1914 should appear by contrast a golden age of stability. But it is too facile to see the same spirit at work in the post-war management of imperial interests in Egypt and the Middle East. The problem that tormented the policy-makers was not, in their view at least, whether the imperial system could survive, nor even how best to prepare for its gradual enfeeblement. It was the more immediate problem of how to contain the side-effects of the war on the internal and international security of the imperial system. All their solutions, whether in Egypt or the Middle East, assumed the necessity of preserving the Empire. But they also reflected a general recognition that old objects must be served by new methods. Thus administrative intervention in Egypt, having reached its climax during the war, had to be brought under much stricter control if the essential collaboration of Egyptian politicians was not to be jeopardised. Similarly, British influence in the strategic sectors of the Middle East would become impossibly expensive to uphold without the cooperation of local allies and the concession of substantial local autonomy. Solutions of this kind were acceptable to ministers because neither seemed to violate that aspect of its imperial control which London held most dear: Britain's ability to prevent the penetration of any rival influence and to use her various dependencies as units in a single system of imperial defence. To preserve that overriding object, the British were prepared to make endless adjustments in their systems of rule and influence.

Thus, in the century after 1850, changes in the international power balance, in the politics and economics of the mother country and in the political and economic development of Britain's dependencies and client states constantly enforced the adoption of fresh or revised techniques of influence and administration. After 1880 a combination of circumstances seemed to propel the policy-makers towards a more vigorous external defence of imperial interests and greater intervention in the internal affairs of colonial societies. The great crisis of 1914–18 saw a repetition and intensification of this tendency. Between 1918 and 1922, by contrast, we can see the beginnings of a reversal as the policy-makers groped for ways of easing the costs and burdens of empire after a phase of extraordinary effort, and of giving themselves more room to manoeuvre in their dealings both with colonial politicians and their own domestic opinion. Ministers and their advisers came gradually to accept that the economic and political effects of the war, both in Britain and in the imperial system, dictated the easing of imperial control, if only for the time being, to allow a new political equilibrium to be established, and to avoid the vicious circle of confrontation and repression. But it is their choice of concessions and their determination to obtain a greater flexibility for the imperial factor that best reveals the tenor of ministerial thinking. Anxious as they were to relieve the pressure on imperial resources and the instruments of imperial power, careless as they were of any 'civilising mission', they were yet determined to preserve in every place that mattered the vital reserves of power and authority that would facilitate British intervention in local politics should it be necessary for imperial reasons. With adequate safeguards against any outside interference, they were ready to tolerate the boisterousness of colonial nationalism with good humour. So long, indeed, as there was no exit from the British world-system (except into the arms of one of Britain's colonial rivals) there was a limit to the damage that local politicians could inflict. Imperial policy, therefore, was less concerned with fending off a final catastrophe than with the more prosaic business of caulking and sealing the political defences that insulated Britain's spheres of rule and influence from external disruption, and, secondly, with the never-ending search for a perfect equilibrium between the aspirations of local politicians and the requirements of the imperial system.

It may be doubted, therefore, whether Britain's experience in Egypt and the Middle East between 1918 and 1922, with all its disappointments and frustrations, can provide a paradigm for the eventual collapse of British world power after 1940. Certainly the failure to exploit the wartime experiments in cooperation to integrate the dominions more fully into the imperial system after the war, the renunciation of the grandiose plans for a far-reaching Middle East supremacy which were framed at the end of 1918, the concessions to Irish and Egyptian nationalism, and the wider scope afforded to Indian politicians in the government of the Indian Empire, all served as portents that victory in 1918 would not be followed by a transformation of the old decentralised character of the imperial system. But the immediate post-war years also provided few clues as to how the descent from imperial power would come about. Britain retained the will and the ability to guard her strategic positions in the Middle East. Secure in her naval power, she could afford to give up her old habit of supervising the internal government of Egypt without jeopardising her ability to use Egypt for her own imperial purposes. Neither in Egypt nor in the rest of the Middle East did nationalism turn out in the inter-war years to be either a potent or an irreconcilable enemy of British imperialism. Rather did it appear to serve involuntarily the purposes of an imperial system anxious to reduce its direct involvement in the hinterland of south-west Asia to the minimum compatible with the exclusion of its rivals.

Indeed, the prospect which most frightened ministers and their advisers after 1918 was not colonial nationalism arrayed in arms against them, but the danger that Britain's imperial rivals would exploit the inevitable tensions between a paramount power and its clients to revive the old cycle of intrigue and counter-intrigue with its pronounced tendency towards veiled annexation. It was the hope that this prime cause of imperial difficulties before 1914 could be liquidated which, as we have seen, encouraged Curzon in his Middle Eastern policies after the war. The same goal of influence without competition largely explains the interest of some ministers in the concept of the international mandate – a device which appeared to British observers not as a criticism of the principle of colonial rule, but as a tribute to the superiority of a free trade empire founded upon the techniques of indirect control over those rival imperial systems which had been established in the three decades before the Great War.

If ministers seemed to pay most attention to the plots and strategems of which they suspected their imperial rivals, it may be that they were right to do so. For the lesson of Middle East policy after 1918 seemed to be that Britain's imperial security lay ultimately not in her capacity to beat down nationalists, but in an ability to divide or defeat those powers whose military and economic strength matched her own, and to prevent them from rupturing the thin skein of naval power and political influence which held the imperial system and its outworks together. Individually, such rivals could be contained by Britain's military power; in combination, as an earlier generation of ministers had recognised in 1900, they threatened to roll up the Empire, formal and informal alike. In the 1920s, those states which were dissatisfied with the results of the Great War lacked both the will and the resources to contemplate a combined assault on the British imperial system. But in the next decade the triple alliance of Britain's enemies, which pre-war diplomacy had successfully averted, exposed the weaknesses of Britain's Empire and laid bare the secrets of its resilience. In the cataclysm which followed, all the essential characteristics of the imperial system, as it had functioned between 1880 and 1940, dissolved and vanished in the birth of a new international order.

Notes

INTRODUCTION

1 M. Beloff, *Imperial Sunset Vol I: Britain's Liberal Empire 1897–1921* (London, 1969) p. 344.
2 Although a confidence mixed with apprehension *c.* 1900. See below ch. 1.
3 See for example Kedourie's penetrating essay 'Sa'd Zaghlul and the British' in his *Chatham House Version and other Middle-Eastern Studies* (London, 1970).

CHAPTER 1. IMPERIAL POLICY AND BRITISH POLITICS

1 The primacy of these political objectives in Turkey, Persia and China has recently been argued in D. McLean, 'Finance and Informal Empire before the First World War', *Economic History Review* 2s. XXIX, 2 (1976) 291–305.
2 A. E. Campbell, *Great Britain and the United States 1895–1903* (London, 1960) esp. pp. 192, 207.
3 S. B. Saul, *Studies in British Overseas Trade 1870–1914* (Liverpool, 1960) chs. III, VIII.
4 On this theme, see D. K. Fieldhouse, *Economics and Empire* (London, 1973), pp. 76–84; E. Stokes, 'Traditional Resistance Movements and Afro-Asian Nationalism', *Past and Present*, 48 (1970) 100–18.
5 For Grey's view, K. Robbins, *Sir Edward Grey* (London, 1971) p. 187.
6 For the background to British policy in Persia, R. L. Greaves, *Persia and the Defence of India* (London, 1959).
7 L. K. Young, *British Policy in China 1895–1902* (Oxford, 1970) pp. 5 ff.
8 For a discussion of this term, D. K. Fieldhouse, *op. cit.*, pp. 80–1.
9 The results of this weakness in Egyptian and Cape Colonial sub-imperialism in the late nineteenth century are described in R. Robinson and J. Gallagher, *Africa and the Victorians* (London, 1961) chs. XII and XIV.
10 For the Liberal imperialists and their views, H. C. G. Matthew, *The Liberal Imperialists* (London, 1973) p. 157.
11 See Hicks Beach to J. Chamberlain, 2 Oct. 1901, in Lady V. Hicks Beach, *The Life of Sir Michael Hicks Beach*, vol. II (London, 1932) p. 157; and E. Stokes, 'Milnerism', *Historical Journal*, V, 1 (1962) 47–60.
12 Milner to Amery, 1 Dec. 1906, in A. M. Gollin, *Proconsul in Politics* (London, 1964) p. 106.
13 On this see G. Monger, *The End of Isolation* (London, 1963) ch. I.
14 For Conservative opposition to tariff reform, N. Blewett, 'Free Fooders, Balfourites, Whole Hoggers: Factionalism within the Unionist Party 1906–1910', *Historical Journal*, XI, 1 (1968) 95–124.

15 R. Hyam, *Elgin and Churchill at the Colonial Office* (London, 1968) ch. 4, pp. 103 ff.
16 See below, ch. 3.
17 For this view, Anil Seal, 'Imperialism and Nationalism in India', *Modern Asian Studies*, 7, 3 (1973) 321–47.
18 *Parliamentary Debates, Commons*, 1909, vol. IV, col. 54.
19 See J. E. Kendle, *The Colonial and Imperial Conferences 1887–1911* (London, 1967) p. 229.
20 Naval expenditure 1898: £20·9 million; 1906: £33·3 million; 1912: £42·9 million. Source: B. R. Mitchell, *Abstract of British Historical Statistics* (Cambridge, 1971) p. 398.
21 An optimism which extended even to Hobson. H. Weinroth, 'British Radicals and the Agadir Crisis', *European Studies Review*, 3, 1 (1973), 54 ff.
22 K. Robbins, *op. cit.*, pp. 265, 270.
23 F. Kazamzadeh, *Russia and Britain in Persia 1864–1914* (New Haven and London, 1968) ch. 9.
24 P. Lowe, *Great Britain and Japan 1911–1915* (London, 1969) pp. 298 ff.
25 As in the restraints on the commercialisation of land introduced by the British in India and Egypt.
26 For the influence of the oil question on post-war policy in the Middle East, see below, ch. 9.
27 *Statistics of the Military Effort of the British Empire* (War Office, London, 1921) pp. 95–7, 104.
28 Recruitment to the Indian Army May 1916–May 1917: 121,000; May 1917–May 1918: 300,000. *Cambridge History of India*, vol. VI, ed. H. H. Dodwell (Cambridge, 1932) p. 481.
29 Sir G. Barrow, *The Life of General Sir Charles C. Monro* (London, 1931) p. 119.
30 *Statistics of the Military Effort* . . . , p. 777.
31 *Ibid.*, pp. 758, 759, 771, 772.
32 See S.S.I. to Viceroy, 1 Feb. 1917, A.C. 20/6/6; Same to sáme, 7 Feb. 1917, A.C. 20/6.
33 V. Anstey, *The Economic Development of India* (London, 1929) pp. 78, 216n.
34 *Report on Indian Constitutional Reforms*, Cd. 9109 (1918) pp. 267–8.
35 Milner to Lloyd George, 9 June 1918, Milner Papers 145.
36 Amery to Lloyd George, ? July 1918, in L. S. Amery, *My Political Life*, vol. 2, *War and Peace 1914–1929* (London, 1953) p. 161.
37 Judith M. Brown, *Gandhi's Rise to Power* (Cambridge, 1972) p. 123.
38 M. L. Dockrill, 'David Lloyd George and Foreign Policy before 1914', in *Lloyd George: Twelve Essays*, ed. A. J. P. Taylor (London, 1971) p. 3.
39 For a discussion of Lloyd George's international ideas, R. Ullman, *The Anglo-Soviet Accord* (London, 1972) ch. XI.
40 The legend of Lloyd George's solitary identification with the Greek policy has recently been attacked in A. E. Montgomery, 'Lloyd George and the Greek Question 1918–1922', in *Lloyd George: Twelve Essays*, ed. A. J. P. Taylor (London, 1971) p. 283.
41 Thomas Jones, *Lloyd George* (London, 1951) p. 279.
42 On this aspect see memo. by Balfour on a conversation with Bonar Law, 22 Dec. 1922, Balfour Papers 49693.

43 For Law's background and origins, R. Blake, *The Unknown Prime Minister* (London, 1955).
44 Lady Dawkins to Milner, 27 Jan. 1912, in J. A. Ramsden, 'The Organisation of the Conservative and Unionist Party in Britain 1910–1930' (Oxford D. Phil., 1974) p. 83.
45 *Ibid.*, pp. 87–9.
46 Austen Chamberlain to George Lloyd, Personal, 7 Dec. 1922, A.C. 18/1/35.
47 As over the need to expel Kamenev to calm Conservative unrest. Bonar Law to Prime Minister, 2 Sep. 1920, B.L.P. 101/4/86.
48 Lloyd George to Bonar Law, 7 June 1921, B.L.P. 107/1/35.
49 For Chamberlain's political career, C. Petrie, *The Life and Times of Austen Chamberlain*, 2 vols. (London, 1939, 1940).
50 See below, ch. 2.
51 A. Chamberlain to Churchill, Personal, 8 Apr. 1921, A.C. 23/9/12; Same to Sir P. Pilditch, 7 Dec. 1921, A.C. 33/1/6; C. Petrie, *op. cit.*, vol. II, p. 163.
52 Ramsden, thesis *cit.*, p. 92.
53 In Oct. 1919 Lloyd George reverted formally to a Cabinet of conventional size.
54 Roberta Warman, 'The Erosion of Foreign Office Influence in the Making of Foreign Policy', *Historical Journal*, XV, 2 (1972) 151.
55 *Parliamentary Debates, Commons*, 1909, vol. IV, col. 54; memo. for War Cabinet, 7 Aug. 1917, copy in Montagu Papers.
56 Sir. I. Malcolm, *Lord Balfour: a Memory* (London, 1930) pp. 11–12.
57 See below, ch. 6.
58 Lord Cromer, *Political and Literary Essays*, third series (London, 1916) p. 3.
59 Earl of Ronaldshay, *The Life of Lord Curzon*, vol. III (London, 1929) p. 24.
60 For two indications of this see Harold Nicolson's tale 'Arketall' in the same writer's *Some People* (London, 1927); and H. Young, *The Independent Arab* (London, 1933) p. 284.
61 Fisher's diary, 19 Oct. 1921, Fisher Papers Box 8A.
62 For a recent view of these defects, A. M. Gollin, *op. cit.*, p. 414.
63 D. Lloyd George, *The Truth about the Peace Treaties*, vol. I (London, 1938) p. 261.
64 A. G. Gardiner, *Pillars of Society* (popular edn, London, 1916) p. 254.
65 Milner to Amery, 30 Dec. 1919, Addit. Milner Papers, Ms. Eng. Hist., c703.
66 Milner to Lloyd George, Confid., 28 May 1919, Curzon Papers F 112/208.
67 Same to same, Strictly Private & Confid., 16 May 1919, Addit. Milner Papers, Ms. Eng. Hist. c700.
68 Montagu was under-secretary for India 1910–14.
69 Speech by Montagu in 1913. S. D. Waley, *Edwin Montagu: a Memoir* (Bombay, 1964) p. 57.
70 Uncompromisingly portrayed in J. M. Keynes, *Essays in Biography* (new edn, London, 1951) pp. 50–2.
71 Bonar Law to Prime Minister, 16 April 1920, B.L.P. 101/4/33.

CHAPTER 2. THE DOMESTIC ORIGINS OF IMPERIAL POLICY

1 Wilson's diary, 12 Nov. 1918, C. E. Callwell, *Field Marshal Sir Henry Wilson: His Life and Diaries*, vol. II (London, 1927) p. 151.
2 Milner to Prime Minister, 13 Nov. 1918, L.G.P. F/38/4/24.
3 Milner to Esher, 28 Nov. 1918, S. Roskill, *Hankey: Man of Secrets*, vol. II (London, 1972) p. 27.
4 Milner to Prime Minister, 7 Dec. 1918, L.G.P. F/38/4/31.
5 Sir E. Geddes to Lloyd George, 7 Jan. 1919, L.G.P. F/18/3/1.
6 On the economic uncertainty of the first months after the German armistice, P. B. Johnson, *Land Fit for Heroes* (Chicago, 1968) pp. 361 ff.
7 Wilson's phrase, Callwell, *op. cit.*, vol. II, p. 161.
8 Bonar Law to Lloyd George (Paris), n.d. but *c.* 15 Jan. 1919, L.G.P. F/30/3/2. On Bonar Law's fear of the House of Commons' reaction, *The Private Papers of Douglas Haig*, ed. R. Blake (London, 1952) p. 350.
9 Thomas Jones to Hankey (Paris), 17 Jan. 1919, L.G.P. F/23/4/4.
10 Callwell, *op. cit.*, vol. II, p. 165.
11 Addison to Lloyd George, 24 Jan. 1919, L.G.P. F/1/5/4.
12 A. Bullock, *The Life and Times of Ernest Bevin*, vol. I (London, 1960) pp. 103, 105.
13 Conclusions of War Cabinet 521, 23 Jan. 1919, CAB. 23/9.
14 Austen Chamberlain to Churchill, Private & Confid., 30 Jan. 1919, A.C. 24/1/24.
15 Conclusions of War Cabinet 606A, 5 Aug. 1919, CAB. 23/15.
16 Churchill's memo. for Cabinet, 16 July 1919, L.G.P. F/170/4/8.
17 See *Conservative and Unionist Campaign Guide for 1922.*
18 Conclusions of Cabinet Finance Committee, 9 Feb. 1920, Appendix III to Cabinet 11 (20), CAB. 23/20.
19 E.g. memoranda by C.I.G.S., 26 April 1919, G.T. 7182, CAB. 24/78; 7 Aug. 1919 (sent to Austen Chamberlain), A.C. 24/1/5.
20 C.I.G.S. memo., 26 April 1919, G.T. 7182, CAB. 24/78.
21 Churchill's memo. for War Cabinet, 16 July 1919, L.G.P. F/170/4/8.
22 C.I.G.S. memo., 7 Aug. 1919, A.C. 24/1/5.
23 Callwell, *op. cit.*, vol. II, p. 182.
24 I. McLean, 'Popular Protest and Public Order: Red Clydeside 1915–1919', in *Popular Protest and Public Order*, ed. R. Quinault and J. Stevenson (London, 1974) pp. 233–9.
25 Conclusions of Ministerial Conference, 11 May 1920, Appendix II to Cabinet 29 (20), CAB. 23/21.
26 Wilson's diary, 11 May 1920, Callwell, *op. cit.*, p. 236.
27 *Ibid.*, vol. II, p. 240 (21 May 1920).
28 Conclusions of Ministerial Conference, 17 June 1920, Appendix II to Cabinet 53 (20), CAB. 23/22.
29 Callwell, *op. cit.*, vol. II, pp. 251–6.
30 Cabinet Finance Committee 27, 12 Aug. 1920, CAB. 27/71.
31 Wilson's diary, 10 Sep. 1920, Callwell, *op. cit.*, vol. II, pp. 261–2.
32 *Ibid.*, vol. II, p. 261.
33 For some discussion of this proposal see memoranda by Worthington-Evans (C.P. 2734, CAB. 24/121) and Fisher (C.P. 2806, CAB. 24/122) in March and

April 1921; see also Fisher's diary, 20 April 1920, Fisher Papers Box 8A.
34 Callwell, *op. cit.*, vol. II, p. 318.
35 See below, ch. 7.
36 Sir B. Mallett and C. O. George, *British Budgets, Second Series, 1913/14 to 1920/21* (London, 1929) p. 178.
37 *The Gold Standard and Employment Policies*, ed. S. Pollard (London, 1970) p. 2; D. Winch, *Economics and Policy* (London, 1969) p. 75.
38 Mallett and George, *op. cit.*, pp. 253 ff.
39 Committee of Imperial Defence, 133rd Meeting, 29 June 1920, CAB. 2/3; memo. by Austen Chamberlain, Secret, 7 June 1920, C.P. 1413, A.C. 34/1/113.
40 Cabinet Finance Committee 23, 22 July 1920, CAB. 27/71.
41 Compared with one ninth of a much smaller total expenditure in 1913.
42 Cabinet Finance Committee 29, 7 Dec. 1920, CAB. 27/71.
43 M. Cowling, *The Impact of Labour* (Cambridge, 1971) pp. 56, 121.
44 Lloyd George to Austen Chamberlain, 10 June 1921, A.C. 23/4/5.
45 *Ibid.*
46 The Geddes Committee proposed reductions of about a quarter in each case. This was modified but not drastically by the Cabinet's own review committee under Churchill.
47 According to a recent study, the establishment of the *Dail Eireann* in Jan. 1919 'caused barely a ripple in England'. D. G. Boyce, *Englishmen and Irish Troubles: British Public Opinion and the Making of Irish Policy 1918–1922* (London, 1972) p. 46.
48 Cowling, *op. cit.*, p. 112.
49 *Ibid.* Seats lost by the coalition are conveniently listed in D. Butler and J. Freeman, *British Political Facts 1900–1967* (2nd edn, London, 1968) p. 152.
50 Bonar Law to Balfour, 5 Oct. 1918, Balfour Papers 49693.
51 *Ibid.*
52 *Ibid.*
53 Law continued to show a qualified enthusiasm for such a fusion until its rejection by the coalition Liberals in March 1920. See Bonar Law to Balfour, 12 March 1920, B.L.P. 96/4.
54 For example in their opposition to protection. K. O. Morgan, 'Lloyd George's Stage Army: the Coalition Liberals 1918–1922' in *Lloyd George: Twelve Essays*, ed. A. J. P. Taylor (London, 1971) pp. 243–5.
55 *Ibid.*, pp. 246–7.
56 Fisher's diary, 31 Jan. 1920, Fisher Papers Box 8A.
57 Some of the sources of which are discussed in Cowling, *op. cit.*, esp. chs. II, III, and IV.
58 Report by Sir M. Fraser, Principal Agent of the Conservative party, 30 Dec. 1921, A.C. 32/4/1b.
59 Fisher's diary, 8 July 1920, Fisher Papers Box 8A. Dyer became a hero for those who believed that Montagu was intent on the destruction of the *Raj*.
60 R. Ullman, *The Anglo-Soviet Accord* (London, 1972) pp. 109–10; Fisher's diary, 7 June 1920, Fisher Papers Box 8A.
61 *Ibid.*, 4 June 1920.
62 R. Ullman, *op. cit.*, p. 303; Bonar Law to Prime Minister, 2 Sep. 1920, B.L.P. 101/4/86.

63 R. Blake, *The Unknown Prime Minister* (London, 1955) p. 424. It is still not clear how far this condition was political.
64 See the complaints of Sir H. Neild (Ealing) on the progress of Anti-Waste in Middlesex: Neild to Austen Chamberlain, 2 Aug. 1921, A.C. 24/3/78.
65 Thomas Jones, *Whitehall Diary*, vol. III, *Ireland 1916–1925*, ed. K. Middlemas (London, 1971) p. 80. The king had appealed in Belfast for Irish reconciliation.
66 Younger to Austen Chamberlain, 9 Nov. 1921, encl. in Chamberlain to Curzon, Secret and Personal, 9 Nov. 1921, Curzon Papers F 112/219. See also Boyce, *op. cit.*, ch. 8.
67 See below, chs. 5, 9.
68 Austen Chamberlain to Curzon, Secret and Personal, 9 Nov. 1921, Curzon Papers F 112/219.
69 Same to same 4 Nov. 1921, Curzon Papers F 112/317.
70 Fisher's diary, 4 Nov. 1921, Fisher Papers Box 8A.
71 Austen Chamberlain to George Lloyd (Bombay), Personal, 7 Dec. 1922, A.C. 18/1/35.
72 Lord Long to Austen Chamberlain, 19 Feb. 1922, A.C. 33/1/32.
73 Austen Chamberlain to Lord Derby, 23 March 1922, A.C. 33/1/52.
74 Austen Chamberlain to Prime Minister, 15 March 1922, A.C./23/7/65.
75 'I should be glad if other work could be found for him,' Chamberlain remarked of Montagu a few days before the latter's enforced resignation. Chamberlain to Long, Confid., 6 March 1922, A.C. 33/1/33.
76 Austen Chamberlain to George Lloyd, Confid., 18 May 1922, A.C. 18/1/28.
77 Cowling, *op. cit.*, pp. 185–9.
78 Derby to Austen Chamberlain, Strictly Confid. and Personal, 1 Sep. 1922, A.C. 33/2/12; Younger to A. Chamberlain, Confid., 16 Sep. 1922, A.C. 33/2/20; Wilson to A. Chamberlain, Private, ? Sep. 1922, A.C. 33/2/26.
79 See below ch. 8. Derby had told Chamberlain that it was Lloyd George's Near Eastern policy which made it impossible for him to support the coalition. Derby to A. Chamberlain, Strictly Confid. and Personal, 1 Sep. 1922, A.C. 33/2/12.
80 Cowling, *op. cit.*, pp. 191–4.
81 Bonar Law's letter to *The Times*, 7 Oct. 1922, carefully distinguished between the necessity of resisting Kemal and Britain's alone bearing the burden of doing it.
82 Faced with this choice, declared Chamberlain, the anti-Lloyd George faction 'would be in a d – d fix'. Chamberlain to Birkenhead, 12 Oct. 1922, A.C. 33/2/52.
83 Austen Chamberlain to George Lloyd, Personal, 7 Dec. 1922, A.C. 18/1/35.
84 See below, ch. 8.
85 Derby to Bonar Law, Confid., 22 Aug. 1922, B.L.P. 107/2/57.
86 See P. S. Gupta, *Imperialism and the British Labour Movement 1914–1964* (London, 1975) p. 36.
87 *Ibid.*, p. 29.

CHAPTER 3. BRITISH POLICY AND THE ORIGINS OF THE POST-WAR CRISIS

1 By 1907 there were approximately 220 000 foreign residents out of a total population of 11 million. See C. Issawi, 'Asymmetrical Development and Transport in Egypt 1800–1914', in *The Beginnings of Modernization in the Middle East*, ed. W. Polk and R. Chambers (Chicago, 1968) p. 391.
2 C. Issawi, 'Egypt since 1800: A Study in Lop-sided Development', *Journal of Economic History*, XXI, 1 (1961) 8.
3 For Mehemet Ali's economic motives, *ibid.*, p. 7; for his relations with foreign commerce, E. R. J. Owen, *Cotton and the Egyptian Economy* (Oxford, 1967) pp. 53 ff.
4 *Ibid.*, p. 60; G. Baer, *A History of Landownership in Modern Egypt 1800–1950* (London, 1962) pp. 17–18.
5 Baer, *op. cit.*, p. 11.
6 P. J. Vatikiotis, *A Modern History of Egypt* (London, 1969) pp. 128 ff.; A. Hourani, 'Ottoman Reform and the Politics of Notables', in Polk and Chambers, *op. cit.*, p. 57.
7 For the ulama, see Afaf Lutfi al-Sayyid, 'The Beginnings of Modernization among the Rectors of Al-Azhar', in Polk and Chambers, *op. cit.*
8 On the survival of popular piety, G. Baer, 'Social Change in Egypt 1800–1914', in *Political and Social Change in Modern Egypt*, ed. P. M. Holt (London, 1968) p. 136.
9 Earl of Cromer, *Modern Egypt*, vol. I (London, 1908) pp. 73, 81.
10 See Sir W. Willcocks and J. I. Craig, *Egyptian Irrigation* (3rd edn, London, 1913) vol. II, pp. 812–14; R. L. Tignor, *Modernization and British Colonial Rule in Egypt 1882–1914* (Princeton, 1966) pp. 36–7.
11 G. Baer, *A History of Landownership . . .*, p. 30.
12 See *idem*, 'Urbanisation in Egypt 1820–1907' in Polk and Chambers, *op. cit.*
13 Issawi, 'Egypt since 1800: A Study in Lop-sided Development', *Journal of Economic History*, XXI, 1 (1961) 12.
14 *Ibid.*, p. 17.
15 Even at the end of the nineteenth century, the royal family remained much the largest landowner in Egypt. Baer, *A History of Landownership . . .*, p. 70.
16 For the Dufferin Report see R. L. Tignor, *op. cit.*, pp. 53–6; A. Colvin, *The Making of Modern Egypt* (Nelson edn, London, n.d.) ch. I; A. Lyall, *The Life of the Marquis of Dufferin and Ava* (Nelson edn, London, ? 1905), ch. X.
17 *Ibid.*, p. 336.
18 Tignor, *op. cit.*, p. 67; Cromer, *op. cit.*, vol. II, p. 351.
19 The gradual entrenchment of this belief in British policy may be traced in R. Robinson and J. Gallagher, *Africa and the Victorians* (London, 1961) chs. VIII, IX.
20 Cromer, *op. cit.*, vol. II, pp. 327–33.
21 *Ibid.*, vol. II, p. 331.
22 A. Milner, *England in Egypt* (8th edn, London, 1901) pp. 208, 209.

23 R. C. Mowat, 'Lord Cromer and his Successors in Egypt' (Oxford D.Phil., 1970) p. 194.
24 *Ibid.*, p. 196.
25 Quoted in Mowat, thesis *cit.*, p. 202.
26 *Ibid.*, p. 203.
27 Tignor, *op. cit.*, p. 181.
28 *Ibid.*, p. 185; Cromer, *op. cit.*, vol. II, pp. 488–9.
29 Milner, *op. cit.*, p. 282.
30 Tignor, *op. cit.*, p. 269.
31 On Mustafa Kamil, see N. Safran, *Egypt in Search of Political Community* (Cambridge, Mass., 1961) pp. 85 ff.
32 Mowat, thesis *cit.*, p. 272; for Gorst's general ideas, Tignor, *op. cit.*, pp. 292 ff.
33 In June 1906, after a fracas between a party of British officers pigeon shooting and Egyptian villagers, one officer had died. After a special tribunal to try the case, four Egyptians were publicly executed and a number of others flogged.
34 R. Storrs, *Orientations* (Defin. edn, London, 1943) p. 69.
35 Annual Report on Egypt for 1910, F.O. 371/1112/11940, p. 2.
36 Mowat, thesis *cit.*, p. 284.
37 Storrs, *op. cit.*, p. 68.
38 Annual Report on Egypt for 1910, p. 2.
39 *Ibid.*
40 Mowat, thesis *cit.*, pp. 296–7.
41 For Kitchener's way of communicating this change, Storrs, *op. cit.*, p. 106.
42 *Ibid.*, p. 116, for a description of these flamboyant progresses.
43 A feddan approximated to an acre.
44 Annual Report on Egypt for 1912, F.O. 371/1638/14764.
45 Kitchener to Grey, 14 April 1912, Documents Collected for the Information of the Special Mission appointed to enquire into the Situation in Egypt [hereafter D.C.S.M.], vol. I, p. 69, Milner Papers 162. For the authoritative nature of this collection as a guide to political events in Egypt, especially between 1915 and Oct. 1919, see minute by Murray, head of Egyptian dept., Foreign Office, 18 March 1920, F.O. 371/5019/1604.
46 Annual Report on Egypt for 1913, F.O. 371/1967/14817.
47 R. Graham, Counsellor at the British Residency.
48 Report by R. Graham on the First Session of the Egyptian Legislative Assembly, Very Confid., 26 June 1914, D.C.S.M., vol. 1, pp. 88–94, Milner Papers 162.
49 *Ibid.*
50 *Ibid.*
51 *Ibid.*
52 Cheetham to Grey, Tel., 10 Sep. 1914, D.C.S.M., vol. I, p. 96, Milner Papers 162.
53 Grey to Cheetham, Tel., 31 Oct. 1914, *ibid.*, vol. I, p. 113.
54 Cheetham to Grey, Tel., 18 Nov. 1914, *ibid.*, vol. I, p. 122.
55 *Ibid.*
56 *Ibid.*
57 Cheetham to Grey, Tel., 8 Dec. 1914, *ibid.*, vol. I, p. 134.

58 Wingate to Balfour, Private and Personal, 11 Feb. 1917, *ibid.*, vol. I, p. 151.
59 Memo. by Sir R. Graham, 2 March 1917, *ibid.*, vol. I, p. 152.
60 Minute by Hardinge, 16 March 1917, *ibid.*, vol. I, p. 157.
61 Hardinge to Wingate, Private, 7 May 1917, *ibid.*, vol. I, p. 160.
62 Note by Brig.-Gen. Clayton, 22 July 1917, enc. in Wingate to Hardinge, 23 July 1917, *ibid.*, vol. I, p. 162.
63 Wingate to Balfour, Secret, 23 July 1917, *ibid.*, vol. I, p. 165.
64 *Ibid.*
65 *Ibid.*
66 *Ibid.*
67 Minute by Hardinge, 6 Sep. 1917, *ibid.*, vol. I, p. 178.
68 As fourth son of the 3rd Marquess of Salisbury, he was brother to Lord Robert Cecil and a cousin of Balfour.
69 Minutes of War Cabinet Egyptian Administration Committee, 26 Sep. 1917, CAB. 27/12.
70 Memo. by Milner, 31 Oct. 1917, appended to report of the Committee, CAB. 27/12.
71 Graham's report on first session of the Egyptian Legislative Assembly, Very Confid., 26 June 1914, D.C.S.M., vol. I, pp. 88–94, Milner Papers 162.
72 In 1914, as part of the transfer of sovereignty, the Khedive had been restyled, for obvious propaganda reasons, 'Sultan of Egypt'.
73 Wingate to Balfour, Tel., Confid., 9 Dec. 1917, D.C.S.M., vol. I, p. 193.
74 Wingate to Hardinge, Private, 24 Dec. 1917, *ibid.*, vol. I, p. 200.
75 Wingate to Balfour, Very Confid., 31 Aug. 1918, *ibid.*, vol. I, p. 209.
76 *Ibid.*
77 Wingate to Balfour, Tel., Private, 8 Nov. 1918, *ibid.*, vol. I, p. 214.
78 Wingate to Balfour, Tel., 17 Nov. 1918, *ibid.*, vol. II, p. 3.
79 *Ibid.*
80 Note on Constitutional Reform by Sir W. Brunyate, 18 Nov. 1918, encl. in Wingate to Balfour, Secret, 24 Nov. 1918, *ibid.*, vol. II, p. 16.
81 Rushdy declared himself 'frappé de stupéfaction' by proposals which he characterised as 'une annexion pur et simple'. Note by Sir H. Rushdy Pasha, n.d., appended to Wingate to Balfour, 5 Dec. 1918, *ibid.*, vol. II, pp. 47–9.
82 V. Chirol, *The Egyptian Problem* (London, 1921) p. 145; see also memo. by 'Anonymous Englishman', 25 March 1919, encl. in Allenby to Curzon, 7 April 1919, D.C.S.M. vol. II, p. 249, Milner Papers 162.
83 Walrond to Milner, 5 Jan. 1919, Milner Papers 164.
84 Chirol, *op. cit.*, p. 146; memo. by A. H. Hooker, 1 April 1919, encl. in Allenby to Curzon, 7 April 1919, D.C.S.M., vol. II, p. 244.
85 Memo. by W. E. Kingsford, 20 June 1919, in the 'Report of the Council of Cairo Non-Official British Community to the British Mission of Enquiry 1920', Milner Papers 164.
86 Report by Political Officer, Zagazig, 14 April 1919, encl. in Allenby to Curzon, 24 May 1919, D.C.S.M., vol. II, p. 299.
87 For the discontents of the Azharites and their part in the subsequent disturbances, see memos. by C. R. Beasley and A. H. Hooker in the 'Report of the . . . Non-Official British Community', Milner Papers 162; and by Chief Political Officer, East Delta, 20 April 1919, encl. in Allenby to

Curzon, 24 May 1919, D.C.S.M., vol. II, pp. 298 ff.
88 Cheetham to Curzon, Tel., 3 Feb. 1919, *ibid.*, vol. II, p. 67.
89 Cheetham to Curzon, Tel., 24 Feb. 1919, *ibid.*, vol. II, p. 76.
90 Cheetham to Curzon, Tel., 5 March 1919, *ibid.*, vol. II, p. 79.
91 Cheetham to Curzon, Tel., Very Urgent, 6 March 1919, *ibid.*, vol. II, pp. 79–80.
92 Cheetham to Foreign Office, Tel., Very Urgent, 17 March 1919, F.O. 371/3714/42905.
93 Baer, *A History of Landownership . . .*, p. 70.
94 *Ibid.*, pp. 24–5.
95 This was consonant with other aspects of British policy.
96 Baer, *op. cit.*, p. 96.
97 See Annual Report on Egypt for 1912, F.O. 371/1638/14764; also R. L. Tignor, *Modernization and British Colonial Rule in Egypt 1882–1914* (Princeton, 1966) p. 143.
98 J. Berque, *Egypt: Imperialism and Revolution* (Eng. trans., London, 1972) p. 130.
99 On the urgency of the labour situation in 1917, see George Lloyd to Austen Chamberlain, Private, 6 Sep. 1917, A.C. 18/1/1.
100 See memo. by Gen. Sir A. Murray (Commander-in-Chief, Egyptian Expeditionary Force), 26 Nov. 1916, Milner Papers 165; P. G. Elgood, *Egypt and the Army* (London, 1924) pp. 199, 202.
101 Elgood, *op. cit.*, pp. 309–10.
102 On the severity of inflation in food prices for 'poorer classes' see Annual Report on Egypt for 1914–1919, F.O. 371/5019/6985.
103 Cheetham to Curzon, Tel., Very Urgent, 20 March 1919, D.C.S.M., vol. II, p. 104.
104 Cheetham to Curzon, Tel., Very Urgent, 17 March 1919, F.O. 371/3714/42905.
105 Wingate to Balfour, 11 Dec. 1918, D.C.S.M., vol. II, Milner Papers 162.
106 *Ibid.*
107 Note on Causes of Unrest, 10 May 1920, Milner Papers 163.
108 *Ibid.*
109 Amine Youssef Bey, *Independent Egypt* (London, 1940) p. 65.
110 *Ibid.*, pp. 43, 76.
111 Our knowledge of the *Wafd*'s organisation in the 1920s and 1930s is very sketchy.
112 Lord Lloyd, *Egypt Since Cromer*, vol. I (London, 1933) p. 56.
113 P. J. Vatikiotis, *Egypt: a Modern History* (London, 1969) pp. 248–9.
114 Duff Cooper, *Old Men Forget* (London, 1953) p. 102.
115 Report by R. Graham, Very Confid., 26 June 1914, D.C.S.M., vol. I, pp. 88–94.
116 Wingate to Balfour, 9 Oct. 1917, *ibid.*, vol. I, p. 193.
117 See Wingate to Hardinge, 19 Nov. 1918, *ibid.*, vol. II.
118 *Ibid.*
119 Wingate to Balfour, 25 Nov. 1918, D.C.S.M., vol. II, Milner Papers 162.
120 Quoted in R. Storrs, *Orientations* (Defin. edn, London, 1943) p. 47.
121 And back to constitutional politics after 1922.
122 Allenby to Curzon, Tel., 4 May 1919, D.C.S.M., vol. II, pp. 180–1.

CHAPTER 4. THE EMERGENCE OF A POLICY

1 Balfour to Wingate, Tel., 27 Nov. 1918, D.C.S.M., vol. II, p. 1.
2 *Ibid.*
3 Wingate to Balfour, Confid., 28 Nov. 1918, *ibid.*, vol. II, p. 35.
4 *Ibid.*
5 Wingate to Balfour, Tel., 26 Dec. 1918, *ibid.*, vol. II, p. 53.
6 Balfour to Wingate, Tel., 1 Jan. 1919, *ibid.*, vol. II, p. 60.
7 Sir R. Graham, assistant under-secretary at the Foreign Office.
8 Graham to Wingate, Private, ? Jan. 1919, Wingate's Account, Milner Papers 162.
9 Wingate to Balfour, Tel., 16 Jan. 1919, D.C.S.M., vol. II, p. 63, Milner Papers 162.
10 Wingate's Account, Milner Papers 162. This narrative with supporting documents was dated 31 Aug. 1919 and sent to Milner.
11 *Ibid.*
12 Curzon's memo. for Balfour, 20 Feb. 1919, D.C.S.M., vol. II, p. 67.
13 Curzon to Cheetham, Tel., 26 Feb. 1919, *ibid.*, vol. II, p. 77.
14 Cheetham to Curzon, Tel., Very Urgent, 6 March 1919, *ibid.*, vol. II, pp. 79–80.
15 See above ch. 3.
16 Balfour to Curzon, Tel., 18 March 1919, F.O.371/3714/42439 Graham minuted sourly: 'this does not help us. . . . '
17 Cheetham to Curzon, Tel., Very Urgent, 20 March 1919, D.C.S.M., vol. II, p. 104.
18 Curzon to Cheetham, Tel., 22 March 1919, *ibid.*, vol. II, p. 108.
19 Allenby was still Commander-in-Chief of the Egyptian Expeditionary Force.
20 As it turned out, Wingate's displacement was permanent and ended his career. In the Milner Papers may be found ample evidence of his bitter resentment.
21 Allenby to Curzon, Tel., Very Urgent, 31 March 1919, D.C.S.M., vol. II, p. 116, Milner Papers 162.
22 Balfour to Curzon, Tel., Very Urgent, 2 April 1919, *ibid.*, vol. II, p. 117.
23 Bonar Law to Lloyd George, Tel., 3 April 1919, L.G.P. F/30/3/42.
24 Foreign Office to Allenby, Tel., 5 April 1919, Wingate's Account, Milner Papers 162.
25 See minute by C.I.G.S. on Allenby's tel. of 4 April 1919, quoted in E. Kedourie, *The Chatham House Version and Other Middle-Eastern Studies: 'Saad Zaghlul and the British'* (London, 1970) p. 115.
26 Minute by Hardinge, 6 Sep. 1917, D.C.S.M., vol. I, p. 178.
27 See above p. 80.
28 Wingate's note, 9 March 1919, Wingate's Account, Milner Papers 162.
29 Minute by R. Graham, 12 March 1919, F.O. 371/3714/39198.
30 *Ibid.*, Curzon's minute, 13 March 1919.
31 Curzon to Balfour (Paris), Confid., 29 March 1919, Curzon Papers F 112/208.
32 Curzon to Balfour, Confid., 1 April 1919, Curzon Papers F 112/208.
33 *Ibid.*, Curzon to Balfour, Confid., 3 April 1919.

34 Bonar Law to Lloyd George, Tel., 3 April 1919, L.G.P. F/30/3/42.
35 Allenby to Curzon, Tel., Very Urgent, 6 April 1919, D.C.S.M., vol. II, p. 123.
36 Curzon to Lloyd George, 15 April 1919, L.G.P. F/12/1/16.
37 Curzon to Allenby, Tel. 18 April 1919, D.C.S.M., vol. II, p. 148.
38 Milner to Curzon, 24 April 1919, Addit. Milner Papers, Ms. Eng. Hist. c699.
39 Milner to Curzon, 25 April 1919, Addit. Milner Papers, Ms. Eng. Hist. c699.
40 *Ibid.*
41 Curzon to Milner, Tel., Private, 15 May 1919, Curzon Collection, F.O. 800/153.
42 Curzon to Balfour, Tel., 23 April 1919, D.C.S.M., vol. II, p. 159.
43 Allenby to Curzon, Tel., 22 Aug. 1919, *ibid.*, vol. III, p. 30.
44 Cheetham to Curzon, Tel., 29 Sep. 1919, *ibid.*, vol. III, p. 81.
45 Allenby to Curzon, Tel., Very Urgent, 11 Nov. 1919, F.O. 371/3720/150982.
46 Milner to Curzon, 25 April 1919, Addit. Milner Papers, Ms. Eng. Hist. c699.
47 Curzon to Lloyd George, 14 July 1919, L.G.P. F/12/1/26.
48 Curzon to Allenby, Personal, 15 Oct. 1919, D.C.S.M., vol. III, p. 111.
49 Curzon to Lloyd George, 14 July 1919, L.G.P. F/12/1/26.
50 Milner to Lloyd George, 19 July 1919, L.G.P. F/39/1/27.
51 J. A. Spender, *Life, Journalism and Politics*, vol. II (London, 1927), p. 87.
52 Milner to Lord Robert Cecil, 2 Nov. 1919, Addit. Milner Papers, Ms. Eng. Hist. c699.
53 Milner to Curzon, 2 Dec. 1919, Curzon Papers F/112/213.
54 Milner's Egyptian diary, 5 Dec. 1919, Milner Papers 289.
55 *Ibid.*
56 *Ibid.*
57 *Ibid.*, 10 Dec. 1919.
58 *Ibid.*
59 Milner's memo., n.d., Milner Papers 164.
60 *Ibid.*
61 *Ibid.*
62 *Ibid.*
63 *Ibid.*
64 *Ibid.*
65 *Ibid.*
66 Milner to Lloyd George, 28 Dec. 1919, L.G.P. F/39/1/52.
67 *Ibid.*
68 Milner's Egyptian diary, 12 Dec. 1919, Milner Papers 289.
69 *Ibid.*
70 Milner's Egyptian diary, 13 Dec. 1919, Milner Papers 289.
71 Milner to Curzon, Private and Confid., 18 Dec. 1919, Milner Papers 162.
72 *Ibid.*
73 Milner's Egyptian diary, 21 Dec. 1919, Milner Papers 289.
74 *Ibid.*, 24 Dec. 1919.
75 *Ibid.*, 23 Dec. 1919.

76 Ingram to Thornton, 23 Dec. 1919, Milner Papers 164.
77 Milner's Egyptian diary, 24 Dec. 1919.
78 Milner to Curzon, Private and Confid., 12 Jan. 1920, Milner Papers 162.
79 Milner to Curzon, Private and Confid., 26 Jan. 1920, Milner Papers 162.
80 *Ibid.*
81 *Ibid.*
82 'General Conclusions' of the Milner Mission, May 1920, F.O. 848/19/1.
83 See E. Kedourie, *The Chatham House Version and Other Middle-Eastern Studies: 'Saad Zaghlul and the British'* (London, 1970) pp. 121, 123.
84 Milner's speech 'The Two Empires', 16 June 1908, in Viscount Milner, *The Nation and the Empire* (London, 1913) p. 293.
85 Milner explicitly recalled this fact of life in Egypt in his diary, 5 Dec. 1919, Milner Papers 289.
86 Milner to Lloyd George, 28 Dec. 1919, Milner Papers 163.
87 *Ibid.*
88 *Ibid.*
89 *Ibid.*
90 *Ibid.*
91 Milner's sketch of a report, dated 12 Feb. 1920, Milner Papers 163.
92 *Ibid.*
93 *Ibid.*
94 *Ibid.*
95 *Ibid.*
96 *Ibid.*
97 Milner to Curzon, Private and Confid., 17 Feb. 1920, Milner Papers 162.
98 Milner's sketch of a report, dated 12 Feb. 1920, Milner Papers 164.
99 *The Times*, 23 March 1920, in F.O. 371/4978/2014.
100 Memo. by J. Murray and J. Loder, 23 Jan. 1920, Milner Papers 164
101 'General Conclusions' of the Milner Mission, May 1920, F.O. 848/19/1.
102 Milner to Chirol, 7 May 1920, Milner Papers 164.
103 Milner to Hurst, encl. in Foreign Office to Derby (Paris), Tel., cypher, No Distribution, 11 May 1920, copy in Milner Papers 164.
104 Record of conversation at the Colonial Office, 21 June 1920, Milner Papers 163.
105 *Ibid.*, 22 June 1920.
106 Memo. by C. J. B. Hurst, 15 June 1920, Milner Papers 163.
107 Record of conversation, 3 July 1920, Milner Papers 163.
108 *Ibid.*, 5 July 1920.
109 *Ibid.*
110 See Zaghlul to Milner, 26 July 1920, Milner Papers 163.
111 This is hinted at in the 'Statement for information of Mission', circulated by Milner, 28 July 1920, Milner Papers 163.
112 See Allenby to Curzon, Tel., 21 May 1920, F.O. 407/186; General Maxwell to Milner, 22 June 1920, Milner Papers 163; J. A. Spender to Milner, 23 June 1920, Milner Papers 163; Milner to Maxwell, 24 June 1920, and to Spender, 27 June 1920, both in Milner Papers 163.
113 The terms of the agreement are set out in Milner's memo. for Cabinet, 18 Aug. 1920, Milner Papers 163, and in Curzon's tel. to Scott (Cairo), 21 Aug. 1920, copy in Montagu Papers.

114 Milner to Chirol, 18 Aug. 1920, Milner Papers 163.
115 *Ibid.*
116 Milner to Spender, 27 June 1920, Milner Papers 163.
117 Milner's minute on Scott to Curzon, Tel., 10 Aug. 1920, F.O. 371/4979/9763.
118 Curzon to Scott, Tel., Very Urgent, 14 Aug. 1920, copy in Milner Papers 163.
119 Milner to Curzon, Confid., 19 Aug. 1920, Milner Papers 162.
120 *Ibid.*
121 *Ibid.*
122 Spender to Milner, 23 June 1920, Milner Papers 163.
123 Milner's memo. for Cabinet, 16 Sept. 1920, (C.P. 4340), copy in Milner Papers 163.
124 *Ibid.*
125 *Ibid.*

CHAPTER 5. EGYPT AND THE CABINET

1 Stenographic Notes of the Proceedings of the Imperial Conference, 6 July 1921, F.O. 371/6301/8245.
2 Curzon to Milner, Confid. and Private, 17 Aug. 1920, Milner Papers 163.
3 Churchill's memorandum for Cabinet, 24 Aug. 1920, copy in Montagu Papers.
4 Churchill to Lloyd George, 5 Aug. 1920, L.G.P. F/9/2/37.
5 The origins of this sense of betrayal are described in Martin Gilbert, *Winston S. Churchill*, vol. III, 1914–1916 (London, 1971) ch. 26.
6 Montagu's memorandum for Cabinet, 19 Oct. 1920, Montagu Papers.
7 Note by Sir W. Duke, 3 Sep. 1920, Montagu Papers.
8 This was, in effect, a debate on Montagu's handling of the political situation in India.
9 Curzon to Milner, Private and Confidential, 18 Aug. 1920, Milner Papers 163.
10 Bonar Law to Curzon, 20 Aug. 1920, F.O. 371/4979/10237.
11 Fisher's diary, 13 Oct. 1920, Fisher Papers Box 8A; Thomas Jones, *Whitehall Diary*, vol. I, ed. K. Middlemas (London, 1969) p. 121.
12 In April 1918. See A. M. Gollin, *Proconsul in Politics* (London, 1964) p. 512.
13 Memorandum by Chief of Naval Staff, 27 Oct. 1920, copy in Montagu Papers.
14 Minutes of Ministerial Conference, 1 Nov. 1920, Appendix I to Cabinet 62(20), CAB. 23/23.
15 Curzon's memorandum for Cabinet, 11 Oct. 1920, copy in Milner Papers 165.
16 Minutes of Ministerial Conference, 4 Nov. 1920, Appended to Cabinet 62(20).
17 *Ibid.*
18 Fisher's diary, 29 Dec. 1920, Fisher Papers Box 8A.
19 *Ibid.*
20 Curzon's memorandum for Cabinet, 11 Oct. 1920, Milner Papers 165.

21 Curzon to Balfour, 13 Oct. 1920, Balfour Papers 49734.
22 Fisher's diary, 29 Dec. 1920, Fisher Papers Box 8A.
23 Earl of Ronaldshay, *The Life of Lord Curzon*, vol. III (London, 1929) pp. 251–3.
24 Curzon to Milner, 13 Feb. 1921, Milner Papers 207.
25 Allenby to Curzon, Tel., Very Urgent, 12 Jan. 1921, F.O. 371/6292/603.
26 Scott to Curzon, Tel., Confid., 9 Feb. 1921, F.O. 371/6292/1803.
27 Memorandum by J. W. Headlam-Morley, 11 July 1921, F.O. 371/6301/8453.
28 Curzon's memorandum for Cabinet, 14 Feb. 1921, C.P. 2589, CAB. 24/119.
29 Milner to Curzon, 19 Aug. 1920, Milner Papers 163.
30 Curzon's memorandum for Cabinet, 14 Feb. 1921, C.P. 2589, CAB. 24/119.
31 Conclusions of Cabinet 9(21), 22 Feb. 1921, CAB. 23/24.
32 Memorandum by J. W. Headlam-Morley, 11 July 1921. F.O. 371/6301/8453.
33 Churchill's memorandum for Cabinet, 22 March 1921, C.P. 2382, CAB. 24/122.
34 Allenby to Curzon, Tel. (188), 21 March 1921. Copy in Montagu Papers.
35 *Ibid.*
36 Memorandum by J. W. Headlam-Morley, 11 July 1921, F.O. 371/6301/8453.
37 *Ibid.*
38 Asserting the need for a new Anglo-Egyptian relationship.
39 Curzon's memorandum for Cabinet, 21 April 1921, C.P. 2871, CAB. 24/122.
40 Verbatim minutes of those meetings at which Egypt was discussed are in F.O. 371/6301.
41 It was widely assumed among ministers without special knowledge of Egypt that the protectorate of 1914 had brought Egypt within the British Empire.
42 F.O. 371/6301.
43 Conclusions of Cabinet 58(21), 11 July 1921, CAB. 23/26.
44 Thomas Jones, *Whitehall Diary*, vol. III, ed. K. Middlemas (London, 1971) p. 85.
45 *Ibid.*
46 *Ibid.*, p. 87.
47 Minutes of Meetings and Correspondence in connection with the Egyptian Official Delegation, F.O. 371/6310/14377.
48 *Ibid.*
49 Conclusions of Cabinet 81(21), 20 Oct. 1921, CAB. 23/27.
50 Minutes of Cabinet sub-committee on Situation in Egypt, 24 Oct. 1921, CAB. 27/134.
51 *Ibid.*
52 Conclusions of Cabinet 85(21), 3 Nov. 1921, CAB. 23/27.
53 *Ibid.*
54 *Ibid.*
55 *Ibid.*
56 For foreign and imperial questions.
57 Kerr to Lloyd George, 28 Oct. 1921, L.G.P. F/34/2/9.
58 *Ibid.*
59 Conclusions of Cabinet 86(21), 4 Nov. 1921, CAB. 23/27.
60 *Ibid.*
61 Minutes of Meetings . . . etc., F.O. 371/6310/14377.
62 *Ibid.*

63 Minutes of Ministerial Conference, 18 Nov. 1921, Appendix III to Cabinet 92(21), CAB. 23/27.
64 *Ibid.*
65 See W. G. Hayter, *Recent Constitutional Developments in Egypt* (Cambridge, 1924).
66 Tyrrell was an assistant under-secretary at the Foreign Office.
67 Letters from British Officials. . . . Copies in Curzon Collection F.O. 800/153.
68 *Ibid.*
69 Allenby to Foreign Office, Tel., Very Urgent, 17 Nov. 1921, Appendix II to Minutes of Ministerial Conference, 18 Nov. 1921, CAB. 23/27.
70 *Ibid.*
71 See Allenby to Curzon, Tel., Very Urgent, Private and Personal, 12 Jan. 1922, Curzon Collection, F.O. 800/153.
72 Conclusions of Cabinet 2(22), 18 Jan. 1922, CAB. 23/29.
73 Churchill to Lloyd George, 13 Jan. 1922, L.G.P. F/10/2/3.
74 Curzon to Allenby, Tel., Strictly Personal and Confid., 18 Jan. 1922, Curzon Collection, F.O. 800/153.
75 Conclusions of Cabinet 2(22), 18 Jan. 1922.
76 Conclusions of Cabinet 4(22), 26 Jan. 1922, CAB. 23/29.
77 Conclusions of Cabinet 5(22), 27 Jan. 1922, CAB. 23/29.
78 Curzon to Lloyd George, 10 Feb. 1922, L.G.P. F/13/3/6.
79 Lloyd George had refused Wingate a peerage on the grounds that he might attack the government in the House of Lords.
80 Curzon to Lloyd George, 10 Feb. 1922, L.G.P. F/13/3/6.
81 Clayton and Amos, respectively Interior and Judicial Advisers to the Egyptian Government, had accompanied Allenby to London.
82 Conclusions of Cabinet 10(22), 16 Feb. 1922, CAB. 23/29.
83 Lord Lloyd, *Egypt Since Cromer*, vol. I (London, 1933) p. 342.
84 *Ibid.*, vol. II (London, 1934) pp. 8–9.
85 Published at the height of the controversy over the India Bill, of which he was a vehement opponent, Lloyd's account was not so much a history as a tract for the times, the credibility of which is weakened not only by his refusal to discuss, let alone criticise, the part played in the 'surrender' by those two heroes of the imperialist pantheon, Curzon and Milner, but even more perhaps by his own readiness in 1925 to serve the system inaugurated by these pathetic and futile endeavours in 1922.
86 Curzon to Milner, 3 Jan. 1920, Curzon Papers, F 112/208.
87 Cf. E. Kedourie, *The Chatham House Version and other Middle-Eastern Studies* (London, 1970) p. 155.
88 For a characteristic instance of this, R. Ullman, *The Anglo-Soviet Accord* (London, 1972) p. 44.
89 Memo. by J. Murray, 23 March 1928, F.O. 371/13118.

CHAPTER 6. WAR AND IMPERIAL POLICY IN THE MIDDLE EAST 1918–1919

1 Cf. S. A. Cohen, 'The Formulation of British Policy towards

Mesopotamia 1903–1914' (Oxford D.Phil., 1972), where it is argued that the occupation of Basra was intended primarily to stimulate Arab opposition to the Turks.

2 See above, ch. 3.

3 V. H. Rothwell, 'Mesopotamia in British War Aims', *Historical Journal*, XIII, 2 (1970) pp. 275, 276; *idem, War Aims and Peace Diplomacy* (Oxford, 1971) pp. 26–7.

4 An inter-departmental committee of officials.

5 J. Nevakivi, *Britain, France and the Arab Middle East 1914–1920* (London, 1969) pp. 19–25.

6 The terms of the Tripartite Agreement are set out in J. C. Hurewitz, *Diplomacy in the Near and Middle East: A Documentary Record*, vol. II (Princeton, 1956) pp. 18–22.

7 J. Nevakivi, *op. cit.*, pp. 34–5.

8 On this see B. C. Busch, *Britain, India and the Arabs 1914–1921* (Berkeley and London, 1971) ch. III.

9 This was the assumption behind the Sykes–Picot Agreement; see B. C. Busch, *op. cit.*, p. 84. For Sykes' appointment as British representative in the Anglo-French discussions, R. Adelson, *Mark Sykes: Portrait of an Amateur* (London, 1975) p. 199.

10 See P. Guinn, *British Strategy and Politics 1914–1918* (London, 1965).

11 H. I. Nelson, *Land and Power* (2nd edn, Newton Abbot, 1971) p. 17.

12 *Ibid.*, p. 18.

13 Rothwell, *op. cit.*, p. 72; W. Roger Louis, *Germany's Lost Colonies* (Oxford, 1967) pp. 81–4.

14 The development of British policy in Persia may be traced in: J. B. Kelly, *Britain and the Persian Gulf 1795–1880* (Oxford, 1968); A. P. Thornton, 'British Policy in Persia 1858–1890', *English Historical Review*, LXIX (1954) and LXX (1955); R. L. Greaves, *Persia and the Defence of India* (London, 1959).

15 P. Avery, *Modern Iran* (London, 1965) p. 192.

16 Memorandum by J. E. Shuckburgh (India Office) 19 Oct. 1917, for Persia Committee, Curzon Papers F 112/271.

17 One of the precursors of the Eastern Committee (for which see below). First met July 1917. Balfour, Curzon and Montagu were its regular ministerial members. Lord Robert Cecil sometimes attended.

18 Persia Committee Minutes, 20 Oct. 1917, Curzon Papers F 112/271.

19 Note by J. E. Shuckburgh, 11 Jan. 1918, Curzon Papers F 112/271.

20 *Ibid.*

21 *Ibid.*

22 *Ibid.*

23 Foreign Office to Marling, Tel., 21 Feb. 1918, communicating the Committee's decision, Curzon Papers F 112/271.

24 *Official History of the War*: F. J. Moberly, *The Campaign in Mesopotamia*, vol. IV (London, 1927) p. 103.

25 Milner's position in the War Cabinet is discussed authoritatively in A. M. Gollin, *Proconsul in Politics* (London, 1964) chs. XVIII, XIX.

26 Milner to Curzon, 26 Feb. 1918, Curzon Papers F 112/122.

27 Persia Committee Minutes, 1 March 1918, Curzon Papers F 112/271.

28 *Ibid.*, 5 March 1918.
29 Moberly, *op. cit.*, p. 138.
30 *Ibid.*
31 Eastern Committee, 15th Minutes, 21 June 1918, Milner Papers 119.
32 *Ibid.*, 16th Minutes, 24 June 1918.
33 *Ibid.*, 15th Minutes, 21 June 1918.
34 *Ibid.*, 16th Minutes, 24 June 1918.
35 *Ibid.*, 5th Minutes, 24 April 1918.
36 *Ibid.*, 21st Minutes, 18 July 1918.
37 *Ibid.*
38 The Articles of the Turkish armistice are reprinted in Moberly, *op. cit.*, pp. 322 ff.
39 Eastern Committee, 46th Minutes, 23 Dec. 1918, Milner Papers 119.
40 *Ibid.*
41 Draft Resolutions, Eastern Committee, 43rd Minutes, 16 Dec. 1918.
42 On these elements, see R. Pipes, *The Formation of the Soviet Union: Communism and Nationalism 1917–1923* (rev. edn, Harvard, 1964).
43 For the diplomatic consequences of this, see R. Ullman, *Britain and the Russian Civil War* (London, 1968).
44 These visions are discussed in W. Roger Louis, *Germany's Lost Colonies* (Oxford, 1967) ch. III.
45 Eastern Committee, 34th Minutes, 3 Oct. 1918, Milner Papers 119.
46 *Ibid.*, 41st Minutes, 5 Dec. 1918.
47 *Ibid.*, 37th Minutes, 29 Oct. 1918.
48 *Ibid.*, 41st Minutes, 5 Dec. 1918.
49 *Ibid.*
50 Louis, *op. cit.*, chs. III, IV.
51 Eastern Committee, 34th Minutes, 3 Oct. 1918, Milner Papers 119.
52 *Ibid.*, 41st Minutes, 5 Dec. 1918.
53 *Ibid.*
54 Resolutions on Syria, Eastern Committee, 43rd Minutes, 16 Dec. 1918, Milner Papers 119.
55 *Ibid.*, 34th Minutes, 3 Oct. 1918.
56 *Ibid.*, 44th Minutes, 18 Dec. 1918.
57 *Ibid.*, 41st Minutes, 5 Dec. 1918.
58 *Ibid.*, 34th Minutes, 3 Oct. 1918.
59 *Ibid.*, 36th Minutes, 24 Oct.1918.
60 *Ibid.*, 38th Minutes, 21 Nov. 1918.
61 *Ibid.*, 45th Minutes, 19 Dec. 1918.
62 *Ibid.*
63 *Ibid.*
64 *Ibid.*
65 *Ibid.*
66 See below ch. 9.
67 Eastern Committee, 48th Minutes, 30 Dec. 1918, Milner Papers 119.
68 Montagu to Curzon, 6 Jan. 1919, Curzon Papers F 112/253.
69 Eastern Committee, 40th Minutes, 2 Dec. 1918; 42nd Minutes, 9 Dec. 1918, Milner Papers 119.
70 *Ibid.*, 43rd Minutes, 16 Dec. 1918.

71 *Ibid.*
72 *Ibid.*, 42nd Minutes, 9 Dec. 1918. This remark was addressed to Montagu.
73 *Ibid.*
74 *Ibid.*
75 *Ibid.*, 43rd Minutes, 16 Dec. 1918.
76 *Ibid.*, 45th Minutes, 30 Dec. 1918.
77 For colonial pressure groups in France *c*. 1918, see C. M. Andrew and A. S. Kanya-Forstner, 'The French Colonial Party and French Colonial War Aims', *Historical Journal*, xvii, 1 (1974) 79–106.
78 This aspect of post-war imperial policy is discussed more fully in ch. 9 below.
79 Hankey's memorandum for the Prime Minister, 19 Dec. 1918, L.G.P. F/23/3/30.
80 Hardinge of Penshurst to Curzon, 11 Feb. 1919, Curzon Papers F 112/212.
81 This 'agreement' was not recorded in a document. D. Lloyd George, *The Truth About the Peace Treaties* (London, 1938) vol. ii, p. 1038; J. Nevakivi, *Britain, France and the Arab Middle East 1914–1920* (London, 1969) pp. 91–2.
82 J. Nevakivi, *op. cit.*, p. 119.
83 Curzon to Derby (Paris), Secret, 12 Feb. 1919, Curzon Papers F 112/278.
84 Nevakivi, *op. cit.*, p. 128.
85 *Ibid.*, pp. 148–9 for some discussion of this.
86 Milner to Lloyd George, Confidential, 8 March 1919, Milner Collection, P.R.O. 30/30/10.
87 Balfour to Curzon, Private, 20 March 1919, Curzon Papers F 112/208.
88 Curzon's memo., 25 March 1919, apparently for departmental circulation, Curzon papers F 112/278.
89 Curzon to Balfour, 22 April 1919, Curzon Papers F 112/278.
90 The so-called King–Crane Commission.
91 Nevakivi, *op cit.*, pp. 144–6.
92 Allenby to Balfour, Tel., 30 May 1919, *D.B.F.P.* Is., iv, p. 256.
93 Assistant Under-Secretary of State, India Office. His province was the India Office's responsibilities in the Middle East.
94 Hirtzel's memo. on France's claim to Syria, 14 Feb. 1919, Montagu Papers; also in Milner Collection, P.R.O. 30/30/10, with attached note showing Milner's 'entire agreement'.
95 Technically known after Jan. 1919 as the Inter-departmental Committee on Middle East Affairs, or I.D.C.E.
96 See above, ch. 2.
97 For example, Milner to Lloyd George, 9 June 1918, Milner Papers 145; Milner had played a decisive role in setting up the Eastern Committee, Gollin, *op. cit.*, p. 562.
98 Ullman, *op. cit.*, pp. 75, 80.
99 Conclusions of War Cabinet 541A, 4 March 1919, CAB. 23/15.
100 I.D.C.E. 11th Minutes, 6 March 1919, Curzon Papers F 112/275.
101 Conclusions of War Cabinet 542, 6 March 1919, CAB. 23/9.
102 Eastern Committee, 38th Minutes, 21 Nov. 1918, Milner Papers 119.
103 Viceroy to S.S.I., Tel., 6 Jan. 1919, Chelmsford Collection, E 264/10 (Tels. to and from S.S.I., vol. iv).

104 Montagu to Curzon, 6 Jan. 1919, Montagu Papers.
105 The War Office displayed a mild enthusiasm for commitments that burdened Indian rather than British resources.
106 I.D.C.E., 3rd Minutes, 14 Jan. 1919, Curzon Papers F 112/275.
107 *Ibid.*, 5th Minutes, 8 Feb. 1919.
108 R. Ullman, *op. cit.*, p. 328.
109 I.D.C.E., 11th Minutes, 6 March 1919.
110 *Ibid.*, 23rd Minutes, 19 June 1919.
111 *Ibid.*, 13th Minutes, 21 March 1919; 14th Minutes, 9 April 1919.
112 Montagu to Curzon, 6 Jan. 1919, Montagu Papers.
113 I.D.C.E., 11th Minutes, 6 March 1919.
114 S.S.I. to Viceroy, Tel., 9 May 1919, Chelmsford Collection, E 264/10 (Tels. to and from S.S.I., vol. IV).
115 I.D.C.E., 18th Minutes, 29 April 1919, Curzon Papers F 112/275.

CHAPTER 7. THE SEARCH FOR SECURITY, 1919–1920

1 For Balfour's attitude, see his memoranda of 22 May 1919, Lothian Collection, G.D. 40/17/38; 26 June 1919, *D.B.F.P.* Is., IV, p. 301; 11 Aug. 1919, *ibid.*, IV, p. 340. Also Balfour (Paris) to Curzon, Tel., 28 July 1919, *ibid.*, IV, p. 321.
2 C. E. Callwell, *Field Marshal Sir Henry Wilson: His Life and Diaries*, vol. II (London, 1927) p. 208.
3 Curzon to Balfour, 20 Aug. 1919, Balfour Papers 49734.
4 *Ibid.* As will be seen, the extent of the proposed Mesopotamian state later became a controversial issue within the Cabinet.
5 *Ibid.* See also Fisher's diary, 20 Aug. 1919, Fisher Papers Box 8A. For Montagu's and Curzon's shared dislike of the project for Jewish settlement in Palestine, Curzon to Montagu, 8 Sep. 1917, Montagu Papers.
6 See Simon (French Minister of Colonies) to Milner, 4 Aug. 1919, Milner Papers 152; Balfour's memo., 11 Aug. 1919, *D.B.F.P.* Is., IV, p. 340.
7 See above p. 164.
8 Curzon to Balfour, 20 Aug. 1919, Balfour Papers 49734.
9 *Ibid.*
10 Fisher's diary, 20 Aug. 1919, Fisher Papers Box 8A.
11 Curzon to Balfour, 20 Aug. 1919, Balfour Papers 49734.
12 Montagu to Prime Minister, Private, 20 Aug. 1919, L.G.P. F/40/2/59.
13 Fisher's diary, 20 Aug. 1919, Fisher Papers Box 8A.
14 Milner to Montagu, 30 Aug. 1919, Montagu Papers.
15 The fullest statement of Curzon's views is in his Cabinet memo. on the Future of Constantinople, 4 Jan. 1920, *D.B.F.P.* Is., IV, pp. 992–1000.
16 Curzon to Balfour, 20 Aug. 1919, Balfour Papers 49734.
17 *Ibid.*
18 See Montagu's angry letter to Lloyd George, 20 Aug. 1919, L.G.P. F/40/2/59.
19 This may be followed in detail in J. Nevakivi, *Britain, France and the Arab Middle East 1914–1920* (London, 1969) ch. IX.
20 W. W. Gottlieb, *Studies in Secret Diplomacy* (London, 1957) pp. 21, 23.

21 Minutes of Anglo-French Conversations in London, 11 Dec. 1919, *D.B.F.P.* Is., II, pp. 728–9, 734.
22 Minutes of Anglo-French Conference, 22–3 Dec. 1919, *D.B.F.P.* Is., IV, p. 963.
23 Fisher's diary, 9, 10 Dec. 1919, Fisher Papers Box 8A.
24 Milner to Montagu, 2 Dec. 1919, Montagu papers.
25 Callwell, *op. cit.*, vol. II, pp. 217–21.
26 *Ibid.*, p. 217.
27 Conclusions of Ministerial Conference, 5 Jan. 1920, Appendix I to Cabinet I(20), CAB. 23/20.
28 Denikin was the White Russian commander in South Russia.
29 Conclusions of Ministerial Conference, 5 Jan. 1920, Appendix I to Cabinet I(20), CAB. 23/20.
30 Conclusions of Cabinet I(20), 6 Jan. 1920, CAB. 23/20.
31 *Ibid.*
32 *Ibid.*
33 Fisher's diary, 6 Jan. 1920, Fisher Papers Box 8A.
34 H. C. Thornton (Milner's Private Sec. at the Colonial Office) to Milner (Egypt), 8 Jan. 1920, Addit. Milner Papers, Ms. Eng. Hist. c703.
35 Conclusions of Cabinet 4(20), 14 Jan. 1920, CAB. 23/20.
36 Amery to Milner, 14 Jan. 1920, Addit. Milner Papers, Ms. Eng. Hist. c703.
37 Draft tel. to High Commissioner, Constantinople, 5 March 1920, *D.B.F.P.* Is., VII, pp. 421–3.
38 Admiral Webb (High Commissioner, Constantinople) to Curzon, Tel., 6 Feb. 1920, *D.B.F.P.* Is., IV, pp. 1085–7; H. C. Luke, *Cities and Men*, vol II (London, 1953) pp. 68–9.
39 Churchill to Curzon, Private, 16 Feb. 1920, Curzon Papers F 112/215; Sir H. Wilson to Curzon, 25 Feb. 1920, Curzon Papers F 112/218.
40 Minutes of First Conference of London, 5 March 1920, 11 a.m., *D.B.F.P.* Is., VII, pp. 411 ff.
41 Curzon to P. H. Kerr, Private, 12 March 1920, Lothian Collection, G. D. 40/17/208; Curzon to Prime Minister, Confid., 9 April 1920, Curzon Papers F 112/216.
42 Conclusions of Cabinet 24(20), 5 May 1920, CAB. 23/21; Fisher's diary, 5 May 1920, Fisher Papers Box 8A.
43 Admiral De Robeck to Curzon, Tel., 17 May 1920, *D.B.F.P.* Is., XIII, p. 73; also Sir A. Block (British Representative, Ottoman Public Debt Administration) to Curzon, 12 June 1920, Curzon Papers F 112/215.
44 De Robeck to Curzon, Tel., Urgent, 15 June 1920, *D.B.F.P.* Is., XIII, p. 86.
45 Minutes of conversation between Lloyd George, Bonar Law, Balfour, Curzon, Milner and Churchill, Downing St., 11 June 1920, Appendix I to Cabinet 37(20), CAB. 23/21.
46 Conclusions of Ministerial Conference, 18 June 1920, App. I to Cabinet 38(20), CAB. 23/21.
47 See *D.B.F.P.* Is., VIII, p. 307.
48 S. R. Sonyel, *Turkish Diplomacy 1918–1923* (London, 1975) p. 82.
49 Rumbold to Curzon, Tel., Urgent, 22 Nov. 1920, *D.B.F.P.* Is., XIII, p. 182.
50 This is the explanation advanced in C. J. Lowe and F. Marzari, *Italian Foreign Policy 1870–1940* (London, 1975) pp. 173–4.

51 Buchanan (Rome) to Curzon, Tel., 29 July 1920, *D.B.F.P.* Is., XIII, p. 109.
52 R. A. Webster, *Industrial Imperialism in Italy 1908–1915* (Los Angeles and London, 1975) pp. 193, 202, 287.
53 S. H. Longrigg, *Syria and Lebanon under French Mandate* (London, 1958) p. 118.
54 *Ibid.*, p. 137.
55 S. H. Roberts, *The History of French Colonial Policy 1870–1925* (new imp., London, 1963) p. 593.
56 These and other more extravagant anxieties are described in Hardinge (Paris) to Curzon, 24 Dec. 1920, *D.B.F.P.* Is., XIII, p. 208.
57 Curzon's memo. for Cabinet, 9 Aug. 1919, *D.B.F.P.* Is., IV, pp. 1119–22.
58 *Ibid.*
59 See above, ch. 6.
60 The Anglo-Persian agreement of 9 Aug. 1919 is printed in *British Foreign and State Papers*, vol. CXII (1919), p. 760.
61 See *D.B.F.P.* Is., IV, pp. 1176–7, 1227; *Ibid.*, XIII, pp. 440–1, 467.
62 Curzon's memo. for Cabinet, 9 Aug. 1919, *D.B.F.P.* Is., IV, pp. 1119–22.
63 A. R. Arasteh, *Man and Society in Iran* (Leiden, 1964); R. Sanghvi, *The Shah of Iran* (London, 1968) pp. 9–11; Sir F. O'Connor, *On the Frontier and Beyond* (London, 1931); Sir P. Sykes, *A History of Persia* (3rd edn, London, 1930) vol. II; Hassan Arfa, *Under Five Shahs* (London, 1962) p.114 and appendix.
64 G. N. Curzon, *Persia and the Persian Question* (2nd imp., London, 1966) vol. II, ch. XXX.
65 Eastern Committee, 45th Minutes, 19 Dec. 1918, Milner Papers 119.
66 For a description of British relations with the largely independent rulers of Fars and Seistan, see O'Connor, *op. cit.*
67 Hassan Arfa, *op. cit.*, p. 75.
68 Sir Clarmont Skrine, *World War in Iran* (London, 1962) p. 60.
69 Skrine says coyly of Vossugh's faction: 'They were known to have the ear of the British Minister, and profited personally from the knowledge.' Skrine, *op. cit.*, p. 75.
70 On the precarious state of Persian revenues, Z. Y. Hershslag, *Introduction to the Modern Economic History of the Middle East* (Leiden, 1964) pp. 135–8.
71 See Cox's reports in late Aug. 1919, *D.B.F.P.* Is., IV, nos. 732, 733, pp. 1138–40.
72 *Ibid.*, IV, pp. 1147–8, Cox to Curzon, Tel., 29 Aug. 1919.
73 *Ibid.*, IV, pp. 1150–1, Cox to Curzon, Tel., 1 Sep. 1919.
74 *Ibid.*, IV, pp. 1170–1, Cox to Curzon, Tel., 19 Sep. 1919.
75 *Ibid.*, IV, pp. 1173–4, for Cox's report to Curzon on his conversation with the editor of a Teheran paper closely associated with Vossugh.
76 Derby (Paris) to Curzon, 30 March 1920, *D.B.F.P.* Is., XIII, p. 459.
77 Norman (Teheran) to Curzon, Tel., Urgent, 13 June 1920, *D.B.F.P.* Is., XIII, p. 513.
78 *Ibid.*, XIII, ch. III, *passim.*
79 Curzon to Cox, Tel., 7 Feb. 1920, *D.B.F.P.* Is., XIII, p. 437.
80 I.D.C.E., 36th Minutes, 17 March 1920, Curzon Papers F 112/275. This

was the remnant of Sykes' expedition to S. Persia to restore British control in 1916.

81 *Ibid.*, 37th Minutes, 13 April 1920.
82 Churchill's memo. for Cabinet, 19 April 1920, C.P. 1101, CAB. 24/104.
83 Viceroy to S.S.I., Tel., 20 Feb. 1920, C.P. 737, CAB. 24/99.
84 *Ibid.*
85 Curzon to Montagu, 15 April 1920, Curzon Papers F 112/217.
86 Conclusions of Cabinet 24(20), 5 May 1920, CAB. 23/21.
87 For the origins of this force see above p. 166.
88 Cox to Curzon, Tel., Clear the Line, 14 May 1920, *D.B.F.P.* Is., XIII, p. 479.
89 *Ibid.*, XIII, pp. 481–2, Same to same, Tel., Extremely Urgent, 14 May 1920.
90 R. Ullman, *The Anglo-Soviet Accord* (London, 1972) p. 359.
91 Wilson's diary, 28 April 1920, Callwell, *op. cit.*, vol. II, p. 255; Churchill to Austen Chamberlain, 10 May 1920, quoted in M. Gilbert, *Winston S. Churchill*, vol. IV: 1917–1922 (London, 1975) p. 483.
92 See R. Ullman, *op. cit.*, pp. 361–2.
93 Conclusions of Ministerial Conference, 18 June 1920, Appendix I to Cabinet 38(20), CAB. 23/21.
94 Finance Committee 27, 12 Aug. 1920, Appendix I to Cabinet 49(20), CAB. 23/22.
95 See Fisher's diary, 21 May 1920, Fisher Papers Box 8A.
96 Milner to Churchill, 1 May 1920, Addit. Milner Papers, Ms. Eng. Hist. c699.
97 Milner's memo. for Cabinet, 24 May 1920, copy in Curzon Papers F 112/253.
98 Fisher's diary, 17 June 1920, Fisher Papers Box 8A.
99 At a meeting of the Cabinet Finance Committee at which Persia was discussed, Lloyd George passed Curzon a note saying that although personally opposed to staying in Persia, he did not want to let him down, 12 Aug. 1920, Curzon Papers F 112/317.
100 Milner to Curzon, Confid., 3 Aug. 1920, Curzon Papers F 112/217.
101 R. Ullman, *op. cit.*, p. 382.
102 For instance, Curzon to Norman, Tel., Most Urgent, 29 Oct. 1920, *D.B.F.P.* Is., XIII, pp. 628–9.
103 *Ibid.*, XIII, pp. 632–3, Curzon to Norman, Tel., Very Urgent, 5 Nov. 1920.
104 *Ibid.*, XIII, p. 643, Norman to Curzon, Tel., 25 Nov. 1920.
105 See below, p. 206.
106 On one occasion, in early June, Lloyd George complained, to Curzon's fury, that the Anglo-Persian agreement had been concluded behind his back. Fisher's diary, 7 June 1920, Fisher Papers Box 8A.
107 Eastern Committee, 44th Minutes, 18 Dec. 1918, Milner Papers 119.
108 Montagu's telegram to Wilson, quoted in A. T. Wilson, *Mesopotamia 1917–1920: A Clash of Loyalties* (London, 1931), p. 114. Wilson was responsible to the India Office for civil administration in Iraq.
109 I.D.C.E., 16th Minutes, 17 April 1919, Curzon Papers F 112/275.
110 S. H. Longrigg, *Iraq 1900–1950* (London, 1953) pp. 92–4; historical note by Sir P. Cox in *The Letters of Gertrude Bell*, edit. Lady Bell, vol. 2 (London, 1927) pp. 518 ff.; Wilson, *op. cit.*, p. 45. H. St. J. Philby, *Arabian*

Days (London, 1948) pp. 98–133 for some description of this relationship in wartime.

111 Ration strength of the Mesopotamian Expeditionary Force (including followers) at 27 March 1920: 204 179. *Statistics of the Military Effort of the British Empire* (War Office, London, 1922) p. 105.

112 P. Sluglett, 'Profit and Loss from the British Mandate: British Influence and Administration in Iraq 1914–1932' (Oxford D.Phil. 1972) p. 64.

113 Wilson, *op. cit.*, p. 120.

114 I.D.C.E., 28th Minutes, 20 Aug. 1919, Curzon Papers F 112/275.

115 *Ibid.*, 30th Minutes, 10 Nov. 1919.

116 See Curzon to Cox, 14 Nov. 1919 and Cox to Curzon, 1 Dec. 1919, both in the file prepared in Aug. 1920 to defend Curzon's record on Mesopotamia, Curzon Papers F 112/257.

117 Cox, having acted as head of civil administration in occupied Mesopotamia for much of the war, was sent to Teheran in 1918. His return to the country as High Commissioner was, however, generally expected.

118 I.D.C.E., 37th Minutes, 13 April 1920, Curzon Papers F 112/275.

119 *Ibid.*

120 A committee, chaired by the Judicial Adviser, set up by the civil administration in Baghdad.

121 I.D.C.E., 38th Minutes, 17 May 1920, Curzon Papers F 112/275.

122 *Ibid.*, 41st Minutes, 16 June 1920.

123 *Ibid.*, 2nd Minutes, 7 Jan. 1919.

124 *Ibid.*, 35th Minutes, 23 Feb. 1920.

125 *Ibid.*, 31st Minutes, 17 Nov. 1919.

126 D. Dilks, *Curzon in India*, vol. I (London, 1969) p. 75; Earl of Ronaldshay, *The Life of Lord Curzon*, vol. II (London, 1928) p. 89; S. Gopal, *British Policy in India 1858–1905* (Cambridge, 1965) p. 255.

127 I.D.C.E., 37th Minutes, 13 April 1920, Curzon Papers F 112/275.

128 Wilson, *op. cit.*, p. 247; Curzon to Allenby, Tel., 19 March 1920, *D.B.F.P.* Is., XIII, p. 232.

129 Churchill's memo. for Cabinet, 1 May 1920, L.G.P. F/205/6/1.

130 *Ibid.* Churchill cited the Sudan as a precedent for temporary withdrawal.

131 Milner's memo. for Cabinet, 24 May 1920, Curzon Papers F 112/253.

132 General staff memo., enc. in Churchill's memo. for Cabinet, 12 June 1920, C.P. 1469, CAB. 24/107.

133 Churchill to Curzon, Private, 22 May 1920, Curzon Papers F 112/215.

134 Churchill to Hankey (for Prime Minister), 22 June 1920, L.G.P. F/9/2/32.

135 Churchill to Lloyd George, 26 Aug. 1920, L.G.P. F/9/2/41.

136 See for instance C. P. 1875, CAB. 24/111.

137 A. T. Wilson to Hirtzel, Private, 19 May 1920. A. T. Wilson Papers 52455.

138 See A. T. Wilson to Hirtzel, 8 July 1919; and Note by A. T. Wilson, 10 June 1920, both in A. T. Wilson Papers 52455.

139 Through the al 'Ahd, a secret society of former officers of the Ottoman army now loyal to Feisal.

140 Ten political officers and officers in the local Iraq levies were killed.

141 A. T. Wilson to S.S.I. Tel. Personal and Confidential for Sir P. Cox, 29 July 1920, A. T. Wilson Papers 52455.

142 Civil Commissioner to S.S.I., Tel., 16 Aug. 1920. A. T. Wilson Papers 52457.
143 P. Sluglett, thesis *cit.*, pp. 324, 331, 334–5.
144 A. T. Wilson to Hirtzel, 26 July 1920, A. T. Wilson Papers 52455; same to Captain Stephenson, 26 July 1920, *Ibid.*, 52456.
145 Nearly 30 000 British and Indian troops were sent to Iraq.
146 A. T. Wilson to Hirtzel, 26 July 1920.
147 A. T. Wilson to Shuckburgh, 4 Aug. 1920, A. T. Wilson Papers 52456.
148 Civil Commissioner to S.S.I., Tel., 16 Aug. 1920, *ibid.*, 52457.
149 *Ibid.*
150 A. T. Wilson to Sir George MacMunn, 10 Sept. 1920, A. T. Wilson Papers 52457.
151 Same to Shuckburgh, 4 Aug. 1920, *ibid.*, 52456.
152 Finance Committee 27, 12 Aug. 1920, Appendix I to Cabinet 49(20), CAB. 23/22.
153 Montagu's memo. for Cabinet, *c.* 18 Aug. 1920, C.P. 1790, CAB. 24/110.
154 Conclusions of Cabinet 51(20), 15 Sep. 1920, CAB. 23/22.
155 Cox's Tel., 24 July 1920, circulated as C. P. 1715, 30 July 1920, CAB. 24/110.
156 *Report on Iraq Administration October 1920 to March 1922*, p. 7.
157 Montagu's memo. for Cabinet, 9 Oct. 1920, enc. in Montagu to J. T. Davies, L.G.P. F/40/3/25.
158 Cox to S.S.I., 16 Oct. 1920, C.P. 1983, CAB. 24/112.
159 Churchill reported Haldane's views to Lloyd George on 10 Nov. 1920, L.G.P. F/9/2/45.
160 Conclusions of Ministerial Conference, 1 Dec. 1920, CAB. 23/23.
161 *Ibid.*
162 Conclusions of Cabinet 67(20), 8 Dec. 1920, CAB. 23/23.
163 Churchill's memo. for Cabinet, 10 Dec. 1920, CAB. 24/116 (C.P. 2275); Conclusions of Cabinet 69(20), 13 Dec. 1920, CAB. 23/23.
164 *Ibid.*
165 *Ibid.*
166 *Ibid.* On the 'most favourable impression' made by A. T. Wilson, see Hankey's diary, 13 Dec. 1920 in S. Roskill, *Hankey: Man of Secrets*, vol. 2 (London, 1972) p. 201.
167 Conclusions of Cabinet 72(20), 17 Dec. 1920, CAB. 23/23.
168 Montagu's memo. for Cabinet, 24 Dec. 1920, C.P. 2356, CAB. 24/117.
169 As C.P. 2343, CAB. 24/117.
170 Curzon's memo. for Cabinet, 26 Dec. 1920, C.P. 2359, CAB. 24/117.
171 Conclusions of Cabinet 82(20), 31 Dec. 1920, CAB. 23/23.
172 Fisher's diary, 31 Dec. 1920, Fisher Papers Box 8A.
173 See memo. by Andrew Ryan (Chief Dragoman at the British High Commission, Constantinople), 23 Sep. 1920, *D.B.F.P.* Is., XIII, pp. 146–50.
174 Conclusions of Ministerial Conference, 2 Dec. 1920, Appendix II to Cabinet 70(20), CAB, 23/23.
175 Churchill to Prime Minister, Private and Secret, 24 March 1920, L.G.P. F/9/2/20.
176 Churchill's memo. for Cabinet, 16 Dec. 1920, C.P. 2387, CAB. 24/117.
177 Note by General Staff, 22 Nov. 1920, *D.B.F.P.* Is., XIII, pp. 183–9.

178 See Appendix II to Cabinet 70(20), CAB. 23/23.
179 The Foreign Office was already toying with these ideas. See memo. by G. P. Churchill, 20 Dec. 1920, *D.B.F.P.* Is., XIII, pp. 666–9.

CHAPTER 8. THE LIMITS OF IMPERIAL POWER

1 For example, Jellicoe's naval mission to India and the dominions, 1919–1920. See S. W. Roskill, *Naval Policy Between the Wars*, vol. I (London, 1968) ch. VII.
2 I. M. Drummond, *Imperial Economic Policy 1917–1939* (London, 1974) ch. 2.
3 Derby (Paris) to Curzon, 18 Nov. 1920, *D.B.F.P.* Is., XII, p. 507.
4 This view was held in the Foreign Office by Sir E. Crowe, and, very vehemently, by Harold Nicolson.
5 Minute by Curzon, 20 Dec. 1920 on a memo. by Nicolson, *D.B.F.P.* Is., XII, pp. 550–3.
6 Conclusions of Cabinet 2(21), 14 Jan. 1921, CAB. 23/24; *D.B.F.P.* Is., XV, pp. 38–9.
7 Conclusions of Ministerial Conference, 18 Feb. 1921, Appendix I to Cabinet 14(21), CAB. 23/24.
8 Correctly, the Third Conference of London.
9 *D.B.F.P.* Is., XV, p. 161.
10 *Ibid.*, XV, p. 449.
11 Curzon to Norman, Tel., 3 Jan. 1921, 5 p.m.; Same to same, Tel., Very Urgent, 5 Jan. 1921, 7 p.m. *D.B.F.P.* Is., XIII, pp. 679, 682.
12 Curzon to Norman, Tel., Very Urgent, 13 Jan. 1921, 2.15 p.m.; Same to same, Tel., Very Urgent, 13 Jan. 1921, 3.05 p.m. *D.B.F.P.* Is., XIII, pp. 692–3.
13 See above ch. 7.
14 Cox to S.S.I., Tel., 29 Jan. 1921, circulated as C.P. 2560, CAB. 23/119.
15 Memo. by Armitage-Smith, 14 Feb. 1921, *D.B.F.P.* Is., XIII, pp.721 ff.
16 *Ibid.*
17 Memo. by Admiralty, 24 Dec. 1920, *D.B.F.P.* Is., XIII, p. 668, n. 2.
18 Chelmsford to Montagu, Tel., Clear the Line, 22 Jan. 1921, *ibid.*, XIII, pp. 704 ff.
19 Norman to Curzon, Tel., 28 Jan. 1921, *ibid.*, XIII, p. 710.
20 Same to same, Tel., 3 Feb. 1921, 12 noon, *ibid.*, XIII, p. 714.
21 Norman to Curzon, Tel., 3 March 1921, *ibid.*, XIII, p. 736.
22 Curzon to Norman, Tel., 20 March 1921, *ibid.*, XIII, p. 746.
23 Curzon to Norman, Tel., Secret, 3 Jan. 1921, 6 p.m., *ibid.*, XIII, pp. 680–1.
24 Same to same, Tel., Private, 21 Jan. 1921, 1.05 p.m., *ibid.*, XIII, p. 703.
25 R. Ullman, *The Anglo-Soviet Accord* (London, 1972) p. 447.
26 *Ibid.*, chs. X, XI, for a survey of ministerial attitudes.
27 Conclusions of Cabinet 61(20), 17 Nov. 1920, CAB. 23/23.
28 The uneasy relations of the Bolsheviks with popular movements in central and south-west Asia are described in Harish Karpur, *Soviet Russia and Asia 1917–1927* (Geneva 1966), and W. Laqueur, *The Soviet Union and the Middle East* (London, 1959).

29 E. H. Carr, *The Bolshevik Revolution 1917–1923*, vol. 3 (Harmondsworth, 1966) ch. 27.
30 H. St. J. Philby, *Arabian Days* (London, 1948) p. 193; historical note by Sir P. Cox in *The Letters of Gertrude Bell*, ed. Lady Bell, vol. 2 (London, 1927).
31 I.D.C.E., 40th Minutes, 1 June 1920; 41st Minutes, 16 June 1920, Curzon Papers F 112/275.
32 S. H. Longrigg, *Iraq 1900–1950* (London, 1953) p. 128.
33 *The Letters of Gertrude Bell*, vol. 2, pp. 497, 528–86 *passim*.
34 *Ibid*., vol. 2, p. 586.
35 Churchill to Lloyd George, 4 Jan. 1921, L.G.P. F/9/2/51.
36 Civil Commissioner (Baghdad) to S.S.I., Tel., 31 July 1920, circulated as C.P. 1723, 2 Aug. 1920, CAB. 24/110.
37 Cox's tel., 27 Dec. 1920, circulated as C.P. 2379, 29 Dec. 1920, CAB. 24/117.
38 S.S.I. to High Commissioner (Baghdad) Tel., 31 Dec. 1920, C.P. 2412 CAB. 24/118.
39 M. Gilbert, *Winston S. Churchill*, vol. IV, 1917–1922 (London, 1975) pp. 511–12.
40 Churchill to Curzon, Private, 12 Jan. 1921, Curzon Papers F 112/275.
41 Churchill to Cox, Tel., 23 Jan. 1921, C.P. 2571, CAB. 24/119.
42 Cox to Churchill, Tel., Clear the Line, 24 Jan. 1921, C.P. 2571.
43 M. Gilbert, *op. cit*., vol. IV, p. 537; B. C. Busch, *Britain, India and the Arabs 1914–1921* (Berkeley and London, 1971) p. 465.
44 General Staff memo., 19 Feb. 1921, circulated as C.P. 2607, CAB. 24/120.
45 The affairs of the Hejaz and the Gulf States were left in practice to the Foreign and India Offices respectively.
46 Churchill to Lloyd George, Tel., 14 March 1921, C.P. 2742, CAB. 24/121.
47 M. Gilbert, *op. cit*., vol. IV, p. 547.
48 *Ibid*., vol. IV, p. 549.
49 Churchill to Lloyd George, Tel., 16 March 1921, C.P. 2743, CAB. 24/121.
50 Conclusions of Cabinet 14(21), 22 March 1921, CAB. 23/24.
51 Fisher's diary, 22 March 1921, Fisher Papers Box 8A.
52 M. Gilbert, *op. cit*., vol. IV, p. 598.
53 144 H.C. Deb. 5s., cols. 1519 ff.
54 This incident is described vividly in H. St. J. Philby, *op. cit*. and dispassionately in E. Monroe, *Philby of Arabia* (London, 1973) p. 108.
55 *Report on Iraq Administration October 1920 to March 1922*, p. 12; S. H. Longrigg, *op. cit*., p. 132.
56 P. Sluglett, 'Profit and Loss from the British Mandate: British Influence and Administration in Iraq 1914–1932' (Oxford D.Phil. 1972) p. 386.
57 *Report on Iraq Administration* . . ., p. 15.
58 C.P. 1754, 3 Aug. 1920, CAB. 24/110.
59 Montagu's memo. for Cabinet, n.d. but *c*. 18 Aug. 1920, C.P. 1790, CAB. 24/110; Churchill's memo. for Cabinet, 30 Sep. 1920, C.P. 1912, CAB. 24/112.
60 For a discussion of politics in the *vilayets* under the Ottomans, A. Hourani, 'Ottoman Reform and the Politics of Notables' in *The Beginnings of*

Modernization in the Middle East, ed. W. R. Polk and R. L. Chambers (Chicago, 1968) pp. 41–68.

61 *The Letters of Gertrude Bell*, vol. 2, pp. 611–16 *passim*.

62 The form of the ballot is described in the *Report on Iraq Administration*. . . .

63 *The Letters of Gertrude Bell*, vol. 2, p. 611.

64 The validity of A. T. Wilson's early plebiscite on this question had never been officially accepted.

65 For British policy towards Palestine and Trans-Jordan at the time of the Cairo Conference, A. S. Klieman, *Foundations of British Policy in the Arab World: the Cairo Conference 1921* (London, 1970); M. Gilbert, *op. cit.*, vol. IV, pp. 560–1.

66 The Turkish National Pact of 1920 is printed in A. J. Toynbee, *The Western Question in Greece and Turkey* (2nd edn, London, 1923), pp. 209–10. For its implications, see memo. by Andrew Ryan, 17 Feb. 1922, *D.B.F.P.* Is., XVII, p. 630.

67 This was implicit in Churchill's calls for realistic concessions to Turkish feeling: Churchill to Lloyd George, 24 March 1920, L.G.P. F/9/2/20; Churchill's memo. for Cabinet, 16 Dec. 1920, C.P. 2387, CAB. 24/117.

68 Churchill to Prime Minister, Tel., 16 March 1921, C.P. 2743, CAB. 24/121.

69 Conclusions of Cabinet, 14(21), 22 March 1921, CAB. 23/24.

70 Conclusions of Cabinet, 45(21), 31 May 1921, CAB. 23/25.

71 On 14 June and 14 July 1921.

72 C. E. Callwell, *Field Marshal Sir Henry Wilson: His Life and Diaries*, vol. II (London, 1927) p. 292.

73 *Ibid.*

74 Garrison commander in Ireland.

75 This memo. of 24 May 1921 (C.P. 2964, CAB. 24/123), is printed in Thomas Jones, *Whitehall Diary*, vol. III, *Ireland 1918–1925*, ed. K. Middlemas (London, 1971) pp. 71–2.

76 Memo. by Sir E. Crowe, 30 May 1921 *D.B.F.P.* Is., XVII, p. 207 ff.

77 Conclusions of Cabinet 44(21), May 1921, CAB. 23/25.

78 Churchill to Lloyd George, 2 June 1921, L.G.P. F/9/3/48; M. Gilbert, *op. cit.*, vol. IV, pp. 590–2.

79 Cabinet Committee on the Future of Constantinople, 9 June 1921, annex to Cabinet 51(21), CAB. 23/26.

80 Recounted in M. Gilbert, *op. cit.*, vol. IV, p. 592.

81 Churchill to Curzon, Private, 15 June 1921, Curzon Papers F 112/219; Lloyd George to Curzon, 16 June 1921, Curzon Papers F 112/220.

82 Owing to a renewed Greek offensive. M. Llewellyn Smith, *Ionian Vision: Greece in Asia Minor 1919–1922* (London, 1973) pp. 223–4.

83 Lloyd George was very angry at the General Staff's reluctance to see the significance of Greek victory at Eskishehir. Lloyd George to Worthington-Evans, 21 July 1921, Worthington-Evans Papers Box I. See also Montagu to Viceroy of India, 19 July 1921, Montagu Papers: 'I am in despair about the Turkish situation . . . the Greeks appear to be winning.'

84 The Irish truce began 11 July 1921.

85 M. Llewellyn Smith, *op. cit.*, p. 234.

86 Churchill's memo., 26 Sep. 1921, *D.B.F.P.* Is., XVII, p. 421, n. 2. On the levies, Churchill to Lloyd George, 28 July 1921, L.G.P. F/9/3/71.

87 Curzon's memo., 7 Oct. 1921, *D.B.F.P.* Is., XVII, pp. 421–3.
88 *Ibid.*
89 *Ibid.*, XVII, pp. 535 ff., Curzon to Hardinge (Paris), 30 Dec. 1921.
90 Pointed out by a Foreign Office memo., 6 Feb. 1922, *ibid.*, XVII, pp. 612–15.
91 See Conclusions of Cabinet 19(22), 20 March 1922, CAB. 23/29.
92 *Ibid.*, *D.B.F.P.* Is., XVII, p. 655.
93 Curzon to Montagu, 29 June 1921, Curzon Papers F 112/221.
94 Conclusions of Cabinet 19(22), 20 March 1922, CAB. 23/29.
95 Or so Churchill told Cox. M. Gilbert, *op. cit.*, vol. IV, p. 811.
96 Churchill's memo. for Cabinet, 'Policy and Finance in Mesopotamia, 1922–23', C.P. 3197, 4 Aug. 1921, CAB. 24/126.
97 *Ibid.*
98 *Ibid.*
99 M. Cowling, *The Impact of Labour* (Cambridge, 1971) p. 121; C. L. Mowat, *Britain Between the Wars* (London, 1966 edn) p. 130. In June 1921 two by-elections in coalition seats were won by 'Anti-Waste' candidates. M. Kinnear, *The Fall of Lloyd George* (London, 1973) p. 95.
100 General Staff memo., 10 May 1921, circulated as C.P. 2925, CAB. 24/123.
101 Montagu to Curzon, 12 May 1921, Curzon Papers F 112/221.
102 In his memo. for Cabinet, 12 Oct. 1921, C.P. 3395, CAB. 24/128.
103 Memo. for Cabinet by Worthington-Evans, 27 Oct. 1921, C.P. 3445, CAB. 24/129 containing views of C.I.G.S.
104 M. Gilbert, *op. cit.*, vol. IV, p. 799.
105 Churchill to Lloyd George, 7 Aug. 1921, L.G.P. F/9/3/75.
106 Churchill's memo., 'Policy and Finance & c.', 4 Aug. 1921, C.P. 3197.
107 This was Churchill's suspicion. Letter to Cox, 2 Aug. 1921, M. Gilbert, *op. cit.*, vol. IV, p. 802.
108 General Staff memo., C.P. 3619, CAB. 24/132.
109 S. W. Roskill, *Naval Policy Between the Wars*, vol. I (London, 1968) pp. 268, 357.
110 Conclusions of Ministerial Conference, 9 Feb. 1922, Appendix IV to Cabinet 14(22), CAB. 23/29; M. Gilbert, *op. cit.*, vol. IV, p. 806.
111 Conclusions of Ministerial Conference, 9 Feb. 1922; Fisher's diary, 9 Feb. 1922, Fisher Papers Box 8A.
112 S. W. Roskill, *op. cit.*, vol. I, p. 233. The other members of the review committee were Birkenhead, Montagu and Baldwin.
113 The phrase was Sir Henry Wilson's; diary, 9 Dec. 1921, Callwell, *op. cit.*, vol. II, p. 316.
114 *The Letters of Gertrude Bell*, vol. 2, p. 619.
115 *Ibid.*
116 *Ibid.*, vol. 2, p. 628.
117 Churchill's minute, 24 Nov. 1921, M. Gilbert, *op. cit.*, vol. IV, p. 809.
118 See Cox's tel. to Churchill of 12 Nov. 1921, circulated as C.P. 3485, CAB. 24/129.
119 For these desiderata, C.P. 3486, n.d. but *c.* 12 Nov. 1921, CAB. 24/129.
120 Churchill's memo. for Cabinet, 17 Feb. 1922, C.P. 3748, CAB. 24/133. Copy in Worthington-Evans Papers.
121 Conclusions of Cabinet, 12(22), 21 Feb. 1922, CAB. 23/29.
122 High Commissioner to S.S.C., Tel., 27 Feb. 1922, C.P. 3804, CAB. 23/134.

123 *Ibid.*
124 *Ibid.*
125 Letter to Archibald Sinclair (his Private Secretary) 9 July 1921, M. Gilbert, *op. cit.*, vol. IV, p. 798.
126 Conclusions of Ministerial Conference, 9 Feb. 1922, Appendix IV to Cabinet 14(22), CAB. 23/29.
127 The question of oil concessions had already caused an Anglo-American dispute. See Churchill's memo. for Cabinet, 13 March 1922, C.P. 3832, CAB. 24/134; and ch. 9 below.
128 Fisher's diary, 14 March 1922, Fisher Papers Box 8A.
129 See above, ch. 7.
130 See above, ch. 7.
131 These joint Allied proposals – the so-called Paris terms – are set out in *D.B.F.P.* Is., XVII, p. 749 ff.
132 Curzon's minute, 25 May 1922, *ibid.*, XVII, p. 834.
133 Curzon's minute on Crowe–Venizelos conversation, 25 May 1922, *ibid.*, XVII, p. 840.
134 *Ibid.*
135 Balfour to Worthington-Evans, 3 July 1922, opposing withdrawal of British contingent at Constantinople, *D.B.F.P.* Is., XVII, p. 874.
136 *Ibid.*, XVII, pp. 898–9, Balfour to Bentinck (Athens) Tel., 28 July 1922; Conclusions of Cabinet 43(22), 3 Aug. 1922, CAB. 23/30.
137 On the unexpected suddenness of the Greek collapse, Lindley (minister at Athens) to Curzon, Private, 8 Sep. 1922, Curzon Papers F 112/224.
138 Conclusions of Cabinet 48(22), 7 Sep. 1922, CAB. 23/31.
139 Conclusions of Cabinet 49(22), 15 Sep. 1922, CAB. 23/31.
140 Conclusions of Ministerial Conference 140, 19 Sep. 1922, CAB. 23/39.
141 Conclusions of Ministerial Conference 142, 20 Sep. 1922, CAB. 23/39.
142 Curzon's telephone message to the Cabinet, 8 p.m. 20 Sep. 1922, C.P. 4202, CAB. 24/139.
143 Conclusions of Ministerial Conference 148, 27 Sep. 1922, held at Colonial Office under Chamberlain's presidency, CAB. 23/39.
144 Conclusions of Ministerial Conference 149, 7 p.m. 27 Sep. 1922, CAB. 23/39.
145 *Ibid.*
146 At Ministerial Conference 145, 23 Sep. 1922, Lord Lee, First Lord of the Admiralty, questioned whether the significance of Chanak had been grasped in the public mind. (CAB. 23/39).
147 Conclusions of Ministerial Conference 149, 7 p.m. 27 Sep. 1922.
148 Conclusions of Ministerial Conference 153, 29 Sep. 1922, CAB. 23/39.
149 See Rumbold to Curzon, Tel., Most Urgent, Private and Secret, 5 Oct. 1922, *D.B.F.P.* Is., XVIII, p. 139.
150 E.g. D. Walder, *The Chanak Affair* (London, 1969) pp. 287–9.
151 That hindsight reveals Kemal in a different light is irrelevant.
152 Memo. respecting the Freedom of the Straits, 15 Nov. 1922, *D.B.F.P.* Is., XVIII, pp. 974–83.
153 Cox to Churchill, Tel., Secret, 15 April 1922, C.P. 4178, Worthington-Evans Papers Box 1.
154 Same to same, Tel., Secret and Personal, 30 April 1922, C.P. 4178.

155 Cox to Churchill, Tel., 15 June 1922, C.P. 4178.
156 Cox to Churchill, Tel., 4 May 1922, C.P. 4178.
157 Cox to Churchill, Tel., 3 June 1922, C.P. 4178.
158 Same to same, Tel., 14 June 1922, C.P. 4178.
159 Cox to Churchill, Tel., Secret and Personal, 10 Aug. 1922, C.P. 4178.
160 See Cox's optimistic telegram to Churchill, 28 June 1922, C.P. 4178.
161 Cox to Churchill, Tel., 28 July 1922, C.P. 4178.
162 Cox to Churchill, Tel., 10 Aug. 1922, C.P. 4178.
163 Cox to Churchill, Tel., Private and Personal, 17 Aug. 1922, C.P. 4178.
164 Conclusions of Cabinet 23(22) 5 April 1922, CAB. 23/30.
165 Fisher and Balfour acted as Britain's ministerial representatives at the League of Nations assembly.
166 Conclusions of Cabinet 23(22) 5 April 1922, CAB. 23/30.
167 *Ibid.*
168 Churchill to Cox, Tel., Private and Personal, 13 July 1922, C.P. 4178.
169 Churchill to Cox, Tel., Secret and Personal, 27 April 1922, C.P. 4178.
170 Churchill to Cox, Tel., Personal and Private, 5 May 1922, C.P. 4178.
171 Cox had fished for such a promise in his tel. of 14 June 1922, C.P. 4178.
172 The best account is in C. J. Edmonds, *Kurds, Turks and Arabs* (London, 1957) pp. 244–62; 296–312. Edmonds was a political officer in Kurdistan at the time.
173 *Ibid.*, p. 248.
174 Cox to Churchill, Tel., Confid., 25 Aug. 1922, C.P. 4178.
175 There seems general agreement that this providential indisposition was genuine.
176 Churchill to Lloyd George, Private, 1 Sep. 1922, L.G.P. F/10/3/41.
177 *Ibid.*
178 Lloyd George to Churchill, 5 Sep. 1922, L.G.P. F/10/3/44.
179 See Cox's letter to a friend, 22 Sep. 1922, P. Graves, *The Life of Sir Percy Z. Cox* (London, 1941) p. 319.
180 C. J. Edmonds, *op. cit.*, ch. XX.
181 Conclusions of Ministerial Conference, 28 Aug. 1922, Appendix II to Cabinet 56(22), CAB. 23/31; Churchill to Cox, Tel., 28 Aug. 1922, C.P. 4178.
182 For Loraine's activity, G. Waterfield, *Professional Diplomat* (London, 1973), chs. 6, 7.
183 *Ibid.*

CHAPTER 9. INDIAN POLICY AND THE OIL QUESTION

1 Eastern Committee, 39th Minutes, 27 Nov. 1918, Milner Papers 119.
2 *Ibid.*, 42nd Minutes, 9 Dec. 1918.
3 *Ibid.*, 44th Minutes, 22 Dec. 1918.
4 Montagu to Prime Minister, 25 Oct. 1918, enc. draft memo. on the Turkish armistice, L.G.P. F/40/2/17.
5 J. M. Brown, *op. cit.*, pp. 139, 191; P. Hardy, *The Muslims of British India* (Cambridge, 1972) pp. 185–9; Note by Sir J. Meston, 21 May 1917, AC 23/1/7.

6 Eastern Committee 45th Minutes, 19 Dec. 1918.
7 Memo. by Sir H. Grant, Secret, 20 Dec. 1918, Curzon Papers F 112/253.
8 Montagu to Curzon, 6 Jan. 1919, Montagu Papers; Montagu to Viceroy, Tel., 9 May 1919, Chelmsford Collection, E 264/10 (Tels. to and from Viceroy, vol. IV).
9 Eastern Committee, 46th Minutes, 23 Dec. 1918.
10 *Ibid.*
11 Francis Robinson, *Separatism Among Indian Muslims* (Cambridge, 1974) pp. 292 ff.
12 Montagu to Prime Minister, Private and Personal, 16 April 1919, L.G.P. F/40/2/50.
13 *Ibid.*
14 Robinson, *op. cit.*, pp. 292, 353.
15 Viceroy to S.S.I., Tel., 17 Nov. 1919, reporting views of Sir Harcourt Butler in the United Provinces, Montagu Papers.
16 Same to same, 15 April 1920, Montagu Papers.
17 Robinson, *op. cit.*, p. 310.
18 J. M. Brown, *op. cit.*, p. 229; Robinson, *op. cit.*, pp. 313 ff.
19 The character and regional variations of the non-cooperation movement are discussed in J. M. Brown, *op. cit.*, ch. 9.
20 Viceroy to S.S.I., Tel., 3 Jan. 1921, Montagu Papers.
21 D. A. Low, 'The Government of India and the First Non-Cooperation Movement 1920–1922', in *Essays in Gandhian Politics*, edit. R. Kumar (Oxford, 1971) pp. 301, 304.
22 Viceroy to S.S.I., Tels., 26 Jan. 1921, 2 Feb. 1921, Montagu Papers.
23 E. Montagu to Curzon, 24 Feb. 1921, encl. tels. from the Viceroy, Curzon Papers F 112/221.
24 Report by Commissioner in Sind, sent by Lloyd (Governor of Bombay) to Montagu, and circulated to Cabinet, 4 Jan. 1922, Montagu Papers.
25 Eastern Committee, 46th Minutes, 23 Dec. 1918, Milner Papers 119.
26 Milner to George Lloyd (Bombay), Private, 2 April 1920, Addit. Milner Papers, Ms. Eng. Hist. c705.
27 Montagu to Reading, 19 July 1921, Montagu Papers.
28 The Cabinet's attitude to the Afghan problem may be followed in R. Ullman, *The Anglo-Soviet Accord* (London, 1972) pp. 341–7; and in Conclusions of Cabinets 66(20), 6 Dec. 1920, CAB. 23/23; 10(21), 3 March 1921, CAB. 23/24; 37(21), 10 May 1921, CAB. 23/24; 63(21), 5 Aug. 1921, CAB. 23/26.
29 Austen Chamberlain to George Lloyd, 13 April 1921, A.C. 18/1/23.
30 B. B. Misra, *The Administrative History of India 1834–1947* (Bombay, 1970) p. 35; R. Coupland, *The Constitutional Problem in India* (Madras, 1945) p. 10.
31 See Anil Seal, 'Imperialism and Nationalism in India', *Modern Asian Studies*, 7, 3 (1973) pp. 330–1.
32 Quoted R. Coupland, *op. cit.*, p. 9.
33 This right, reserved in the Government of India Act 1858, was not exercised to great effect. See Lord Hartington's judgment in 1878, in R. Robinson and J. Gallagher, *Africa and the Victorians* (London, 1961) pp. 12–13.
34 Eastern Committee, 16th Minutes, 24 June 1918, Milner Papers 119.

35 Government of India Act 1919 (9 and 10 Geo. 5 c. 101), S. 25, reprinted in A. B. Keith, *Speeches and Documents on Indian Policy 1750–1921*, vol. II (London, 1922) p. 311.

36 In the House of Commons, 9 June 1919. The reasons for Montagu's caution are suggested in Curtis's obituary notice in *Round Table*, 182 (1956) p. 107.

37 Lionel Curtis, *Letters to the People of India on Responsible Government* (London, 1918) p. 61.

38 *Report on Indian Constitutional Reforms*, Cd. 9109 (1918) p. 130.

39 Montagu's Private Notes on his Indian Tour 1917–1918, Montagu Papers.

40 Montagu to Prime Minister, n.d. but Oct. 1919, Montagu Papers.

41 R. Coupland, *op. cit.*, pp. 83–4.

42 Montagu to Prime Minister, 28 Feb. 1919, L.G.P. F/40/2/40.

43 The course and outcome of this controversy may be traced in J. S. Mangat, *The History of the Asians in East Africa c. 1886–1945* (Oxford, 1969) p. 120 ff.

44 Montagu to Austen Chamberlain, 17 Feb. 1919, Montagu Papers.

45 Lloyd George to Montagu, 25 April 1920, in S. D. Waley, *Edwin Montagu: a Memoir* (Bombay, 1964) p. 246.

46 The Indian Army and the British contingents were termed collectively the 'Army in India'.

47 Sir G. Barrow, *op. cit.*, p. 246.

48 *Report of the Committee Appointed to Enquire into the Administration and Organisation of the Army in India*, Cmd. 943 (1920) p. 3.

49 *Ibid.*, p. 4.

50 *Ibid.*, p. 8.

51 *Ibid.*, p. 101.

52 *Ibid.*, p. 102.

53 Viceroy to S.S.I., Tel., 3 Sep. 1920, C.P. 1844, CAB. 24/111.

54 Montagu's memo. for Cabinet, 24 Dec. 1920, C.P. 2362, CAB. 24/117.

55 *Ibid.*

56 *Ibid.*

57 *Ibid.*

58 *Ibid.*

59 Churchill's memo. for Cabinet, 10 Feb. 1921, C.P. 2564, CAB. 24/119.

60 Viceroy to S.S.I., Tel., 30 March 1921, circul. as C.P. 2799, CAB. 24/121.

61 *Speeches by the Earl of Reading*, vol. I (Simla, 1926) p. 77.

62 Conclusions of Ministerial Conference, 20 Dec. 1921, Appendix II to Cabinet 93(21), CAB. 23/27.

63 Conclusions of Cabinets 78(21), 12 Oct. 1921, CAB. 23/27; and 8(22), 6 Feb. 1922, CAB. 23/29.

64 Austen Chamberlain to Montagu, Private, 27 Jan. 1922, A.C. 21/5/30.

65 The Indian military budget for 1922–3, although below the peak figure of 1919–20, was double that of 1914–15. See *The Official History of the Indian Armed Forces in the Second World War 1939–45: Indian War Economy*, ed. N. C. Sinha and P. N. Khera, pp. 293–5.

66 These proposals are in C.P. 3929, printed for Cabinet April 1922, copy in Worthington-Evans Papers.

67 Conclusions of Ministerial Conference, 9 Feb. 1922, Appendix I to Cabinet 12(22), CAB. 23/29.

68 This was how Chamberlain interpreted the timing of the telegram's publication, which was held back until the eve of Gandhi's arrest. See A. Chamberlain to Curzon, Confid., 13 March 1922, A.C. 23/7/33.
69 Curzon to Austen Chamberlain, 9 March 1922, Curzon Papers F 112/232.
70 L. F. Rushbrook Williams, *India in 1922–23: A Statement prepared for presentation to Parliament* (Calcutta, 1923) pp. 273, 108 ff.
71 Summary of Conclusions, Committee of Imperial Defence Sub-Committee on Indian Military Requirements, 1 Aug. 1922, C.P. 4141, CAB. 24/138.
72 Around 1 per cent in 1920. S. H. Longrigg, *Oil in the Middle East* (3rd edn, London, 1968) p. 48.
73 The title of a polemic by Louis Fischer published in 1926.
74 M. Jack, 'The Purchase of the British Government Shares in the British Petroleum Company 1912–1914', *Past and Present*, 39 (1968) p. 154; see also H. Longhurst, *Adventure in Oil: The Story of British Petroleum* (London, 1959).
75 B. R. Mitchell, *Abstract of British Historical Statistics* (Cambridge, 1962) p. 301.
76 *War Cabinet Report for the Year 1917*, Cd. 9005 (1918) p. 136.
77 *Ibid.*
78 On the 'economics of siege' see W. K. Hancock, *Survey of British Commonwealth Affairs*, vol. II, *Problems of Economic Policy 1918–1939*, Part 1 (London, 1940) pp. 94–110.
79 Mitchell, *op. cit.*, p. 301.
80 J. A. De Novo, 'The Movement for an Aggressive American Oil Policy Abroad 1918–1920', *American Historical Review*, LXI, 4 (1956) p. 136.
81 At its peak in 1919 over £500 million.
82 Slade's memo., 30 July 1918, S. W. Roskill, *Naval Policy Between the Wars*, vol. I (London, 1968) p. 220.
83 D. J. Payton-Smith, *Oil: A Study of Wartime Policy and Administration* (History of the Second World War, U.K. Civil Series, H.M.S.O., 1971) p. 13. For the sustained official interest in bringing Royal Dutch Shell under British control, M. R. Kent, 'British Government interest in Middle East Oil Concessions' (London Ph.D., 1968) pp. 276–89; 301–6.
84 For the fate of some of these ideas, I. M. Drummond, *Imperial Economic Policy 1917–1939* (London, 1974).
85 J. A. De Novo, *op. cit.*, p. 857.
86 *Ibid.*, p. 860; J. Ise, *United States Oil Policy* (New Haven, 1926) p. 460; Roskill, *op. cit.*, vol. I, p. 219.
87 Taking 69 per cent of Persia's exports and providing 58 per cent of her imports. For Britain the figures were 13 per cent and 24 per cent respectively. Naval Intelligence Division, *Persia: a Handbook* (1945) p. 481.
88 The shortest route to Europe was Teheran–Resht–Enzeli–Baku–Batum–Constantinople.
89 For Curzon's earlier views on the contribution of British trade and investment to the strengthening of Persia, G. N. Curzon, *Persia and the Persian Question*, vol. II (London, 1892) p. 620.
90 R. Robinson and J. Gallagher, *op. cit.*, pp. 201, 241, 388–9.
91 See above, ch. 8.
92 Note by L. Oliphant (Foreign Office) on conversation with Sir C. Greenway

(Chairman of Anglo-Persian Oil Company), 19 May 1921, F.O. 371/6414/5835.

93 The first big strike at Kirkuk did not come until 1927.

94 For the negotiation of these agreements, see M. R. Kent, thesis, *cit.*

95 J. Nevakivi, *Britain, France and the Arab Middle East 1914–1920* (London, 1969) pp. 90–1, 94–5, 154–5.

96 See R. Ullman, *The Anglo-Soviet Accord* (London, 1972) p. 463 for Lloyd George's 'commercial conception' of international affairs.

97 See above, ch. 6.

98 For the text of the Cadman–Berthelot Agreement concluded at San Remo in April 1920, Nevakivi, *op. cit.*, p. 245. In effect, the French were given the holding of the *Deutsche Bank*.

99 In a well-known phrase, Curzon had declared that the Allies were 'floating to victory on a sea of oil'. Quoted in J. Rowland and Basil, 2nd Baron Cadman, *Ambassador for Oil* (London, 1960) p. 81.

100 See memoranda by Long of 18 March 1920 (C.P. 903), 29 June 1920 (C.P. 1554); and by Kellaway of 21 June 1920 (C.P. 1524), 15 Nov. 1920 (C.P. 2110), all in F.O. 371/5086.

101 Value of oil imports into Britain 1920: £66·6 million; 1921: £54·5 million; 1922: £39·1 million. B. R. Mitchell, *op. cit.*, p. 301.

102 See minutes by Tyrrell, 3 Nov. 1920, and Tilley, 3 Nov. 1920; initialled by Curzon, 6 Nov. 1920. F.O. 371/5086/13385.

103 The U.S. government claimed the same rights as all League members in the mandates and employed delaying tactics and diplomatic pressure on the League Council in protest against the exclusiveness of Anglo-French oil policy. See H. W. V. Temperley, *A History of the Peace Conference at Paris*, vol. VI (London, 1924) p. 188; and B. Gerig, *The Open Door and the Mandates System* (London, 1930), p. 140.

104 See Churchill's memo. for Cabinet, 13 March 1922, C.P. 3832, CAB. 24/134.

105 D. J. Payton-Smith, *op. cit.*, p. 18; A. Beeby-Thompson, *Oil Pioneer* (London, 1961) pp. 406, 408. For the gradual recognition of this interdependence on both sides of the Atlantic, M. J. Hogan, 'Informal Entente: Public Policy and Private Management in Anglo-American Petroleum Affairs 1918–1924', *Business History Review*, XLVIII, 2 (1974).

106 Minutes of Cabinet Committee on Oil Companies Amalgamation, March–June 1922, CAB. 27/180.

107 A point made with emphasis by Curzon at the Lausanne Conference in 1923. H. Nicolson, *Curzon: The Last Phase* (London, 1934) p. 337; Earl of Ronaldshay, *The Life of Lord Curzon*, vol. III (London, 1928) p. 337.

108 Memorandum by the General Staff on the Proposed New Treaty between the Allies and Turkey, 19 Oct. 1922, *D.B.F.P.* Is., XVIII, Appendix II, p. 985.

CHAPTER 10. CONCLUSION

1 Lothrop Stoddard, *The Rising Tide of Colour* (London, 1922) p. 83.

2 Leonard Woolf, *Imperialism and Civilisation* (London, 1928) p. 13.

3 *Ibid.*, p. 17.

4 Hirtzel to Wilson, 17 Sep. 1919, in J. Marlowe, *The Late Victorian* (London, 1967) p. 166.
5 Same to same, 16 July 1919, *ibid.*, p. 165. Hirtzel was Assistant Under-Secretary of State at the India Office.
6 See above ch. 2.
7 'Historical Summary Oct. 1925 to Nov. 1926', F.O. 371/12354.
8 Lampson to Foreign Office, 13 March 1935, F.O. 371/19070.
9 See J. G. Darwin, 'The Chanak Crisis and the British Cabinet', *History*, 65, 213 (1980) 32–48.

Bibliography

A. Manuscript Sources

I. Official and Private Papers

Public Record Office

1. Cabinet Records
Minutes and Conclusions of Cabinets (CAB. 23)
Minutes of Ministerial Conferences (CAB. 23)
Minutes and Memoranda of Cabinet Committees (CAB. 27)
Cabinet Memoranda (CAB. 24)
Minutes of Committee of Imperial Defence (CAB. 2/3. The Committee was without influence or importance in this period.)

2. Foreign Office Records
Correspondence and Memoranda relating principally to Egypt and Persia.
Balfour collection (F.O. 800).
Curzon Collection (F.O. 800). Contains some correspondence on Egypt.

3. Milner Collection (P.R.O. 30). A small collection but with some important correspondence and memoranda.

Scottish Record Office

1. Papers of P. H. Kerr, later 11th Marquess of Lothian (G.D. 40/17). A disappointing collection for this period and topic.

House of Lords Record Office

1. Papers of 1st Earl Lloyd George ('F' Series only).
2. Papers of Andrew Bonar Law. These contain very little on foreign and imperial affairs for this period but are useful for domestic politics.

British Library

1. Papers of 1st Earl of Balfour. Mainly useful for 1919.

2. Papers of A. T. Wilson.

India Office Library and Records

1. Papers of 1st Marquess Curzon (Mss. Eur. F 112). As well as private correspondence, these contain Curzon's collection of the minutes and memoranda of the Persia Committee, the Eastern Committee, the Middle East Committee, and the Inter-departmental committee on Middle East Affairs. An indispensable source.
2. Papers of Lord Chelmsford, Viceroy of India 1916–1921 (Mss. Eur. E 264/10 only: telegrams to and from Secretary of State for India vol. IV).

Bodleian Library, Oxford

1. Papers of 1st Viscount Milner. These contain Milner's private and official correspondence and memoranda relating to the Milner Mission 1919–1920, as well as other correspondence, his special Egyptian diary, and a bound copy of the minutes of the Eastern Committee 1918–1919. [Consulted 1970–71]
2. Papers of H. A. L. Fisher (principally Box 8A, Fisher's Cabinet diary for 1918–1922).
3. Papers of Sir L. Worthington-Evans. Not of great value for this period or topic.
4. Additional Milner Papers (Ms. Eng. Hist.). A supplementary collection of Milner's papers containing some important correspondence.

Library of Trinity College, Cambridge

1. Papers of E. S. Montagu. These contain copies of official papers relating to India, Egypt and Turkey as well as private correspondence. There is a wealth of material relating particularly to the Khilafat agitation.

Birmingham University Library

1. Papers of Sir Austen Chamberlain. These are particularly important for the internal politics of the Lloyd George coalition 1921–22.

II. Unpublished Theses

S. A. Cohen, 'The Formulation of British Policy towards Mesopotamia 1903–1914' (Oxford D.Phil. Thesis 1972).

M. R. Kent, 'British Government Interest in Middle East Oil Concessions' (London Ph.D. Thesis 1968).

R. C. Mowat, 'Lord Cromer and His Successors in Egypt' (Oxford D.Phil. Thesis 1970).

J. A. Ramsden, 'The Organisation of the Conservative and Unionist Party in Britain 1910–1930' (Oxford D.Phil. Thesis 1974).
P. Sluglett, 'Profit and Loss from the British Mandate: British Influence and Administration in Iraq 1914–1932' (Oxford D.Phil. Thesis 1972).
B. M. J. Wasserstein, 'British Officials and the Arab-Jewish Conflict in Palestine 1917–1929' (Oxford D. Phil. Thesis 1974).

B. Printed Sources

I. Primary Sources

1. Parliamentary Papers

War Cabinet Report for the Year 1917, Cd. 9005 (1918).
War Cabinet Report for the Year 1918, Cmd. 325 (1919).
Report on Indian Constitutional Reforms, Cd. 9109 (1918).
Report of the Committee appointed to enquire into the Administration and Organisation of the Army in India, Cmd. 943 (1920).
Review of Civil Administration of Mesopotamia, Cmd. 1061 (1920).
2. Report on Iraq Administration October 1920 to March 1922.
3. Parliamentary Debates, Fifth Series, House of Commons (mainly Persia and Iraq 1920–1921).
4. British Foreign and State Papers 1919, Vol. CXII.
5. *Documents on British Foreign Policy*, edited by R. Butler and E. L. Woodward (subsequently R. Butler and J. P. T. Bury; W. N. Medlicott and D. Dakin), First Series, vols. II, IV, VII, VIII, XII, XIII, XV, XVII, XVIII.

II. Secondary Sources

1. Books and Articles cited in references

Adelson, R., *Mark Sykes: Portrait of an Amateur* (London, 1975).
Amery, L. S., *My Political Life*, vol. 2, *War and Peace 1914–1929* (London, 1953).
Andrew, C. M. and Kanya-Forstner, A. S., 'The French Colonial Party and French Colonial War Aims 1914–1918', *Historical Journal*, XVII, 1 (1974), 79–106.
Anstey, V., *The Economic Development of India* (London, 1929).
Arasteh, A. R., *Man and Society in Iran* (Leiden, 1964).
Arfa, Hassan, *Under Five Shahs* (London, 1962).
Avery, P., *Modern Iran* (London, 1965).
Baer, G., *A History of Landownership in Modern Egypt 1800–1950* (London, 1962).
——, 'Social Change in Egypt 1800–1914', in *Political and Social Change in Modern Egypt*, ed. P. M. Holt (London, 1968).
——, 'Urbanisation in Egypt 1820–1907', in *Beginnings of Modernization in the Middle East*, ed. W. R. Polk and R. Chambers (Chicago, 1968).

Barrow, Sir G., *The Life of General Sir Charles C. Monro* (London, 1931).
Beeby-Thompson, A., *Oil Pioneer* (London, 1961).
Bell, Lady (ed.), *The Letters of Getrude Bell*, 2 vols. (London, 1927).
Beloff, M., *Imperial Sunset*, vol. 1: *Britain's Liberal Empire 1897–1921* (London, 1969).
Berque, J., *Egypt: Imperialism and Revolution* (Eng. trans., London, 1972).
Blake, R., *The Private Papers of Douglas Haig* (London, 1952).
——, *The Unknown Prime Minister* (London, 1955).
Blewett, N., 'Free Fooders, Balfourites, Whole Hoggers: Factionalism within the Unionist Party 1906–1910', *Historical Journal*, XI, 1 (1968), 95–124.
Boyce, D. G., *Englishmen and Irish Troubles: British Public Opinion and the Making of Irish Policy 1918–1922* (London, 1972).
Brown, Judith M.,*Gandhi's Rise to Power* (Cambridge, 1972).
Bullock, A., *The Life and Times of Ernest Bevin*, vol. 1 (London, 1960).
Busch, Briton Cooper, *Britain, India and the Arabs 1914–1921* (Berkeley and London, 1971).
Butler, D., and Freeman, J., *British Political Facts 1900–1967* (2nd edn, London, 1968).
Callwell, C. E., *Field Marshal Sir Henry Wilson: His Life and Diaries*, 2 vols. (London, 1927).
Cambridge History of India, vol. VI, ed. H. H. Dodwell (Cambridge, 1932).
Campbell, A. E., *Great Britain and the United States 1895–1903* (London, 1960).
Carr, E. H., *The Bolshevik Revolution 1917–1923*, vol. 3 (Harmondsworth, 1966).
Chirol, V., *The Egyptian Problem* (London, 1921).
Colvin, Sir A., *The Making of Modern Egypt* (Nelson edn, London, n.d.).
Conservative and Unionist Party Campaign Guide 1922.
Coupland, R., *The Constitutional Problem in India* (Madras, 1945).
Cowling, M., *The Impact of Labour* (Cambridge, 1971).
Cromer, Earl of, *Modern Egypt*, 2 vols. (London, 1908).
——, *Political and Literary Essays*, third series (London, 1916).
Curtis, Lionel, *Letters to the People of India on Responsible Government* (London, 1918).
Curzon, G. N., *Persia and the Persian Question*, 2 vols. (London, 1892; 2nd imp. 1966).
De Novo, J. A., 'The Movement for an Aggressive American Oil Policy Abroad 1918–1920', *American Historical Review*, LXI, 4 (1956), 854–76.
Dilke, C. W., *Greater Britain* (3rd edn, London, 1869).
Dilks, D., *Curzon in India*, vol. 1 (London, 1969).
Dockrill, M. L., 'David Lloyd George and Foreign Policy before 1914', in *Lloyd George: Twelve Essays*, ed. A. J. P. Taylor (London, 1971).
Drummond, I. M., *Imperial Economic Policy 1917–1939* (London, 1974).
Edmonds, C. J., *Kurds, Turks and Arabs* (London, 1957).
Elgood, P. G., *Egypt and the Army* (London, 1924).
Fieldhouse, D. K., *Economics and Empire* (London, 1973).
Fischer, L., *Oil Imperialism* (London, 1926).
Gardiner, A. G., *Pillars of Society* (pop. edn, London, 1916).
George, D. Lloyd, *The Truth About the Peace Treaties*, 2 vols. (London, 1938).
Gerig, B., *The Open Door and the Mandates System* (London, 1930).

Gilbert, M., *Winston S. Churchill*, vol. III, 1914–1916; vol. IV, 1917–1922 (London, 1971, 1975).
Gollin, A. M., *Proconsul in Politics* (London, 1964).
Gopal, S., *British Policy in India 1858–1905* (Cambridge, 1965).
Gottlieb, W. W., *Studies in Secret Diplomacy* (London, 1957).
Graves, P., *The Life of Sir Percy Z. Cox* (London, 1941).
Greaves, R. L., *Persia and the Defence of India* (London, 1959).
Greenberg, M., *British Trade and the Opening of China* (Cambridge, 1951).
Guinn, P., *British Strategy and Politics 1914–1918* (London, 1965).
Gupta, P. S., *Imperialism and the British Labour Movement 1914–1964* (London, 1975).
Hancock, W. K., *Survey of British Commonwealth Affairs*, vol. II: *Problems of Economic Policy 1918–1939*, Part 1 (London, 1940).
Hardy, P., *The Muslims of British India* (Cambridge, 1972).
Hayter, W. G., *Recent Constitutional Developments in Egypt* (Cambridge, 1924).
Hershslag, Z. Y., *Introduction to the Modern Economic History of the Middle East* (Leiden, 1964).
Hicks Beach, Lady V., *The Life of Sir Michael Hicks Beach*, 2 vols. (London, 1932).
Hogan, M. J., 'Informal Entente: Public Policy and Private Management in Anglo-American Petroleum Affairs 1918–1924', *Business History Review*, XLVIII 2 (1974) 187–205.
Hoskins, H. L., *British Routes to India* (London, 1928).
Hourani, A., 'Ottoman Reform and the Politics of Notables', in *Beginnings of Modernization in the Middle East*, ed. W. R. Polk and R. Chambers (Chicago, 1968).
Hurewitz, J. C., *Diplomacy in the Near and Middle East: a Documentary Record*, vol. II (Princeton, 1956).
Hyam, R., *Elgin and Churchill at the Colonial Office* (London, 1968).
Ise, J., *United States Oil Policy* (New Haven, 1926).
Issawi, C., 'Egypt since 1800: a Study in Lop-sided Development', *Journal of Economic History*, XXI, 1 (1961) 1–25.
——, 'Asymmetrical Development and Transport in Egypt 1800–1914', in *Beginnings of Modernization in the Middle East*, ed. W. R. Polk and R. Chambers (Chicago, 1968).
Jack, M., 'The Purchase of the British Government Shares in the British Petroleum Company 1912–1914', *Past and Present*, 39 (1968) 139–68.
Johnson, P. B., *Land Fit For Heroes* (Chicago, 1968).
Jones, Thomas, *Lloyd George* (London, 1951).
——, *Whitehall Diary*, 3 vols., ed. K. Middlemas (London, 1969–71).
Karpur, Harish, *Soviet Russia and Asia 1917–1927* (Geneva, 1966).
Kazemzadeh, F., *Russia and Britain in Persia 1864–1914* (New Haven and London, 1968).
Kedourie, E., *England and the Middle East: The Destruction of the Ottoman Empire 1914–1921* (London, 1956).
——, *The Chatham House Version and Other Middle-Eastern Studies* (London, 1970).

Keith, A. B., *Speeches and Documents on Indian Policy 1750–1921*, 2 vols. (World's Classics edn, London, 1922).
Kelly, J. B., *Britain and the Persian Gulf 1795–1880* (Oxford, 1968).
Kendle, J. E., *The Colonial and Imperial Conferences 1887–1911* (London, 1967).
Keynes, J. M., *Essays in Biography* (new edn, London, 1951).
Kinnear, M., *The Fall of Lloyd George* (London, 1973).
Klieman A. S., *Foundations of British Policy in the Arab World: The Cairo Conference 1921* (London, 1970).
Laqueur, W., *The Soviet Union and the Middle East* (London, 1959).
Llewellyn Smith, M., *Ionian Vision: Greece in Asia Minor 1919–1922* (London, 1973).
Lloyd, Lord, *Egypt Since Cromer*, 2 vols. (London, 1933–4).
Longhurst, H., *Adventure in Oil* (London, 1959).
Longrigg, S. H., *Iraq 1900–1950* (London, 1953).
——, *Syria and Lebanon under French Mandate* (London, 1958).
——, *Oil in the Middle East* (3rd edn, London, 1968).
Louis, W. R., *Great Britain and Germany's Lost Colonies* (Oxford, 1967).
Low, D. A., 'The Government of India and the First Non-Cooperation Movement 1920–1922', in *Essays in Gandhian Politics*, ed. R. Kumar (Oxford, 1971).
Lowe, C. J. and Dockrill, M. L., *The Mirage of Power*, vol. 2 (London, 1972).
Lowe, C. J. and Marzari, F., *Italian Foreign Policy 1870–1940* (London, 1975).
Lowe, P., *Great Britain and Japan 1911–1915* (London, 1969).
Luke, H. C., *Cities and Men*, vol. II (London, 1953).
Lutfi al-Sayyid, Afaf, 'The Beginnings of Modernization among the Rectors of Al-Azhar', in *Beginnings of Modernization in the Middle East*, ed. W. R. Polk and R. Chambers (Chicago, 1968).
Lyall, Sir A., *The Life of the Marquis of Dufferin and Ava* (Nelson edn, London, n.d.).
Malcolm, Sir I., *Lord Balfour: a Memory* (London, 1930).
Mallett, Sir B. and George, C. O., *British Budgets, Second Series 1913/14 to 1920/21* (London, 1929).
Mangat, J. S., *The History of the Asians in East Africa c. 1886–1945* (Oxford, 1969).
Marlowe, J., *Late Victorian* (London, 1967).
Matthew, H. C. G., *The Liberal Imperialists* (London, 1973).
McLean, D., 'Finance and Informal Empire before the First World War', *Economic History Review*, second series, XXIX, 2 (1976) 291–305.
McLean, I., 'Popular Protest and Public Order: Red Clydeside 1915–1919', in *Popular Protest and Public Order*, ed. R. Quinault and J. Stevenson (London, 1974).
Milner, Viscount, *The Nation and the Empire* (London, 1913).
Milner, A., *England in Egypt* (8th edn, London, 1901).
Misra, B. B., *The Administrative History of India 1834–1947* (Bombay, 1970).
Mitchell, B. R., *Abstract of British Historical Statistics* (Cambridge, 1962, 1971).
Monger, G., *The End of Isolation* (London, 1963).
Monroe, E., *Philby of Arabia* (London, 1973).
Montgomery, A. E., 'Lloyd George and the Greek Question 1918–1922' in

Lloyd George: Twelve Essays, ed. A. J. P. Taylor (London, 1971).
Morgan, K. O., 'Lloyd George's Stage Army: the Coalition Liberals 1918–1922', in *Lloyd George: Twelve Essays*, ed. A. J. P. Taylor (London, 1971).
Mowat, C. L., *Britain Between the Wars* (London, 1966).
Naval Intelligence Division, *Persia: a Handbook* (London, 1945).
Nelson, H. I., *Land and Power* (2nd edn, Newton Abbot, 1971).
Nevakivi, J., *Britain, France and the Arab Middle East 1914–1920* (London, 1969).
Nicolson, H., *Some People* (London, 1927).
——, *Curzon: The Last Phase* (London, 1934).
Nish, I. H., *Alliance in Decline: a Study in Anglo-Japanese Relations 1908–1923* (London, 1972).
O'Connor, Sir F., *On the Frontier and Beyond* (London, 1931).
Official History of the Indian Armed Forces in the Second World War 1939–1945: Indian War Economy, ed. N. C. Sinha and P. N. Khera.
Official History of the War, F. J. Moberly, *The Campaign in Mesopotamia*, vol. IV (London, 1927).
Owen, E. R. J., *Cotton and the Egyptian Economy* (Oxford, 1967).
Payton-Smith, D. J., *Oil: a Study of Wartime Policy and Administration* (History of the Second World War, U.K. Civil Series, H.M.S.O., 1971).
Petrie, C., *The Life and Times of Austen Chamberlain*, 2 vols. (London, 1939, 1940).
Philby, H. St. J., *Arabian Days* (London, 1948).
Pipes, R., *The Formation of the Soviet Union: Communism and Nationalism 1917–1923* (revised edn, Harvard, 1964).
Pollard, S. (ed.), *The Gold Standard and Employment Policies* (London, 1970).
Reading, Earl of, *Speeches*, vol. 1 (Simla, 1926).
Robbins, K., *Sir Edward Grey* (London, 1971).
Roberts, S. H., *The History of French Colonial Policy 1870–1925* (new imp., London, 1963).
Robinson, F., *Separatism Among Indian Muslims* (Cambridge, 1974).
Robinson, R. and Gallagher, J., *Africa and the Victorians* (London, 1961).
Ronaldshay, Earl of, *The Life of Lord Curzon*, vol. III (London, 1929).
Roskill, S., *Naval Policy Between the Wars*, vol. I (London, 1968).
——, *Hankey: Man of Secrets*, vol. II (London, 1972).
Rothwell, V. H., 'Mesopotamia in British War Aims 1914–1918', *Historical Journal*, XIII, 2 (1970) 273–94.
——, *British War Aims and Peace Diplomacy* (Oxford, 1971).
Rowland, J. and Basil, 2nd Baron Cadman, *Ambassador for Oil* (London, 1960).
Rushbrook Williams, L. F., *India in 1922–23: a Statement prepared for presentation to Parliament* (Calcutta, 1923).
Safran, N., *Egypt in Search of Political Community* (Cambridge, Mass., 1961).
Sanghvi, R., *The Shah of Iran* (London, 1968).
Saul, S. B., *Studies in British Overseas Trade 1870–1914* (Liverpool, 1960).
Seal, A., 'Imperialism and Nationalism in India', *Modern Asian Studies*, 7, 3 (1973) 321–47.
Seeley, J. R., *The Expansion of England* (2nd edn, London, 1897).
Skrine, Sir C., *World War in Iran* (London, 1962).
Smith, Goldwin, *The Empire* (Oxford, 1863).

Sonyel, S. R., *Turkish Diplomacy 1918–1923* (London, 1975).
Spender, J. A., *Life, Journalism and Politics*, vol. II (London, 1927).
Stoddard, Lothrop, *The Rising Tide of Colour* (London, 1922).
Stokes, E., 'Milnerism', *Historical Journal*, v, 1 (1962) 47–60.
——, 'Traditional Resistance Movements and Afro-Asian Nationalism', *Past and Present*, 48 (1970) 100–18.
Storrs, R., *Orientations* (definitive edn, London, 1943).
Sykes, Sir P., *A History of Persia*, 2 vols. (3rd edn, London, 1930).
Temperley, H. W. V., *A History of the Peace Conference at Paris*, vol. VI (London, 1924).
Thornton, A. P., 'British Policy in Persia 1858–1890', *English Historical Review*, LXIX (1954) 554–99; LXX (1955) 55–71.
——, *The Imperial Idea and its Enemies* (London, 1959).
——, *For the File on Empire* (London, 1968).
Tignor, R. L., *Modernization and British Colonial Rule in Egypt 1882–1914* (Princeton, 1966).
Toynbee, A. J., *The Western Question in Greece and Turkey* (London, 1922).
Trumpener, U., *Germany and the Ottoman Empire 1914–1918* (Princeton, 1968).
Ullman, R., *The Anglo-Soviet Accord* (London, 1972).
Vatikiotis, P. J., *A Modern History of Egypt* (London, 1969).
Walder, D., *The Chanak Affair* (London, 1969).
Waley, S. D., *Edwin Montagu: a Memoir* (Bombay, 1964).
War Office, *Statistics of the Military Effort of the British Empire* (London, 1922).
Warman, R., 'The Erosion of Foreign Office Influence in the Making of Foreign Policy 1916–1918', *Historical Journal*, xv, 1 (1972) 133–59.
Waterfield, G., *Professional Diplomat* (London, 1973).
Weber, F. G., *Eagles on the Crescent: Germany, Austria and the Diplomacy of the Turkish Alliance* (Ithaca and London, 1970).
Webster, R. A., *Industrial Imperialism in Italy 1908–1915* (Los Angeles and London, 1975).
Weinroth, H., 'British Radicals and the Agadir Crisis', *European Studies Review*, 3, 1 (1973) 39–61.
Willcocks, Sir W. and Craig, J. I., *Egyptian Irrigation*, 2 vols. (London, 1931).
Wilson, A. T., *Mesopotamia 1917–1920: A Clash of Loyalties* (London, 1931).
Winch, D., *Economics and Policy* (London, 1969).
Woolf, Leonard, *Imperialism and Civilisation* (London, 1928).
Young, H., *The Independent Arab* (London, 1933).
Young, L. K., *British Policy in China 1895–1902* (Oxford, 1970).

2. *Select List of other works consulted*

Addison, C., *Four and a Half Years*, 2 vols. (London, 1934).
Balfour, Earl of, *Chapters of Autobiography*, ed. E. Dugdale (London, 1930).
Barnes, J. and Middlemas, K., *Baldwin* (London, 1969).
Beaman, A. H., *The Dethronement of the Khedive* (London, 1929).
Boyle, C., *A Servant of the Empire* (London, 1938).
Bullard, R., *The Camels Must Go* (London, 1961).
Burrell, R. M., 'Britain, Iran and the Persian Gulf: Some Aspects of the

Situation in the 1920s and 1930s', in *The Arabian Peninsula: Society and Politics*, ed. D. Hopwood (London, 1972).
Butler, J. R. M., *Lord Lothian* (London, 1960).
Carthill, Al (pseud.), *The Lost Dominion* (London, 1924).
Cecil, Lord Edward, *The Leisure of an Egyptian Official* (7th edn, London, 1938).
Churchill, Randolph S., *Lord Derby* (London, 1959).
Coen, Terence Creagh, *The Indian Political Service* (London, 1971).
Cole, D. H., *Imperial Military Geography* (8th edn, London, 1935).
Cook, G. L., 'Sir Robert Borden, Lloyd George and British Military Policy 1917–1918', *Historical Journal*, xiv, 2 (1971) 371–95.
Cooper, Duff, *Old Men Forget* (London, 1953).
Davenport, E. H. and Cooke, S. R., *The Oil Trusts and Anglo-American Relations* (London, 1923).
Dearle, N. B., *An Economic Chronicle of the Great War for Great Britain and Ireland 1914–1919* (London, 1929).
Delaisi, F., *Oil. Its Influence on Politics* (Eng. trans., London, 1922).
Dugdale, B. E. C., *Arthur James Balfour*, vol. II (London, 1936).
East, W. G. and Spate, O. H. K., *The Changing Map of Asia* (4th edn, London, 1961).
Farnie, D. A., *East and West of Suez* (Oxford, 1969).
George Lloyd, D., *War Memoirs*, 6 vols. (London, 1933–6).
Gilbert, M., *Sir Horace Rumbold* (London, 1973).
Graves, P. P., *The Question of the Straits* (London, 1931).
Harington, Sir C., *Tim Harington Looks Back* (London, 1940).
Headlam, C. (ed.), *The Milner Papers*, vol. 1 (London, 1931): biographical introduction.
Howard, H. N., *The Partition of Turkey* (new edn, New York, 1966).
Kinross, Lord, *Ataturk* (London, 1964).
Landes, D. S., *Bankers and Pashas* (London, 1958).
Lewis, B., *The Emergence of Modern Turkey* (London, 1961).
Lockwood, P. A., 'Milner's Entry into the War Cabinet, December 1916', *Historical Journal*, vii, 1 (1964) 120–34.
Loder, J. de V., *The Truth About Mesopotamia, Palestine and Syria* (London, 1923).
Monroe, E., *Britain's Moment in the Middle East, 1914–1956* (London, 1965).
Montgomery, A. E., 'The Making of the Treaty of Sèvres 10 August 1920', *Historical Journal*, xv, 4 (1972) 775–87.
Morgan, K. O., 'Lloyd George's Premiership: a Study in "Prime Ministerial Government"', *Historical Journal*, xiii, 1 (1970) 130–57.
Mowat, R. C., 'From Liberalism to Imperialism: the case of Egypt 1875–1887', *Historical Journal*, xvi, 1 (1973) 109–24.
Naylor, J. F., 'The Establishment of the Cabinet Secretariat', *Historical Journal*, xiv, 4 (1971) 783–803.
O'Dwyer, Sir M., *India as I Knew it* (London, 1925).
Owen, E. R. J., 'The attitudes of British Officials to the Development of the Egyptian Economy 1882–1922', in *Studies in the Economic History of the Modern Middle East*, ed. M. A. Cook (London, 1970).
Rawlinson, A., *Adventures in the Near East 1918–1922* (London, 1924).

Reading, Marquess of, *Rufus Isaacs*, 2 vols. (London, 1942, 1945).
Robinson, K., *Dilemmas of Trusteeship* (London, 1965).
Rowland, P., *Lloyd George* (London, 1975).
Royal Institute of International Affairs, *Political and Strategic Interests of the United Kingdom* (London, 1939).
Russell, Sir T., *Egyptian Service 1902–1946* (London, 1949).
Ryan, A., *The Last of the Dragomans* (London, 1951).
Semmel, B., *Imperialism and Social Reform* (London, 1960).
Steiner, Z., *The Foreign Office and Foreign Policy 1898–1914* (Cambridge, 1969).
'Tawwaf' (pseud.), *Egypt 1919, Being a Narrative of Certain Incidents of the Rising in Upper Egypt* (Alexandria, 1925).
Townshend, C. J. N., *The British Campaign in Ireland 1919–1921* (London, 1975).
Ullman, R., *Intervention and the War* (London, 1961).
——, *Britain and the Russian Civil War* (London, 1968).
Wavell, A. P., *Allenby in Egypt* (London, 1943).
Wilson, T., *The Downfall of the Liberal Party* (London, 1966).
Wingate, R., *Not in the Limelight* (London, 1959).
Wrench, J. E., *Alfred Lord Milner: the Man of No Illusions* (London, 1958).
Young, K., *Arthur James Balfour* (London, 1963).
Zeine, Z. N., *The Struggle for Arab Independence* (Beirut, 1960).

Index